The inside scoop fro

STREETWISE GUIDE

BEIJING

FOREIGN LANGUAGES PRESS

Second Printing 2008

Authors: G.C.A. (Glenn) Alexander, Ouyang Weiping

Contributing Authors: Samantha Wilson, Yan Hong

Managing Editors: Ouyang Weiping, He Yongyan

Editors: Sue Duncan, Han Qingyue, May Yee, Chad Pearson, M. Tyson Darius, Chellis Ying

Designers: Edison Flores, He Yongyan, Ouyang Weiping

Illustrator: Li Shiji

Photographers: Cui Yanxing, Zhang Jian, Han Dequn, Justin Hirschkorn, Tom Carter, Jeff Wang

Consultants: Andy Mckillop, Howard Aster, Tony McGlinchey, Stephen Horowitz, Paul White, Gregor Kneussel

ISBN: 978-7-119-04621-1
© Foreign Languages Press, Beijing, China, 2007
Published by Foreign Languages Press
24 Baiwanzhuang Road, Beijing, 100037, China
Website: http://www.flp.com.cn
Email Address: Info@flp.com.cn
Sales@flp.com.cn
Distributed by China International Book Trading Corporation
35 Chegongzhuang Xilu, Beijing 100044, China
P. O. Box 399, Beijing, China

Printed in the People's Republic of China

Contents

6-39

AREA GUIDE

42-297

"Patriotic" Southwest

PP120-131

"Wild" West

PP132-157

"Academic" Northwest

PP158-189

"Olympic" North

PP190-213

"Arty" Northeast

PP214-239

"Modern" East

PP240-267

"Antiques" Southeast

PP268-277

Beyond the Fifth Ring Road

PP278-297

TRAVELERS' SURVIVAL GUIDE

300-350

APPENDIX

352-357

How to Use the Book

Streetwise Guide Beijing was written to be a comprehensive and user-friendly guide to China's exciting and ever-changing capital. Take a moment to familiarize yourself with the book's design and layout, so that you can take full advantage of the wealth of information contained inside.

You'll find the city very well organized in a clear manner with color-coded sections, detailed maps, sample itineraries, accommodation choices, transportation options and symbols to denote pricing, discounts and more! Enjoy!

1. Pick an area

Explanation of Beijing's layout.

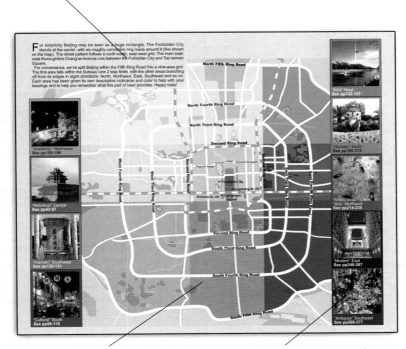

Each area is color coded for convenience.

Quick reference to color-coded areas.

2. Fold-out area map

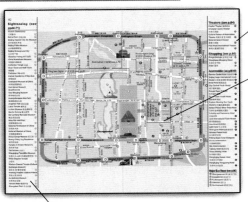

Color-coded numbered/lettered circles correspond to locations marked on Area Map and in the content.

Denotes food and entertainment hot spots.

Quick reference to main section's content.

Introduction and highlight information to the sight.

3D map of the attraction.

3. Sights

Streetwise star rating
★★★= Sights that you can't miss.
★★ = Sights that you should visit.
★ = Sights that you can visit if you have time.

✕ Symbol for recommended nearby restaurants.

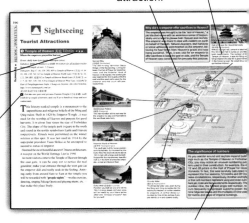

Introduction to the hot spot.

Quick and interesting facts.

4. The finer detail

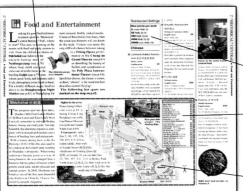

Price guide with symbols to denote price range.

Quick reference to the area's listings and map locations.

Detailed hot spot map.

5. Set your home base

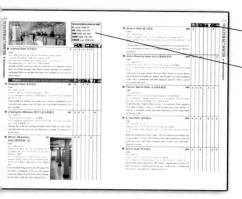

Accommodation/amenities chart.

Price guide with symbols to denote price range.

Key spots to take notice of on your route.

6. Recommended itineraries

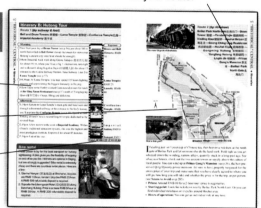

Step-by-step itinerary.

Suggested itinerary route map.

Total expense of this itinerary.

Area's major bus stops which can be also found on the fold-out map.

7. Transportation

Bus routes complete with bus type, hours of operation and highlighted spots of interest.

The fast-disappearing siheyuan compound houses give us a clear look at urban life from days of old.

INTRODUCING BEIJING

Beijing Layout Map

For simplicity Beijing may be seen as a huge rectangle. The Forbidden City stands at the center, with fairly concentric ring roads surrounding it (four shown on the map). The street pattern follows a north-south, east-west grid. The main east-west thoroughfare, Chang'an Jie, cuts between the Forbidden City and Tian'anmen Square.

For convenience, we've split Beijing within the Fifth Ring Road into a nine-area grid. The first area falls within the Subway Line 2 (the Loop Line), with the other areas branching off from its edges in eight directions: North, Northeast, East, Southeast and so on. Each area has been given its own descriptive nickname and color to help with your bearings and to help you remember what this part of town provides. Happy trails!

"Academic" Northwest
See pp158-189

"Historical" Central
See pp42-97

"Patriotic" Southwest
See pp120-131

"Cultural" South
See pp98-119

West Fourth Ring Road

West Third Ring Road

North Fifth Ring Road

h Fourth Ring Road

aird Ring Road

Ring Road

ng'an Dajie

Second Ring Road

East Third Ring Road

East Fourth Ring Road

bidden City

Chang'an Jie

an'anmen
Square

I Ring Road

hird Ring Road

ourth Ring Road

South Fifth Ring Road

"Wild" West
See pp132-157

"Olympic" North
See pp190-213

"Arty" Northeast
See pp214-239

"Modern" East
See pp240-267

"Antiques" Southeast
See pp268-277

Welcome to Beijing

Beijing opens itself to you.

ADVENTURE AWAITS!

Arriving from Canada in 2003, and having traveled extensively around the world, it didn't take long for me to grasp that Beijing is unlike any other city in the world.

Yes, you can say this is due to 5,000 years of history, you can argue it's because China is full throttle in the midst of really "opening up," you may even cite entrance to the WTO, or the awarding of the 2008 Olympic Games as reasons for this. In truth, it is all these reasons and more! Consider also rising family incomes, add explosive growth in the Internet, stir in

Beijing is unlike any other city in the world.

awareness of the outside world, and finally a pinch of Chinese curiosity, and you begin to understand the dynamic, and sometimes confusing, recipe that has produced today's Beijing.

Talking with many Beijingers, they recount times not so long ago when a simple house, simple clothes and a reliable bike were measures of wealth. While this may still be true in some rural areas, it is increasingly rare in today's Beijing. Everyone is in on the expansion; businessmen now demand not just a space to do business, but buildings that fuse old with new, creating corporate identities for their enterprises.

This view from the Kunming Lake can be seen by climbing to the top of the Longevity Hill.

Demands on education are also rising, as parents insist on preparing their children to do business in today's world. Schools of every type, at every level, are opening at the same furious pace as everything else. You can find Chinese who have learned English, German, French, Italian, Spanish and more!

Bright city lights shine in Beijing's Jianguomen area.

The Chinese government struggles daily with these challenges and is trying many innovative potential solutions. One example is wisely choosing not to develop a single "downtown." Instead, Beijing has created certain "zones" for different businesses. Need electronics? You will find yourself in Zhongguangcun. This area of Haidian District (in northwest Beijing) was created for this, aided by attractive tax incentives and relaxed import-export regulations. The business community has responded by moving and opening related companies here—the result is Beijing's "Silicon Valley."

Want big business? You'll find yourself in Chaoyang District (east Beijing). Chaoyang is home to the Central Business District (CBD). Here corporate headquarters, office space and meeting rooms abound, but few showrooms are to be seen and absolutely no factories. Here you will find not only most of the embassies in Beijing, but also many foreign companies and restaurants, as well as the SOHO buildings and the China World Trade Center (and hotel).

In today's Beijing, relocation is a part of life for people and for businesses alike. Environmental responsibility is becoming an increasingly critical issue. Automobiles, expanding population, mass housing, gigantic malls and factories that surround Beijing compound the problem. The Fourth Ring Road, once considered the "Outer Limits," has given way to the Fifth and now the Sixth Ring Road, and many factories fall well within

Beijing has worked to create certain "zones" for doing different business.

what most consider the city itself.

798 is one such factory area. It was once one of Beijing's largest state factories. An active plant until the late 1980s, its Bauhaus style buildings are now home to cutting-edge art studios, galleries and loft apartments. Recent contemporary art auctions in London and New York saw works by artists based at 798 fetch impressive prices.

Ancient Greek and Arabian myths tell of the phoenix. As the legend goes, after a life of 500 to 600 years, the phoenix would build a nest that would also be its own funeral pyre, from the ashes of which a new bird would emerge. The Chinese also speak of the phoenix, representing the *yin* (female) complement to the dragon's *yang* (male). It is the highest ranking of birds and said to land on only the greatest of treasures. Perhaps the phoenix could serve as a metaphor for today's Beijing. A city resting on its rich architectural and cultural past, rising from its pell-mell rebuilding, all the while emerging, reborn as a truly world class city!

So get your feet into some durable, comfortable shoes, grab your camera and your sense of adventure, and make your way through the sights, sounds and experiences of this amazing city!

As the 2008 Olympic mascots would say: "Beijing Welcomes You!"

G.C.A. (Glenn) Alexander
Beijing 2007

Fast Facts

A ● **Area and Administration:** 16,808 sq km (6,489 sq miles) covering 16 districts and two counties.
● **Area Code:** 010 when dialing from another city in China, but drop the first 0 if dialing from abroad. The country code for China is 86.

B ● **Business Hours (average range)**
Banks: daily 9am-5pm
Bars: daily 2pm-2am (some open until 6am)
Drugstores/pharmacies: daily 9am-5pm (some are 24 hours)
Hair salons: daily 9am-midnight
Hospitals: 7am-5pm, emergency 24 hours
Major sights: daily 8.30am-5pm (Apr 16-Oct 15, last entry at 4pm), 8.30am-4.30pm (Oct 16-Apr 15, last entry at 3.30pm)
Markets: daily 9am-4pm or 6pm
Government offices: daily 9am-5pm (closed on weekends)
Post offices: daily 9am-5pm
Restaurants: daily 10am-11pm (some are 24 hours)
Shopping malls: daily 9am-9pm
Stores: daily 9am-9pm
Supermarkets: daily 9am-9pm

Visiting time alternatives

Autumn is often recommended as prime visiting time, but you won't be the only one taking advantage of the favorable climate. And remember that the National Day holiday (Oct 1-7) is a favorite time for the Chinese to travel. Over-crowding and inflated prices can be avoided by visiting off-season. April, June and November are good alternatives as crowds are thinner, the weather is decent, and prices more reasonable.

C ● **Climate:** Beijing's temperate, monsoonal climate results in four distinct seasons. Temperatures plummet in January, while we see high temperatures in July and August with a splash of rain. Autumn (early September-late October) is considered an optimum time to visit, with the city's windy springs, hot, humid summers and cold, dry winters (late October-late March) being less tourist-friendly.

● **Currency:** Renminbi (人民币 people's money, 元 yuan or ¥) approximately USD 1=RMB 7.3, EUR 1=RMB 10.6 (as of January, 2008). The People's Bank of China issues RMB bills in denominations of one, two and five jiao (one jiao= $^1/_{10}$ RMB) and one, two, five, 10, 20, 50 and 100 yuan, and coins in denominations of one, two and five fen (cent), one jiao and one yuan.

Months		Jan	Feb	Mar	Apr	May	June	July	Aug	Sept	Oct	Nov	Dec
Temperature (°C)	Average	-4.6	-2.1	4.7	13	19.9	23.6	25.8	24.4	19.1	12.2	4.3	-2.5
	Max	10.7	15.5	22.6	31.1	36.6	38.9	39.6	38.3	32.3	29.3	23.3	13.5
	Min	-22.8	-17.6	-12.5	-2.4	3.7	11.2	16.1	12.3	4.9	-1.4	-11.6	-18
Rainfall (mm)		2.6	7.7	9.1	22.4	26.1	70.4	196.6	243.5	63.9	21.1	7.9	1.6
Wind speed (m/s)		2.4	2.7	3	3.3	2.8	2.2	1.7	1.6	1.8	2.1	2.2	2.5
Seasons		Spring Apr. 1-May. 25 (55 days)			Summer May. 26-Sept. 5 (103 days)			Autumn Sept. 6-Oct. 25 (50 days)			Winter Oct. 26-Mar. 31 (157 days)		

E
● **Economy/GDP:** USD 6,210 per capita (permanent residents) in 2006, with an increase of 8.8% over 2005.
● **Education:** There are over 100 colleges and universities in Beijing, most of them state-run or affiliated, with just a handful of private institutions. Education levels in Beijing are among the highest in China, with an average university enrollment rate of 73.6% in 2007.
● **Electricity:** 220V 50Hz. Transformers (220V to 110V) are available in all major hotels for hair dryers and electric shavers.
● **Environment:** Increasing urbanization, traffic volume and pollution are major environmental threats, but awareness and environmental action are both on the increase.
● **Ethnic Groups:** 95.7% of Beijing's population is of the Han group, but you may run into someone from any of China's 56 ethnic groups.

G
● **Geographic Features:** Mountains occupy 62% of Beijing's total area, fringing the north, east and west sides. Five rivers cross the city on their way toward the Bohai Sea. The flatness of the city makes it great for cycling.

K
● **Kids:** The single-child policy is not in effect for couples who both come from a single-child family. In rural areas, couples can have a second child if their first is female. Ethnic minorities are not limited to one child at all.

L
● **Language:** Mandarin (Putonghua 普通话), China's official language, is spoken in Beijing and by 70% of China's population, the remainder speaking an array of regional dialects. Some dialects vary drastically from each other and can hardly be mutually understood.

O
● **Official City Flowers and Trees:** Rose (月季) and chrysanthemum (菊花); sophora (国槐) and cypress (侧柏)

P
● **Population:** By the end of June 2007, the permanent resident population in Beijing reached 17 million, in addition to 5.107 million of floating population. (Source: Beijing Municipal Statistics Bureau, March 2005)

T
● **TCM:** Abbreviation for Traditional Chinese Medicine. While Western medicine forms an important role in China's healthcare, most people opt for TCM treatment such as herbal medicine, acupuncture and massage therapy.
● **Time Zone:** GMT +8 (Standard Time), Noon in Beijing = 4 am in London (same day) and 11 pm in New York (day before). Beijing Time is universal throughout China.
● **Tipping:** Generally, tipping is not necessary, but upmarket restaurants (e.g. in hotels) may add a 10-15% service fee. Tour guides and bellhops also expect a tip.
● **Traffic:** Beijing's streets were home to 1.56 million private cars by October 2006. With approximately 1,000 new motor vehicles a day squeezing onto the streets, traffic jams are a fact of life! Avoid traveling in the city during rush hours between 8am-9am, 5pm-7pm. Friday evenings are particularly hellish.

W
● **Water:** Beijing tap water is not drinkable unless boiled, however bottled water is cheap and widely available.
● **Work:** Beijing urban citizens have an average 5.9-day working week, and an average monthly salary of RMB 1,878. (Source: National Bureau of Statistics, November 2006)

Best of Beijing

There's so much to Beijing that realistically you won't get around it all in a few days, or months even! But to help you get the best out of your trip, we kick off with some of the city's unique and must-see experiences. To really appreciate what makes the list, you need to understand a bit more about this unique city. From the age of Kublai Khan to Mao Zedong, this city had been the center of Chinese political life. Since 1978 (the start of economic reform), Beijing has become an international metropolis. A city that attracts people from around the world to do business, see its many sights, eat its fantastic food, find outrageous bargains and, come for the 2008 Olympics!

No. 1 on our list, the Forbidden City, was the imperial home of emperors for 491 years. The Temple of Heaven was where emperors appeased their gods; the Summer Palace and Yuanmingyuan were where foreign invasions accelerated the demise of the imperial system. The Great Wall served to protect from nomad incursions even before the whole country was unified. Then there are the imperial tombs and parks, Peking Man, giant pandas and more, all echoing China's 5,000 years of history. The leafy *hutong* areas should not be missed, still preserved (just) in the wholesale modernization of the city. And of course now on this list of "must-sees" are the modern Olympic facilities, the shopping malls and markets, and urban nightlife.

This is a city of contrasts—the historic cheek-by-jowl with the ultra-modern, and the traditional with the so-cool-it-hurts!

1 **Forbidden City**（故宫）Also known as the Palace Museum, it housed 24 of China's emperors, laying hidden from the world for centuries. **See p.44**

2 Tian'anmen Square（天安门广场）One of Beijing's most famous landmarks. **See p.50**

3 Great Wall（长城）A symbol of China, it snakes its way majestically across dramatic landscapes. **See p.280**

4 Hutong or alleys（胡同）These fast-disappearing neighborhoods preserve the true ancient flavor of Beijing. **See p.64**

5 Summer Palace（颐和园）Regal and beautiful at any time of the year. **See p.160**

6 Temple of Heaven(天坛) Where ancient Chinese emperors whispered to heaven. **See p.100**

8 Zhoukoudian Peking Man （周口店猿人遗址） Dating back 500,000 to 600,000 years. **See p.294**

7 Giant pandas at Beijing Zoo （北京动物园大熊猫）China's furriest national symbol. **See p.134**

9 Olympic venue— Bird's Nest （鸟巢） Centerpiece of Beijing Olympics. **See p.353**

10 **National Museum** (国家博物馆) Recording 5,000 years of Chinese history. **See p.65**

11 **Beihai Park** (北海公园) A royal park in the heart of Beijing. **See p.54**

12 **Lama Temple** (雍和宫) Inhale the burning incense amid the tranquility of this Tibetan Buddhist temple. **See p.57**

13 **Yuanmingyuan** (圆明园) Ruins of the Old Summer Palace, looted by foreign forces in 1860 and 1900. Now a park. **See p.164**

14 **Peking Opera** （京剧）
An ancient art form, where costumes, make-up and masks speak louder than words. **See p.22**

17 **Peking Roast Duck**
（北京烤鸭）Beijing's very own roast duck recipe is a cultural heritage, with tantalizing crispy skin and tender meat. For more recommended dishes, **see Picture Menu on p.35**

15 **Ming Tombs** （十三陵） The final resting place of 13 Ming Dynasty emperors. **See p.286**

16 **Dashanzi Art District** （大山子艺术区）
Home to 798 art area, now the hottest art center in Beijing. Art studios, gallery space, trendy restaurants and loft apartments have transformed industrial into avant-garde. **See p.220**

18 Shopping
Beijing is a shopper's paradise, but always be ready to bargain at the Pearl Market (红桥 see p.111), Silk Street (秀水 see p.260), Tianyi (天意 see p.149) and Panjiayuan Antique Market (潘家园 see p.273).

19 Nightlife
Sanlitun Bar Street (三里屯酒吧街 see p.248), Wudaokou (五道口 see p.168) area and Shichahai (什刹海 see p.72)…after dark fun, Chinese-style.

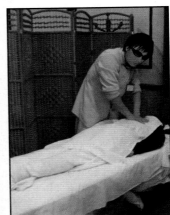

20 Blind massage
（盲人按摩）Where healing hands become eyes. **See p.330**

21 Public squares
The heart of Chinese life, where singing, dancing and entertainment abound. Join in. It's free. Try Beijing Exhibition Center Square, close to the Zoo. **See p.133**

Qianmen Dajie (early 20th century). The gatehouse is 42 m tall, making it the tallest one in Beijing.

Brief History

NAME CHECK

What's in a name? Beijing means "northern capital," but the city has had quite a few different names during its long history. Yanjing (as in the beer) and Dadu (as in the hotel) are present-day clues to some of this great city's previous IDs. Contrary to appearances, Beijing has not always been the capital of China.

For thousands of years it was an important northern stronghold, but the actual center of national political power rested further south. For long periods, under the powerful dynasties of the Qin (221-206 BC), Han (206 BC-220 AD) and Tang (618-907), all China was under unified rule from dynastic capitals further south along the Yellow River. But in the Song Dynasty (960-1279), large areas of northern China were actually under the control of nomadic tribes who ruled under dynasties of the Liao (916-1125) and Jin (1115-1234).

What we now call Beijing was the capital of these northern regimes, but national capital status (and the name Dadu) did not come until the Mongol Yuan Dynasty (1271-1368) finally defeated the Southern Song Dynasty (1127-1279) in the south. The Ming court initially set their capital in Nanjing, but later thought better of their decision and transferred it to Beiping (i.e. Beijing). The Qing put their own stamp on the city, which, apart from during the War of Resistance Against Japanese Aggression (1937-1945) and the War of Liberation (1946-1949), has remained capital of China ever since 1421.

So, names apart, how did the city change during its succession of rulers? Read on!

Earliest Inhabitants

Beijing's earliest recorded fossil remains are those of the Peking Man dating back 500,000 years. The remains providing evidence of daily life, including stone tools and the use of fire as well as decorative items were found at Zhoukoudian, in Beijing's southwestern suburbs, but today's environment and climate are a world away from what the Peking Man would have experienced.

This is no ordinary rock. It's the fossilized cranium of the Peking Man.

A warmer, more humid, forested environment would have been able to support vast numbers of wildlife, providing an ideal ecosystem in which man could flourish.

- **Where to see the Peking Man fossils**
  Cave of Peking Man at Zhoukoudian (周口店猿人遗址), see p.294
- **The mystery of the missing skull**
  In 1929 in Beijing, archeologists unearthed five humanoid skulls and dozens of other fragments thought to be half a million years old. During World War II, however, they went missing soon after being shipped to the United States in an attempt to keep them safe. China, the United States and Japan have been searching for the fossils ever since.

500,000-600,000 years ago	1045 BC	214 BC	618-938
Fossils records prove human activities in Beijing in this period.	City of Ji built, the initial stage of Beijing takes shape.	Construction of the Great Wall in Beijing begins.	Youzhou of the Tang Dynasty.

City of Ji, Beijing's First Phase

The founding of Beijing can most probably be attributed to the Yellow Emperor, a formidable leader of the surrounding agricultural settlements. As the story goes, 4,000-5,000 years ago the Yellow Emperor fought his arch rival Chiyou in the prefecture of Zhuo and hence the city of Zhuolu (west of present-day Beijing) was born. His successor Emperor Yao built his capital Youdu on the site where the city of Ji was later established.

Ji was claimed as capital during the Warring States Period (475-221BC) by the victorious Marquis of Yan, and the remains of that old city are believed to lie beneath the busy traffic of today's Guang'anmen (广安门).

In the early 3rd century BC, the all-conquering Emperor of Qin systematically unified China, and named Ji capital of Guangyang Commandery (part of China's first feudal empire). And so it stood, through war and peace, building and rebuilding, for the next 1,000 years to the end of the Tang Dynasty, as the country's fundamental trade and military stronghold.

The First Emperor of Qin (259 - 210 BC) unified China and commissioned the Great Wall to be built.

Capital of the Liao and Jin Dynasties

By the early 10th century, the Tang Dynasty was on the verge of collapse, and the strong feudal city of Ji was left vulnerable. Grasping their chance, the Khitan around the Liaohe River in the northeast moved south and garrisoned in Ji, making it their second capital. It hence became known as Nanjing (Southern Capital) and Yanjing. During his reign, Emperor Taizong of the Liao Dynasty ordered the building of several palaces, using his new city as a stronghold for conquering the heartlands further to the south.

The Liao was subsequently conquered in the early 12th century by the Nüzhen who founded the Jin Dynasty. In 1153, the Jin transferred their capital to Yanjing, renaming it Zhongdu (Central Capital) in an attempt to succeed in their war against the Southern Song Dynasty that was later forced to move south.

In 1151, sorely needed renovation and rebuilding began, as the city of Zhongdu expanded in all directions. Palaces sprang up in the style of the Northern Song (the power ruling most of China 960-1127) capital on the Yellow River. The city of Zhongdu was laid out around a core of imperial buildings and its population was estimated at around one million.

21st-16th century BC	16th-11th century BC	11th century-771 BC	770-256 BC	770-476 BC	475-221 BC	221-206 BC
Xia Dynasty	Shang Dynasty	Western Zhou	Eastern Zhou	Spring and Autumn Period	Warring States Period	Qin Dynasty

BEIJING KEY DATES

938-1153	1153-1215	1267-1285	1368	1406-1420	16
Nanjing, capital of the Liao Dynasty.	Beijing, the Central Capital (Zhongdu) of the Jin Dynasty.	Kublai Khan, grandson of Genghis Khan, has the city rebuilt as his new capital Dadu.	Ming Dynasty armies conquer the city, subsequently called Beiping.	Emperor Yongle has the Forbidden City built. Capital is transferred from Nanjing and Beiping is renamed Beijing.	Li Zichen takes Be in the fall

Reconstruction of the City under the Yuan

In 1215, Mongol armies from their capital in what is today Inner Mongolia, invaded and conquered Zhongdu. In 1271, Kublai Khan named the new dynasty

Kublai Khan (1215 - 1294). This founder of the Yuan Dynasty welcomed foreign trade.

Yuan and declared Zhongdu as his capital Dadu (Great Capital). With the final defeat and elimination of the Southern Song in 1127, China was finally reunified and Dadu was promoted to the political center of the entire country.

During Kubai Khan's rule (1260-1294), the city was drastically remodeled and rebuilt to include imperial palaces, city walls, moats and a canal. Mansions for the imperial princes, government offices, the Imperial Ancestral Temple, the Altar of Land and Grain and the Tonghui Canal all owe their roots to this period.

The Yuan Dynasty (1271-1368), with its beautiful new capital, enjoyed flourishing and booming trade with Europe, Asia and Africa, proudly showing off the city's assets to all visitors. Marco Polo himself wrote the emperor's palace at Dadu a glowing review:

"*You must know that it is the greatest palace that ever was! The roof is very lofty and the walls of the palace are all covered with gold and silver. They are adorned with dragons, beasts and birds, knights and idols, and other such things!…No man on earth could design anything superior to it.*"

Kublai Khan's new and improved rectangular Dadu measured 28 km around the perimeter, with a grid-system street pattern providing order and logic, and major streets measuring 24 paces across.

Capital of the Ming and Qing Dynasties

The restoration of the rule of the Han people came with the Ming Dynasty (1368-1644) whose armies conquered Dadu in 1368, later renaming the city Beiping (Northern Peace). The Ming capital however was initially in Nanjing on the Yangtze River. In 1406, Emperor Yongle put in motion the construction of massive fortification walls around Beiping; they were 12 m high and 10 m thick and took a dozen years to complete, during which time palaces and gardens were constructed for the transfer of capital status from Nanjing to Beiping in 1421. Along with its new title, Beiping was finally renamed Beijing, meaning "Northern Capital." The original city plan was laid out during the Yuan Dynasty.

Emperor Yongle (1360 - 1424) built the Forbidden City (Palace Museum).

CHINA KEY DATES

206 BC-24 AD	25-220	220-280	265-316	317-420	420-589	386-581	581-618	618-9
Western Han	Eastern Han	Three Kingdoms (Wei, Shu, Wu)	Western Jin	Eastern Jin	Southern Dynasties (Song, Qi, Liang, Chen)	Northern Dynasties (Northern Wei, Eastern Wei, Northern Qi, Western Wei, Northern Zhou)	Sui Dynasty	Tang I

...but it was under the Ming and the subsequent Qing Dynasty (founded in 1644 by the Manchus) that the city really started to become an impressive architectural masterpiece. The most notable Qing Dynasty contribution was the creation of gardens, complete with meticulously planned open-air pavilions and magnificent palaces.

The Forbidden City, thus named during the Ming Dynasty, is now called the Palace Museum. It stood then, as it does today, in the heart of the city, a symbol of the great power and wealth of China.

Capital of New China

B eijing's most recent chapter began on January 31, 1949 as the Chinese People's Liberation Army marched into the city under the command of Chairman Mao Zedong. In his famous speech from the Tian'anmen Rostrum on the following October 1, he declared the founding of the People's Republic of China.

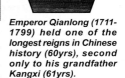

Emperor Qianlong (1711-1799) held one of the longest reigns in Chinese history (60yrs), second only to his grandfather Kangxi (61yrs).

After years of turmoil following the collapse of China's last dynasty, the chaos of the Republic of China (1912-1949) years, the War of Resistance Against Japanese Aggression and the War of Liberation, citizens looked forward to a new sense of direction and identity.

In the years that have passed, Beijing has undergone a more drastic transformation than at any other time in its history. The city has burst out of the nine gates of the Inner City wall and now spreads to the Fifth Ring Road and beyond.

Beijing's facelift has been drastic, but some of the city's features have retained their original place in the big picture. Tian'anmen Square still remains the heart of Beijing, the palaces and watchtowers are under strict cultural relic protection, old *hutong* alleys and housing have been renovated and conserved, and imperial palaces and gardens still hold a special place in the hearts of Beijingers.

Inner City gates

There were nine gates along the Inner City wall. Of the original Ming wall, only two gates survive, Deshengmen and Zhengyangmen (now Qianmen). Their names remain however, and many of the stations on today's Subway Line 2 incorporate the word *men* (门 gate), a reminder of where the ancient gates once stood. In their heyday, the gates all served different purposes: the troops marched through Deshengmen (德胜门) to battlefield and later returned through Andingmen (安定门); the city's fresh drinking water entered through Xizhimen (西直门), while construction materials made their way in through Dongzhimen (东直门); Fuchengmen (阜成门) was reserved for coal import and grains were brought in through Chaoyangmen (朝阳门); Zhengyangmen (正阳门) was reserved for the exclusive use of emperors, while the two most unpopular gates were Xuanwumen (宣武门) and Chongwenmen (崇文门) via which prisoners walked to their death and merchant taxes were paid, respectively.

Art and Culture

Intricate carvings in stone or wood. Pick your fancy.

When pausing to consider the art and culture of Beijing, no doubt Peking Opera springs to mind. This unique style of performance is 200 years old. Tea ceremonies, painted (from the inside!) glassware, papercuts, *yangge* dancing, kite making and calligraphy all have a rich history too.

But not everything about Beijing art and culture belongs to days gone by; vibrant, modern art galleries are an ever-increasing sight in today's Beijing. Peking Opera is still performed in its original form, but you can also find performances with modern musical accompaniment and style in this cosmopolitan city. As craftsmen attract a new, urban clientele, the "inside-out" painted glassware also features contemporary scenes. Kite makers have not turned their backs on the brightly colored birds, faces and styles of the past, but now include modern themes in their repertoire.

Beijing is a city where you can tour a modern art gallery in the morning, take part in an ancient tea ceremony in the afternoon, and enjoy up-dated-style Peking Opera as you eat your dinner. Traditional and modern forms of art and culture co-exist and sometimes merge in a city that is proud of them all. No matter where your tastes lie, Beijing is the place to find "something old, something new, something fusion, something you!"

Peking Opera

The world-famous Peking Opera, China's national opera style, has been an integral part of Chinese culture for over 200 years. Originating from humble beginnings in rural communities, it was brought to the capital by the Qing Emperor Qianlong who, during his periodic inspections of the southern regions, discovered and fell in love with the vibrancy and life in performances there. As an 80th birthday gift to himself, he ordered local companies to perform for him and had the Anhui and Hubei groups incorporated into the palace

The painted faces in Peking Opera represent characters and their specific characteristics. Left to right: Xiaosheng, Huadan, Hualian.

opera. Thus, Peking Opera was born.

Peking Opera is not the only style performed in Beijing today (enthusiasts can also find Kunqu, Pingju and many other styles), but it remains the one that touches people's hearts, and a trip to the city would not be complete without taking in a show. Peking Opera's diverse ingredients—song, dance, martial arts, exotic facial make-up and outlandish costumes—form an ever-changing kaleidoscope of color and movement. Faces are painted to portray a character's personality, temperament and age. The female roles are called *dan* (旦), male roles are *sheng* (生), and clowns are *chou* (丑). Each role, according to their sex, age and disposition, is characterized by particular make-up, for example *jing* (净) rep-

resenting a rough, frank character and *hualian* (花脸) representing a cruel or sinister character.

The costumes, make-up and extravagant traditional headdresses are cultural treasures handed down from generation to generation. It is a living tradition so important in the history of Beijing—a real treat for the eyes, ears and mind to enjoy a performance first-hand.

Venues where you can see Peking Opera performances are listed on p.84, p.110.

Modern Art—Songzhuang Village and 798

Songzhuang Village exemplifies the emerging trend of avant-garde art being produced outside urban life. This

Displayed art pieces at Dashanzi galleries. From left to right: oil painting, sculpture and photo.

trend started in the 1980s, when a community of free-thinking and unconventional poor artists living in the Yuanmingyuan area made an exodus out of the city, aiming for a life less complicated and stressful. Rent was cheaper too. Free of the shackles of city life, pioneering talents like Yue Mingjun and his contemporary Fang Lijun gave birth to new artistic expression and style. From this community lifestyle emerged work that challenged and provoked a re-evaluation of society. Taking on subjects such as gender roles, how to define success, the meaning and purpose of art, the evolution and opening up of society... and all were tackled with passion, vision and brilliance. The concept is simple enough: remove distractions, concentrate talent, promote reflection, challenge preconceptions, encourage expression, provide workspace and art will follow. Follow it has!

Songzhuang Village is a community where artists of today have chosen to embrace this lifestyle and focus their passion into producing quality art. For those who make an appointment and/or arrange to visit, you will see these talented artists at work in their home/studio space. You will find many of them eager to share their vision with you if your Chinese is good enough, or through an interpreter. Small galleries showcase their watercolors, sculptures, oil paintings and designs, many of which are for sale. Even if you are not in the market to acquire anything, a trip to Songzhuang is a worthwhile and interesting way to get "up close and personal" with art.

Another example of Beijing's cutting-edge art area is 798. Details are on p.220.

How to get to Songzhuang: Take Bus "938 支 9" at Beijing Railway Station (北京站) to Songzhuang (宋庄).

Festivals

There are many traditional festivals in China that are celebrated on the Chinese lunar calendar, which is about one month different from the solar calendar. It would be really fun to visit Beijing during one of these festivals as special activities are held and more ancient culture and customs can be enjoyed.

In addition to Chinese festivals dating from time immemorial, Western holidays like Christmas and occasions such as Valentine's Day and Halloween are being embraced with enthusiasm, and as in the West, shoppers can enjoy sales and bargains at such times.

Lantern Festival (元宵节) (*15th of first lunar month. Usually in February*) End of the lunar new year celebrations. Beautiful shining lanterns and *yuanxiao* (glutinous rice dumplings) are the focus, as well as riddle telling, feasting and dancing.

Tomb-sweeping Festival (清明节) (*Usually falls on April 5*) A day off to honor the dead with offerings and the burning of incense and paper money.

New Year's Day (元旦) (*Jan 1*) Locals enjoy one day off; parties are everywhere.

nuary	February	March	April

Spring Festival (春节) (*First day of the first lunar month. Usually in January or February*) This is an exciting time of year in China. Fireworks fill the air; dragons and lions dance in the streets; and temple fairs are enjoyed during this week-long holiday.

International Women's Day (妇女节) (*Mar 8*) Half day off for women only; shopping malls usually have special sales for women.

Where to enjoy traditional temple fairs

White Cloud Temple Fair
白云观庙会
The White Cloud Temple Fair is a buzz of colorful, traditional folk art performances and a very worthwhile Taoist culture exhibition. Sample from a bewildering array of freshly-cooked snacks with typical local flavors. See White Cloud Temple on p.122.

Chinese Spring Festival in Beijing means two things: crowded trains and temple fairs.

International Labor Day (劳动节) (*May 1*) Or May Day holiday. A day off work for all Chinese working people.

International Children's Day (儿童节) (*Jun 1*) Children under 14 have the day off school, and have fun with their parents at parks.

Birthday of the Communist Party of China (建党节) (*Jul 1*) Exhibitions about the Communist Party and commemorative activities are held.

Birthday of the People's Liberation Army (建军节) (*Aug 1*) It is usually celebrated by the army.

May	June	July	August

Chinese Youth Day (青年节) (*May 4*) Commemorating the patriotic and democratic May 4 Movement launched by college students in 1919 to protest the northern warlord government's agreeing to sign an unequal treaty with foreign powers. Schools often organize commemorative activities on this day.

Dragon Boat Festival (端午节) (*Fifth day of fifth lunar month. Usually in June*) Exciting dragon boat races are an activity commemorating a patriotic poet more than 2,000 years ago. Holiday food is *zongzi* (粽子), glutinous rice dumplings wrapped in bamboo or reed leaves.

Double-seventh Festival (七夕节) (*Seventh of seventh lunar month. Usually in August*) Traditional lovers' day in China when romance fills the air and you'll see flower bouquets and couples hand in hand. A Chinese Valentine!

Changdian Temple Fair 厂甸庙会
Transport: Bus 7, 14, 15 to Liulichang (琉璃厂)
Nanxinhua Jie, Liulichang, Xuanwu District.
宣武区南新华街东西琉璃厂
If you wish to visit to Beijing's oldest temple fair, then Changdian should be your first port of call. Boasting the oldest history of any of the city's many fairs, tradition is its middle name!

Ditan Temple Fair 地坛庙会
Enjoy the swirl of vibrant folk performances and fashion shows exhibited at Ditan Temple Fair in Chaoyang District. Their food street is also an eye-pleasing, stomach-rumbling sight to behold! See Ditan (Temple of the Earth) on p.194.

National Teachers' Day (教师节) (*Sep 10*) Teachers enjoy high respect in China. Besides a day off, they may also receive cards, flowers and greeting calls from students.

National Day (国庆节) (*Oct 1*) Holiday celebrating the founding of the People's Republic of China in 1949. Most people get seven days off to spend as they please. A popular time for travel.

September | **October** | **November** | **December**

Mid-autumn Festival (中秋节) (*15ᵗʰ of eighth lunar month. Usually in September or October*) Traditional moon cakes are enjoyed on this new official holiday, as is the full moon in the sky.

Double-ninth Festival (重阳节) (*Ninth of ninth lunar month. Usually in October*) Also called Height-ascending Festival, this is for the seniors, who spend the day climbing mountains or enjoying chrysanthemum wine and Double-ninth Cake.

Cultural Festivals

"Meet in Beijing" Arts Festival "相约北京"联欢活动

The "Meet in Beijing" Arts Festival was born in 2000 and has become an annual international event exploding with cultural diversity. It usually lasts 30-40 days from April to May. Bringing together cultures and traditions from all over the world, this festival stages various art performances, from traditional Chinese operas to Western concerts. You'll find any kind you like at this festival. Time and venues for performances vary. For show info, see www.piao.com.cn.

In Dashanzi, the former factories are revitalized as art galleries.

Chaoyang Pop Music Festival 北京流行音乐节 (朝阳流行音乐周)

Proudly proclaiming its status as Asia's biggest music festival, the Chaoyang Pop Music Festival held during the May Day holiday (May 1-7) at Chaoyang Park welcomes an impressive selection of China's top performers, with international stars too. Chaoyang Park almost buckles under the weight of the 300,000 people who flock to enjoy the pumping music. See Chaoyang Park on p.242.

Dashanzi International Art Festival 北京大山子国际艺术节

Exhibitions, performances, video displays. If it's avant-garde you're after, then the Dashanzi International Art Festival won't disappoint. Featuring renowned artists from China and abroad, this month-long springtime festival epitomizes Beijing's emergence and flourishing on the international art scene. See Dashanzi on p.220.

or check http://www.diaf.org/ (in English and Chinese) for more info.

Beijing International Cultural Tourism Festival 北京国际旅游文化节

To promote greater understanding between China and the rest of the world, this annual festival (usually in September) was first held in 1998. The central feature, a carnival-style parade, displays an assortment of national and international folk artists, performances and exhibitions.

"Beijing 2008" Olympic Culture Festival "北京2008"奥林匹克文化节

After China made its successful Olympic bid in 2003, this festival was created to plan for the future event, with the unveiling of venues, mascots, slogans and all things Olympic! Concerts, exhibitions, dancing and performances are amongst the treats on offer. Now it's held annually in June and July.

A beautiful snow carving of the Great Wall.

Street Culture

Beijing's diversity is readily evident walking down any street. You will find people playing enthusiastic games of chess, mahjong or checkers, often located quite near to local merchants with their wares spread out on blankets. Look for bicycle repair shops, barbershops, shoe repair or street massage services on sidewalks all over the city. Follow the "sound of music" to find street dancers out in full force, in almost any kind of weather. When you're feeling a bit peckish you are sure to find a variety of food (if you're brave and of sound stomach) to sample. In this section, we introduce you to the street culture of Beijing to help make you "Streetwise."

Walking in Reverse
Among the countless ways the Chinese exercise is the mysterious practice of walking backward. Why do they do it? To exercise muscles not used in normal walking, to reduce impact on their knees and to increase leg endurance.

Outdoor Barber
For a cheap haircut you could do worse than to visit one of Beijing's traditional outdoor barbers. Most of them are skilled and can give you a simple haircut, a taste of culture and a great story to tell your friends for a few RMB.

Umbrella? It's not raining...
Umbrellas have become a common accessory in China as women strive to keep their skin as white as possible, pale skin being associated with affluence. It's common to see umbrellas used as parasols in an effort to block the sun.

"Don't walk!"

Traffic Assistants
These under-appreciated city employees act as crosswalk guards. They're the ones who will warn you to stay on the sidewalk just as you're about to step into oncoming traffic. Just listen for a loud whistle and one will be nearby.

Migrant Workers
The heavy lifters, laborers, construction trade guys, working long hours for little money. The majority are from the countryside or other areas of low employment, trying for a better life. The government is trying to better their welfare through improvements in social security, insurance and job training.

"Just a little off the top, please."

A relaxing afternoon with Tweety.

Sword Sharpener

Preserving a piece of Chinese culture with their trade, these craftsmen can sharpen all your knives and scissors to a razor's edge with just a piece of whetstone, a bottle of water and a lot of experience.

"Dance in the street?" Well, yes...

Originally, for the upper class, ballroom dance came to China in the 1930s, however today you will find it taught and practiced in the street. Open squares and large streets become ideal, and more importantly, free "dance halls" often in early morning or just following dinner. You will receive a warm welcome should you decide to join in the fun!

"Walking the bird, I'm just a'walking the bird..."

Older men in Beijing enjoy taking their caged birds for a walk early in the morning. It's a hobby that dates back to the Qing Dynasty when keeping birds for pleasure was a rich man's practice. Nowadays it's a re-minder of the past and an opportunity for the elderly to relax and remain active. Some birds are quite striking and have interesting calls. If you're polite about it, a closer look is often welcome.

Exhibition Chess—All Over Town!

Chinese chess is a local favorite played with enthusiasm in parks and courtyards. Outdoor games are often loud and animated; onlookers cheer or groan as their neighbors attempt to best each other in friendly competition.

Somewhat differing from international chess, here a river separates the opponents.

Food and Drink

"Why did the Peking Duck cross the road?"

There is no such thing as "Chinese food." The sheer enormity and diversity of this country has created regional cuisines that reflect the availability of materials and the tastes of their people. This is aptly summed up in this common saying "sweet in the East, sour in the West, salty in the North, and spicy in the South." Though not 100% accurate, it highlights the diverse flavors of this vast country. Luckily for visitors to Beijing, everything is on offer, ranging from small eateries to fancy five-star establishments. Street food is delicious, filling and cheap and shouldn't be missed. Kebab, roast sweet potato, and fried pancake with egg are some of our favorites! Expect to see beer (Tsingtao is one of locals' favorites), Western wine, whisky and the famous Chinese *baijiu* (白酒), potent white spirit with a high alcohol content. A Beijing favorite is *erguotou* (二锅头), which boasts 56% alcohol.

Eating and Drinking Habits

In China the dining hours are usually just a bit earlier than you are used to. At 11.30am most people are already sitting down ready to dig in. And as for dinner, most people would never dream of arriving any later than 8.30pm to eat, the usual is about 5-6pm. Dinner time in a Chinese restaurant is also served "family-style," with many dishes coming to the center of the table as people eat as they please. While eating in a restaurant, people are never shy and often are rather joyful and rowdy. Shouts of "*Ganbei*!" thunderously carry across the room. This equivalent to "Cheers!" means "drain your glass," and an evening with friends is incomplete without it. Tea is an indispensable part of Chinese people's life; they drink tea at home, in restaurants, or at office. This being the case in most of the street-side restaurants, free tea is served while you wait for your food to come.

How to Order

It's not an easy job for foreigners who don't speak any Chinese to order food in a restaurant. The easiest way is to point at the dishes on their menu. But the cheaper the restaurant, the less likely they have an English menu; more upmarket ones may have pictured menus to give you an idea of what you're ordering. No English menu? No pictures? Fear not. Use our **Picture Menu** on p.35.

Another good way is to look at what the next table is eating. This will give you a clear picture of what the dishes really are. The third way is to ask their staff to recommend dishes to you. But you might end up with something you wouldn't want to eat, like frogs or animals' kidneys. At this time, a phrasebook is always helpful. Ask them to point out the ingredients of the dish on your phrasebook.

Lottery invoice

The government, to encourage people to request receipts, has introduced a lottery-invoice system. Ask your waiter for a *fapiao* (发票 invoice) and scratch off the silver box, you can win up to RMB 5,000 (this system works on the invoice used by the service trades like restaurants and bars), so be sure to ask for one on all purchases!

Beijing Specialties

Royal Cuisine 宫廷菜
The recipes and dishes of the imperial Qing Dynasty kitchens were closely guarded and cherished secrets, but they are still served up today by skilled and talented chefs at several restaurants around town, most notably the **Fangshan Restaurant** (仿膳餐厅 see p.55) in Beihai Park. Highly decorative and artistic pieces are the signature of this style of cooking, a treat for the eyes as well as

for the palate.

The **Manchu-Han Banquet** (满汉全席) can only be described as the ultimate blow-out, taking over three days to complete all 108 dishes. Designed originally as a court banquet for the Manchu and Han people, it can now be experienced at the Fangshan Restaurant on special occasions for those with a hearty appetite!

Peking Roast Duck 北京烤鸭
One of Beijing's most famous culinary exports, Peking Roast Duck is certainly a must-try experience in this city. Wrap the juicy, tender, slow roasted meat in small pancakes, top with dipping sauce and vegetables, wrap the pancake and tuck in for a mouthwatering (and rich) meal.

Bianyifang (便宜坊 86-10-67120505, in Hademen Hotel, No. A2, Chongwenmenwai Dajie, 崇文门外大街甲2号哈德门饭店内) is one of the oldest restaurants, which began to sell Peking Roast Duck in 1855. **Quanjude** (全聚德 see p.108) boasts the most popular place in town.

Roast Mutton and Beef 烤肉
Referred to as the "tent or field food" for centuries, roasted meat was originally the food of northern nomads. Through an improvement in cooking methods, the taste was honed to perfection and it became a staple dish in Beijing. **Kaorou Ji** (烤肉季 see p.73) is famous for its mutton.

The Emperor's food

While there were no hard and fast rules (after all, he was the emperor!), a Qing Dynasty emperor ate two meals a day, one in the morning and the other at lunchtime. According to imperial protocol, the emperor was always to eat alone, not even his wife or mother was allowed to accompany him at the dinner table! A meal would consist of anything between a dozen and several hundred dishes, which the emperor would eat at a place of his choosing.

Fear of poisoning meant precautions; a silver needle was inserted into each dish, which, it was said, would turn dark if the food was poisoned. Furthermore, each dish had to be tasted by the eunuch who delivered the food to the emperor's table.

Hotpot Mutton 涮羊肉

Mutton has been present in the northern diet for many, many years, and hotpot was, and still is a favorite way to enjoy it. The dish is completed with a dipping sauce, a successful mix of unlikely ingredients (sesame paste, fermented bean curd, salty chive, Shaoxing rice wine, pepper oil and bitter shrimp oil) together with sweet garlic and flat bread to soak it up. **Donglaishun** (东来顺 see p.147) is a top spot for this food. The mutton season is generally from October to April.

Hotpot, a fresh alternative to a burger and fries.

Beijing Snacks 小吃

Beijing snacks are yet another living relic handed down through the years, and still play an integral part in gastronomic life. They come in every shape, size and cooking style—steaming, deep and shallow frying, boiling…. Listing every snack would be a near impossibility, these are some of the most common: *douzhi* (豆汁 soy bean milk), *aiwowo* (艾窝窝 steamed cone-shaped cake made of glutinous rice or millet with a sweet filling), *chatang* (茶汤 paste or custard made of millet or sorghum flour), *wandouhuang* (豌豆黄 pea flour cake), and *lüdagun* (驴打滚 pastry made of steamed glutinous millet flour or soybean flour mixed with sugar).

You won't have to look hard for places to buy these. Here are some good starting points: **Nanlaishun** (南来顺 *86-10-63534720, by the west gate of Grand View Garden* 大观园西门旁) in Xuanwu District, where you can find over 70 different kinds; **Longfusi** (隆福寺) and **Niujie** (牛街 see p.109) which sell predominantly Muslim snacks; and

The sweet tanghulu is a great treat from the street.

Donghuamen Night Market (东华门 夜市 see p.83) off Wangfujing with a multifarious collection of snack dishes from all over China.

World Cuisine

If you crave something a little familiar then fear not, Beijing is packed to the hilt with Western restaurants serving anything you could think of: American, Mediterranean, European, South American… The list is endless. Most Western restaurants can be found in areas where expats congregate, notably the east and the northeast. Some long-standing favorites are **Fish Nation** (English, see p.76, p.250), **Peter's Tex-Mex Grill** (US, see p.258), **Grandma's Kitchen** (US, see p. 256), **Pili Pili** (African, see p.230) and **Lotus Root** (Thai, see p.75).

The Chinese love affair with Western-style fast-food joints means that, whatever part of town you are in, you won't have to look hard for McDonald's or KFC, if that's what you're in the mood for.

Korean, Japanese, Indian, Thai and Arabian restaurants have also made a foothold, being popular with Chinese and foreign diners alike.

Vegetarian Food

Most Beijingers are carnivores, though more and more young people, especially white-collar employees, are following vegetarianism to keep their bodies healthy and in shape. Some strict Buddhist believers also don't eat meat at all. Vegetarian restaurants are few and far between and can also be expensive as they try intricate cooking methods to make vegetarian food taste like meat to cater to the fervent meat-eaters. You might not notice them as they don't always have an English name next to the Chinese. Keep your eyes open for the Chinese character "素" (vegetarian) on restaurant signs. It is a good indicator. If you are vegan and don't want to go to expensive vegetarian restaurants, your best bet is to order tofu dishes and vegetables which can be found in all Chinese restaurants. Indian restaurants also serve tasty vegetable dishes. Vegetarian restaurants (see p.82, p.108, and p.229) are listed as one separate category in our restaurant listings.

Food and Drink Hot Spots

Located in many residential and commercial areas, food and drink hot spots have become increasingly popular. Almost every area has one or two. Each has its own style, and features eating and drinking places (we have listed many throughout this guide), and the atmosphere is as intoxicating as the unusual array of foods and drinks. Among the best-known are **Guijie** (see p.79), **Wudaokou** (see p.168), **Yayuncun** (see p.198) and **Sanlitun** (see p.248).

Enjoying Western meals on a night out is a favorite among couples.

Picture Menu

The following are commonly ordered snacks and dishes in a restaurant or at a street-side stand. Chinese and English names, explanations and general prices are given for the ease of your use.

Street Snacks

串儿 Kebabs
RMB 1/stick

煎饼 Jianbing
RMB 2.5/each
Thin pancake with egg and deep-fried crispy crust.

肉夹馍 Roujiamo
RMB 3/each
Mo is a type of bun, and this is sort of Chinese meat sandwich.

红薯 Sweet Potato
RMB 1/each

鸡蛋灌饼 Fried Pancake with Egg Filling
RMB 1/each

驴打滚 Rolling Donkey
RMB 1/each
A kind of Islamic cake made of bean flour.

糖葫芦 Tanghulu
RMB 1/stick
Sugar-coated haws (and nowadays also bananas, grapes, strawberries, yams, etc.) on a stick.

茶鸡蛋 Tea Eggs
RMB 0.7/each

麻辣烫 Malatang
RMB 0.5/stick
Skewers of meat, vegetables or tofu boiling in a tray of spicy broth.

Breakfast

馄饨 Wonton Soup
RMB 1/bowl
Savory little Chinese dumplings stuffed with meat are simmered in broth. Cheap, healthy and tasty.

小笼包 Steamed Stuffed Buns
RMB 0.4/each
These thin wrapped stuffed buns are bursting with flavor. Simple but elegant, they are enjoyed at all times of the day.

油条 Fried Bread Stick
RMB 0.4/each
This morning favorite is a golden brown rectangle of Chinese fried dough.

豆腐脑 Boiled Tofu
RMB 1/bowl
A healthy breakfast choice made from tofu, mushrooms, coriander and chili. Flavorful and warm for winter mornings.

Pork, Beef, and Lamb Dishes

回锅肉 Twice Cooked Pork
RMB 12
Boiled pork slices stirfried with hot sauce.

糖醋排骨 Pork Ribs in Sweet and Sour Sauce
RMB 22

鱼香肉丝 Fish-flavored Shredded Pork
RMB 12

This shredded pork and black fungus dish doesn't actually contain any fish. It's cooked in sumptuous spicy garlic sauce.

菠萝咕老肉 Pineapple Pork with Sweet and Sour Sauce
RMB 16

蚝油牛肉 Beef in Oyster Sauce
RMB 20

Strips of fresh beef served in oyster sauce, sometimes with vegetables. Not very spicy, but definitely scrumptious.

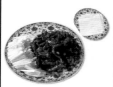

京酱肉丝 Shredded Pork with Beijing Sauce
RMB 10

Shredded pork in Beijing sauce served with tofu wraps and spring onions. Make wondrous little tacos and use your fingers!

糖醋里脊 Sweet and Sour Pork Tenders
RMB 18

铁板牛肉 / 羊肉 Sizzling Beef/Lamb
RMB 22

A sizzling beef/lamb platter with pepper or tomato flavor. You can smell the mouth-watering aroma before it reaches your table.

火锅 Hotpot
RMB 40/person

A soup base boils in the center of the table, to which you can add meat or vegetables of your choice! Vegetarian/vegan safe if requested.

Chicken and Duck Dishes

宫保鸡丁 Kung Pow Chicken
RMB 12

A delightful blend of cubed chicken, peanuts and vegetables stir fried with red chili bean paste. Great with a bowl of rice.

烤鸭 Peking Roast Duck
RMB 48/each

This dish dates back at least 1,500 years and is Beijing's most famous and revered delicacy. You simply must try it.

Vegetable

脆皮日本豆腐 Crispy Tofu
RMB 16

蚝油生菜 Lettuce in Oyster Sauce
RMB 8

Never had cooked lettuce? Try this one. The Chinese cook their lettuce in oyster sauce, and it's quite nice actually.

清炒荷兰豆 Fried Pea Pods
RMB 12

These are great, fresh and a little sweet, cooked in almost buttery-tasting oil. Crispy and flavorful.

干煸四季豆
Dry-fried String Beans
RMB 14
These beans are truly savory, soaking up the flavor of the pork they're prepared with.

西芹炒腰果
Celery with Cashew
RMB 16

松仁玉米 Pine Nuts with Sweet Corn
RMB 20
Crunchy, fresh and a little salty.

西红柿炒鸡蛋
Scrambled Eggs with Tomatoes
RMB 8
Visitors to China seem to love this simple dish, perhaps because it's uncomplicated and the name says it all.

Staple Food

什锦炒饭
Assorted Fried Rice
RMB 10

饺子 Dumplings
RMB 0.5/each
Filled with vegetables or meat, these bite-sized treats are usually served with vinegar and soy sauce. Quick and easy.

锅贴 Fried Dumplings
RMB 12
Savory pan-fried dumplings.

春卷 Spring Rolls
RMB 2/each
Crispy little appetizers, these thin rolls are filled with meat and vegetables and then deep-fried till delicious.

金银馒头
Gold and Silver Buns
RMB 12
Deep-fried and original steamed buns accompanied with a sweet dipping sauce.

For the Brave Only

臭豆腐 Stinky Tofu
RMB 8/plate
Deep-fried fermented tofu.

毛蛋 Fuzzy Eggs
RMB 1/stick
It is fully-formed, unhatched chick.

红烧猪蹄
Marinated Pig's Feet
RMB 28

Sport and Entertainment

Tai Chi: martial art or moving meditation? You decide.

Chinese people love sport and exercise. All across Beijing in communities of every size, the government has installed exercise equipment and encouraged its use. The awarding of the 2008 Olympic Games saw an even bigger push in encouraging Beijingers to get active. Billiards, table tennis, badminton, volleyball, aerobics, dance, Tai Chi and more are "played," mostly in early mornings and evenings, often led by local community members who love to teach.

In addition to lively bars, nightclubs and KTV (karaoke) rooms right in your face, Beijing's entertainment life also involves traditional acrobatic shows and kungfu extravaganzas, both featuring dazzling displays of human agility and strength; as well as quick mask-changing (变脸), shadow puppet show (皮影戏), theater shows and movies.

Martial Arts/Wushu 武术

Martial arts of every kind exist in Beijing. Kungfu, Taijiquan (Tai Chi) and Wushu to name only three. Wushu's popularity has soared since the announcement to include it as an Olympic sport for the 2008 games in Beijing. Martial arts enthusiasts from all over the world have come to study here, many of them at the prestigious Beijing Sports University (北京体育大学 http://219.242.208.2/jgsz/htm/xzbm/wsc/htm/wsc_lbww.html). The Red Theater (see p.110) is a good place for kungfu shows.

Yangge Dance 秧歌

If you hear rhythmic drumming and see a group of people dancing in unison to the music and wielding fans on the street or a public square, you have stumbled across *yangge* (秧歌). Originating in the rural north, *yangge* now is beloved by senior urbanites, who take the vigorous movements as a way to keep fit.

"Am I doing it right?"

Bars and Nightclubs

From seedy to sensational, from almost free to insanely pricey, there is a bar for you in Beijing! Check our section on bars and nightclubs where we feature a wide selection of places to relax, unwind and socialize. To find choices to suit any taste and/or budget, we wandered and drank our way through most of the city (no thanks required, it's our job). With new locations opening every day and others packing up and moving on, you may not always find what we've written about, but you will no doubt find a place where fun is on the menu and the drink flows free (even if not cheap). Most bars don't charge entrance fee unless there are special performances. Dance clubs and discos charge RMB 10-100 for entrance, depending on the time and events.

Many bars continue the party into the early hours of the morning.

KTV

KTV is wildly popular in China, where it is most often enjoyed with a group of friends or business associates, not in a bar with all the other patrons as in the West, but in one's own private (sometimes very large) room. Many KTV places have a good selection of English songs available. Don't be at all surprised to find Chinese people who cannot speak English able to belt out a famous English song pretty well. Decent KTV locations include **Melody** and **Partyworld** (featuring buffet style lunches and dinners as a part of their room rental fee. See p.143).

Cinemas and Theaters

Beijing has massive movie houses and top-notch concert halls which continue to open despite the well over 100 locations currently in business. Major theaters are: **Capital** (see p.84), **Tianqiao** (see p.110), **Chang' an** (see p.84) and **Poly** (see p.84). And now Beijing boasts a world-class **National Grand Theater** (see p.84) to the west of the Tian'anmen Square which will be open in 2008.

These venues not only host traditional Peking Opera and acrobatic shows, but also western dramas, ballets and concerts. Star names have made appearances in Beijing, including Sarah Brightman, Nora Jones, David Copperfield, Luciano Pavarotti; even the Broadway musical *CATS* played here. The **UME Cinema** opposite the Shuang'an Department Store is among the many where you can catch the latest Hollywood movies (dubbed or in the original language with subtitles), as well as Chinese blockbusters. Interested in Chinese "arthouse" movies? Check out **Cherry Lane Movies** which on Fridays and Saturdays features Chinese "arthouse" films with English subtitles. Check their website at www. cherrylanemovies.com.cn for listings. You can also check upcoming events and book tickets of all kinds through www. piao.com.cn, which offers service in Chinese, English, Japanese and Korean, or by calling ticket hotlines: 86-10-64177845, 400-810-3721/800-810-3721 (in English).

"Historical" Central

"Historical Central" refers to the area encompassed by Subway Line 2 (the Loop Line), which follows the outline of what was once Beijing's Inner City wall (see **Layout of old Beijing** on p.53).

This dynamic area is a showcase of the cultural and political lifeblood of both modern and ancient Beijing. Many of Beijing's crème-de-la-crème tourist sites are found in this area. From **Tian'anmen Square** (see p.50) in the heart of the city, you are a few short steps from the **Forbidden City** (see p.44), the **National Museum of China** (see p.65) and the **Memorial Hall of Chairman Mao** (see p.51). A short bus, subway or taxi ride will bring you to **Wangfujing** (see p.85), both a subway stop and a huge shopping area, the imperial **Beihai Park** (see p.54) and **Shichahai** (see p.72) where you can enjoy a unique *hutong* (ancient alleys, see p.64) tour. When you are visiting Beijing, "Central" is certainly the ideal place to start.

Highlights

- **Tian'anmen Square** 天安门广场 One of the best-known landmarks of Beijing. Imagine 63 soccer fields end-to-end to grasp the sheer scale of one of the world's largest public squares (440,000 sq m). **See p.50**
- **Forbidden City** 故宫 Also called Palace Museum, this former dwelling of Chinese emperors is the most amazing royal palace complex. **See p.44**
- **Beihai Park** 北海公园 Oldest and best-preserved imperial garden in the downtown area. **See p.54**
- **Lama Temple** 雍和宫 Pray in this biggest lamasery in Beijing and bring good luck back home. **See p.57**
- **Drum Tower and Bell Tower** 钟鼓楼 Back in the Ming Dynasty, they were used to mark time, an equivalent to Big Ben in London. **See p.56**

- **Beijing Underground City** 北京地下城 An underground rabbit warren of tunnels, built to protect Chinese people from nuclear threat in the 1960s. **See p.62**
- **National Museum of China** 中国国家博物馆 Soak yourself in 5,000 years of Chinese history. **See p.65**
- **Hutong** 胡同 Ancient alleys keep the most authentic flavor of old Beijing. Enjoy a rickshaw tour among the grid-pattern *hutong* alleys. **See p.64**
- **Wangfujing Shopping Street** 王府井步行街 This over-700-year-old commercial street offers a wide variety of bargain shops, posh boutiques and a great place to hang out. **See p.85**
- **Donghuamen Night Market** 东华门夜市 Offering some of the best street food in town, it's like Chinatown, in China. **See p.83**

Sightseeing

Tourist Attractions

❶ Forbidden City
故宫 Gùgōng ★★★

Imperial palace

Hours: daily 8.30am-5pm (Apr 16-Oct 15, last entry at 4 pm), 8.30am-4.30pm (Oct 16-Apr 15, last entry at 3.30pm)

Entrance: RMB 60 (Apr 1-Oct 31), RMB 40 (Nov 1-Mar 31), free (children under 1.2 m), half price with a student card or for women on Women's Day (March 8); Clock and Watch Hall and Treasure Gallery require an additional RMB 10; audio tour RMB 40 with a RMB 100 deposit.

Suggested length of visit: 2 hours-1 day, and the earlier start the better.

Transport: Bus 1, 2, 10, 20, 52, 120, 126, 203, 205, 728, 802 or Subway Line 1 to Tian'anmen East (天安门东) or Tian'anmen West (天安门西), then go through the Tian'anmen Rostrum to the south gate; or Bus 202, 211, 810, 814, 846, 101, 103, 109, 124 to Palace Museum (故宫)

North of Tian'anmen Square. (86-10-65132255) http://www.dpm.org.cn/
天安门北侧

❌ *Wangfujing Food Street (王府井小吃一条街)*

🔪 *A deposit is required for audio tour rentals and can only be refunded where paid, which means a long walk back at the end of the tour. A guidebook is a way around this and you can keep it for posterity!*

Today the Forbidden City, or Palace Museum, a **World Cultural Heritage** site since 1987, still abounds with its original sense of grandeur and wealth, an aura of pomp and majesty passed down through the eras, a secret city closed off from the world for about 500 years. 720,000 sq m of courtyards, pavilions, great halls, flourishing gardens and nearly 10,000 rooms combine to form one of the best preserved historical sites in China. Built by tens of thousands of people, it took over 14 years and 32 million bricks to complete.

Owing its origins to the 24 Ming and Qing dynasty emperors who worked and lived here, few of the original buildings remain. The last emperor **Puyi** (known in the West through the movie *The Last Emperor*) moved out of this complex in 1925. Today only 1/3 of this palace complex is open to the public; the latest renovations, started in 2002, will however make it possible to display almost half of the palace by the time of the 2008 Beijing Olympics.

The entire palace sits on a north-south axis, or the meridian line, with halls and houses symmetrically arranged on the sides. It consists of three parts: the **outer court** (外廷) where the emperor received high officials and administered state affairs; the **inner court** (内廷) where the emperor, empress and concubines lived; and the **Imperial Garden** (御花园) for the imperial family to entertain and relax.

Visits to the Forbidden City can be conducted via four routes, and three are listed in the book. The palace is huge and it's hard to see everything in a day. So follow one of our routes to make the best use of your time.

Kept full of water, these were to be used in case of fire.

● How did all the stone for the Forbidden City get there?

Constructing the Forbidden City called for monumental quantities of high quality stone, much of it white marble quarried in the outer limits of Beijing and granite from neighboring Hebei Province. Transporting enormous blocks of stone to the capital was a Herculean feat, for there was no machinery to lighten the load. Hundreds of men were needed for this huge task, in a never-ending process of sliding stone over wooden rollers in summer; and over homemade ice-blocks in winter.

● Too many rooms for one man?

The legendary Jade Emperor in Heaven was believed to have enjoyed a palace of "10,000 rooms" ("room" here refers to the space between two pillars). Regarded as Sons of Heaven, all earthly Chinese emperors showed due respect for the Jade Emperor by stopping short of this number—hence the deferential number of 9,999.5 rooms in the Forbidden City.

● How many concubines did an emperor have?

Chinese emperors were well-known for their staggering numbers of concubines. One example was the Qing Emperor Kangxi (r. 1662-1723) who had eight categories of empress and imperial concubines: one empress, one *Huangguifei* (first-rank), two *Guifei* (second-rank), four *Fei* (third-rank) and six *Pin* (fourth-rank), plus an unknown number of *Guiren* ("honorable concubines"), *Changzai* ("always there") and *Daying* ("answering"). Emperor Kangxi had 55 empresses and concubines, while Emperor Guangxu was the most modest with only one empress and two concubines.

Many concubines fell into disfavor with the emperor and were banished to a secluded portion of the palace, forbidden to see other men. The emperor might not even have slept with some of these women, or perhaps only once. The dream of every imperial concubine was to become pregnant and bear a son who might one day become emperor himself.

● Eunuch system

Surrounded by legions of beautiful concubines and maids, the emperor nevertheless could tolerate no intermingling, so to prevent affairs in the Imperial Palace, male servants were castrated. This dangerous and inhumane practice took many lives. Those that survived lived a fairly privileged life, but at great personal cost.

Differently ranked, some eunuchs achieved considerable power, holding a relationship of trust with the emperor, no doubt partially because of their lack of a certain appendage. It was not rare that high-ranking eunuchs interfered with the imperial laws and this had a destructive effect on the imperial court.

It is said there are almost 10,000 rooms in Forbidden City. Do you dare count?

Hall of Celestial and Terrestrial Union (交泰殿 Jiaotaidian)
Signifying the happy and long marriage of the emperor and empress, this hall served as the reception point for her majesty's birthday parties. Today 25 imperial seals are kept here.

Palace of Terrestrial Tranquility (坤宁宫 Kunninggong)
In the Ming Dynasty this was where the empress lived. In the Qing Dynasty, it was used for offering sacrifices to the Manchu gods and its east wing room was used as bridal chamber of the newly wed emperor and empress.

Route A: two hours

Meridian Gate (午门)→ Gate of Prosperous Harmony (熙和门)→ Gate of Supreme Harmony (太和门)→ Hall of Enlarging Right Conducts (弘义阁)→ Hall of Supreme Harmony (太和殿)→Hall of Central Harmony (中和殿)→ Hall of Preserved Harmony (保和殿)→ Grand Council (军机处)→ Gate of Celestial Purity (乾清门)→ Palace of Celestial Purity (乾清宫)→ Hall of Celestial and Terrestrial Union (交泰殿)→Palace of Terrestrial Tranquility (坤宁宫)→ Imperial Garden (御花园)→ Hall of Imperial Peace (钦安殿)→ Gate of Divine Might (神武门)

Hall of Mental Cultivation (养心殿 Yangxindian)
Historically important hall where the Qing emperors lived, studied, and worked after Emperor Yongzheng (1677-1735). Empress Dowager Cixi attended to state affairs behind a curtain in the east chamber of this hall.

Hall of Preserved Harmony (保和殿 Baohedian)
In the Ming Dynasty, the emperor put on ritual clothing here before the ceremonies. In the Qing Dynasty, it was used for imperial banquets and examinations.

Route C: one day

Meridian Gate (午门)→ Gate of Prosperous Harmony (熙和门)→ Hall of Martial Valor (武英殿)→ Gate of Prosperous Harmony (熙和门)→ Gate of Supreme Harmony (太和门)→Hall of Enlarging Right Conducts (弘义阁)→ Hall of Supreme Harmony (太和殿)→ Hall of Central Harmony (中和殿)→ Hall of Preserved Harmony (保和殿)→ Grand Council (军机处)→ Hall of Mental Cultivation (养心殿)→ Six Western Palaces (西六宫)→ Imperial Garden (御花园)→ Palace of Terrestrial Tranquility (坤宁宫)→ Hall of Celestial and Terrestrial Union (交泰殿)→Palace of Celestial Purity (乾清宫)→Gate of Celestial Purity (乾清门)→Hall for Ancestral Worship (Clock and Watch Hall) 奉先殿 (钟表馆)→Xiqing Gate (锡庆门)→ Nine-dragon Screen (九龙壁)→Gate of Imperial Supremacy (皇极门)→Hall of Imperial Supremacy (Treasure Gallery) 皇极殿 (珍宝馆)→Music Corner (畅音阁)→ Hall of Character Cultivation (养性殿)→ Qianlong Garden (乾隆花园)→Hall of Joyful Longevity (乐寿堂)→ Pavilion of Sustained Harmony (颐和轩)→Hall of Infinite Happiness (符望阁)→ Well of Concubine Zhen (珍妃井)→ Dongtongzi (东筒子)→ Cangzhen Gate (苍震门)→ Palace of Abstinence (斋宫)→ Six Eastern Palaces (东六宫)→Imperial Garden (御花园)→Hall of Imperial Peace (钦安殿)→ Gate of Divine Might (神武门)

Meridian Gate (午门 Wumen)
This enormous gate stands nearly 40 m tall and guards entrance to the Forbidden City. In the Qing Dynasty, c officials would wait inside this gate every morning for the peror to appear in court.

Imperial Garden (御花园 **Yuhuayuan**)
This largest garden in the Forbidden City was a serene place for generations of the imperial families to relax on their own.

Palace of Celestial Purity (乾清宫 **Qianqinggong**)
This was where emperors of the Qing and Ming dynasties slept. After, Emperor Yongzheng, the third Qing emperor, moved to the Hall of Mental Cultivation, it was used for handling routine state affairs, receiving officials and occasional banquets.

Six Eastern Palaces (东六宫 **Dongliugong**)
These concubine living quarters are now exhibition areas for treasures of former imperial families.

Hall of Imperial Supremacy (皇极殿 **Huangjidian**)
A smaller model of the Palace of Celestial Purity. Now it is the first exhibition hall of the Treasure Gallery.

Nine-dragon Screen (九龙壁 **Jiulongbi**)
A symbol of the emperor's supreme power. When the screen was being fired in the kiln, a piece broke and was replaced with a bit of wood. If the emperor had known, death would have resulted. However, the imperial inspectors missed the flaw on the belly of the third dragon. Can you see it?

Hall of Central Harmony (中和殿 **Zhonghedian**)
A private study for the emperor and a place for him to rest a while and receive officials before important ceremonies.

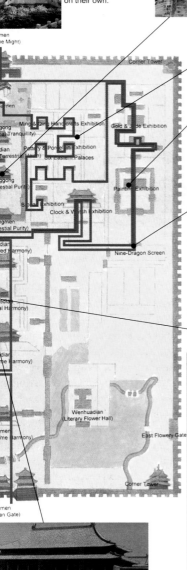

Supreme Harmony (太和殿 **Taihedian**)
...ghest hall in the Forbidden City is also called "the..." Used for the emperor's accession to the throne, ...se of the rule over the country and important cer... ...s like weddings and New Year's banquet.

Route B: half day

Meridian Gate (午门)→ Gate of Supreme Harmony (太和门)→ Hall of Enlarging Right Conducts (弘义阁)→ Hall of Supreme Harmony (太和殿)→ Hall of Central Harmony (中和殿)→Hall of Preserved Harmony (保和殿)→ Grand Council (军机处)→ Hall of Mental Cultivation (养心殿)→ Six Western Palaces (西六宫)→Imperial Garden (御花园)→Palace of Terrestrial Tranquility (坤宁宫)→ Hall of Celestial and Terrestrial Union (交泰殿)→Palace of Celestial Purity (乾清宫)→ Gate of Celestial Purity (乾清门)→ Gate of Prospering Fortune (景运门)→ Hall for Ancestral Worship (Clock and Watch Hall) 奉先殿 (钟表馆)→Xiqing Gate (锡庆门)→Nine-dragon Screen (九龙壁)→ Gate of Imperial Supremacy (皇极门)→ Hall of Imperial Supremacy (Treasure Gallery) 皇极殿 (珍宝馆)→Palace of Tranquil Longevity (宁寿宫)→Music Corner (畅音阁) →Hall of Character Cultivation (养性殿)→Qianlong Garden (乾隆花园)→Hall of Joyful Longevity (乐寿堂)→Pavilion of Sustained Harmony (颐和轩)→ Hall of Infinite Happiness (符望阁)→ Well of Concubine Zhen (珍妃井)→ Gate of Divine Might (神武门)

Join the fun, and fly your kite on Tian'anmen Square.

❷ Tian'anmen
天安门 Tiān'ānmén ★★★

Landmark of Beijing

Hours: daily, except special events
Entrance: Tian'anmen Square free, Tian'anmen Rostrum (天安门城楼) RMB 15 for adults, RMB 5 for those over 70
Suggested length of visit: 1 hour
Transport: Bus 1, 2, 10, 20, 52, 120, 126, 203, 205, 728, 802 or Subway Line 1 to Tian'anmen East (天安门东) or Tian'anmen West (天安门西)
Chang'an Jie, west of Wangfujing. (86-10-63095745) 长安街, 王府井西侧

❌ *Laijin Yuxuan (来今雨轩, 86-10-66056676), inside the west gate of Zhongshan Park, RMB 50-60/ person, famous for the dishes described in the classic novel, A Dream of Red Mansions. Or try Tianyuan Fast Food Restaurant (天苑快餐厅, 86-10-65597692) on Guangchang Donglu (广场东路), south of Tian'anmen Shopping Center (天安门购物中心)*

📝 *Make the most of your visit by entering Tian'anmen Square from the south at Qianmen. From here you are central to the square as well as the Qianmen Gate Tower and Dazhalan (Dashilan in Beijing dialect), a traditional shopping street.*

With the Forbidden City to the north and the **Memorial Hall of Chairman Mao** (毛主席纪念堂) to the south, the **National Museum of China** (中国国家博物馆) to the east and the **Great Hall of the People** (人民大会堂) to the west, the square surrounds the central **Monument to the People's Heroes** (人民英雄纪念碑) bearing the inscription "The People's Heroes Are Immortal." Built in 1958, the Square is the world's largest public square (440,000 sq m) and has witnessed many historical events.

Across the street to its north end is the **Tian'anmen Rostrum** where imperial edicts were issued in the Ming and Qing dynasties. Standing on the rostrum to view the expanse of Tian'anmen Square, one may remember Chairman Mao's declaration to the world on October 1, 1949: "The People's Republic of China and the central people's government are founded!"

Flag ceremonies

Getting up at the crack of dawn isn't everyone's idea of fun, but watching the People's Liberation Army guard of honor march on Tian'anmen Square to perform the flag ceremony is certainly worth the effort. Timed to occur at exactly sunrise (and sunset for the lowering ceremony), the ceremony lasts two minutes and seven seconds: the exact time it takes the sun to rise and set each day. Vehicles driving down Chang'an Jie stop as a mark of honor; an impressive sight and certainly the quietest the square ever gets. Flag-raising ceremony time varies (exact time is posted next to the flagpole): around 4.30am in summer and 7am in winter. If you can't make the flag-raising ceremony, try the flag-lowering ceremony some time between 4.30pm-6.30pm.

Memorial Hall of Chairman Mao
毛主席纪念堂 Máozhǔxí jìniàntáng

Contains body of Chairman Mao

Hours: 8.30am-11.30am (Tue-Sun); 2pm-4pm (Tue & Thur) (closed on Mondays; check hours on special holidays)
Entrance: free
Suggested length of visit: 45 minutes
South side of Tian'anmen Square. (86-10-65132277 ext.80)
天安门广场南部

⚡ Bags and cameras are not allowed through and have to be stored across the road in a separate building for a small fee.

Join the line to file past the body of Chairman Mao, displayed lying in a crystal coffin. In the north hall stands a grand and smiling statue of Chairman Mao against *Throughout China*, a huge piece of embroidery depicting China's cultural and historical ancestry. The hall also displays the achievements of veteran Chinese revolutionaries. An impressive collection of cultural relics, historical texts, letters and photos fill the halls.

❸ Working People's Cultural Palace 劳动人民文化宫 Láodòng rénmín wénhuàgōng ★

Once the place for emperors to pay respects to their ancestors

Hours: daily 6am-9pm (summer), 6.30am-7.30pm (winter)
Entrance: RMB 2
Suggested length of visit: 45 minutes
Transport: see transport to Tian'anmen on p.50
East of Tian'anmen Rostrum. (86-10-65252189/ 65250474)
天安门城楼东侧

On May 1, 1951, International Labor Day, Mao Zedong declared the opening of the Beijing Working People's Cultural Palace, bringing to an end 500 years of near abandon of the Imperial Ancestral Temple (太庙 Taimiao), first built in 1420 to serve as a repository. It was here that the Ming and Qing emperors offered sacrifices to their ancestors when they were enthroned, married, received prisoners of war or returned triumphantly from battles. The imperial halls remain today having been turned into a public park with lovely ancient pine trees and flowerbeds.

❹ Zhongshan Park 中山公园
Zhōngshān gōngyuán ★★

Where emperors worshipped the gods of Land and Grain

Hours: daily 6am-10pm (summer, last entry at 9pm), 6.30am-9pm (winter, last entry at 8pm)
Entrance: RMB 3 for adults, free for children under 1.2 m
Suggested length of visit: 1/2 hour
Transport: see transport to Tian'anmen on p.50
West of Tian'anmen Rostrum. (86-10-66055431)
天安门城楼西侧

Zhongshan Park arches are inscribed with "Defend the Peace" (Baowei Heping).

This little park has a long, tumultuous history: starting life 1,000 years ago as a temple. In 1421, the Ming Emperor Yongle had the sacrificial **Altar of Land and Grain** (社稷坛 Shejitan) built on the temple site, its location perfectly symmetrical to the Imperial Ancestral Temple. The altar sits at the north end of the park today. It is a three-tiered square terrace. The top tier is filled with five different types of soil, red, white, black, green and yellow. 1914 saw the opening of the altar to the public as Central Park, which in 1928 was renamed Zhongshan Park, as tribute to Dr. Sun Yat-sen. While many of the early phases of the temple have long gone, its ancient cypress trees are silent witness to the years of change.

❺ Jingshan Park 景山公园
Jǐngshān gōngyuán ★★

Best view over the Forbidden City

Hours: daily 6am-10pm (summer), 6.30am-8pm (winter)
Entrance: RMB 2, RMB 5 during flower exhibitions

From atop the 48-m-high Jingshan Hill you get a royal view of Beijing.

Imperial suicide at Jingshan Hill

It is said that the last Ming emperor Chongzhen hanged himself on an old pagoda tree at the eastern foot of Jingshan Hill after insurgent peasants conquered Beijing in 1644. Now a new tree has been planted to mark what is thought to be the site of the suicide.

Suggested length of visit: 1-1.5 hours
Transport: Bus 5, 810 to Jingshan Houjie (景山后街); or 812, 814, 846, 101, 103, 109, 124 to Palace Museum (故宫)
Opposite the north gate of the Forbidden City, Xicheng District. (86-10-64044071)
西城区故宫北门对面

Jingshan, or Coal Hill since coal was once heaped at the foot of the hill, provides a wonderful view over the Forbidden City. The highest point in town in ancient times, now dwarfed by skyscrapers, it was created using earth from the moat when it was dug, and was situated to enhance the Forbidden City's *fengshui*, blocking the northern winds and providing an aesthetic and spiritual link to the mountains of the Ming Tombs.

❻ Huangchenggen Site Park
皇城根遗址公园 Huángchénggēn yízhǐ gōngyuán ★

Imperial city wall

Hours: daily 24 hours
Entrance: free
Suggested length of visit: 1 hour
Transport: Bus 60, 112 to Shatan Lukoubei (沙滩路口北)
Along Nanheyan Dajie and Beiheyan Dajie.
南河沿大街和北河沿大街东侧

The park lies between Forbidden City and Wangfujing Street, on the site where the centuries-old east **Imperial City Wall** had stood. With a length of 2.8 km and a width of 30 m, it provides seven cultural spots including maps of Beijing in the Ming and Qing dynasties carved in stone.

This park connects Ping'an Dajie and Chang'an Jie.

Layout of old Beijing

One of the most surprising things about Beijing is that the 21st century city still follows the basic Ming and Qing dynasty street pattern. During that time, the city center was, like today, the oblong Forbidden City surrounded by a turreted 10-m-high wall and a deep moat. Home to the emperor, it was completely off limits to all but the elite, as was the Imperial City, the next "ring" in the sequence. Also walled, it contained the still standing Imperial Ancestral Temple and Altar of Land and Grain. The Inner City, inhabited by royal families and high-ranking officials, formed the third oblong "ring," today's loop subway line. Further to the south was the Outer City, an anomaly in the symmetry and the living space of ordinary people.

Along the central axis running north-south through the Forbidden City, are arranged symmetrically shops and houses, in addition to major altars: Temple of Heaven in the south (Tiantan), Temple of the Earth (Ditan) in the north, Temple of the Moon (Yuetan) in the west and Temple of the Sun (Ritan) in the east.

❼ Beihai Park 北海公园
Běihǎi gōngyuán ★★★

Oldest and best-preserved imperial garden downtown

Hours: Park: daily 6am-9pm (Apr 1-May 31, Sep 1-Oct 31), 6.30am-8pm (Nov 1-Mar 31), 6am-10pm (Jun 1-Aug 31); Jade Island (琼华岛): daily 8.30am-6pm (summer), 9am-4.30pm (winter)
Entrance: RMB 10 (summer) and RMB 5 (winter); all-inclusive ticket RMB 20 (summer) and RMB 15 (winter)
Suggested length of visit: 2 hours
Transport: Bus 5, 812, 814, 846, 101, 103, 109, 124 to Beihai (北海); or 13, 701, 107, 111, 118 to Beihai Park North Gate (北海北门)
East side of Andingmenwai Dajie. (86-10-64038054)
安定门外大街路东

❌ *Ri Chang Restaurant (日昌茶餐厅, 86-10-64058205), about 200 m east of Beihai Park North Gate, RMB 30-45/person. Cheap Cantonese food.*
🛥 *Boats are available for getting around: north bank to Fangshan (仿膳) (RMB 10); west bank to Jade Island (琼华岛) (RMB 5).*

Beihai Park remains one of China's oldest and best-preserved imperial gardens, and a true haven in the midst of urban hustle. Dating back 1,000 years, it has survived the Liao, Jin, Yuan, Ming and Qing dynasties, and is a perfect example of the ancient Chinese art of garden landscaping. This park covers an area of over 700,000 sq m and more than half is water. Its hills and manicured lawns boast many species of trees and plants fringing a large lake, with pavilions and towers hidden in between. Today, it is a great place for boating in summer and a huge ice rink in winter.

The park has four gates, leading in four different directions. Most visitors enter the park through its south gate, tour the island, and then walk all the way along the eastern bank of the lake to its north gate if they have time.

White Dagoba (白塔 Baita)
An onion-shaped shrine dagoba in Tibetan style in the center of Jade Island, built to honor the fifth Dalai Lama when he visited Beijing in 1651.

Round Town (团城 Tuancheng)
Round Town is a small castle enclosure on the south of Beihai Park. In its heyday, the main building here, **Hall of Receiving Light** (承光殿 Chengguangdian), was a spot favored by Ming emperors for watching fireworks; it was made a Buddha hall in the Qing Dynasty. The huge jade urn in the Jade Urn Pavilion was believed to be Kublai Khan's wine vessel.

Nine-dragon Screen (九龙壁 Jiulongbi)
One of a trio of similarly designed, equally famous walls in China, it is built completely of glazed tiles and actually has 635 carved dragons, an impressive feat of Qing Dynasty craftsmanship. It is 5 m high and 27 m long.

Five-dragon Pavilions (五龙亭 Wulongting)
This area was named after the magical impression of five pavilions linked up by winding bridges. It was a favorite place of imperial families, where they could relax, enjoy a spot of fishing or watch the moon.

Tranquil Mind Study (静心斋 Jingxinzhai)
On the north shore of the lake. Built in 1757 and once a study of Qing Dynasty Emperor Qianlong, this is Beihai's crowning glory. In front of the building, Empress Dowager Cixi even had a railway built that led to Zhongnanhai.

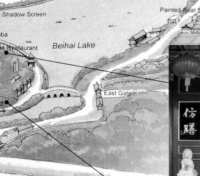

Fangshan Restaurant (仿膳)
To dine like a royal, there is no other choice than Fangshan Restau-rant. "Fangshan" means meals cooked to the same specifications as those prepared in the imperial kitchen, and this restaurant was founded in 1925 by several cooks from the imperial kitchen.

Temple of Eternal Peace (永安寺 Yong'ansi)
Built in 1651 together with the White Dagoba. Once a temple for Lamas to read sutras, later it was also used for imperial families to pay respects to Buddha.

Jade Island (琼华岛 Qionghuadao)
The most impressive part of Beihai Park. Based on a legendary immortals' land, this 66,000-sq-m islet is especially beautiful in summer when lotus blossoms flourish. In its center stands a giant white dagoba, with many temple halls dotted around.

❽ Prince Gong's Mansion
恭王府 Gōngwángfǔ ★★★

The best example of a prince's mansion

Hours: daily 7.30am-5pm (summer), 8.30am-4.30pm (winter)

Entrance: RMB 20; RMB 60 (including a guide and a Peking Opera show in its theater)

Suggested length of visit: 1 hour

Transport: Bus 13, 701, 107, 111, 118 to Beihai Park North Gate (北海北门), walk west 200 m, then turn north.

No. A14, Liuyin Jie, Xicheng District. (86-10-66180573)

西城区柳荫街甲14号

✖ *See "Food and Entertainment" around the Shichahai lake area on p.72*

This beautifully preserved mansion near Shichahai Lake owes its name to Prince Gong, who helped Empress Dowager Cixi assume power; in 1851 he received this complex as a gift from his brother, the Qing Emperor Xianfeng (r.1851-1862). Originally built in 1777, it was once home to He Shen, one of the most corrupt ministers of Emperor Qianlong's reign period. It has been well loved and well preserved ever since. Today only its garden is open to visitors; by 2008, however, visitors will be able to see the main part of the mansion.

The garden in Prince Gong's Mansion.

❾ Drum Tower and Bell Tower
钟鼓楼 Zhōnggǔlóu ★★

Ancient timekeeping

Hours: daily 9am-5.30pm

Entrance: RMB 15 for Bell Tower and RMB 20 for Drum Tower

Suggested length of visit: 45 minutes

Transport: Bus 5, 60, 124, 834, 107 to Drum Tower (鼓楼)

Gulou Xidajie, Dongcheng District. (Bell Tower: 86-10-64012674; Drum Tower: 64075176)

东城区鼓楼西大街

✖ *Walk south from the Drum Tower to Di'anmenwai Dajie (地安门外大街). Try Wangdelou Muslim Restaurant (望德楼穆斯林餐厅, 86-10-64041818), RMB 40-50/person.*

✐ *Visitors can beat the drums and bells on New Year's Day and Spring Festival. With the Museum Pass you can get two free admissions to the Bell Tower.*

The original Drum Tower goes back over 700 years to the Yuan Dynasty reign of Kublai Khan. Back in the Ming Dynasty, the drums in the Drum Tower were beaten to give the correct time of day. Today, on the second floor, there is a drum-beating performance every half hour, lasting about three minutes each time.

100 m north sits the Bell Tower, which dates back to 1420. The tower's original iron bell was deemed too quiet, so it was replaced with a huge bronze one, whose casing was over 10 inches thick. The bronze bell, which is still there and in perfect condition, can be heard as far as 20 km away.

Standing on the Drum Tower or the Bell Tower, you'll get the best aerial view of the surrounding *hutong* alley community.

⑩ Lama Temple
雍和宮 Yōnghégōng ★★★

Biggest lamasery in Beijing

Hours: daily 9am-4.30pm (summer), 9am-4pm (winter)

Entrance: RMB 25, English audio tour for an additional RMB 25 plus a RMB 200 deposit. RMB 12 for students

Suggested length of visit: 1-1.5 hours

Transport: Bus 13, 116, 117, 807 or Subway Line 2 to Lama Temple (雍和宮)

East side of Beixinqiao Beijie, Dongcheng District. (86-10-64044499)

东城区北新桥北街路东

✗ *Jin Ding Xuan (金鼎轩, 86-10-64296888), north of the Yonghegong Bridge, RMB 40, one of the most popular dim sum restaurants in Beijing and offering discounts between 6am-11am, 2pm-5pm and 10pm-6am.*

✐ *Regular religious ceremonies are held 9am-11am on the 1ˢᵗ, 15ᵗʰ and 30ᵗʰ day of each lunar month; grand ceremonies are held on the 15ᵗʰ of the fourth lunar month and the 25ᵗʰ of the 10ᵗʰ lunar month; largest-scale ceremony lasts from the 23ʳᵈ of the first lunar month to the 1ˢᵗ of the second lunar month. (Check this site to find the solar dates http://chinesefortunecalendar.com/CLunarCal1.htm)*

B uilt in 1694, this temple was originally the home of Qing Emperor

Lamaseries in Beijing

Political reasons prompted the Qing regime to build lamaseries in Beijing, as the emperors, especially Qianlong, believed the support of organized religion essential to effective control over Tibet and Mongolia. The lamaseries (today only Yonghegong and West Yellow survived) acted as the temporary accommodation for visiting officials and monks from these places.

Yongzheng before he became emperor. In 1723, Emperor Yongzheng contributed half of the grounds to the Tibetan monks of the Yellow (Geluk) sect and left the other half as his temporary palace residence. The Buddhist buildings in this peaceful complex are topped with ornately decorated, yellow roofs. Yellow was the imperial color of that time, which denotes the high status of this temple, a scaled-down imperial palace.

A 6-m-tall bronze **statue of Tsongkapa**, founder of the Yellow sect rests in the **Hall of the Wheel of Law** (法轮殿 Falundian), but the temple's crowning glory is the breathtaking 18-m-tall **statue of Maitreya** (Buddha of Future) carved from a single tree trunk in the **Pavilion of Eternal Happiness** (万福阁 Wanfuge), the tallest building in the lamasery.

During Spring Festival, this temple is extremely busy with devout worshipers. If you come here for one of its religious ceremonies, you'll see a lot more.

Lamas chant during religious ceremonies.

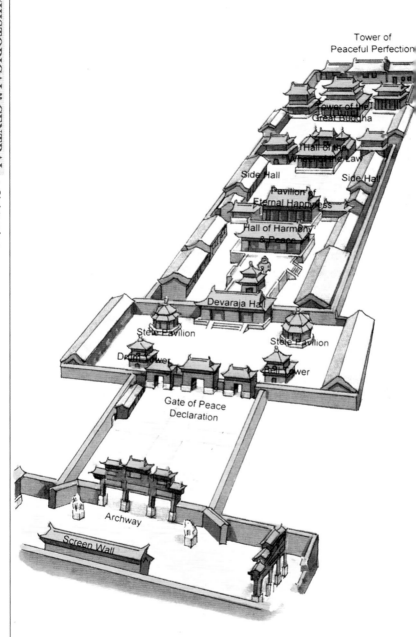

Lama Temple Layout

The *Buddha of Future, Maitreya. 18m tall.*

⑪ Confucius Temple
孔庙 Kǒngmiào ★★

Second largest Confucius temple in China

Hours: daily 8.30am-5pm
Entrance: RMB 10
Suggested length of visit: 45 minutes
Transport: Bus 13, 807, 116 to Guozijian (国子监)
or 108, 104 to Fangjia Hutong (方家胡同) or Sub-
way Line 2 to Lama Temple (雍和宫)
No. 13, Guozijian, Dongcheng District. (86-10-
84011977)
东城区国子监13 号

Free on Wednesdays; with the Museum Pass you can get two tickets for half price.

China's second largest temple built in honor of Confucius (the largest is in Qufu, Shandong Province, hometown of the Sage). In the compound of four courtyards, you'll find 14 **stele pavilions** bearing precious historical records of the Ming and Qing dynasties. The **198 stone tablets** in the front courtyard, carved with the names of all scholars who passed the imperial exams during the Ming, Qing and part of Yuan dynasties, are a must-see.

198 tablets times how many names on each... Wow, that's a lot of scholars!

Social spectrum reflected in color

As with all aspects of life in ancient Beijing, even color denoted a person's status in society. It was a taboo to use colors beyond that of one's "rank." The most honorable colors were yellow, gold and red, which were reserved exclusively for the imperial families and their palaces. One step below were green and blue, and today you will still see princely mansions decorated with these colors. Down at the bottom were black, grey and white, which were allocated to common people. Hence the grey walls of *hutong* alleys between the courtyard homes.

The one exception is the Confucius Temple, the roof of which was repainted gold during the Qing Dynasty to show respect for the Sage.

⑫ White Dagoba Temple
白塔寺 Báitǎsì ★★

Housing the largest Tibetan-style Buddhist dagoba of the Yuan Dynasty in Beijing

Hours: daily 9am-5pm
Entrance: RMB 20
Suggested length of visit: 1/2-1 hour
Transport: Bus 7, 13, 103, 409, 603, 812, 823, 846
to White Dagoba Temple (白塔寺)
No. 171, Fuchengmennei Dajie. (86-10-66139073)
阜成门内大街171 号

Free on Wednesdays; with the Museum Pass, you can get two free admissions.

There are only two dagobas in Beijing: one is in Beihai Park, the other in this temple. The temple is officially called Temple of Resourceful Response (妙应寺 Miaoyingsi) and commonly known as White Dagoba Temple.

Designed and built in 1271 by a Nepalese architect under Kublai Khan's order, the 50.9-m-tall dagoba is much older and more famous than the temple itself. The temple has undergone destruction by fire and subsequent reconstruction several times; it is now a beautifully presented collection of Tibetan Buddhist

You can't miss the White Dagoba Temple. It's the one shaped like an upside down ice-cream cone.

artifacts and art. A magnitude 7.8 earthquake in 1976 (the world's deadliest in 400 years that took 240,000 lives in Tangshan, 140 km from Beijing) actually unearthed artifacts that are now on display. The **Hall of Great Enlightenment** (大觉宝殿 Dajue Baodian) houses an optically impressive collection of thousands of tiny Buddhas.

Why do people burn incense in temples?

While the burning of incense in temples may today be a spiritual ritual, the origins of this trend were probably much more mundane and utilitarian—to get rid of bad smells inside a temple that might accumulate when large numbers of praying monks congregated for long periods. It was only later that incense became imbued with ritual significance. In Buddhist temples for example, the burning of three incense sticks represents Abstinence, Calmness and Wisdom.

⓭ Temple of Ancient Monarchs
历代帝王庙 Lìdài dìwángmiào ★★

houses 188 emperors' tablets

Hours: 8.30am-4.30pm
Entrance: RMB 20, half price for students
Suggested length of visit: 30-45 minutes
Transport: see transport to White Dagoba Temple (白塔寺) on p.60
North side of Fuchengmennei Dajie, Xicheng District (east of White Dagoba Temple). (86-10-66185405/66120186)
西城区阜成门内大街北侧(白塔寺东侧)
✓ *With the Museum Pass, you can get two tickets for half price.*

This temple was built in 1530 to house the ancestral tablets of emperors and loyal officials. It was expanded during the Qing Emperor Qianlong's reign to enshrine the tablets of 188 emperors, 79 officials and Guan Yu (160-219, a general in the period of the Three Kingdoms, renowned for his loyalty). Since 1925, it was kept for other uses, including a memorial ceremony to mark Sun Yat-sen's death, and as a school from 1931. It was reopened to the public in 2004 after 10 years of renovation.

The temple also holds regular exhibitions, including the temple's history and the origins of "100 Chinese surnames."

⑭ Beijing Underground City
北京地下城 Běijīng dìxiàchéng ★★

Fascinating construction
Chinese and English tour guide

Hours: daily 8.30am-6pm
Entrance: RMB 20
Suggested length of visit: 15-30 minutes
Transport: Bus 9, 848, 744, 729, 820 to Taijichang (台基厂)
No. 62, Xidamochang Hutong, Chongwenmen Dongdajie, Chongwen District. (86-10-67022657)
崇文区崇文门东大街西打磨厂胡同62号

Labyrinth-like tunnels beneath Beijing streets.

Little-known but very interesting. In the 1960s, seeing the nuclear threat getting stronger, Chairman Mao decided the future and protection of the Chinese people lay below the surface. A task force of thousands set to work creating an underground rabbit warren of tunnels, working solidly for 10 years. 90 entrances have been recorded, all of which now lie below shops in Qianmen area. It accesses the Forbbiden City and even Subway Lines 1 and 2, but of course these accesses are sealed today. Much of this "shadow city" was put to use as warehouses, hotels and restaurants and today only a small portion is open to visitors.

You may find this place difficult to find with even many local residents unsure of its location.

⑮ Ming City Wall Park 明城墙
遗址公园 Míngchéngqiáng yízhǐ gōngyuán ★

A testament to Ming history

Hours: 24 hours (park); daily 8am-5pm (Southeast Corner Tower)
Entrance: free for the park; RMB 10 for the Southeast Corner Tower
Suggested length of visit: 1/2 hour
Transport: Bus 25, 820, 44, 43, 39, 713 to Dongbianmen (东便门)
Chongwenmen Dongdajie, Chongwen District. (86-10-65270574)
崇文区崇文门东大街

This mile-long city wall has its origins in the Ming Dynasty. The present wall, stretching east-west from Dongbianmen (东便门) to Chongwenmen (崇文门), was rebuilt using original Ming Dynasty bricks reclaimed from local residential areas. Following the wall's destruction in the 1950s, the bricks had been used for various purposes. At its **Southeast Corner Tower** (东南角楼) an informative exhibition on the history of Chongwen District and a gallery can be found.

Very little original city wall still remains.

Stargazers welcome.

⑯ Ancient Observatory
古观象台 Gǔguānxiàngtái ★★

500-year record of Chinese astronomy

Hours: daily 9am-11.30am, 1pm-4.30pm (closed on Mondays)
Entrance: RMB 10
Suggested length of visit: 1/2 hour
Transport: Subway Line 1 or 2 to Jianguomen (建国门), Exit C.
No. 2, Dongbiaobei Hutong, Jianguomen, Dongcheng District (southwest corner of Jianguomen Qiao). (86-10-65242202)
东城区建国门东裱褙胡同 2 号 (建国门桥西南)
🔽 *With the Museum Pass, you can get two tickets for half price.*

On the site of a former watchtower at Jianguomen, the Ancient Observatory dates back to 1442. It was the imperial observatory of the Qing and Ming dynasties and is also one of the oldest observatories in the world.

It houses a fascinating collection (some of which are replicas) of a Ming Dynasty star chart and eight astronomical instruments such as the Armillary Sphere and Azimuth Theodolite designed by **Jesuit missionaries** who tried to convert the Chinese emperor and officials to Catholicism 300 years ago. These instruments were looted by the foreign troops of the Eight Powers, and fortunately were returned following world condemnation.

⑰ Wisdom Convert Temple (Cultural Exchange Museum)
智化寺 (文博交流馆) Zhìhuàsì ★

Beijing's best-preserved Ming Dynasty wooden construction

Hours: daily 8.30 am-4.30pm
Entrance: RMB 20
Suggested length of visit: 1/2-1 hour
Transport: Bus 44, 750, 800, 810, 820, 特2 to Yabao Lu (雅宝路) or 24, 713 to Lumicang (禄米仓)
No. 5, Lumicang Hutong, Dongcheng District. (86-10-65253670)
东城区禄米仓胡同 5 号
🔽 *Free on Wednesdays; with the Museum Pass you can get two free admissions.*

Originally a family shrine built by Ming eunuch Wang Zhen in 1443, this complex has 10 halls arranged in a traditional Buddhist temple layout. Its buildings are the best-preserved Ming wooden construction in Beijing.

The two-story main hall includes a towering carved image of Thathagata and over 9,000 Buddhist statues, all 13 cm high. The world's only official wood blocks for printing *Great Buddhist Scriptures* are housed here.

Jing music, a musical form that is 500 years old and combines Ming Dynasty tradition with Buddhist and folk music, can be experienced for free four times a day (15 minutes each at 9am, 10am, 11am and 3pm).

Hutong 胡同 ★★★

At first glance Beijing may seem like a sprawling mass of highways, busy intersections and vast amounts of traffic, but look a little closer and you will see a very different side to the city's transport network—*hutong*. Beijing's *hutong*, built during the Yuan Dynasty (1271-1368), were alleys designed originally as a way to prevent fires from spreading from one *siheyuan* (四合院 courtyard house) to another.

Drum-like stone guarding a traditional siheyuan house.

They quickly became an integral means of getting around, and today, over 1,000 *hutong* still remain, providing wonderful insights into the city's ancient architecture and lifestyle. Walking or biking around the *hutong* areas is a lovely experience, although for the less energetic there is always the option of taking a rickshaw (see **Hutong Tour** on p.92).

The *hutong* listed below are marked on the map on p.42.

18 Yandai Xiejie 烟袋斜街

Tucked behind Houhai Lake, this is one of Beijing's oldest *hutong* lanes. It got its name from the many tobacco pipe (烟袋 yandai) shops mushrooming with the arrival of the Manchu rulers. With a combination of residential buildings and traditional shopfronts displaying carved windows and selling an assortment of antiques, it is a quaint and charmingly old-fashioned area.

19 Chaodou Hutong 炒豆胡同

This *hutong*, once serving as an integral part of the Yuan Dynasty street grid pattern, stands today as one of the best preserved in the city. Its proximity to the Imperial City wall hidden deep within Nanluoguxiang (南锣鼓巷) has ensured its preservation.

20 Mao'er Hutong 帽儿胡同

Mao'er Hutong is one of the city's famous alleys that most visitors fall in love with. Literally meaning "Hat-maker Lane," the lane dates back to the Ming Dynasty (1368-1644) when it was known as Wenchang Gong.

Mao'er Hutong is home to several places that have received cultural relic status. Sadly, none are open to the public. **Wanrong's Residence**, home of China's last empress, stands at No.s 35 and 37, while a little further down is No. 11, the former residence of **Feng Guozhang**, president of

Antique knick-knacks galore! — a small store on Yandai Xiejie.

the Beijing government 1917-1918. Lastly, the **Keyuan Garden**, which was once home to a Qing Dynasty scholar.

Visitors can, however, visit the houses at No.s 14 and 16, which provide a fascinating insight into the architectural styles of the time.

This *hutong* runs west to east from Di'anmenwai Dajie to Nanluoguxiang. If you get lost, just ask around—someone will point you in the right direction!

Notes for maximizing your *hutong* trip

To get the most out of your *hutong* trip, we recommend following tips:

First, big groups are not well received by local residents, so keep group size down to three or four people.

Second, never open closed doors, which could be someone's house! If the door is open, it's ok to have a quiet peek inside. If a resident asks you to leave, do so!

Third, taking photos is normally no problem, but always be polite and considerate to the people who live there.

Last, many tour guides offer services that can often be informative and worthwhile. Just be sure to agree on the price before heading off.

Don't be camera shy.

Museums

㉑ National Museum of China
中国国家博物馆 ★★★

5,000 years of Chinese culture
English tour guide

Closed for expansion & scheduled to re-open in 2010. No.16, Dongchang'an Jie (east side of Tian'anmen Square). (86-10-65128901)
东长安街16号(天安门东侧)

China's 5,000+ years of history is the focus here, including the arts that help make this country so unique and respected. An amalgamation of two: the National Museum of Chinese History and the National Museum of Chinese Revolution, the museum displays a diversified range of items: from pottery dating back as early as the Neolithic era to as late as the 1800s; from 14th century BC *ding* wine vessels to Tang Dynasty calligraphy, painting and shadow puppets; from Mao's hat to Xu Haifeng's gold medal won in the men's 50 m pistol event in the 23rd Los Angeles Olympics. You will certainly find the most important Chinese relics here.

In addition to its permanent collection, there is a **Wax Gallery** where visitors can be photographed with China's most important figures (e.g. Mao) and a few foreign faces (e.g. David Beckham).

At the time of printing, all exhibits were

The grandiose National Museum of China.

closed for renovations with the intention of being re-opened in 2010. By then, the museum will be expanded from 65,000 sq m of floor space to 192,000 and more items are expected to be added to its permanent collection.

㉒ Beijing Imperial City Art Museum 北京皇城艺术馆 ★★

Showcase of the imperial city

Hours: daily 10am-5.30pm
Entrance: RMB 20
Suggested length of visit: 30-45 minutes
Transport: Bus 1, 2, 4, 10, 20, 37, 52, 59, 120, 728, 802, or Subway Line 1 to Tian'anmen East (天安门东)
Inside Changpuhe Park. (86-10-85115114)
菖蒲河公园内

🎫 *With the Museum Pass, you can get two tickets for half price.*

The museum, opened in 2003, is the only museum in Beijing that displays and researches the government offices, temples, storehouses, gardens, security systems, ceremonial offerings and operas of the Imperial City. Its two-story *siheyuan*-style buildings contain three exhibition halls which house the city wall bricks, playbills, lampshades and other historical items, as well as a scale model of the Imperial City of the Ming and Qing dynasties.

㉓ National Art Museum of China 中国美术馆 ★★

Display of fine arts
English tour guide

Hours: daily 9am-5pm (closed on Mondays, last entry at 4pm)
Entrance: RMB 20
Suggested length of visit: 1 hour
Transport: Bus 103, 111, 202, 211, 814 to Meishuguan (美术馆)
No. 1, Wusi Dajie. (86-10-64012252/7076)
五四大街1号

With an area of 27,000 sq m, this museum was constructed in 1959 as one of the "10 great buildings" at that time and is China's largest showcase of paintings, sculpture, calligraphy and handicrafts by modern and contemporary Chinese and foreign artists. It also holds temporary exhibitions of special themes or artists, calligraphy and photos. Young artists consider it a great career breakthrough if their work is displayed here.

㉔ Wangfujing Paleolithic Museum 王府井古人类文化遗址博物馆 ★

Rivals the Zhoukoudian Peking Man discovery
English tour guide

Hours: 10am-4.30pm (weekdays); 10am-6.30pm (weekends)
Entrance: RMB 10
Suggested length of visit: 1/2-1 hour
Transport: Bus 10, 37, 41, 59, 120, 126, 203, 420, 802 or Subway Line 1 to Wangfujing (王府井)
Oriental Plaza W1P3, No. 1, Dongchang'an Jie, Dongcheng District. (86-10-85186306)
东城区东长安街1号, 东方广场W1P3

🗝 *With the Museum Pass, you can get two tickets for half price.*

Unearthed on the construction site of a downtown plaza in 1996 were ruins of human activities about 25,000 years ago. This is another important palaeoanthropologic find after Peking Man remains were discovered at Zhoukoudian in Beijing. It is also the first time in the world that a palaeoanthropologic relic was discovered within the confines of a major city. Evidence of fire use, remains of stone axes and spades made of animal bones are on display.

㉕ Geological Museum of China 中国地质博物馆 ★★

Honored as best museum by a British museum delegation
English audio tour

Hours: daily 9am-4.30pm (closed on Mondays)
Entrance: RMB 30
Suggested length of visit: 1 hour
Transport: Bus 13, 102, 42, 603, 604, 812, 823, 846 to Xisi Lukouxi (西四路口西)
Xisi, Xicheng District. (86-10-66557858)
西城区西四

🗝 *With the Museum Pass, you can get two tickets for half price.*

China's first geological museum is also the best of its kind in Asia. It has five permanent exhibition halls: the Earth Sciences Hall, the Ore Hall, the Paleobotanical Hall, the Gems Hall, and the Land and Resources Hall.

The museum's collection is extremely rich, with 120,000 specimens. Its crowning glory is the world's **largest quartz crystal** (3.5 tons). Other eye-catching pieces such as the **earliest hominid fossil** in China—Yuanmou-Man tooth from Yunnan Province—are also on display.

Don't get stuck between a rock and a hard place at the Geological Museum of China.

㉖ China Numismatic Museum
中国钱币博物馆 ★

Evolution of Chinese currency

Hours: daily 9am-4pm (last entry at 3.30pm; closed on Mondays)

Entrance: RMB 10

Suggested visiting duration: 1 hour

Transport: Bus 5, 20, 48, 120, 301, 803, 826, 特4, or Subway Line 2 to Qianmen (前门)

No.17, Xijiaominxiang, Xicheng District (by an office building of the Bank of China). (86-10-66081385)
西城区西交民巷17号

With the Museum Pass, you can get two free tickets.

Lovers of money, look no further! This is a national museum dedicated to the study of China's history of currency.

The three-story museum has two permanent exhibits: **Ancient Chinese Currency** on the second floor and **Contemporary Chinese Currency** on the third.

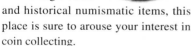

Temporary exhibits are usually held on the third. With a collection of over 300,000 Chinese and foreign coins and historical numismatic items, this place is sure to arouse your interest in coin collecting.

㉗ Beijing Police Museum
北京警察博物馆 ★

Interesting history of Beijing police

Hours: daily 9am-4pm (last entry at 3.30pm; closed on Mondays)

Entrance: RMB 5

Suggested length of visit: 45 minutes

Transport: Bus 3, 6, 8, 9, 41, 44, 48, or 110 to Dongjiaominxiang (东交民巷) or Qianmen (前门) or Subway Line 1 to Tian'anmen East (天安门东) or Line 2 to Qianmen (前门)

No. 36, Dongjiaominxiang, Dongcheng District. (86-10-85222223/2282)

"Stop, in the name of the law!"

东城区东交民巷36号

With Museum Pass, you can get one free ticket.

The museum was originally a Beijing branch of the National City Bank of New York, a typical Western-style building. There is a lot of fun in this museum: equipment and uniforms used by the Beijing police from the Han Dynasty (206 BC-220 AD) to high-tech modern times. History, criminal investigation and specifics of Chinese police responsibilities through the ages are detailed. The **fingerprint forensics exhibit** is a must-see highlight.

㉘ Guo Moruo Museum
郭沫若纪念馆 ★

A well-preserved *siheyuan* within Prince Gong's Mansion

Hours: daily 9am-4.30pm (closed on Mondays)

Entrance: RMB 20

Suggested length of visi: 45 minutes

Transport: Bus 13, 107, 111, 118, 701 to Beihai Park North Gate (北海北门)

No.18, Qianhai Xijie. (86-10-66125392/59842789)
前海西街18号

With the Museum Pass, you can get two tickets for half price.

This historical courtyard was where Chinese writer Guo Moruo (1892-1978) lived his last 15 years. Guo was also an influential poet and historian of his time. One of his most famous works is *Goddess*.

The real attraction here is the courtyard itself, part of Prince Gong's Mansion.

㉙ Soong Ching Ling Residence 宋庆龄故居 ★

The place witnessing a great woman's last years

Hours: daily 9am-4.30pm (closed during Spring Festival)
Entrance: RMB 20
Suggested length of visit: 45 minutes
Transport: Bus 5, 210, 819, 834 to Guozishi (果子市)
No. 46, Houhai Beiyan, Xicheng District. (86-10-64044205)
西城区后海北沿 46 号

Madam Soong Ching Ling (1893-1981) was the widow of Dr. Sun Yat-sen, founder of the Republic of China and she herself was Vice-president of the People's Republic of China.

Formerly the mansion of the father of China's last emperor, this quiet and beautiful compound became the residence of Soong Ching Ling after the People's Republic of China was founded. It was turned into a museum in 1981 dedicated to the memory of her and Dr. Sun Yat-sen. On display are her library, furniture and personal belongings. The house is kept as it was when she was alive. Historical photos are also displayed, serving as a great insight into China's modern history.

Soong Ching Ling's house.

㉚ Mei Lanfang Memorial Museum 梅兰芳纪念馆 ★

Life of a legendary opera star

Hours: daily 9am-4pm (closed on Mondays)
Entrance: RMB 10
Suggested length of visit: 45 minutes
Transport: Bus 22, 38, 47, 409, 626, 726, 826 to Huguosi (护国寺)
No. 9, Huguosi Jie, Xicheng District. (86-10-66183598)
西城区护国寺街 9 号

Mei Lanfang (1894-1961) was the most accomplished and renowned Peking Opera star in China's modern times. In his 50-year career he played over 100 different roles, and as a "cultural ambassador" he made Peking Opera known to the world.

Mei Lanfang

The year after Mei Lanfang passed away, his family donated a great number of his works to the government. In 1986, his former residence was turned into a museum, displaying more than 32,000 stage photos, librettos, letters, playbills, calligraphy, paintings and books about or collected by the Peking opera artist, as well as his furniture and costumes.

㉛ Former Residence of Mao Dun 茅盾故居 ★

Home of a literary giant

Hours: 9am-4pm (closed on Mondays)
Entrance: RMB 5
Suggested length of visit: 45 minutes
Transport: Bus 104, 108, 113, 201, 758, 803, 850 to Jiaodaokou Nan (交道口南) or 107, 124, 204, 815 to Baochao Hutong (宝钞胡同)
Jiaodaokou Houjie, Dongcheng District (No. 13,

Mao Dun, widely considered one of the PRC's greatest novelists.

Yuan'ensi Hutong). (86-10-64044089)

东城区交道口后街 (圆恩寺胡同 13 号)

🗹 *With the Museum Pass, you can get two free admissions.*

Mao Dun (1896-1981) started his literary activities after he graduated from Peking University in 1916. In 1921, he became the first author to join the Communist Party. He joined the League of Chinese Left-wing Writers in 1930, and years later, published his most famous novel *Midnight*, mirroring real life in Shanghai at that time. He also worked as the first Minister of Culture for New China. In accordance with his will, the Mao Dun Literature Award was founded with his donation of RMB 250,000.

Mao Dun spent his last seven years in this compound, which is preserved as it was when he lived here. Even the calendar on his desk remains to the last page he turned. His furniture, personal belongings, original manuscripts, letters and family photos are also displayed.

This compound and *hutong* neighborhood give you a glimpse into the past; even if you are not interested in the exhibition, take a gander.

㉜ Lu Xun Museum
鲁迅博物馆 ★

The place to learn about the greatest modern novelist and critic

Hours: daily 9am-4pm (closed on Mondays)
Entrance: RMB 5

Suggested length of visit: 1 hour
Transport: Bus 13, 101, 102, 103, 42, 335, 489, 603, 714, 814, 846, 850 or Subway Line 2 to Fuchengmen (阜成门)
No. 19, Gongmenkou Ertiao, Fuchengmennei. (86-10-66156549/8)

阜城门内宫门口二条 19 号

🗹 *With the Museum Pass, you can get two free entries.*

Lu Xun (1881-1936) is respected as one of the pioneer writers of China's modern literature. Living in Beijing between 1912 and 1926, he played a great role in the May Fourth Movement of 1919. Known for his essays contrasting traditional and modern China, he became famous in the West in 1926 for his critical work—***The True Story of Ah Q***.

The museum, opened in 1956, displays his manuscripts, poems, letters, translation works, books published in different languages, and his own collections. You can also buy copies of Lu Xun's works in different languages, including *The Diary of a Mad Man* and *The True Story of Ah Q*.

Watch your step on your way into Lu Xun's home.

㉝ Xu Beihong Museum
徐悲鸿纪念馆 ★

Showcase of China's best-known modern artist

Hours: daily 9am-11am, 1pm-4pm (closed on Mondays)
Entrance: RMB 5; free for students
Suggested length of visit: 45 minutes-1 hour
Transport: Bus 27, 206, 331, 347, 800, 820, 939, 运通104 to Xinjiekou Huokou (新街口豁口)
No. 53, Xinjiekou Beidajie. (86-10-62252042)
新街口北大街53号

📝 *Free on Wednesdays; with the Museum Pass, you can get two free entries.*

Xu Beihong (1895-1953) is considered one of the best-known master painters in contemporary China and the father of China's modern art. Xu learned Western painting in Paris in his early years and successfully mixed Chinese and Western art styles into his paintings. He founded the Central Academy of Fine Arts in 1950. You may not know his name, but you will certainly be familiar with his horse paintings. Some of his works are priceless.

The museum displays his Chinese paintings, oil paintings, sketches, books, and his personal collections.

Another masterpiece by Xu Beihong.

㉞ Guo Shoujing Museum
郭守敬纪念馆 ★

Dedicated to a great astronomer

Hours: daily 8.30am-5pm
Entrance: RMB 0.5
Suggested length of visit: 1/2-1 hour
Transport: Bus 55, 305, 315, 815, 946 to Deshengmen (德胜门)
No. A60, Deshengmen Xidajie, Xicheng District. (86-10-66183083)
西城区德胜门西大街甲60号

Guo Shoujing (1231-1316) was a true genius, astronomer and scientist. When he was 14, he designed a water clock. He worked at Kublai Khan's observatory and there he invented the 365.2425-day calendar (same as the Gregorian calendar) and made a dozen astronomical instruments such as the abridged

Guo Shoujing looking toward the heavens.

armilla, almost 300 years before Europe reached the same level of knowledge.

Guo Shoujing's major achievements were in water conservancy, readily visible in the exhibit of "Guo Shoujing and Dadu Water Resources." He remains best known for constructing the artificial Kunming Lake in the Summer Palace as a reservoir.

The museum itself, built on a site of a Yuan temple, has beautiful garden-like scenery. It is certainly worth spending some time strolling through the man-made hills, lanes and bridges after a visit to this great man's life accomplishments.

🍴 Food and Entertainment

Looking for good food and enter-tainment spots in "Historical" Central Beijing? Well, where to start? This area is bursting at the seams with food and party centers to visit. From the chilled out shores of **Shichahai** (see below) or the ancient *hutong* area of **Nanluoguxiang** (see p.76) where food, drink and great views are all on the menu, to the bustling **Guijie** (see p.79) area where good food, red lanterns and a lively atmosphere come hand in hand. For a totally different angle, head on down to the **Donghuanmen Night Market** (see p.83) at Wangfujing for

The Chinese yo-yo, a.k.a Diabolo.

more unusual, freshly cooked snacks. If none of these tickle your fancy, then the countless theaters will no doubt do the trick. Visitors can make the very difficult choice between taking in a **Peking Opera** perfor-mance at the **Chang'an Grand Theater** (see p.84) or absorbing the beauty of ballets and symphonies at the **Poly Plaza Interna-tional Theater** (see p.84). Spoilt for choice; the choice is yours; in short, "choice" is the word that best describes central Beijing!

The following hot spots are marked on the map on p.42.

Shichahai 什刹海

This gorgeous spot has three lakes, Qianhai (前海 Front Lake), Houhai (后海 Rear Lake) and Xihai (西海 West Lake) all surrounded by old-style Beijing houses, *hutong* and courtyards. Not only beautiful, this charming expanse is com-plete with historical architecture and a bunch of bustling bars and restaurants.

With a history dating back to the Jin Dynasty (1115-1234), this area used to be a station on the Grand Canal, resulting in Shichahai's prosperity. When using waterways became passé as a way of doing business, the area changed from a business hub to a place of leisure where people could relax amidst pleasant and natural scenery. In 2005, Shichahai was listed as one of the five most beautiful city districts in China by *Chinese Na-tional Geography* magazine.

Sights in the area:
Prince Gong's Man-sion (see p.56), Soong Ching Ling Residence (see p.69), Guo Moruo Museum (see p.68) and Yandai Xiejie (see p.64)
Transport: take Bus 5, 60, 107, 124, 210, 815, 819, 834 to Gulou (鼓楼), then walk to Yandai Xiejie (烟袋斜街) which runs to Yinding Qiao (银锭桥) at Houhai. Or you can take Bus 13, 701, 107, 111, 118 to Beihai Park North Gate (北海北门), then walk over Lotus Lane (荷花市场), t south end of Shichahai.

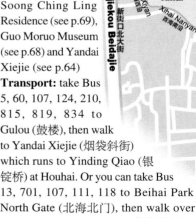

Xihai Beiyan
Xinjiekou Beidajie
新街口北大街
Xihai Xiyan 西海西沿
Xihai
Xihai Nanyan 西海南沿

Restaurant listings

Meal prices per adult

¥ under RMB 29
¥¥ RMB 30-49
¥¥¥ RMB 50-69
¥¥¥¥ RMB 70-99
¥¥¥¥¥ over RMB 100

Chinese

Laohanzi
老汉字客家菜馆
Hakka
English menu   ¥¥
Hours: 10.30am-10.30pm
East bank of Shichahai, Xicheng District (east of Lotus Lane by Beihai Park North Gate). (86-10-64042259) 西城区什刹海东岸 (北海北门门荷花市场东侧)

Good (if often a little on the salty side) Qianhai style restaurant specializing in Foil-wrapped fish (纸包鲈鱼) and Three-cup duck (三杯鸭).

ⓑ Shuaifu Restaurant
帅府饭庄
Sichuan & Cantonese cuisine
English menu   ¥¥
Hours: 10am-2am
Transport: Bus 13, 701, 107, 111, 118 to Beihai Park North Gate (北海北门)
No. A19, Qianhai Beiyan, Xicheng District. (86-10-66185347) 西城区前海北沿街甲 19 号

Dine like a general on Sichuan and Cantonese dishes prepared under the instruction of a former cook of the late Marshal Nie Rongzhen. If it was good enough for him...

ⓒ Fu Ku 福库
Sichuan cuisine
English menu   ¥¥¥
Hours: 10.30am-10.30pm
Transport: Bus 5, 55 to Deshengmen (德胜门)
No. A4, Binhai Hutong, Denei Dajie,

Come in for some home-cooked food at Fu Ku.

Xicheng District (Northwest bank of Houhai). (86-10-64024093) 西城区德内大街滨海胡同甲4号(后海西北沿)
Fu Ku offers spicy Sichuan food with a difference. Brilliant sunshine (阳光灿烂), Mashed mango and corn (芒果玉米泥), Curry beef with butter cake (咖喱牛肉配黄油饼) are just some of their creative variations.

ⓓ Kaorou Ji 烤肉季
Muslim barbecue
English menu   ¥¥¥
Hours: 11am-11pm
No. 14, Qianhai Dongyan, Xicheng District (close to Yinding Qiao).
(86-10-64045921/2554) 西城区前海东沿 14 号(靠近银锭桥)

One of Beijing's longest-established restaurants. It has been serving up Muslim dishes since the Qing Dynasty. Their barbecued lamb and steamed sesame buns are big favorites with Beijingers.

BBQ beef and mutton at Kaorou Ji.

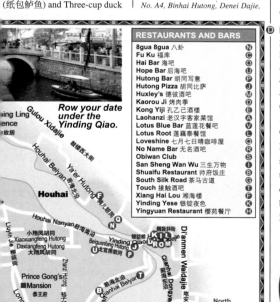

Row your date under the Yinding Qiao.

RESTAURANTS AND BARS

8gua 8gua 八卦	Ⓝ
Fu Ku 福库	Ⓒ
Hai Bar 海吧	Ⓤ
Hope Bar 后海吧	Ⓓ
Hutong Bar 胡同写意	Ⓟ
Hutong Pizza 胡同比萨	Ⓙ
Huxley's 接彼酒吧	Ⓜ
Kaorou Ji 烤肉季	Ⓓ
Kong Yiji 孔乙己酒楼	Ⓔ
Laohanzi 老汉字客家菜馆	Ⓐ
Lotus Blue Bar 蓝莲花餐吧	Ⓥ
Lotus Root 莲藕泰餐馆	Ⓛ
Loveshine 七月七日晴咖啡屋	Ⓠ
No Name Bar 无名酒吧	Ⓡ
Obiwan Club	Ⓢ
San Sheng Wan Wu 三生万物	Ⓘ
Shuaifu Restaurant 帅府饭店	Ⓑ
South Silk Road 茶马古道	Ⓖ
Touch 接触酒吧	Ⓣ
Xiang Hai Lou 湘海楼	Ⓕ
Yinding Yese 银锭夜色	Ⓚ
Yingyuan Restaurant 樱苑餐厅	Ⓗ

Ⓔ Kong Yiji 孔乙己酒楼

Jiangsu & Zhejiang cuisine
English menu ¥¥¥
Hours: 10am-2am
Transport: Subway Line 2 to Jishuitan (积水潭), Exit C. Head south and turn east at the first hutong. It is within 500 m. South bank of Houhai, Deshengmen, Xicheng District (across the lake from the Soong Ching Ling Residence). (86-10-66184917) 西城区德胜门什刹海后海南岸 (对岸即宋庆龄故居)

For a long, tranquil dinner and great southeastern style food, the immaculately decorated Kong Yiji is the place. Well-known for its Flavored broad beans (茴香豆), Stir-fried shrimp (油爆小河虾) and Fried stinky tofu (臭豆腐).

Ⓕ Xiang Hai Lou 湘海楼

Hunan cuisine
English menu ¥¥¥
Hours: 10.30am-10.30pm
No. A21, Ya'er Hutong, Shichahai, Xicheng District. (86-10-64028408) 西城区什刹海鸦儿胡同甲21号

Typical spicy Hunan food in traditional surroundings. Ask for a table on the third floor overlooking the lake and neighboring *hutong*.

Ⓖ South Silk Road 茶马古道

Yunnan cuisine

Inside South Silk Road.

English menu ¥¥¥¥
Hours: noon-10pm
12-13, No. A19, Lotus Lane, Qianhai Xiyan, Xicheng District. (86-10-66155515/66164261) 西城区前海西沿荷花市场甲19号12-13室

Owned by an artist, this fashionable little restaurant is a creation of minimalist décor twinned with Yunnan specialties and a great house rice wine. Traditonal Yunnan dishes such as Crossing-the-bridge rice noodle (过桥米线) and Steaming pot chicken (气锅鸡) are scrumptious.

Ⓗ Yingyuan Restaurant 樱苑餐厅

Hangzhou cuisine
English menu ¥¥¥¥
Hours: 10am-2am
Transport: Bus 13, 701, 107, 111, 118 to Beihai Park North Gate (北海北门) No. 54, Qianhai Xijie, Xicheng District. (86-10-66112597) 西城区前海西街54号

The plastic bamboo and non-matching furniture can either be seen as quaint or tacky. Either way the Hangzhou-style dishes and views of Qianhai are top-notch.

Ⓘ San Sheng Wan Wu 三生万物

Taoist

English menu ¥¥¥¥
Hours: 10am-12am
Transport: Bus 5, 60, 107 to Drum Tower (鼓楼)
No. 37, Yandai Xiejie, Di'anmen, Xicheng District (inside Guangfuguan Temple). (86-10-64042778) 西城区地安门烟袋斜街37号 (广福观内)

Once a Ming Dynasty Taoist temple (now sporting faux-antique furniture), this well-hidden restaurant serves up an interesting selection of rustic yet elegant Taoist food. They only serve two tables a day: lunch and supper, so make sure you reserve two or three days in advance.

Let the Hutong Pizza tantalize your taste buds.

Italian

Ⓙ Hutong Pizza 胡同比萨

Pizza
English menu ¥¥¥
Hours: 11am-11pm
No. 9, Yindingqiao Hutong, Xicheng District. (86-10-66175916) 西城区银锭桥胡同9号

Serving up fresh pizzas as well as specialties like Roasted potato skins (烤薯皮) and Cream of mushroom soup (奶油蘑菇汤), this chilled out restaurant offers not only great food but one of the best bathrooms you will find in a *hutong*!

Russian

Ⓚ Yinding Yese 银锭夜色

Russian

Find comfortable surroundings at Yinding Yese.

English menu ¥¥¥¥

Hours: 11am-2am

No. A75, Yandai Xiejie, Xicheng District. (86-10-84040616) 西城区烟袋斜街甲75号 (靠近后海银锭桥)

☑ *Carlsberg, buy a dozen get half a dozen free.*

This interesting restaurant and bar is two-tiered in all respects: the first floor is home to Russian cuisine, some eccentric décor (complete with his and hers chairs) and live bands (after 9pm); the second floor boasts a themed dance bar.

Thai

Lotus Root 莲藕泰餐馆

Thai food

English menu ¥¥¥

Hours: 11am-2am

Transport: Bus 108 to Di'anmen (地安门)

No. 29 & 32, Yandai Xiejie, Xicheng District (turn west at the south intersection of the Bell and Drum Towers). (86-10-84015544) 西城区烟袋斜街29, 32号 (钟鼓楼南路口向西)

☑ *Drinks are 30 percent off before 8.30pm.*

The backpacker-style Lotus Root restaurant and bar offers spicy Thai favorites such as Curry chicken (咖哩鸡) and Spicy lobster (香辣虾). Really great food in intimate surroundings.

Bar listings

Prices for a bottle of Tsingtao beer (青岛啤酒), a favorite local beer

¥ under RMB 14
¥¥ RMB 15-24
¥¥¥ RMB 25-34
¥¥¥¥ over RMB 35

Ⓜ Huxley's 德彼酒吧

Light rock

English menu & service ¥

Hours: 2pm-3am

Entrance: free

No. 16, Yandai Xiejie, Houhai, Xicheng District. (86-10-64027825) 西城区后海烟袋斜街16号

Drink up, rock out and wind down. Huxley himself serves some of the cheapest drinks around in funky surroundings and a relaxed, comfortable atmosphere.

Ⓝ 8gua 8gua 八卦

Jazz

English menu ¥¥

Hours: 11am-2am (Mon-Fri), 1pm-2am (Sat and Sun)

Entrance: free

No. C6, Ya'er Hutong, Houhai Beiyan, Xicheng District. (86-10-64018080) 西城区后海北沿鸦儿胡同后丙6号

Do as the sign says, gossip ("bagua" means to gossip)! Settle down on the invitingly squishy

sofas in modern-traditional Chinese surroundings, or in one of the curtained-off rooms for really juicy secrets.

Ⓞ Hai Bar 海吧

Western pop music

English menu ¥¥

Hours: 10am-2am

Entrance: free

No. 36, Yandai Xiejie, Xicheng District. (86-10-64034913) 西城区地安门烟袋斜街36号

Watch the world go by with a drink in your hand from this lovely terrace bar. For a really great view of Houhai ask for the table in the attic.

Ⓟ Hutong Bar 胡同写意

Botswana music

English menu and service ¥¥

Hours: 2pm-2am

Entrance: free

No. 8, Houhai Nanyan, Xicheng Distict. (86-10-66158691) 西城区后海南沿8号

Uniquely designed, this small courtyard house bar has created breezy open rooms, one of the few lakeside bars that have successfully invested as much effort inside as outside.

Hutong Bar patio.

Ⓠ Loveshine 七月七日晴咖啡屋

French music, movie screening

English menu and service ¥¥

Hours: 1pm-3am

Entrance: free

No. 12, Houhai Beiyan, Xicheng District. (86-10-84002941) 西城区后海北沿12号

What the staff lack in smiles

Loveshine makes up for in comfort and entertainment. With two screenings a night you can snuggle up on sofas with a beer and unwind.

No Name Bar 无名酒吧

Western pop music, jazz
English menu and service ¥¥
Hours: noon-2am
Entrance: free
No. 3, Qianhai Dongyan, Xicheng District (next to Kaorou Ji Restaurant).
(86-10-64018541) 西城区前海东沿3号 (烤肉季隔壁)

Fronting Shichahai's historic area, No Name Bar was among the earliest to move their sofas outside along the river. This funky little hip bar is a foreigners' favorite.

Obiwan Club

Western pop music
English menu and service ¥¥
Hours: 1pm-2am
Entrance: free
Transport: Subway Line 2 to Jishuitan (积水潭), Exit C.
No. 4, Xihai Xiyan, Xicheng District (near Jishuitan Subway Station). (86-10-66173231) 西城区西海西沿4号 (积水潭地铁附近)

Weave your way through the jungle of staircases and balconies of this rooftop three-story club until you find your spot. For a great view keep going all the way to the top.

Touch 接触酒吧

Blues
English menu and service ¥¥
Hours: 1.30pm-6am
Entrance: free
No. 8, Qianhai Beiyan, Xicheng

District. (86-10-66180809) 西城区前海北沿8号

Located in a traditional courtyard house a "touch" (!) of creativity has been added to its architecture. Rooftop decking, glassed central courtyard (together with ancient tree and fishpond), big windows and indoor water features create a refreshing summer hideaway.

Hope Bar 后海吧

Western music
English menu and service ¥¥¥
Hours: 2pm-2am
Entrance: free
No. 20, Houhai Nanyan, Xicheng District (50 m west of Yinding Qiao). (86-10-66136209) 西城区后海南沿20号 (银锭桥往西50米)

Sporting tropical plants, rattan chairs and chart-topping tunes– you'd be forgiven for thinking you'd arrived in a botanical garden. Really cheap drinks make the sunshine much brighter though!

Lotus Blue Bar 蓝莲花餐吧

Light music
English menu and service ¥¥¥
Hours: 1.30am-2am (Mon-Fri), 11.30am-2am (Sat-Sun)
Entrance: free
No. 51-6, Qianhai Xiyan, Di'anmen Xidajie, Xicheng Distirct. (86-10-66172599/2733) 西城区地安门大街前海西沿51-6号

As the aroma of Thai dishes floats around the sound of live music and the waters of Shichahai, sit back and take in the mood of this lovely novel bar.

Get in touch at Touch.

Nanluoguxiang 南锣鼓巷

If you are looking for a historical and interesting area with a few drinking hole options, don't miss Nanluoguxiang. Over 700 years old, this alley dates back to the Yuan Dynasty and was designed at the behest of Kublai Khan.

It is a perfect place for a stretch of unique cafes and bars. While the rest of Beijing's entertainment districts become more crowded and more grating on the nerves, this alley retains its calm charm.

Sights in the area (see p.94-95): Suo's Mansion (索家宅院), Keyuan Garden (可园), Wanrong's Residence (婉容故居), Beijing Artists Association (北京市美术家协

Restaurant listings

Meal prices per adult
¥ under RMB 29
¥¥ RMB 30-49
¥¥¥ RMB 50-69
¥¥¥¥ RMB 70-99
¥¥¥¥¥ over RMB 100

British

Fish Nation 鱼邦

English menu ¥¥¥¥
Hours: 11am-midnight
Transport: Bus 124, 107 to Xiaojingchang (小经厂)

会), Central Academy of Drama (中央戏剧学院), Prince Seng's Mansion (僧王府) and Former Residence of Mao Dun (茅盾故居)

Transport: take any of the following buses to Luoguxiang (锣鼓巷): 13, 118, 823, 834, 850. When you get off the bus, make your way to your final destination on foot.

Gulou Dongdajie 鼓楼东大街 North

Houguloyuan Hutong 后鼓楼苑胡同

Nanxiawazi Hutong 南下洼子胡同

Ju'er Hutong 菊儿胡同

F

Qiangulouyuan Hutong 前鼓楼苑胡同 **A**

Ju'er Hutong 菊儿胡同

Heizhima Hutong 黑芝麻胡同

Houyuan'ensi Hutong 后圆恩寺胡同

Nanluoguxiang 南锣鼓巷

Shajing Hutong 沙井胡同 **C**

Qianyuan'ensi Hutong 前圆恩寺胡同

Jingyang Hutong 景阳胡同

Qinlao Hutong 秦老胡同 **J**

G **B**

Mao'er Hutong 帽儿胡同

Beibingmasi Hutong 北兵马司胡同

H

Yu'er Hutong 雨儿胡同

Dongmianhua Hutong 东棉花胡同 **D** **I** **E**

Suoyi Hutong 蓑衣胡同

Banchang Hutong 板厂胡同

Fuxiang Hutong 福祥胡同

Chaodou Hutong 炒豆胡同

Di'anmen Dongdajie 地安门东大街

RESTAURANTS AND BARS

Danyanpi Bar 单眼皮吧	**F**
Down Town Restaurant 东堂食馆	**C**
Fish Nation 鱼邦	**A**
Here Bar 这里吧	**G**
Hongrenfang 红人坊	**H**
Luogu Dongtian 锣鼓洞天	**D**
Pass By Bar 过客	**I**
Pass By Restaurant 与食巨近	**E**
Salud 老伍	**J**
Xiao Xin's Café 小新的店	**B**

No. 31, Nanluoguxiang, Dongcheng District (near Qiangulouyuan Hutong). (86-10-64013249) 东城区南锣鼓巷31号(近前鼓楼苑胡同)

Boasting traditional English fare this popular chain restaurant even offers a children's play zone. Treat yourself to scones, Earl Grey tea, seafood mix, pizzas or barbecues.

Cafés

Xiao Xin's Café 小新的店
English menu and service ¥¥
Hours: 10am-2am

No. 103, Nanluoguxiang, Dongcheng District. (86-10-64036956) 东城区南锣鼓巷103号

🔲 *Wireless internet available.*

This café is famous for cheesecakes and other pastries made by

Xiao Xin, a Beijing baking legend. A relaxed atmosphere to enjoy coffee and a delectable baked delight from a master.

Chinese

C Down Town Restaurant 东堂食馆

Cantonese ¥
Hours: 10am-midnight
No. 85, Nanluoguxiang, Dongcheng District (next to Peking Down Town Backpackers Accommodation). (86-10-84002429) 东城区南锣鼓巷85号(紧挨东堂客栈)

Take advantage of the bicycle rental for an economical mode of transport!

Part of the adjacent, comfortable hotel, this restaurant is ideal for foreign travelers looking for value for money.

ⓓ Luogu Dongtian

锣鼓洞天

Home-cooking Sichuan cuisine

English menu ¥¥

Hours: 11am-11pm (Sun-Thu), 10am-1am (Fri-Sat)

No. 102, Nanluoguxiang, Dongcheng District. (86-10-84024729) 东城区南锣鼓巷102号

An exciting fusion of Asian dishes with an emphasis on Sichuan cuisine. Very reasonably priced and bursting with flavor.

French

ⓔ Pass By Restaurant

与食巨近

English menu ¥¥¥¥¥

Hours: 11am-midnight

No. 114, Nanluoguxiang, Dongcheng District (beside Pass By Bar). (86-10-64006868) 东城区南锣鼓巷114号 (过客酒吧旁) .

Inspired by its French-influenced cuisine, this two-story *hutong* restaurant provides for the perfect romantic evening. Elegant décor, intimate lighting and immaculate service combine for a lovely dining experience.

Pass By Restaurant.

Friends are always welcome at the Pass By Bar.

Bar listings

Prices for a bottle of Tsingtao beer (青岛啤酒), a favorite local beer

¥ under RMB 14
¥¥ RMB 15-24
¥¥¥ RMB 25-34
¥¥¥¥ over RMB 35

ⓕ Danyanpi Bar 单眼皮吧

Pop, jazz

English menu and service ¥

Hours: 2pm-2am

Entrance: free

No.17-1, Nanluoguxiang, Dongcheng District. (86-10-84022050) 东城区南锣鼓巷17-1号

With tasty authentic wine and an Italian coffee machine, you can tell that the owners of this bar appreciate the European lifestyle. The bar even features a "coffee show."

ⓖ Here Bar 这里吧

Light music

English menu ¥

Hours: 9am-1pm

Entrance: free

No. 97, Nanluoguxiang, Dongcheng District. (86-10-84014246) 东城区南锣鼓巷97号

A perfect place for backpackers looking for good food and drinks, this comfortable bar is decorated with photos taken by the owner. Nice house plants add to the relaxing atmosphere.

ⓗ Hongrenfang 红人坊

Traditional Chinese music

English menu and service ¥¥

Hours: 12pm-late

Entrance: free

No. 111, Nanluoguxiang, Dongcheng District. (86-10-68511489) 东城区南锣鼓巷111号

You might find yourself feeling a little tipsy earlier than usual in the strange atmosphere of this ancient Chinese-style bar. Its unique drinking experience not to be missed. Very spacious.

ⓘ Pass By Bar 过客

English menu ¥¥

Hours: 10am-2am

Entrance: free

No. 108, Nanluoguxiang, Dongcheng District. (86-10-84038004) 东城区南锣鼓巷108号

Expats and backpackers love this place for its intellectual vibe. There's reading material available, and amazing Tibetan prints on the walls. It's also a restaurant. Authentically and delicately prepared Italian dishes including traditional cheeses, pizzas and salads (be sure to try the tuna!).

ⓙ Salud 老伍

Jazz, Spanish music

English menu and service ¥¥

Hours: 1pm-2am

Entrance: free

No. 66, Nanluoguxiang, Dohgcheng District. (86-10-64025086) 东城区南锣鼓巷66号

With reasonably priced cocktails (RMB 25) and house Spanish Montrose (RMB 40) combined with a good kitchen capable of pizza or traditional Chinese fare, this is a safe bet for a nice night. Interesting photography and treasures collected by the owner from all over the world are on display.

"Ghost" Street 簋街 Guijie

Don't let the name fool you, there's nothing to be scared of here. That is, unless you're scared of delicious food, because there's plenty of that on Dongzhimennei Dajie (东直门内大街). This street is packed with over 100 restaurants, some open all night. There are also shops, so you can walk off dinner with a little shopping.

The ghostly moniker comes from times past when outdoor vendors would set up kerosene lamps and sell their wares all night long. Red lanterns along the street today remind us of this old tradition. Visit at night and you'll surely be able to imagine how it was.

Besides its official name on the map, this food street is often referred to as Guijie, which has the same pronunciation as Ghost Street in Chinese. But the actual character "簋" (gui) means a round mouthed pot used in ancient times. You'll see a bronze statue of this character at the eastern end of the street.

Known for great food at low prices, Guijie is also highly entertaining. Let the polite staff bring you a steaming tray of the street specialty, spicy, tongue-numbing crayfish (小龙虾).

Sights nearby: Lama Temple (see p.57) and Confucius Temple (see p.60)
Transport: the most convenient is to take Subway Line 2 to Dongzhimen (东直门), leave through Exit A or D, then walk. Bus 107, 106, 24, 117 all directly go to Guijie.

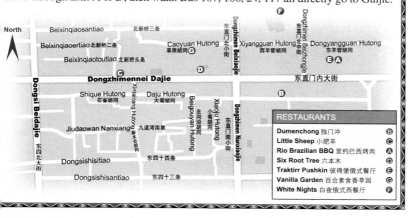

RESTAURANTS

Dumenchong 独门冲	Ⓑ
Little Sheep 小肥羊	Ⓒ
Rio Brazilian BBQ 里约巴西烤肉	Ⓐ
Six Root Tree 六本木	Ⓓ
Traktirr Pushkin 彼得堡俄式餐厅	Ⓔ
Vanilla Garden 百合素食香草园	Ⓖ
White Nights 白夜俄式西餐厅	Ⓕ

Restaurant listings

Meal prices per adult

¥ under RMB 29

¥¥ RMB 30-49

¥¥¥ RMB 50-69

¥¥¥¥ RMB 70-99

¥¥¥¥¥ over RMB 100

Brazilian

Ⓐ Rio Brazilian BBQ
里约巴西烤肉

BBQ ¥¥¥

Hours: 11am-3pm, 5pm-midnight

Dongzhimennei Dajie, Dongcheng District (west of 7-11). (86-10-84064368/9) 东城区东直门内大街

(7-11 西侧)

Enough to satisfy any hunger, this all-you-can-eat buffet (RMB 48 per person for lunch, RMB 58 for dinner) offers a colorful salad bar as well as sizzling chicken, beef, lamb and seafood served directly from the skewer to your plate.

Chinese

❻ Dumenchong 独门冲

Sichuan cuisine ¥¥¥

Hours: 24 hours
No. 15, Dongzhimennei Dajie,
Dongcheng District. (86-10-84062040)
东城区东直门内大街15号

Owned by a cool Chinese male model, it specializes in Chongqing-style fish and ribs served in the authentic way—spicy!

❼ Little Sheep 小肥羊

Hotpot ¥¥¥

Hours: 11am-11pm
No. 209, Dongzhimennei Dajie,
Dongcheng District. (86-10-84001669) 东城区东直门内大街209号

Part of a nationwide chain made famous by its special mutton hotpot. Their secret lies in its cumin-based broth, so flavorful! It makes you forget to use the dipping sauce!

The sign of Little Sheep.

Japanese

❽ Six Root Tree 六本木

English menu ¥¥¥

Hours: 10am-2am
No. 177, Dongzhimennei Dajie,
Dongcheng District. (86-10-64011797)
东城区东直门内大街177号

The all-you-can-eat (and drink!) menu is the best way to go in this stylish Japanese restaurant. Choose from an eye-popping selection including Fruit sushi (水果寿司), Fruit tempura (水果天

妇罗), Six root tree salad (六本木沙拉).

Russian

❿ Traktirr Pushkin 彼得堡俄式餐厅

English menu ¥¥¥

Hours: 11am-2am
No. 5-10, Dongzhimennei Dajie,
Dongcheng District. (86-10-84078158) 东城区东直门内大街5-10号

In a cuisine not renowned for its delicacy, this menu offers traditional Russian dishes with a bit of ritz. Enjoy their special pickled cherry tomatoes washed down with Russian beer (RMB 20) whilst enjoying the nightly performance.

ⓕ White Nights 白夜俄式西餐厅

English menu ¥¥¥¥

Hours: 10.30am-midnight
No. A13, Dongzhimen Beizhongjie,
Dongcheng District. (86-10-84029595) 东城区东直门北中街甲13号

Strong, sturdy Russian dishes served in strong, sturdy Russian surroundings, complete with collection of matyoshka dolls. Menu offers classics like Chicken Kiev, Black bread and their speciality, Arabian mutton.

Vegetarian

ⓖ Vanilla Garden 百合素食香草园

English menu ¥¥¥

Hours: 10.30am-10pm
No. 23, Caoyuan Hutong,
Dongzhimen Beixiaojie,
Dongcheng District. (86-10-64052082) 东城区东直门北小街草园胡同23号

Veg out (so to speak) and enjoy vegetarian dishes, imported organic coffees and herbal teas in comfortable surroundings.

RESTAURANTS AND BARS	
Cihai Suxin 慈海素心	❶
Dalian Seafood Dumplings 大连海鲜饺子	Ⓐ
Fujialou 福家楼	Ⓑ
Huaiyangfu 淮扬府	Ⓒ
Ku'ai Chuanba 酷爱串吧	Ⓒ
Latinos 拉提诺	Ⓓ
Qilu Hotel 齐鲁饭店	Ⓓ
Ri Chang 日昌茶餐厅	Ⓔ
Xihu Chuancai 西湖船菜	Ⓕ

Restaurant listings

Meal prices per adult

¥ under RMB 29

¥¥ RMB 30-49

¥¥¥ RMB 50-69

¥¥¥¥ RMB 70-99

¥¥¥¥¥ over RMB 100

Chinese

Ⓐ Dalian Seafood Dumplings 大连海鲜饺子

Northeast cuisine
English menu ¥

Hours: 10am-10pm
Transport: Bus 13, 42, 118, 701, 850, 823 to Di'anmen Dong (地安门东)
No. 119, Di'anmen Dongdajie, Xicheng District (300 m south of Drum Tower). (86-10-64043054) 西城区地安门东大街119号 (鼓楼南300米)

Dumplings are to northeast China what spaghetti is to Italy. This restaurant offers a great selection to try, along with some mouth-watering seafood thrown in for good measure.

Ping'an Dajie 平安大街

Ping'an Dajie is the second largest east-west thoroughfare in central Beijing that runs parallel to Chang'an Jie (长安街). It consists of four sections: Ping'anli Xidajie (平安里西大街), Di'anmen Dajie (地安门大街), Zhangzizhong Lu (张自忠路) and Dongsishitiao (东四十条). Despite a lack of parking space and serious traffic congestion, the old-Beijing mix of authentic and faux-Qing Dynasty low-rise buildings and a great selection of restaurants are worth exploring.

Sights in the area: Shichahai (see p.72) and Beihai Park (see p.54).

Transport: the best to make your way is to take Bus 701 or Trolley bus 118. Both run along the avenue.

Fujialou 福家楼

Beijing cuisine

English menu   ¥¥

Hours: 11am-2pm, 5pm-9.30pm

Transport: Bus 118, 701, 823, 834 or Subway Line 2 to Dongsishitiao (东四十条)

No. 23, Dongsishitiao, Dongcheng District (200 m west of Poly Plaza). (86-10-84037831) 东城区东四十条23 号(保利大厦西200 米)

Specializing in old Beijing favorites, this extremely popular and busy restaurant offers a classic selection of noodles, soups and cold dishes cooked just the way Beijingers like them.

Intestines, anyone?

Ku'ai Chuanba 酷爱串吧

Kebabs

English menu   ¥¥

Hours: 11am-2am

Transport: Bus 13, 118, 823, 850 to

Luoguxiang (锣鼓巷)

No. 60, Di'anmen Dongdajie, Xicheng District. (86-10-84014525) 西城区地安门东大街60 号

📋 *10% discount on reservations made through www.fantong.com (in Chinese).*

Give your taste buds (and your partner) a real treat at this romantic restaurant. Kebabs such as golden needles mushrooms with bacon (培根金针菇), corn (烤玉米), chicken wings (烤鸡翅) are highly recommended.

Qilu Hotel 齐鲁饭店

Shandong, Sichuan, Hangzhou and Cantonese cuisine

English menu   ¥¥

Hours: 24 hours

Transport: Bus 111, 107, 13, 118, 810, 823 to Dongguanfang (东官房)

No. 103, Di'anmen Xidajie, Xicheng District. (86-10-66180966 ext. 6008) 西城区地安门西大街103 号

The hotel boasts 13 restaurants under one big roof. Whether it's Shandong, Sichuan, Cantonese or vegetarian that takes your fancy (or all of them, we don't judge), you'll definitely find it

here. RMB 38 hotpot buffet is available too.

Curry chicken clay-pot at Ri Chang.

Ri Chang 日昌茶餐厅

Cantonese cuisine

English menu   ¥¥

Hours: 10am-3am

Transport: Bus 13, 42, 118, 701, 850, 823 to Di'anmen (地安门)

No. 14, Di'anmen Xidajie, Xicheng District (close to Beihai Park North Gate). (86-10-64058205) 西城区地安门西大街14 号(近北海北门)

A cheap, boot filling, tasty selection of Cantonese style dishes and hotpot. The clay-pot dishes (煲仔饭) and Bifengtang (避风塘) in particular shouldn't be missed.

Xihu Chuancai 西湖船菜

Hangzhou cuisine

English menu   ¥¥

Hours: 10am-2pm, 4.30pm-11pm

Transport: Bus 13, 42, 118, 701, 850,

Huaiyangfu (listed below)

823 to Di'anmen (地安门)
No. 6, Di'anmen Xidajie, Xicheng District. (86-10-84002929) 西城区地安门西大街6号

📋 *10% discount on reservations made through www.fantong.com (in Chinese).*

Traditional Hangzhou dishes served nicely in unconventional minimalist surroundings. The Duck noodle (老鸭面 a bargain at RMB 20) and West lake fish in vinegar sauce (西湖醋鱼) should definitely be on the must-try list.

⑥ Huaiyangfu 淮扬府
Jiangsu & Zhejiang cuisine ¥¥¥¥
Hours: 10.30am-2pm, 5pm-9pm
Transport: Bus 701, 107, 118 to Ping'an Hospital (平安医院)
1/F, China Peking Opera Theater, No. 22, Ping'anli Xidajie, Xicheng District. (86-10-58519988) 西城区平安里西大街22号中国京剧院一楼

📋 *10% discount with a VIP card.*

Traditional wood-carvings decorate Huaiyangfu and bring that extra flavor of tradition. Chinese *Erhu* and dulcimer performances are available at 6.30pm every night.

Vegetarian

⑭ Cihai Suxin 慈海素心
English menu ¥¥¥¥
Hours: 9.30am-11pm
Transport: Bus 111, 107, 13, 118, 810, 823 to Dongguanfang (东官房)

Inside Qilu Hotel, No. 103, Di'anmen Xidajie, Xicheng District. (86-10-66571898) 西城区地安门西大街103号齐鲁饭店内

📋 *12% discount on reservations made through www.fantong.com (in Chinese).*

Not so easy to find but definitely worth the forage, this vegetarian restaurant offers an extensive and creative selection of tofu related and vegetable dishes.

Bar listings

Prices for a bottle of Tsingtao beer (青岛啤酒), a favorite local beer
¥ under RMB 14
¥¥ RMB 15-24
¥¥¥ RMB 25-34
¥¥¥¥ over RMB 35

ⓘ Latinos 拉提诺
Latin dance ¥¥
English menu and service
Hours: 8pm-late
Entrance: free
Transport: Bus 46 to Dongsishitiao Qiao (东四十条桥)
No. A12, Historical Complex, Nanxincang, Dongsishitiao, Dongcheng District. (86-10-64096997) 东城区东四十条南新仓饮食特色街A12铺

Come to dance salsa and check out live music from Colombia or top Latin DJs. Can't dance? Don't worry; this place has teachers on tap.

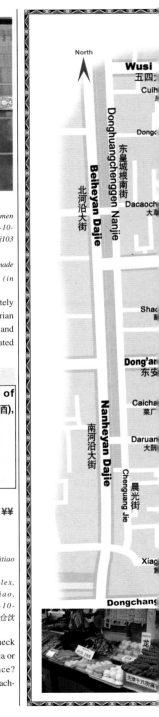

Dongsi Xidajie 东四西大街

Duofu Xiang 多福巷

Baofang Hutong 报房胡同
Guanfang Dayuan
官房大院

Xiaoboge Hutong
小鹁鸽胡同

灯市口北巷
DengshiKou
Beixiang

hikou Dajie 灯市口大街

Baishu Hutong 柏树胡同

Ganyu Hutong 甘雨胡同

Xitangzi Hutong 西堂子胡同

nghuamen Night Market

Jinyu Hutong
金鱼胡同

Xiaowei Hutong
校尉胡同

Meizha Hutong
煤渣胡同

北帅虎胡同
Beishuaihu Hutong
Dongshuaihu Hutong
东帅虎胡同

Dongdansantiao
东单三条

Wangfujing Dajie 王府井大街

安街

Donghuamen Night Market 东华门夜市

Fancy biting into some delicious scorpion skewers? Or maybe you prefer boiled silkworms?

Donghuamen has it all, from sweet to sour, salty to spicy. Offering some of the best street food in town, this 200-m-long stretch of outdoor stalls, lined with red lanterns and animated vendors sizzles to life every evening—it's like Chinatown, in China.

Donghuamen is not as cheap as it used to be, but all the prices are clearly indicated. Just make sure the vendor points to the price on the board, before you order. It's also a good idea to take a stroll and see what's on offer before allowing your eyes to get the better of your stomach. There are over 100 regional dishes and desserts to choose from, though the most popular are kebabs, meat, vegetable and fish dishes. Alternatively, try the pancakes, dumplings and stews. Even if you've already eaten, it's worth checking out Donghuamen for its bustling atmosphere.

Sights nearby: Forbidden City (see p.44) and Tian'anmen Square (see p.50).

Transport: Subway Line 1 to Wangfujing (王府井), head north along Wangfujing Dajie (王府井大街) till you hit Dong'anmen Dajie (东安门大街), turn left at the intersection.

Theaters

The theaters listed below are marked on the map on p.42.

㉟ Capital Theater 首都剧场

Drama

Hours: 7.30pm-9.30pm

Price: RMB 80-500

Transport: Bus 108, 104, 111 to Dengshi Xikou (灯市西口)

No. 22, Wangfujing Dajie, Dongcheng District. (call for event info: 86-10-65249847) 东城区王府井大街22 号

The stars of China and abroad shine in Beijing's most respected theater. For the very best in drama and dance, this is where the pulse is.

㊱ Chang'an Grand Theater 长安大戏院

Peking Opera

English subtitles

Hours: 7.30pm

Price: RMB 50-280

Transport: Subway Line 2 to Beijing Railway Station (北京站)

No. 7, Jianguomennei Dajie, Dongcheng District. (call for event info: 86-10-65101307/1309/1310) 东城区建国门内大街7 号

This cabaret-style theater has exciting live performances of traditional Peking Opera with English subtitles. Relax with a drink and something to eat at one of the tables.

㊲ Cultural Palace of Nationalities Theater 民族文化宫大剧院

Drama, concerts & cross-talking

Hours: 7.30pm

Price: RMB 80-600

Transport: Bus 395, 702 or Subway Line 1 or 2 to Fuxingmen (复兴门)

No. 49, Fuxingmennei Dajie, Xicheng District. (call for event info: 86-10-66022770) 西城区复兴门内大街49 号

Here's a chance to learn about China's many fascinating minority groups. In addition to performances there is a library, a hotel and a recreational center.

㊳ National Grand Theater 国家大剧院

Concert, Western and Chinese operas

Hours: varied play schedule

Transport: Bus 1, 2, 10, 20, 52, 120, 126, 203, 205, 728, 802 or Subway Line 1 to Tian'anmen East (天安门东) or Tian'anmen West (天安门西)

West of the Great Hall of the People. (86-10-66550000) 人民大会堂西侧

This huge and complex theater is a structural and architectural phenomenon. You'll see the

Poly Plaza.

amazing exterior, made of titanium panels that frame a glass curtain. An enormous pool and lush greenery surrounds the dome-like structure.

㊴ Poly Plaza International Theater 保利大厦国际剧院

Hours: 7.30pm

Price: RMB 80-480

Transport: Bus 118, 701, 823, 834 or Subway Line 2 to Dongsishitiao (东四十条)

Poly Plaza, No. 14, Dongzhimen Nandajie, Dongcheng District. (call for event info: 86-10-65001188/65065343) 东城区东直门南大街14 号保利大厦

This well-known theater showcases fabulous Chinese and international concerts. The Poly Plaza also hosts ballets and musicals, making it a diverse entertainment venue.

Chang'an Grand Theater.

🛒 Shopping

W hether you're a shopaholic or shopaphobic, no one should skip Wangfujing. While this is Beijing's main commercial street, the atmosphere and people-watching opportunities add a certain something that is definitely worth experiencing. The night food market on **Donghuamen** is an experience too!

Beyond Wangfujing, there are the funky boutiques along the **Dongsi Beidajie**, the massive **Beijing Books Building**, the cell phone market at **Xidan Sci-Tech Square** …. literally something to suit everyone. Don't be afraid to bargain in the markets though, the vendors aren't!

The places listed below are marked on the map on p.42.

Famous Wangfujing Street.

Dongsi Beidajie
东四北大街
Various unique shops
Hours: 8am-7pm
Transport: Bus 106, 116 to Dongsishi'ertiao (东四十二条)
Between Dongzhimennei Dajie and Chaoyangmennei Dajie, Dongcheng District 东城区东直门内大街和朝阳门内大街之间

Unusual shops, clothing shops especially, differentiate this north-south shopping street from the other "big two." Those looking for something special shouldn't miss it.

Wangfujing Shopping Street 王府井步行街
Clothing, shoes, jewelry, food
Hours: 8am-10pm
Transport: Bus 10, 37, 41, 59, 120, 126, 203, 420, 802 or Subway Line 1 to Wangfujing (王府井), North Exit.
Stretches from Dongchang'an Jie to National Art Museum of China. 南到东长安街, 北到中国美术馆

This 700-year-old commercial street features a wide variety of shops and posh boutiques where you can find world famous brands.

Xidan 西单
Clothing, shoes, jewelry, electronics
Hours: 8am-10pm
Transport: Bus 22, 47, 726, 808, 826 to Xidan Department Store (西单商场) or Subway Line 2 to Xidan (西单) One km west of Tian'anmen Square. 天安门广场西1公里

Xidan features clothes stores, food markets, a cell phone mall and a lot more. If you are looking for shopping and dining in an international atmosphere, it's all right here.

Overlooking Xidan.

Accommodation

For most visitors to Beijing, "Historical" Central is generally the first place to stay, and with good reason. With many of the city's top sights within a stone's throw of each other, and others within easy reach by bike, bus, taxi or subway, it seems a logical choice. Accommodation can be found to suit any preference and pocket, from RMB 50 hostel beds to more cultural abodes such as **Beijing Lüsongyuan Hotel** (see p.90), located in a traditional *siheyuan*.

The places listed below are marked on the map on p.42.

(see p.90) ... on p.42.

Accommodation prices per night
¥ under RMB 99
¥¥ RMB 100-199
¥¥¥ RMB 200-299
¥¥¥¥ RMB 300-399
¥¥¥¥¥ over RMB 400

Dorms/Hostels	🚐	☎	▦	👫	⛩	@	👕
Ⓐ Beijing Saga International Youth Hostel 北京实佳国际青年旅舍 ¥				■	■		
Ⓑ City Central Youth Hostel 城市青年酒店 ¥	■	■	■	■	■	■	■
Ⓒ Drum Tower Youth Hostel 鼓韵青年酒店 ¥	■	■	■	■	■	■	■

Ⓐ Beijing Saga International Youth Hostel
北京实佳国际青年旅舍 ¥

Price: RMB 40-60 (dorm beds), RMB 160 (singles), RMB 180 (doubles), RMB 210 (triples)

Transport: Bus 24, 713 to Lumicang (禄米仓)

No. 9, Shijia Hutong, Nanxiaojie, Dongcheng District. (86-10-65272773)
东城区南小街史家胡同9号

One of the best hostels in the downtown *hutong* area, near Beijing Railway Station and Tian'anmen, this friendly place is clean, quiet and affordable.

Ⓑ City Central Youth Hostel 城市青年酒店 ¥

Price: RMB 60 (dorm beds), RMB 120 (singles), RMB 160 (doubles)
Transport: Bus 24 or Subway Line 2 to Beijing Railway Station (北京站)
No. 1, Beijingzhan Qianjie, Dongcheng District. (86-10-85115050) 东城区北京站前街1号

With high standards and a great location, this newly opened hostel is near Tian'anmen Square, Forbidden City, Temple of Heaven, Ancient Observatory, Behai Park, Wangfujing Shopping Street.

Ⓒ Drum Tower Youth Hostel 鼓韵青年酒店 ¥

Price: RMB 40-70 (dorm beds), RMB 228 (singles), RMB 100-258 (doubles), RMB 298 (triples)
Transport: Bus 60, 206, 27 to Liupukang (六铺炕) or Subway Line 2 to Gulou Dajie (鼓楼大街)
No. 51, Jiugulou Dajie, Xicheng District. (86-10-84029787)
http://www.guyunhostel.com 西城区旧鼓楼大街51号

Ideally located and highly regarded by foreign travelers, this hostel is within walking distance of the Bell and Drum Towers and close to other major sights in the central area. It offers all sizes of rooms. Tourist information and bicycle rental are also available.

Eastern Morning Sun Youth Hostel 东方晨光青年旅社 ¥

Price: RMB 80 (singles), RMB 120/140 (doubles), RMB 180 (triples)
Transport: Subway Line 1 to Dongdan (东单)
No. 8-16, Dongdansantiao, Dongcheng District (opposite the south gate of Peking Union Medical College Hospital). (86-10-65284347) http://www.hostelsbeijing.com/en/index.html 东城区东单三条8-16 (协和医院南门对面)

Very close to Tian'anmen, this specially equipped hostel is right in the middle of Beijing.

Jade International Youth Hostel 西华智德饭店 ¥

Price: RMB 50-80 (dorm beds), RMB 240-380 (doubles)
Transport: Bus 819, 60 to Fuchan Yiyuan (妇产医院)
No. 5, Zhide Beixiang, Beiheyan Dajie, Dongcheng District (Near Wangfujing Dajie). (86-10-65259966) http://www.xihuahotel.com-chinesehome.html

东城区北河沿大街智德北巷5号(王府井大街附近)

Centrally located with easy transportation to all the best tourist attractions, this hostel is also near Huangchenggen Site Park and Wangfujing. Just a 10-minute walk away is the Donghuamen Night Market. Take advantage of its bicycle rental and tourist information desk.

Peking Down Town Backpackers Accommodation ¥ 东堂青年旅社

Price: RMB 50 (dorm beds), RMB 130 (singles), RMB 170 (doubles)
Transport: Bus 13, 118, 823, 850 to Luoguxiang (锣鼓巷)
No. 85, Nanluoguxiang, Dongcheng District. (86-10-84002429)
downtown@backpackingchina.com 东城区南锣鼓巷85号

Well situated in one of Beijing's beautiful *hutong* neighborhoods, this hostel is geared to backpackers' needs. It offers an attached restaurant /library and bike rental for RMB 20/day.

Hotels (prices based on double-occupancy rooms)

Tailong Hotel 泰龙宾馆 ¥¥¥

Price: RMB 218-238
Transport: Bus 103, 104, 803 to Sun Dong An Plaza (新东安市场)
No. 51, Dong'anmen Dajie, Dongcheng District (at the Donghuamen Night Market). (86-10-65518836) 东城区东安门大街51号(东华门夜市)

Very near to Wangfujing Shopping Street and the surrounding famous sites. You can smell the good food of Donghuamen Night Market from your room.

Accommodation prices per night	
¥	under RMB 99
¥¥	RMB 100-199
¥¥¥	RMB 200-299
¥¥¥¥	RMB 300-399
¥¥¥¥¥	over RMB 400

	🏨	@	✕	🍴	🍸	🐾	🛏

🄷 Industry and Commerce Hotel 工商宾馆 ¥¥¥

| | ■ | ■ | ■ | | | | |

Price: RMB 238-278
Transport: Bus 2, 210 to Shatan Lukounan (沙滩路口南)
No. 95, Beiheyan Dajie, Dongcheng District (close to National Art Museum of China). (86-10-65277544) 东城区北河沿大街95号(中国美术馆附近)
Right next to the Palace Museum, and near the Eastern Church, Beihai Park and Jingshan Park. Tourism and airport shuttle services are available for your convenience.

🄸 Oriental Peace Hotel 东方和平宾馆 ¥¥¥

| | ■ | ■ | ■ | | ■ | ■ | ■ |

3 star
Price: RMB 248-308
Transport: Bus 10, 120, 203, 420, 802 or Subway Line 1 to Wangfujing (王府井)
No. A33, Dongdansantiao, Dongcheng District (beside McDonald's). (86-10-82058493) 王府井东单三条甲33号(麦当劳旁边)
An ideal place for those who want to stay in Beijing's center on a budget. Within walking distance to major spots in the Central area, including Beijing Railway Station, you can get to most parts of the city easily from here.

🄹 Wangfujing Yongguang Hotel 王府井永光宾馆 ¥¥¥

| | ■ | | ■ | | ■ | ■ | ■ |

3 star
Price: RMB 230-380
Transport: Bus 103, 104, 803 to Sun Dong An Plaza (新东安市场)
No. 43, Dong'anmen Dajie, Wangfujing, Dongcheng District (at the Donghuamen Night Market). (86-10-65265558) 东城区王府井东安门大街43号(东华门夜市)
Near all the spots of interest in Central, this hotel has single rooms, doubles and suites.

🄺 Dongsi Super 8 Hotel 东四速8酒店 ¥¥¥

| | ■ | ■ | | | ■ | ■ | |

Price: RMB 248-338
Transport: Bus 106, 116, 204, 804 to Qianliang Hutong (钱粮胡同)
No. 137, Dongsiwutiao, Dongcheng District. (86-10-64065688) 东城区东四五条137号
In courtyard surroundings, this hotel is a relaxing place to make your home away from home.

🄻 Wangfujing Dawan Hotel 王府井大万酒店 ¥¥¥

| | ■ | ■ | ■ | | ■ | | |

3 star
Price: RMB 260-300
Transport: Bus 106, 110, 803 to Mishi Dajie (米市大街)
No. A2, Ganyu Hutong, Dongdan Beidajie, Dongcheng District (near Peking Union Medical College Hospital). (86-10-85112266) 东单北大街甘雨胡同甲2号(北京协和医院附近)

A great place to stay if shopping is on your agenda, as Wangfujing is close. It's also near Tian'anmen and other major sights of "Historical" Central.

Lien Hotel 丽恩酒店 ¥¥¥

2 star

Price: RMB 268

Transport: Bus 113, 118, 701, 823 to Dongsishitiaoqiao Dong (东四十条桥东) or Subway Line 1 to Dongsishitiao (东四十条)

No. A3, Xinzhong Xijie, Dongcheng District (close to Poly Theater). (86-10-65531516) www.lien.com.cn (in Chinese) 东城区新中西街甲3号 (保利剧院附近)

Just 15 minutes' drive from the city center and Beijing Railway Station, and 25 minutes from the airport, this comfortable hotel is also close to Beijing's hottest night scene—Sanlitun. The restaurant speciality is Sichuan cuisine.

Lishi Hotel 礼士宾馆 ¥¥¥

2 star

Price: RMB 270-390

Transport: Bus 24, 713 to Yanyue Hutong (演乐胡同)

No.18, Lishi Hutong, Dongsi Nandajie, Dongcheng District (close to Sanyou Shopping Mall). (86-10-65220033) http://www.lishi-hotel.com (in Chinese) 东城区东四南大街礼士胡同18号 (三友商场附近)

Close to Wangfujing and National Art Museum of China, this hotel is only a short taxi ride from Tian'anmen and other Central sights.

Botai Hotel 博泰宾馆 ¥¥¥

3 star

Price: RMB 288-348

Transport: Bus 113, 823, 701, 118 to Kuanjie (宽街)

No. 140, Jiaodaokou Nandajie, Dongcheng District (near National Art Museum of China). (86-10-64079911) 东城区交道口南大街140号 (中国美术馆附近)

Close to key parts in the Central area, the rooms here are small but well equipped. There's also a Chinese restaurant with a large menu. A great place to see Beijing in style while on a budget.

Qilu Hotel 齐鲁饭店 ¥¥¥¥

3 star

Price: RMB 298-368

Transport: Bus 111, 107, 13, 118, 810, 823 to Dongguanfang (东官房)

No. 103, Di'anmen Xidajie, Xicheng District (close to Beihai Park). (86-10-66180966) 西城区地安门西大街103号 (北海公园附近)

Close to Beihai Park and Prince Gong's Mansion, this hotel provides a haven of comfort and convenience. With 168 rooms and suites, there are plenty of features to enjoy here while you aren't out sightseeing.

🏨 @ ✕ 🍸 👕 🏃 🏊

◉ Golden Palace Silver Street Hotel ¥¥¥¥
王府井金府银街大酒店

4 star

Price: RMB 378-418

Transport: Bus 106, 110, 807 to Mishi Dajie (米市大街)

No. 31, Ganyu Hutong, Wangfujing Dajie, Dongcheng District (near Dawan Hotel).
(86-10-85110388) 东城区王府井大街甘雨胡同 31 号 (大万酒店附近)

This clean and comfortable hotel with 233 rooms has classic Chinese decoration and stylish surroundings.

® Times Holiday Hotel 时代假日酒店 ¥¥¥¥

3 star

Price: RMB 380

Transport: Bus 108, 111, 420, 803 to Dengshi Xikou (灯市西口)

No. 57, Dengshikou Dajie, Dongcheng District (close to Beijing Crowne Plaza Hotel).
(86-10-65269955) http://www.sdjr.cn/index1-english.htm 东城区灯市口大街57号 (北
京皇冠假日酒店附近)

This international standard hotel is perfect for business or pleasure. It's
right in the middle of Wangfujing, Beijing's most famous shopping area.
Nicely furnished rooms with all the important amenities.

Siheyuan/Garden-style Hotels 🏨 @ ✕ 🍸 👕 🏃 🏊

ⓢ Lüsongyuan Hotel 侣松园宾馆 ¥¥¥¥¥

Price: RMB 500-600

Transport: Bus 108, 104, 113, 850 to Beibingmasi (北兵马司)

No. 22, Banchang Hutong, Kuanjie, Dongcheng District. (86-10-64040436) 东城区宽
街板厂胡同 22 号

A historical building in a traditional *siheyuan* compound, it is favored by
foreign guests, especially for its open-air seats under grapevines or beside
swaying bamboos.

ⓣ Bamboo Garden Hotel 竹园宾馆 ¥¥¥¥¥

3 star

Price: RMB 616-880

Transport: Bus 60 or Subway Line 2 to Drum Tower (鼓楼)

No. 24, Xiaoshiqiao Hutong, Xicheng District. (86-10-58520088) http://www.bbgh.
com.cn/en1.htm 西城区小石桥胡同24 号

Close to the Drum Tower in the center of old Beijing, this hotel has typical
Chinese courtyard style with American-standard modern facilities. It also
offers airport bus service.

Itineraries

Itinerary A: Imperial Palace Tour

Morning

8am Start your day at **Tian'anmen Square** (see p.50), allowing for a 30-minute stroll around the world's largest public square.

8.30am Explore the sites around the square. After a photo stop at **Monument to the People's Heroes**, head south to the **Memorial Hall of Chairman Mao** (see p.51), where his body is preserved. 45 minutes is plenty of time to explore.

9.20am Carry on northward to **Tian'anmen Rostrum** (see p.50) guarded by the enormous portrait of Mao above. Allow yourself a 20-minute breather to take a spectacular view of the entire square before entering **Zhongshan Park** (see p.52), the original place where Chinese emperors prayed to the God of Land and Grain. Half an hour is enough to enjoy this park.

10.10am Exit the park and head north to the **Forbidden City** (see p.44). Allow yourself at least three hours to wander around in this most amazing imperial architecture.

Afternoon

1.30pm Leave the palace through its north gate and take Bus 109, 124 or 103 to **Beihai Park** (see p.54) (about 5 minutes). Or just walk westward to the park and eat at any small restaurant on your way.

2.30pm Leave the restaurant with a full tummy. Spend two hours walking, or rowing, around one of China's best-preserved imperial gardens.

4.30pm Exit the park through the south gate and take Bus 103 (about 15 minutes) to **Wangfujing** (see p.85) for a slice of modern Beijing. Jump on one of the electric tour buses for a 45-minute tour of the area. That leaves a good hour for shopping!

5.30pm After completing a full circle, walk north up Wangfujing and turn left at the intersection by the Foreign Language Book Store. Head west to **Donghuamen Night Market** (see p.83), and tuck into some of the hundreds of freshly prepared specialities on offer in Beijing's most famous food market. About one hour should be enough.

7pm End of tour.

Expenses

Tian'anmen Rostrum: RMB 15

Zhongshan Park: RMB 3

Lunch: RMB 40

Forbidden City: RMB 60

Beihai Park: RMB 20

Wangfujing tour bus: RMB 15

Dinner at Donghuamen Night Market: RMB 30

Transport: RMB 2

Total: RMB 185 (USD 24)

Itinerary B: Hutong Tour

Route 1 (by subway & foot)

Bell and Drum Towers 钟鼓楼—**Lama Temple** 雍和宫—**Confucius Temple**孔庙—**Imperial Academy** 国子监

Morning	Expenses
9am Start your day at **Drum Tower** (see p.56), just about 100 m north from which is **Bell Tower** (see p.56). Go up the towers for views over Beijing's ancient city (one hour should be enough).	**Drum and Bell Towers:** RMB 35
10am Descend, walk west along Gulou Xidajie (鼓楼西大街) for about 150 m, where you'll see a big T-intersection, turn right and walk north along Jiugulou Dajie (旧鼓楼大街) for about 15 minutes to the Gulou Subway Station. Take Subway Line 2 to **Lama Temple** (see p.57).	
10.30am At Lama Temple, you may spend 1.5 hours lighting incense and appreciating the biggest lamasery in Beijing.	**Lama Temple:** RMB 25

Afternoon	
12pm Enjoy some freshly cooked Cantonese dim sum for lunch at **Jin Ding Xuan Restaurant** (see p.57) north of Yonghegong Qiao (雍和宫桥). Cheap, filling and delicious.	**Lunch:** RMB 40
1.30pm Return to Lama Temple's main gate and head west and through a decorated archway at the entrance to the leafy *hutong*, you'll pop into the **Confucius Temple** (see p.60). Spend an hour looking around China's second largest temple dedicated to the revered Sage.	**Confucius Temple:** RMB 10
2.45pm A few meters to the west is **Imperial Academy**. Within China's traditional education system, this was the highest and most prestigious institute. Explore it for about 45 minutes.	**Imperial Academy:** RMB 10
3.30pm End of the tour.	**Transport:** RMB 3

Total: RMB 123 (USD 16)

Bike rental

Pedal power is by far the best transport for *hutong* sightseeing. A bike gives you the flexibility of hopping on and off as you like. Helmets are optional in Beijing, but are strongly suggested! Bike rental is extremely cheap and there are countless rental places. Here are a few:

1. Qianhai Nanyan (前海南沿) at Shichahai, bicycles are RMB 10/hour, tandem bicycles RMB 20/hour. A RMB 500 refundable deposit is required.
2. Opposite the Lüsongyuan Hotel (侣松园宾馆) along Banchang Hutong. Price is a mere RMB 5/hour or RMB 30/day. A RMB 200 refundable deposit is required.

The new bicycle rickshaws.

Route 2 (*by rickshaw*)

Beihai Park North Gate 北海门门—Drum Tower 鼓楼 —Yandai Xiejie 烟袋斜街 — Yinding Qiao 银锭桥—Houhai Beiyan 后海北沿 —Soong Ching Ling Residence 宋庆龄故居—Houhai Xiyan 后海西沿— **Dongming Hutong** 东明胡同 — **Yangfang Hutong** 羊房胡同 — **Liuyin Jie** 柳荫街 —**Prince Gong's Mansion** 恭王府 —**Beihai Park North Gate** 北海门门

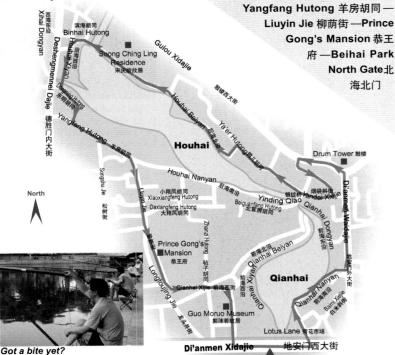

Got a bite yet?

If cycling just isn't your cup of Chinese tea, then hop on a rickshaw at the north gate of Beihai Park and let someone else do the hard work. Hold tight as you get whizzed down the winding, narrow alleys, quaintly stuck in a long-past age. See *sihueyuan* houses, check out the two ancient towers or simply absorb the culture of local people. You can wind up at **Prince Gong's Mansion** (see p.56), the best preserved Qing Dynasty prince mansion. Be sure to have properly bargained for the entire price of your trip and make sure that you have clearly agreed to where you will go, how long you will take and whether the price is for the trip, or per person (see **Scams to Avoid** on p.335).

- **Prices:** Around RMB 80 for a 2-hour tour (price is negotiable).
- **Starting point:** Look for rickshaws nearby Beihai Park North Gate. Or you can find individual rickshaws or tricycles around the Houhai area.
- **Hours of operation:** You can get an individual ride at any time.

Route 3 (*by bicycle*)

Nanluoguxiang 南锣鼓巷 —**Ju'er Hutong** 菊儿胡同 —**Houyuan'ensi Hutong** 后圆恩寺胡同 —**Heizhima Hutong** 黑芝麻胡同 —**Qinlao Hutong** 秦老胡同 —**Beibingmasi Hutong** 北兵马司胡同 —**Mao'er Hutong** 帽儿胡同 —**Yu'er Hutong** 雨儿胡同 —**Dongmianhua Hutong** 东棉花胡同 —**Banchang Hutong** 板厂胡同 —**Chaodou Hutong** 炒豆胡同

Keyuan Garden (可园), No. 9, Mao'er Hutong.
This grand and impressive abode was home to Wen Yu (?-1884), a Qing Dynasty secretary to the Grand Secretariat. Today it has been designated a cultural relic under state protection. It's regarded as the Qing Dynasty's most artistic garden.

Former Residence of Mao Dun (茅盾故居), No. 13, Houyuan'ensi Hutong. **See p.69**
An amalgamation of East and West, you will see a traditional *siheyuan* courtyard standing alongside Western-style.

Wanrong's Residence (婉容故居), No. 35, 37, Mao'er Hutong.
Wanrong's claim to fame is that she was empress of China's last ever emperor, Puyi.

Beijing Artists Association (北京市美术家协会), No. 13, Yu'er Hutong.
The place used to be home of Qi Baishi (1864-1957), China's most famed traditional painter.

Qiangulouyuan Hutong
前鼓楼苑胡同

Heizhima Hutong
黑芝麻胡同

Shajing Hutong
沙井胡同

景阳胡同 Jingyang Hutong

Mao'er Hutong
帽儿胡同

Yu'er Hutong
雨儿胡同

Suoyi Hutong
蓑衣胡同

Fuxiang Hutong
福祥胡同

Nanluoguxiang prides itself on being ancient Beijing's most wealthy area and modern Beijing's best-preserved *hutong* grid pattern. Eight parallel *hutong* strike off from this 800-m-long stretch of authentic architecture. This tour will take you, by pedal power, through these *hutong* and the *siheyuan* courtyards along the sides.

Expenses

Bike rental: RMB 20

Former Residence of Mao Dun: RMB 5

Total: RMB 25 (USD 3.2)

Suo's Mansion (索家宅院), No. 35, Qinlao Hutong.
This beautiful southern-style garden was once home of an elite Qing Dynasty official. Its garden style is unique in this part of the city.

r Hutong 菊儿胡同

yuan'ensi Hutong 后圆恩寺胡同

nyuan'ensi Hutong 前圆恩寺胡同

lao Hutong 秦老胡同

ibingmasi Hutong 北兵马司胡同

ngmianhua Hutong 东棉花胡同

nchang Hutong 板厂胡同

haodou Hutong 炒豆胡同

Central Academy of Drama (中央戏剧学院)
Dongmianhua Hutong.
The academy has produced several internationally known stars: Gong Li (*Farewell My Concubine* and *Memoirs of a Geisha*) and Zhang Ziyi (*Crouching Tiger, Hidden Dragon* and *Memoirs of a Geisha*)

Prince Seng's Mansion (僧王府), No. 77, Chaodou Hutong.
In its original state this vast mansion sprawled from Chaodou Hutong to Banchang Hutong. Since 1912, sections were sold off and smaller, individual complexes thus formed. To see the original sections of the mansion, visit Nos. 71, 73, 75 and 77 along Chaodou Hutong and Nos. 30, 32 and 34 along Banchang Hutong.

Bus Details

Major Bus Stops

Most of the major bus stops in the central area sit along the loop subway line, such as Qianmen, Fuchengmen, Xizhimen, Beijing Railway Station and Dongzhimen. At each of these there are direct routes to key destinations. **They are marked on the map on p.42.**

Chongwenmen Xi (崇文门西), west of Chongwenmen Subway Station, on Chongwenmen Xidajie (崇文门西大街)

To Beihai Park (北海公园): 103
To Beijing West Railway Station (北京西站): 820 内, 特 2, 848 支
To Beijing Zoo (动物园): 103
To Forbidden City (故宫): 103
To Grand View Garden (大观园): 59
To Pearl Market (红桥市场): 60, 723
To Temple of Heaven (天坛): 744

Dongzhimen (东直门), close to Dongzhimen Subway Station

To Beijing Railway Station (北京站): 24
To Beijing Zoo (动物园): 107
To Drum Tower (鼓楼): 107
To Forbidden City (故宫): 107
To Lama Temple (雍和宫): 117
To Olympic Park (奥林匹克公园): 18, 858
To Pearl Market (红桥市场): 106
To Temple of Heaven (天坛): 106

Fuchengmen (阜成门), close to Fuchengmen Subway Station

To Beihai Park (北海公园): 101, 103, 814, 846
To Forbidden City (故宫): 101, 103, 814, 846
To Jingshan Park (景山公园): 101, 103, 814, 846
To Summer Palace (颐和园): 运通 106
To Beijing Zoo (动物园): 103, 714, 814, 102
To Yuanmingyuan (圆明园): 814

To Zhongguancun (中关村): 运通 106

Qianmen (前门), south of Tian'anmen Square, close to Qianmen Subway Station

To Beihai Park (北海公园): 5
To Beijing Amusement Park (北京游乐园): 8
To Beijing Railway Station (北京站): 729, 744, 126
To Beijing West Railway Station (北京西站): 301
To Beijing Zoo (动物园): 特 4
To Drum Tower (鼓楼): 819, 5
To Grand View Garden (大观园): 59, 819
To Jingshan Park (景山公园): 5
To Ox Street (牛街): 48
To Pearl Market (红桥市场): 723
To Summer Palace (颐和园): 726, 826
To Temple of Heaven (天坛): 803, 120
To Yuanmingyuan (圆明园): 特 4, 726, 826
To Zhongguancun (中关村): 特 4

Xizhimenwai (西直门外), close to Xizhimen Subway Station, on Xizhimenwai Dajie (西直门外大街)

To Beijing Zoo (动物园): 105, 111, 27, 360, 601
To Forbidden City (故宫): 111
To Fragrant Hill (香山): 634, 360
To Jingshan Park (景山公园): 111
To Summer Palace (颐和园): 634, 运通 106
To Temple of Heaven (天坛): 7, 105
To Yuanmingyuan (圆明园): 运通105, 运通205
To Zhongguancun (中关村): 808, 运通 105, 运通 106, 运通 205

Useful Bus Routes

The following is a list of specially selected bus routes passing through the "Central." These are not all depot-to-depot routes and many less important stops have been omitted. Sights of interest are in bold type. Bus type and times of first and last buses of the first depot are also indicated.

Suggestion: If you are unsure you have the right stop, point out the Chinese characters below for where you want to go and ask another passenger, conductor or driver for help. Many young Chinese have OK English and will be able to help.

1 (standard bus, 5am-11pm)

Gongzhufen Nan 公主坟南 -**Military Museum** 军事博物馆 -Nanlishi Lu 南礼士路 - Fuxingmennei复兴门内-Xidan Lukoudong 西单路口东 -**Tian'anmen West** 天安门西 -Dongdan Lukouxi 东单路口西 -Ritan Lu 日坛路

2 (standard bus, 5am-11pm)

Muxiyuanqiao Bei 木樨园桥北 -**Temple of Heaven West Gate** 天坛西门 -**Dazhalan** 大栅栏 -**Tian'anmen East** 天安门东 -**Donghuamen** 东华门 -Shatan Lukounan 沙滩路口南 -Kuanjie Lukounan 宽街路口南

特4 (double-decker, 6am-8.30pm)

Qianmen 前门 -Santasi 三塔寺 -Beijing Exhibition Center 北京展览馆 -**Beijing Zoo** 动物园 -Baishiqiao Dong 白石桥东 -**Weigongcun** 魏公村 -Renmin Daxue 人民大学 -**Zhongguancun** 中关村 -**Yuanmingyuan East Gate** 圆明园东门

5 (standard bus, 5am-12am)

Qianmen 前门 -**Tian'anmen West** 天安门西 -Nanchang Jie 南长街 -Xihuamen 西华门 -**Beihai Park** 北海 -Jingshan Houjie 景山后街 -Di'anmennei 地安门内 -**Drum Tower** 鼓楼 -Deshengmen 德胜门

13 (standard bus, 5am-11pm)

Yuetan Park 月坛公园 -Fuchengmen 阜成门 -**White Dagoba Temple** 白塔寺 -**Beihai Park North Gate** 北海北门 -Luoguxiang 锣鼓巷 -Kuanjie Lukoudong 宽街路口东 -**Guozijian** 国子监 -Yonghegongqiao Dong 雍和宫桥东

17 (standard bus, 5.05am-11.30pm)

Qianmen 前门 -Zhushikou Nan 珠市口南 -**Tianqiao** 天桥 -**Temple of Heaven** 天坛 -Xiannongtan 先农坛 -Muxiyuanqiao Bei 木樨园桥北

37 (standard bus, 6am-10pm)

Ganjiakou Dong 甘家口东 -Yuetan Beijie Beizhan 月坛北街北站 -Fuxingmennei 复兴门内 -Cultural Palace of Nationalities 民族文化宫 -Xidan Lukoudong 西单路口东 -**Tian'anmen West** 天安门西 -**Wangfujing** 王府井

101 (trolley bus, 5.30am-10pm)

Chaoyangmennei 朝阳门内 -Meishuguan Dong 美术馆东 -**Forbidden City** 故宫 -**Beihai Park** 北海 -Xisi Lukoudong 西四路口东 -**White Dagoba Temple** 白塔寺 -Fuchengmennei 阜成门内 -Zhanlan Lu 展览路 -Ganjiakou Bei 甘家口北

103 (trolley bus, 4.50am-11pm)

Beijing Railway Station West 北京站西 -

Wangfujing Lukoubei 王府井路口北 -Sun Dong An Market 新东安市场 -Meishuguan 美术馆 -**Forbidden City** 故宫 -**Beihai Park** 北海 -**White Dagoba Temple** 白塔寺 -**Beijing Zoo** 动物园

109 (trolley bus, 5am-11pm)

Guang'anmen 广安门 -Niujie Lukouxi 牛街路口西 -**Xidan Department Store** 西单商场 -Gangwashi 缸瓦市 -**Beihai Park** 北海 -**Forbidden City** 故宫 -Meishuguan Dong 美术馆东 -Chaoyangmennei 朝阳门内

118 (trolley bus, 5am-11pm)

Workers' Stadium 工人体育场 -Luoguxiang 锣鼓巷 -**Beihai Park North Gate** 北海北门 -Ping'anli 平安里 -**Guanyuan** 官园 -Santasi 三塔寺 -**Purple Bamboo Park South Gate** 紫竹院南门

124 (trolley bus, 6am-10pm)

Yanhuang Art Museum 炎黄艺术馆 -**Olympic Sports Center East Gate** 奥体东门 -**Temple of the Earth West Gate** 地坛西门 -Baochao Hutong 宝钞胡同 -**Drum Tower** 鼓楼 -Jingshan Park East Gate 景山东门 -**Forbidden City** 故宫 -Beihai Park 北海

726 (standard bus, 6am-10pm)

Qianmen 前门 -**Tian'amen Square East** 天安门广场东 -**Xidan Department Store** 西单商场 -Huguosi 护国寺 -Xinjiekou Bei 新街口北 -**Beijing Language and Culture University** 北京语言大学 -Wudaokou 五道口 -Tsinghua University West Gate 清华西门 -**Yuanmingyuan South Gate** 圆明园南门 -**Summer Palace** 颐和园

810 (A/C, 5.30am-9pm)

Yabao Lu 雅宝路 -Chaoyangmennei 朝阳门内 -Meishuguan Dong 美术馆东 -**Forbidden City** 故宫 -Jingshan Houjie 景山后街 -**Beihai Park North Gate** 北海北门 -Xinjiekou Bei 新街口北 -Beijing Normal University 北京师范大学

823 (A/C, 5.40am-8pm)

Dongzhimenwai 东直门外 -Workers' Stadium 工人体育场 -**Dongsishitiao** 东四十条 -Luoguxiang 锣鼓巷 -**Beihai Park North Gate** 北海北门 -Xisi Lukouxi 西四路口西 -**White Dagoba Temple** 白塔寺 -**Yuetan Park** 月坛公园 -Beijing West Railway Station 北京西站

Dazhalan shopping street, where you can buy things from traditional to modern.

"Cultural" South

Looking for some genuine Beijing folk culture? Head south!

Part of "South" was once the "Outer City" (see p.53 for **Layout of old Beijing**). Because of a decree by the Qing court that only Manchus could live within the "Inner City," "South" became the major residential area for ordinary people. It was home to Beijing's first racetrack and photographic studio and where the first, brave foreign students lived. **Peking Opera** (see p.22) artists and **acrobats** found this the best place to fulfill their dreams and win fame; in fact, today's **Tianqiao** area, not far from the **Temple of Heaven** (see p.100), is still the best place to go for these arts.

Peking Opera mask.

Markets appeared (and disappeared) according to the needs of the people. For some of the ancient markets, street names may be all that remain (such as **Huashi Dajie** 花市大街, or **Flower Market**), but plenty of shopping can still be found at places such as **Hongqiao Market** (commonly called **Pearl Market**, and a firm favorite with foreigners, see p.111). It is located directly next to the Temple of Heaven, which could prove quite convenient, since after being jostled and overwhelmed with "Hello, lookie-lookie" from the stall holders, you may just want to offer up a prayer of your own.

Another sight worth seeing is the **Eight Grand Hutong** (see p.102), an ancient red light district. The brothels of this place are no longer in business, but you will still find buildings here as a testament to days (and nights) gone by.

To experience some Muslim culture, you don't have to go to far Arabian lands as **Niujie** (see p.109) provides it all. It has the biggest mosque in Beijing, where the Chinese Hui ethnic people offer regular prayers.

Highlights

- **Temple of Heaven** 天坛 Offerings to Heaven were made here by emperors to benefit crops and harvests. **See p.100**

- **Eight Grand Hutong** 八大胡同 The city's ancient red light district. Hundreds of brothels once dotted these alleys that now pull in the tourists. **See p.102**

- **Temple of the Origin of the Dharma** 法源寺 Built in the 7th century, this is the oldest temple in Beijing city proper. Currently home to the Chinese Buddhist Academy. **See p.103**

- **Niujie (Ox Street)** 牛街 You could call this street Muslim Central. Lots of things Muslim to be found, food especially. **See p.109**

- **Niujie Mosque** 牛街礼拜寺 The oldest Beijing mosque, also the largest. Visitors are welcome to view during non-prayer times. **See p.103**

- **Qianmen Dajie** 前门大街 One of the truly ancient streets in Beijing. Shopping, dining and busy people are all in the mix here. **See p.106**

- **Liyuan Theater** 梨园剧场 Subtitled Peking Opera on stage. **See p.110**

- **Wansheng Theater (Tianqiao Acrobatic Theater)** 万胜剧场 (天桥杂技剧场) Flips, spins, balancing and more... **See p.110**

- **Red Theater** 红剧场 Ready for some real action? Come here and check out Chinese martial arts. **See p.110**

Sightseeing

Tourist Attractions

❶ Temple of Heaven 天坛 Tiāntán ★★★

Where the emperors prayed for harvest

Hours: daily 6am-8pm (park), 8am-6pm (sites)
Entrance: RMB 50 (summer) or RMB 30 (winter) for all-inclusive ticket
Suggested length of visit: 2-3 hours
Transport: Bus 17, 36, 120, 203, 803 to Temple of Heaven (天坛); 6, 34, 35, 106, 110, 743, 822 to Temple of Heaven North Gate (天坛北门); 53, 122, 208, 特3, 运通102 to Temple of Heaven South Gate (天坛南门); or 2, 7, 20, 707, 729, 744, 826 to Temple of Heaven West Gate (天坛西门)
East of Yongdingmennei Dajie, Chongwen District. (86-10-67028866)
http://www.tiantanpark.com/cn/
崇文区永定门内大街东侧

✖ *Exit the east gate and get onto Tiantan Donglu (天坛东路), walk south for a couple of minutes, and you'll see a bunch of cheap and nice restaurants.*

This history-soaked temple is a monument to the superstitions and religious beliefs of the Ming and Qing rulers. Built in 1420 by Emperor Yongle, it was used for the worship of Heaven and prayers for good harvests. It is about four times the size of Forbidden City. The shape of the temple park (square in the south and round in the north) symbolizes Earth and Heaven respectively. Rituals were performed on the winter solstice at this spot. It was last used in 1914 by the unpopular president Yuan Shikai as he attempted to ascend to status of emperor.

Deemed the most beautiful ancient Chinese architecture, it was put on the World Heritage List in 1998.

As most visitors come to the Temple of Heaven through the east gate, it can be easy not to notice the real grandeur; make your entrance through the west gate (as the emperor did) and really soak in the feeling. Arriving early from around 6am to 8am at the temple you will be rewarded with "**people sights**"—wushu exercise, dancing, singing Peking Opera and playing music, etc.— that make this place lively.

Sacred Way
(丹陛桥 Danbiqiao)
The 360-m-long Vermilion Ste Bridge, or the Sacred Way, running tween the Hall of Prayer for Good H vests and the Imperial Vault Heaven. In its heyday, the central p was reserved for divine gods while east and the west paths were for emperor and the court officia respectively.

Abstinence Palace
(斋宫 Zhaigong)
The main function of this hall was the emperor to stay and fast be the sacrificial ceremony.

Imperial Vault of Heaven
(皇穹宇 Huangqiongyu)
This vault was built to house woo worship tablets. Surrounded by Echo Wall, the wood structure sta 19.5 m high with a large vault bene Support for the impressively beau roof is in the form of entwined bra ets—a real architectural feat.

Echo Wall (回音壁 Huiyinbi)
Position yourself at one end of 193.2-m-long, speak, and your v will be heard by your friend at other end. Chinese whispers? for yourself!

Why did the emperor offer sacrifices to Heaven?

The emperor was thought to be the "son of Heaven," a job title that came with an enormous sense of responsibility and a need to please both Heaven and mortals. The emperor was there to deal with matters on earth on behalf of Heaven. Natural disasters, bad harvests or social upheavals were blamed on the emperor, believing he had fallen from Heaven's grace and was being punished. Thus, it was vital for an emperor to offer sacrifices to keep the god on side, and the Temple of Heaven was constructed for precisely this purpose.

Hall of Prayer for Good Harvests
(祈年殿 Qiniandian)
Without a single nail, cement or steel rod, this 38-m-high hall is surely an architectural masterpiece. The symbol of the Temple of Heaven, it was for Ming and Qing emperors to pray for a good harvest in the following year. Its cobalt-blue roof symbolizes Heaven.

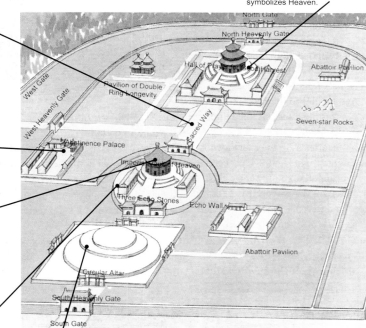

Circular Altar
(圜丘坛 Huanqiutan)
This three-tier altar was used during the Ming and Qing dynasties for the worship to Heaven on winter solstice by emperors. A central stone surrounded by nine circles echoes if anyone stands on it and speaks loudly.

The significance of numbers

As you wander around and explore imperial buildings such as the Temple of Heaven or Forbidden City, you may notice an unusual numbering pattern used in their construction, for example, the 4, 12 and 28 pillars in the Hall of Prayer for Good Harvests. In fact, this was carefully calculated to represent the four seasons, 12 months and 28 Chinese constellations, respectively. Another example is that odd numbers represent *yang* and even numbers *yin,* male and female elements respectively. The number nine, the highest single odd number, recurs frequently to represent supreme power: the nine ridge-tile beasts and the multiples of nine used for rooms and steps of imperial buildings.

❷ Eight Grand Hutong
八大胡同 Bādà hútòng ★★★

Red light district in ancient Beijing

Suggested length of visit: half day
Transport: Bus 2, 120, 201, 48, 729, 744,
826 to Dazhalan (大栅栏) or 5, 23, 57, 105,
715, 743 to Zhushikou Xi (珠市口西)
North of Zhushikou Dajie and south of Tieshu
Xiejie.
珠市口大街以北铁树斜街以南

Guanyinsi Jie provides access to the Eight Grand Hutong.

This fast-disappearing area tucked behind Dazhalan was a renowned red light district in late Qing Dynasty and the Republic of China (1912-1949). The founding of the People's Republic of China in 1949 put an end to the brothel business in this area, leaving the buildings for residential or office uses.

Differing theories as to the exact identification of the Eight Hutong have been put forward, and the age-old debate continues to rage on. However, it is generally accepted that the following, from west to east, formed the famous Eight: **Baishun** (百顺胡同), **Yanzhi** (胭脂胡同), **Hanjia** (韩家), **Shaanxixiang** (陕西巷), **Shitou** (石头胡同), **Zongshu Xiejie** (棕树斜街), **Zhujia** (朱家胡同) and **Xiaoli and Dali** (小力、大力胡同).

The east-west Baishun Hutong is the area's best-known and elite, and some well-preserved Western-style buildings and guild halls stand as testament that this was one of Beijing's top recreation spots.

Cheap tour-guide driven rickshaws are abundant here. RMB 10-15 will ensure you a full view of this *hutong* neighborhood.

Currently undergoing renovation, it is losing its original flare. So make sure to drop by this area when you are visiting Beijing and snap some photos of the old streets and houses which could end up being valuable one day.

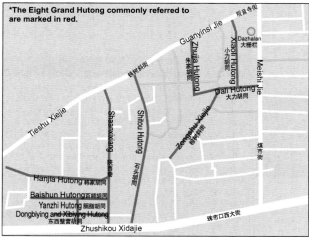

Sketch Map of the Eight Grand Hutong

❸ Niujie Mosque
牛街礼拜寺 Niújiē lǐbàisì ★★

A thousand years of Muslim worship

Hours: daily 7am-7pm
Entrance: RMB 10
Suggested length of visit: 45 minutes
Transport: Bus 10, 48, 626, 717 to Niujie Mosque
(牛街礼拜寺)
No. 18, Niujie, Xuanwu District. (86-10-63532564)
宣武区牛街18号

❌ *Try one of the local Muslim restaurants in Niujie (see p.109)*

📝 *This is a serious place of worship, so respect is needed, including wearing suitable dress. Non-Muslim visitors are welcome, but arrangements must be made in advance. No non-Muslim is allowed inside when prayers are in progress.*

This oldest and largest mosque in Beijing is a mixture of Islamic and Chinese cultures and also a major gathering place for Beijing's Muslims. Dating back to 996 in the Liao Dynasty after Islam was first introduced into China, it was enlarged and lifted to the status of one of the four official temples in Beijing in the Ming Dynasty, and further renovated by Qing Emperor Kangxi (r. 1662-1722). The latest facelift in 2005 almost doubled its floor space.

The mosque has 42 rooms in total, the most important being the **Prayer Hall** which is paved with mats and has striking gold-inscribed Arabic-style arches and pillars, and can accommodate 1,000 worshippers. Nearby is a minaret where the call to prayer is announced five times a day. **The Tower for Observing the Moon** (望月楼 Wangyuelou) (that can easily be seen from the street) is used to determine the time for **Ramadan**, an important Muslim festival of fasting.

Also home to several stone tablets inscribed in Chinese and Arabic, the mosque complex draws over 600 Muslims on Fridays. So visiting on this day allows a better experience of this religious place.

The main gate of the mosque only opens during Ramadan and **Corban** (an important Muslim festival); worshippers and visitors usually take the side gate.

❹ Temple of the Origin of the Dharma 法源寺 Fǎyuánsì ★★

Oldest temple in Beijing city proper

Hours: daily 8am-3.30pm
Entrance: RMB 5
Suggested length of visit: 45 minutes
Transport: Bus 109 to Caishikou Xi (菜市口西)
No. 7, Fayuansi Qianjie, Xuanwu District. (86-10-83517182)
宣武区法源寺前街7号

📝 *With the Museum Pass, you can get two free admissions to the Museum of Buddhist Literature and Heritage of China in this temple.*

The temple was decreed to be built by Tang Emperor Taizong in 645 in memory of his generals and soldiers who died in wars, and it was initially named Temple to Mourn the Loyal. Over the last millennium, it has been nearly destroyed many times by fire, wars and earthquakes, and renamed and renovated several times too. The oldest buildings are still standing, and the present temple name is from 1734.

Being the oldest and second largest temple within the confines of the city, this temple has a hall that other temples don't have—**the Vairochana Hall** (毗卢佛殿 Pilufodian). Formerly a memorial hall for the eminent Tang Dynasty monk Xuanzang (a major figure in the novel *Journey to the West*) who went to India to learn Buddhism, it

Reverent Muslim prayer.

contains a five-in-one bronze image of Vairochana seated on a lotus throne.

The temple is also home to the **Chinese Buddhist Academy** (中国佛学院) and the **Museum of Buddhist Literature and Heritage of China** (中国佛教图书文物馆) which displays some valuable relics, including Buddhist manuscripts, bronze statues and stone tablets.

Every April the **lilacs** bloom here, this temple draws numerous visitors with its **Lilac Fair** where people enjoy beautiful lilacs, create paintings and write poems. So visit during this time, when you can catch a glimpse of Beijing people's cultural life.

❺ Grand View Garden
大观园 Dàguānyuán ★

Garden from a novel

Hours: daily 8.30am-4pm
Entrance: RMB 40
Suggested length of visit: 1 hour
Transport: Bus 59, 122, 458, 717, 744, 819 to Grand View Garden (大观园)
No. 12, Nancaiyuan Jie, Xuanwu District. (86-10-63544994)
宣武区南菜园街12号

With the Museum Pass, you can get two free admissions.

A new garden based on descriptions in the classic novel *A Dream of Red Mansions* which tells a tragic love-story in a noble family and is the equivalent of *Romeo and Juliet* in the West. The book has been around for over 200 years, but the garden didn't become a reality until 1984. More than 40 attractions and a large lake are surrounded by trees and flowers, making for an authentic *Dream* experience.

There is a permanent exhibit on the culture and art of *A Dream of Red Mansions*. And a trip to this garden is incomplete without trying the food described in the novel, at the **Red Mansion Hotel** outside the east gate of the garden.

❻ Joyous Pavilion Park
陶然亭 Táorántíng ★

Public park

Hours: daily 6am-9pm
Entrance: RMB 2; free for children under 1.2 m
Suggested length of visit: 1 hour
Transport: Bus 40, 59, 613, 819 to Taoranting North Gate (陶然亭公园北门)
No. 19, Taiping Jie, Xuanwu District. (86-10-63532385) http://www.trtpark.com/index.htm
宣武区太平街19号

This lovely park was built in 1695 by a Qing official named Jiang Zao as a common people's recreation spot, while most of the gardens in Beijing at that time were exclusive for imperial family use. The temple inside was built in the Yuan Dynasty, being the oldest construction in the park.

The park got the name from Tang poet Bai Juyi's words about golden chrysanthemums, mature home-brewed wine and the joys and indulgences of life. Providing an ideal place to go boating or for picnics on weekends, it lives up to its name as a pleasant, joyous park.

You can get a glimpse of this great story on TV —A Dream of Red Mansions.

Museums

❼ Beijing Museum of Natural History 北京自然博物馆 ★★

Natural science
English tour guide

Hours: daily 8.30am-4pm
Entrance: RMB 30 for adults, RMB 15 for students
Suggested length of visit: 1 hour
Transport: Bus 2, 6, 17, 20, 35, 59, 102, 105, 106, 110, 120, 707, 803, 826 to Tianqiao (天桥)
No. 126, Tianqiao Nandajie (near Temple of Heaven West Gate). (86-10-67024431)
http://www.bmnh.org.cn/
天桥南大街126 号 (近天坛西门)

This enormous museum of natural science, the biggest in China, contains four major exhibits—"**Animal, the Friend of Human Beings**," "**the Green Homeland**," "**Paleontology**" and "**the Mystery of Humans**." There are also a dinosaur world and an aquarium house. Although old and in need of some updating, the museum provides great visuals illustrating China's natural wonders through the ages with its collection of 200,000 items in terms of paleontology, ornithology, mammals and invertebrates.

The history of the world.

❽ Museum of Ancient Pottery Civilization 古陶文明博物馆 ★

The only museum specializing in Chinese pottery
English, Japanese and Chinese tour guides

Hours: daily 10am-5pm (closed on Mondays)
Entrance: RMB 20, students RMB 10
Suggested length of visit: 45 minutes
Transport: Bus 59, 122, 458, 717, 744, 819 to Grand View Garden (大观园)
No. 12, Nancaiyuan Xijie, Xuanwu District (near Grand View Garden North Gate). (86-10-63538884/8811)
北京宣武区南菜园西街12 号 (大观园北门)
✍ *With the Museum Pass, you can get two adult tickets for half price.*

This museum features potteries by ancient Chinese: painted potteries from the Neolithic Age, the Zhou, Qin, Han and Tang dynasties, and tiles and sealing clay from the Warring States Period, Qin and Han dynasties. More than 3,000 other types of pottery are also on display. There is another interesting exhibit on Chinese written characters: from the earliest forms inscribed on tortoise shells to emperors' seals. It's a lot of fun and worth your time.

❾ Beijing Museum of Traditional Opera 北京戏曲博物馆 ★

All about Peking Opera

Hours: 9am-7.30pm
Entrance: RMB 10
Suggested length of visit: 1 hour
Transport: Bus 14, 15, 66, 102, 23, 603 to Hufangqiao Lukounan (虎坊桥路口南)
Inside Huguang Guild Hall, No. 3, Hufangqiao Lu. (86-10-63518284)
虎坊桥路3 号湖广会馆内
✍ *With the Museum Pass, you can get two free admissions.*

This museum sits inside the Huguang Guild Hall which was built in 1807. It chronicles the fascinating and colorful history of Peking Opera. There are daily performances. The clever use of vocals, the eye-catching costumes and the brilliant masks will make this a memorable visit.

Food and Entertainment

For the richest collection of restaurants in southern Beijing, **Niujie** (see p.109) and **Qianmen Dajie** (see below) should be a first port of call. Boasting an impressive array of Muslim eateries, Niujie is definitely the best-known area to savor these authentic flavors and home-cooking. Take your pick of places to dine and be sure to try traditional desserts such as rice cake, as a sweet climax to a fabulous meal. Qianmen enjoys the reputation of a centuries-old food Mecca. **Quanjude** (see p.108) has made its name as one of the best

Fresh cotton candy.

places to eat a succulent and juicy Peking roast duck.

Eating isn't all that's on offer. Apart from countless shops to browse your way around, this area also has lots of theaters. Plonk yourself down and let your full belly rest while jugglers, acrobats or even kungfu performers strut their stuff for your entertainment. The **Red Theater** (see p.110) puts on great kungfu shows. While they may break some bricks, it certainly won't break the bank!

The following hot spots are marked on the map on p.98.

Qianmen Dajie 前门大街

For over 500 years this has been one of Beijing's main shopping streets and today is no different. You will find anything and everything to suit any budget or preference. Located just south of Tian'anmen Square, it's easily accessible, so you won't need to carry your purchases too far!

Be sure to visit **Dazhalan** (大栅栏 Beijingers pronounce it "Dashilanr"), a *hutong* running west from Qianmen Dajie. There you will find a colorful and lively array of food stalls, silk shops, theaters, Chinese medicine shops and clothes shops, some being 400 years old.

Currently Qianmen Dajie is undergoing a large-scale reconstruction in order to improve living conditions for local people. For this reason, some time-honored restaurants have temporarily moved elsewhere. The project will be completed in 2008. By then this old street will be reformed into a pedestrian street, blended with sights, Chinese and Western restaurants, and shops.

Sights nearby: Tian'anmen Square (see p.50), Temple of Heaven (see p.100)

Transport: Bus 特 4, 5, 301, 120, 726 or Subway Line 2 to Qianmen (前门), then walk south.

Qianmen Xiheyan Jie

Dongbeiyuan Hutong
东北园胡同

Liulichang Dongjie
琉璃厂东街   Yang

櫻桃斜街

Yingtao Xiejie

North

Yanzhi
Hutong
姐胭脂
胡同

Restaurant listings

Meal prices per adult
¥ under RMB 29
¥¥ RMB 30-49
¥¥¥ RMB 50-69
¥¥¥¥ RMB 70-99
¥¥¥¥¥ over RMB 100

Chinese

Jinyang Restaurant
晋阳饭庄

Shanxi cuisine
English menu ¥¥¥

Hours: 10.30am-2pm, 5pm-9pm
Transport: Bus 57, 105, 715 to
Hufangqiao Lukoudong (虎坊桥路口东)
No. 241, Zhushikou Xidajie, Xuanwu
District. (86-10-63037636 ext. 100)
宜武区珠市口西大街241号

Beijingers come for Crispy roast
duck (香酥鸭) and Taiyuan lamb

(太原羊肉). When in Rome…

B Jinzhaimen Restaurant
金宅门食府

Sichuan, Beijing and Cantonese
cuisine ¥¥¥
Hours: 10am-10pm
Transport: Bus 9, 201, 703, 729 to
Qianmen East (前门东)
1/F, Guanqi Hotel, No.18, Qianmen
Dongdajie, Chongwen District. (86-
10-67058229) 崇文区前门东大街18
号观旗宾馆一层

15% discount if reserved through
www.ziye114.com (in Chinese).

Serving up an assortment of
Chinese cuisines, the food at
Jinzhaimen is well-priced and
well-cooked. The house specials,
Spicy and tongue-numbing tofu
(麻婆豆腐), Beijing roast duck
(烤鸭) and Dongjiang salted
chicken (东江盐焗鸡) are
delicious.

C Fengzeyuan Restaurant
丰泽园饭庄

Shandong cuisine
English menu ¥¥¥¥¥
Hours: 11am-2pm, 5pm-9pm
Transport: Bus 23, 57, 66, 105, 715 to
Zhushikou Xi (珠市口西)
No. 83, Zhushikou Xidajie, Xuanwu
District. (86-10-63186688)宜武区珠
市口西大街83号

10 percent off if reserved through
www.qingke800.com (in Chinese and
English).

For an elite opportunity to eat
like the aristocracy, visit the
Fengzeyuan Restaurant where

Fried meatballs at Fengzeyuan.

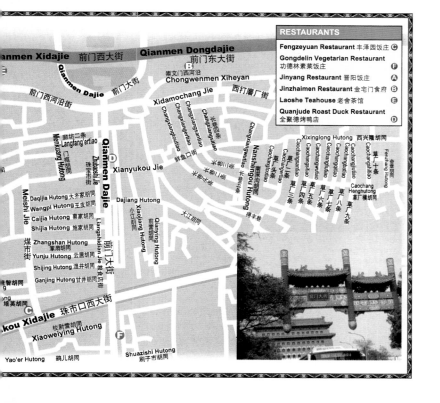

RESTAURANTS	
Fengzeyuan Restaurant 丰泽园饭庄	C
Gongdelin Vegetarian Restaurant 功德林素菜饭庄	F
Jinyang Restaurant 晋阳饭庄	A
Jinzhaimen Restaurant 金宅门食府	B
Laoshe Teahouse 老舍茶馆	E
Quanjude Roast Duck Restaurant 全聚德烤鸭店	D

the apprentice of Chairman Mao's own chef will cook you up the house specials of Sea cucumber with spring onion (葱烧海参) and Baby cuttlefish with egg soup (烩乌鱼蛋汤).

Ⓓ Quanjude Roast Duck Restaurant
全聚德烤鸭店
Beijing roast duck
English menu ¥¥¥¥¥
Hours: 11am-1.30pm, 4.30pm-8pm
Transport: Bus 59, 120 to Dazhalan (大栅栏)
No. 32, Qianmen Dajie, Chongwen District. (86-10-65112418)
崇文区前门大街32号
📍 *10% off through www.ctrip.com, and reserve a table or get there early, otherwise you won't get a table.*

If you only get to try Beijing's famous roast duck once, let it be here at Quanjude. Locals attest to it being the very best the city has to offer. Its famous duck feast consists of dishes made from almost every part of the

Cutting it right takes true skill.

duck, such as the duck's tongue and liver.

Teahouse

Ⓔ Laoshe Teahouse
老舍茶馆
Beijing cuisine, imperial cuisine & teahouse with entertainment
English menu ¥¥¥¥
Hours: 10am-10pm (first floor), 10.30am-1pm (second floor), 8.30am-9pm (third floor)
Transport: 特2, 特4, 特7, 9, 212, 301, 703, 808, 848 to Qianmen West (前门西)
Building 3, Zhengyang Shichang, Qianmen Xidajie, Xuanwu District. (86-10-63036506) 宣武区前门西大

The Laoshe Teahouse is a hub for Chinese culture.

街正阳市场3号楼
📍 *Discount is given if reserved through www.dianping.com (in Chinese).*
This three-floor teahouse offers an elegant variety of teas and restaurants serving up imperial and traditional Beijing cuisine. Some truly entertaining magic, acrobatic and Peking Drum performances are also given on the third floor. Performances are nightly and begin at 7.50pm, tickets range between RMB 60-180 per person.

Vegetarian

Ⓕ Gongdelin Vegetarian Restaurant
功德林素菜饭庄
English menu ¥¥
Hours: 10.30am-8.30pm
Transport: Bus 110, 120, 703, 729 to Zhushikou (珠市口)
No.158, Qianmen Nandajie, Chongwen District (50 m south of Zhushikou Church). (86-10-67020867)
崇文区前门大街158号(珠市口教堂向南50米)
Beijing's only Buddhist-style restaurant, Gongdelin serves up tasty and imaginative vegetarian dishes in temple-like surroundings. Due to the renovation at the Qianmen area, the restaurant is currently closed and please call before you go.

RESTAURANTS

Bai's Rice Cake 白记年糕
Hongshunxuan 鸿顺轩
Jianghu Renjia Restaurant 江湖人家食府
Mudelou Muslim Restaurant 穆德楼清真餐厅
Niujie Dashuntang Restaurant 牛街大顺堂食府
Turpan Restaurant 吐鲁番餐厅
Wei's Chinese Cheese 奶酪魏

Restaurant listings

Meal prices per adult
¥ under RMB 29
¥¥ RMB 30-49
¥¥¥ RMB 50-69
¥¥¥¥ RMB 70-99
¥¥¥¥¥ over RMB 100

Chinese

Ⓐ Bai's Rice Cake
白记年糕
Muslim snacks ¥
Hours: 8.30am-8.30pm
Transport: see transport to Niujie on p.109
1/F, Niujie Muslim Supermarket, Niujie Beikou, Xuanwu District. 宣武区牛街北口牛街清真超市1层
Come here for the famous Muslim rice cake dessert at bargain prices. Just RMB 5-10 will get you a kilo of this fresh and fan-

u Hutong
入胡同
Jiaozi Hutong
教子胡同
F
Xijie 南横西街
orth

Niujie (Ox Street) 牛街

The name might be misleading; you won't find any ox on this street. It's actually where the biggest and oldest mosque is located, a relic that represents the prosperity of Muslims in ancient Beijing and today. Home to 12,000 Muslims, Niujie is the biggest residential area for Muslims. You may run into people wearing white hats. They are Hui ethnic people, the major Muslim population here.

Providing the locals some cheap but tasty Muslim restaurants, it also gives Muslims a safe place to preserve their religion while making a few bucks from tourists!

Sights in the area: Niujie Mosque (see p.103).

Transport: Bus 10, 48, 626, 717 to Niujie (牛街), then on foot.

Now it is hard to tell it from any other street.

tastic dessert. Your sweet tooth will thank you.

Wei's Chinese Cheese 奶酪魏

Beijing snacks ¥

Hours: 8.30am-8.30pm

Transport: see transport to Niujie above

2/F, Niujie Muslim Supermarket, Niujie Beikou, Xuanwu District. 宣武区牛街北口牛街清真超市2层

Traditional Beijing snacks. You've got to try super snacks like Wei's cheese roll (奶卷), Two-layered milk (双皮奶) and Chinese cheese with almond (杏仁奶酪).

奶酪魏

Milk and cheese the way it is supposed to be.

Ⓒ Hongshunxuan 鸿顺轩

Muslim ¥¥

Hours: 9.30am-9.30pm

Transport: see transport to Niujie above

Building 3, Niujie Beikou, Xuanwu District (beside the Niujie Muslim Supermarket). (86-10-83548892) 宣武区牛街北口3号楼（牛街清真超市旁）

Always on the cutting edge of Muslim cuisine, this place has a great reputation among restaurants around Niujie. New dishes are constantly added to the extensive menu.

Ⓓ Jianghu Renjia Restaurant 江湖人家食府

Sichuan cuisine ¥¥

Hours: 10am-10pm

Transport: see transport to Niujie above

1/F, Guangtong Hotel, No. 9, Dequan Hutong, Niujie, Xuanwu District. (86-10-63568619) 宣武区牛街德泉胡同9号广通酒店1楼

! 10% off if reserved through www.ziye114.com (in Chinese).

This tasty and low-priced Sichuan place is famous for Spicy boiled fish (水煮鱼) and Boiled shrimp (盆盆虾).

Ⓔ Mudelou Muslim Restaurant 穆德楼清真餐厅

Xinjiang cuisine ¥¥

Hours: 9.30am-10.30pm

Transport: see transport to Niujie above

*East of Niujie Dongli Xiaoqu,
Xuanwu District.* (86-10-83545481)
宣武区牛街东里小区东侧

Looking to satisfy a major hunger while not busting your wallet? These big portions of savory Xinjiang grilled meat and noodles will leave a smile on your face.

ⓕ Niujie Dashuntang Restaurant
牛街大顺堂食府
Muslim　　　　　　¥¥

*Hours: 10am-9.30pm
Transport: Bus 特5 to Niujie Lukouxi (牛街路口西)
1/F, Building 5, Fayuansi Xili, Xuanwu District.* (86-10-63530644)
宣武区法源寺西里5号楼1层

Serving old-time foods like Sweet wheat cake (糖火烧) and Boiled ox stomach (爆肚), this place is a historical Muslim restaurant featuring high-quality eats.

Succulent rack of lamb.

ⓖ Turpan Restaurant
吐鲁番餐厅
Xinjiang cuisine　　　¥¥

*Hours: 6am-9am (breakfast), 11am-2pm (lunch), 5pm-9pm (dinner)
Transport: see transport to Niujie on p.109
No. 6, Niujie Beikou, Xuanwu District (near Guang'anmennei Dajie).* (86-10-83160247) 宣武区牛街北口6号 (近广安门内大街)

A meat-eater's paradise, this place serves traditional Xinjiang dishes like Big plate chicken (大盘鸡) and Shouzha (hand-grab) lamb (手抓羊肉).

Theaters

The theaters listed below are marked on the map on p.98.

Huguang Guild Hall's performance stage.

⑩ Huguang Guild Hall
湖广会馆
Peking Opera

*Hours: 7.30pm
Price: RMB 150-280
Transport: Bus 14, 15, 66, 102, 23, 603 to Hufangqiao Lukounan (虎坊桥路口南) No. 3, Hufang Lu, Xuanwu District (look for a colorful opera mask sculpture at the intersection of Luomashi Dajie).* (86-10-63518284/63529134) 宣武区虎坊路3号 (骡马市大街路口，门口有彩色京剧脸谱雕塑)

This museum/theater dates back to 1807. It's located in a cluster of traditional tiled-roof buildings and features traditional Peking Opera at a reasonable price.

⑪ Liyuan Theater 梨园剧场
Peking Opera with English subtitles

*Hours: daily 6pm-9pm (performance from 7.30pm-8.40pm)
Price: RMB 180-480
Transport: Bus 6, 15, 822 to Yong'an Lu (永安路)
Qianmen Hotel, No. 175, Yong'an Lu, Chongwen District.*
(86-10-63016688-8860/8864) 崇文区永安路175号前门饭店

Liyuan has won over foreign audiences with its English subtitles and traditional atmosphere. Exciting acrobatics are also staged.

⑫ Red Theater 红剧场
Kungfu

*Performance: daily 7.30pm-8.50pm
Price: RMB 180-680
Transport: Bus 116, 35, 60, 705, 822 to Beijing Tiyuguan (北京体育馆)
Workers' Cultural Palace, No. 44, Xingfu Dajie, Chongwen District.* (86-10-67142473) 崇文区幸福大街44号工人文化宫

The fantastic kungfu shows presented by the China Heaven Creation International Performing Arts Company are put on here. The show is a must-see production in Beijing

for tourists and kungfu lovers.

⑬ Tianqiao Theater
天桥剧场
Opera, ballet, drama

*Hours: performances start at 7.30pm
Price: RMB 80-880
Transport: Bus 120, 110 to Beiwei Lu (北纬路)
No. 30, Beiwei Lu, Xuanwu District.* (86-10-83156170) 宣武区北纬路30号

Featuring perhaps the best facilities in Beijing, this three-floor theater offers great comfort, with more than 1,200 soft seats.

⑭ Wansheng Theater (Tianqiao Acrobatic Theater) 万胜剧场 (天桥杂技剧场)
Acrobatics

*Hours: daily 7.15-8.35pm
Price: RMB 100-200
Transport: Bus 2, 7, 15, 17, 20, 34, 35, 59, 105, 106, 707, 729, 803, 819, 822, 48, 917 to Tianqiao (天桥)
No. 95, Tianqiao Shichang, Xuanwu District (opposite Tianqiao Theater).* (86-10-63037449) 宣武区天桥市场95号 (天桥剧场对面)

⑮ Zhengyici Theater
正乙祠戏楼
Peking Opera

*Hours: varied play schedule
Price: RMB 380-680
Transport: Subway Line 2 to Hepingmen (和平门)
No. 220, Qianmen Xiheyan Dajie, Xuanwu District.* (86-10-83151649) 宣武区前门西河沿大街220号

☑ *Reserve early; shows are only staged if the number of audience reaches 15.*

Authentic Peking Opera, this place is the first choice for fans of the art form. Contributing to the atmosphere are the knowledgeable staff, who are big fans themselves.

Shopping

"South" claims itself as Beijing's shopping paradise. Markets strive to meet all people's needs. From paper clips, to ancient-style furniture at the macro end, you'll find everything in this area. After strolling around Tian'anmen Square, you'll have to drop by **Qianmen Dajie** (see below) and **Dazhalan** (see below), two of Beijing's most ancient commercial streets. Walking through the ancient buildings and bargaining with the street vendors, you'll find these areas a lot of fun. South from Qianmen, just 10 minutes by bus, is the **Pearl Market** (see below), Beijing's best-loved one-stop shopping destination. Because of its popularity with foreign visitors, the vendors here try suggesting outrageously high prices: be sure to haggle, you'll overpay for sure if you don't (don't be offended—it's all part of the experience!). Head west from Dazhalan and you can find **Liulichang** (see p.112), packed with traditional Chinese curios and art for the most part, expert shoppers can find some genuine antiques if they have a discerning eye.

Coming "South" to shop? Make sure you bring an empty suitcase!

The markets and supermarkets listed below are marked on the map on p.98.

Commerce at its best on Dazhalan.

⑯ Qianmen Dajie and Dazhalan
前门大街和大栅栏
Antiques, jewelry, craft, clothing
Hours: 8.30am-6pm
Transport: Bus 特4, 5, 301, 120, 726 or Subway Line 2 to Qianmen (前门) or 2, 120, 201, 48, 729, 744, 826 to Dazhalan (大栅栏)
Qianmen Dajie, Xuanwu District (south of Tian'anmen Square). 宣武区前门大街（天安门广场南）

Heading south from Tian'anmen Square, you'll see a straight north-south street. This is the Qianmen Dajie, the oldest market street in Beijing, over 500 years old. An east-west lane opening onto the street on its west side is the famous Dazhalan, literally meaning Great Fence. This ancient market features many traditional and time-honored shops, including: Tongrentang Traditional Chinese Medicine Shop (同仁堂中药 86-10-63031155), Dongsheng Hat Shop (东升帽店 86-10-63035955), Ruifuxiang Satin, Silk and Fur Shop (瑞蚨祥丝绸 86-10-63041702), Neiliansheng Shoemaker's (内联升鞋店 86-10-63013041).

The current renovation has resulted in the relocation of some time-honored stores, but the busy shopping atmosphere remains.

⑰ Hongqiao Market (Pearl Market) 红桥市场
One-stop shopping
Hours: 8.30am-7.30pm
Transport: Bus 43, 41, 39, 60, 116, 208, 610, 707, 807 to Fahuasi (法华寺) Tiantan Donglu, Chongwen District. (86-10-67119130) 崇文区天坛东路

Known as the Pearl Market, this is a one-stop shopping place, featuring two floors of pearls and jewelry and much more. Also, this market carries everyday items. Close to the east gate of the Temple of Heaven, tourists usually come to shop here after visiting the beautiful temple. Bargain on everything!

Three-foot stone carvings sold at Liulichang. No kidding!

⑱ Liulichang 琉璃厂

Curios, old and rare books, calligraphy and paintings

Hours: 8am-6pm

Transport: Bus 7, 14, 15 to Liulichang (琉璃厂)

No. 115, Liulichang Dongjie, Hepingmenwai, Xuanwu District. (86-10-63047749) 宣武区和平门外琉璃厂东街115号

With a history of over 300 years, this place is lined with historical buildings decorated with gorgeous carved columns. It is one of two street markets that still bear the appearance of a Qing Dynasty market street (the other is Suzhou Street in the Summer Palace mainly for show purposes).

A great place to get traditional Chinese items, particularly old and rare books and "four treasures of the study (brush, ink stick, paper and inkstone)."

⑲ Baoguosi Temple Market 报国寺文化工艺品市场

Antiques, old books and newspapers

Hours: 6am-4pm

Transport: Bus 617 to Guang'anmen (广安门)

No.1, Baoguosi, Guang'anmennei Dajie, Xuanwu District. (86-10-63173214/63017719) 宣武区广安门内大街报国寺1号

It was home to the China Association of Collectors and today a collectors' favorite. This market displays and sells antique paintings, calligraphy and ancient coins. It is best known for old books and newspapers. Sharp-nosed art lovers can find nice surprises here. Regular exhibitions and activities for collectors are also held, such as the "World Coins Exhibit," "Chinese Stamps Exhibit," and "Chinese Storybooks Exhibit."

⑳ Tianya Building 天雅服装大厦

Clothing

Hours: 6.30am-5pm

Transport: Bus 107, 103 to Muxiuyan Nanzhan (木樨园南站)

No. 9, Nanyuan Lu, Fengtai District (500 m south of Muxiyuan Roundabout). (86-10-51363308/3399) http://www.sino-tianya.com/home.asp (in Chinese) 丰台区南苑路9号(木樨园环岛南侧500米)

This is one of the largest clothes wholesale centers in Beijing. The building has nine floors. One to five are all clothing at low prices, with more than 800 shops that will make your eyes hurt. The ninth floor features a huge stage for fashion shows.

㉑ Tianwaitian Commodities Wholesale Market 天外天小商品批发市场

The oldest commodities wholesale market in Beijing

Hours: 6am-5pm

Transport: Bus 366, 运通107 to Muxiuyan (木樨园)

No. 101, Yongdingmenwai, Chongwen District (6th floor of Bairong World Trade Building, at the intersection of Yongdingmenwai Dajie). (86-10-68027601) 崇文区永定门外101号(永定门外大街路口百荣世贸大厦内6层)

Being Beijing's earliest commodities wholesale market, Tianwaitian still stands strong. Renowned for its accessory wholesale business, its vendors also sell a selection of clothing and home wares. Business and retail prices can be arranged.

㉒ Walmart 沃尔玛

Supermarket

Hours: 7am-10pm

Transport: Bus 109, 102, 105, 603, 604 to Xuanwumen (宣武门)

B1, 1/F, Fuzhuo Garden Square, Xuanwumenwai Dajie, Xuanwu District.(86-10-63168905) 宣武区宣武门外大街富卓花园广场地下一层和首层

Accommodation

O nce upon a time this area was the last place Beijingers would choose to buy a home. Densely populated by poor local folk and immigrants from around China, living conditions were bad to say the least. But today the landscape looks very different. Gone are the dirty, undeveloped streets and shabby housing and in their place a prosperous cultural and commercial zone has emerged. Hotels have reared their heads, catering to ever-growing tourist demand, the **Qianmen** area having the greatest concentration. Located between "Central" and "South," it is perfectly situated on some of the city's prime real estate, close to Qianmen subway and bus stations, within walking distance of **Dazhalan** and easy reach of many of Beijing's top spots.

All places listed below are marked on the map on p.98.

Accommodation prices per night
¥ under RMB 99
¥¥ RMB 100-199
¥¥¥ RMB 200-299
¥¥¥¥ RMB 300-399
¥¥¥¥¥ over RMB 400

Dorms/Hostels	🛏	☎	☰	🚻	🏕	@	👕
Ⓐ Changgong Youth Hostel 长宫饭店 ¥	■	■	■	■	■	■	■
Ⓑ Feiying International Youth Hostel 飞鹰国际青年旅舍 ¥			■	■	■	■	■
Ⓒ Fenglong (Phoenix and Dragon) International Youth Hostel 凤龙国际青年旅社 ¥	■	■	■		■		

Ⓐ Changgong Youth Hostel 长宫饭店 ¥

Price: RMB 35-50 (dorm beds), RMB 70-100 (doubles), RMB 105 (triples)
Transport: Bus 7, 14, 15 to Liulichang (琉璃厂); or 特4, 5, 301, 120, 726 or Subway Line 2 to Qianmen (前门)
No. 11, Yingtao Xiejie, Xuanwu District (close to Qianmen Subway Station). (86-10-63032665) 宣武区樱桃斜街11号 (前门地铁站附近)

A great low-budget option, this hostel offers the basics plus a whole lot more; Internet, information desk, barbecues and several well-priced trips to the Great Wall are all available.

Ⓑ Feiying International Youth Hostel 飞鹰国际青年旅舍 ¥

Price: RMB 30-50 (dorm beds), RMB 220 (doubles), RMB 260 (triples)
Transport: Subway Line 2 to Changchun Jie (长椿街)
Behind Building 10, Xuanwumen Xidajie (close to Changchunjie Subway Station). (86-10-63171116) 宣武门西大街10号楼后街 (靠近长椿街车站)

A recent refurbishment and tie-up with Youth Hostelling International have seen this hostel shoot up the popularity chart. Offering dormitories, twin or triple-bed rooms, it is one of the best budget choices in town. Take advantage of the bicycle rental here.

Ⓒ Fenglong (Phoenix and Dragon) International Youth Hostel 凤龙国际青年旅社 ¥

Price: RMB 120 (doubles), RMB 300 (triples)
Transport: Bus 19, 48, 414, 运通102 to You'anmen (右安门)
No. 5, You'anmen Dongjie, Xuanwu District. (86-10-63545836) 宣武区右安门东街5号

Well kitted out, this hostel has all those little home comforts plus a helpful, reliable tour service downstairs (along with the mini bar!). Bicycle rental is available.

Accommodation prices per night
¥ under RMB 99
¥¥ RMB 100-199
¥¥¥ RMB 200-299
¥¥¥¥ RMB 300-399
¥¥¥¥¥ over RMB 400

Jinghua Hotel

Ⓓ Jinghua Hotel 京华饭店 ¥

2 star

Price: RMB 50 (dorm beds), RMB 300-380 (double-occupancy rooms)

Transport: Bus 运通 103, 运通 108 to Yangqiao (洋桥)

Xiluoyuan Nanli, Yongdingmenwai, Fengtai District. (86-10-87812211)

www.jinghua-hotel.com 丰台区永定门外西罗园南里

Standard double rooms are nicely decorated and well equipped with all mod cons. With, amongst other things, a sauna, massage, bar, nightclub and banquet hall you can dance the night away and then get your sore feet rubbed better!

Hotels (prices based on double-occupancy rooms)

Ⓔ Huayuan Hotel 华苑饭店 ¥¥

2 star

Price: RMB 160-180

Transport: Bus 366, 729, 854 to Sanyingmen (三营门)

No.111, Sanyingmen, Nanyuan Lu, Fengtai District. (86-10-67991188) 丰台区南苑路三营门 111 号

Clean, bright twin and three-bed rooms come complete with bathtub so you can soak weary sightseeing feet! Basic but clean budget dormitories are also available.

Ⓕ Jinjiang Inn (Majiapu) 锦江之星马家堡店 ¥¥

Price: RMB 189

Transport: Bus 485 to Majiapu Lu (马家堡路)

No. 65, Majiapu Lu, Fengtai District. (86-10-67589412) http://www.jj-inn.com/Default.aspx 丰台区马家堡路 65 号

Jinjiang Inn is the first and largest budget hotel chain in China. Well-equipped and with great services, this hotel is suitable for business or leisure stays.

Ⓖ 365 Inn (Qianmen) ¥¥
安怡之家宾馆前门店

2 star

Price: RMB 198-208

Transport: Bus 特4, 5, 301, 120, 726 or Subway Line 2 to Qianmen (前门) or 2, 120, 201, 48, 729, 744, 826 to Dazhalan (大栅栏)

No. 55, Dazhalan Xijie, Xuanwu District (close to Qianmen Subway Station). (86-10-63085956) www.365inn.com.cn 宣武区大栅栏西街55号(前门地铁站附近)

Located smack-bang in the heart of Beijing, 365 Inn offers a multitude of services. The quaint rooms are enhanced by the hotel's tour booking facility, bike rental and safety deposit boxes.

Guoren Hotel 国人宾馆 ¥¥¥

2 star

Price: RMB 160-298

Transport: Bus 特4, 5, 301, 120, 726 or Subway Line 2 to Qianmen (前门)

No. A2, Qianmen Dajie, Chongwen District. (86-10-67025398) 崇文区前门大街甲2号

Offering almost everything you'll need, this hotel's crowning glory however is its location so close to Tian'anmen Square that you can walk there in minutes.

Jintan Bowling Hotel 金坛大厦保龄宾馆 ¥¥¥

3 star

Price: RMB 168-368

Transport: Bus 39, 43, 705, 723, 813, 957, 958 to Dongce Lu (东侧路)

No. 31, Tiantan Donglu, Chongwen District. (86-10-67023708) 崇文区天坛东路31号

Geared up for foreign visitors, this hotel offers cheap beer, good Chinese and Western food, English newspapers and bar games, as well as computer (with USB2 compatibility and multi-language support). There's a great beer garden next door!

Tiantan Sports Hotel 天坛体育宾馆 ¥¥¥

3 star

Price: RMB 180-320

Transport: Bus 35, 34, 41, 116 to Beijing Tiyuguan Xi (北京体育馆西)

No. 10, Tiyuguan Lu, Chongwen District (close to Pearl Market). (86-10-87183888)

www.tianti.com 崇文区体育馆路10号 (红桥市场附近)

Neighboring the Temple of Heaven, this 350-room hotel offers a plethora of creature comforts; rooms even sport in-house movie and satellite TV systems! A multitude of cafés, bars and restaurants can all be found within its four big walls.

Ai Hua Hotel 爱华饭店 ¥¥¥

3 star

Price: RMB 198, 290, 360

Transport: Bus 43, 39, 25, 812, 705, 957 to Dongce Lu (东侧路)

No. B48, Tiantan Dongli, Chongwen District. (86-10-67112255) 崇文区天坛东里乙48号

Situated equidistant from the Temple of Heaven and the Pearl Market, this is a great choice. Rooms offer all those little material pleasures while the conference room, coffee shop, restaurant and recreation center offer something for everyone.

Qinian Hotel 祈年饭店 ¥¥¥

2 star

Price: RMB 258

Transport: Bus 35, 6, 106, 707, 822 to Jinyuchi (金鱼池)

No. 91, Tiantan Lu, Chongwen District. (86-10-67021339) 崇文区天坛路91号

This friendly and inviting hotel offers many complimentary facilities for that extra touch—a temple and *hutong* tour, a folk art show, satellite and DVD shows—the staff here really do spoil you!

🖼️ @ ✕ 🍸 🍷 🐟 🏠

Ⓜ Yongdingmen Hotel 永定门饭店 ¥¥¥

3 star

Price: RMB 258

Transport: Bus 2, 17, 40, 729, 854 to Shazikou (沙子口)

No. 77, Anlelin Lu, Chongwen District. (86-10-51076688) www.ydmhotel.com (in Chinese) 崇文区安林路77号

One hundred fully equipped rooms offer all modern amenities plus a 200-seat conference and multi-function hall. If you are after pleasure, not business, there is a karaoke and dance hall too!

Ⓝ Xiaoxiang Building 潇湘大厦 ¥¥¥¥

3 star

Price: RMB 380

Transport: Bus 59, 15 to Friend-ship Hospital (友谊医院)

No. 42, Beiwei Lu, Xuanwu District (close to Joyous Pavilion Park). (86-10-83161188) 宜武区北纬路 42号(陶然亭公园附近)

Clean, bright, spacious rooms offer all the comforts of home (plus room service) while some great Hunan food is dished up in the dining room downstairs.

Ⓞ Hademen Hotel 哈德门饭店 ¥¥¥¥¥

3 star

Price: RMB 498

Transport: Subway Line 2 to Chongwenmen (崇文门)

No. A2, Chongwenmenwai Dajie, Chongwen District (50 m southeast of Chongwenmen Subway Station). (86-10-67112244) www.hademenhotel.com 崇文门外大街甲2号 (崇文门地铁站东南50米处)

Offering standard and deluxe rooms, suites and business offices, this centrally located hotel knows what guests need. Their laundry, taxi, exchange and bike rental services are top notch.

Accommodation prices per night

¥ under RMB 99

¥¥ RMB 100-199

¥¥¥ RMB 200-299

¥¥¥¥ RMB 300-399

¥¥¥¥¥ over RMB 400

Itinerary

Itinerary C: Culture and Shopping Tour

Morning

8am Start your day at **Niujie Mosque** (see p.103), the biggest and oldest mosque in Beijing. 40 minutes should be enough.

8.40am Head to **Niujie Muslim Supermarket**, diagonally opposite Niujie Mosque, and dive in for some authentic Muslim snacks. Follow up with a relaxing half-hour walk along **Niujie** (牛街) (see p.109), and experience the unique customs of the Hui people.

9.30am Take Bus 48 at Niujie Mosque and get off at Dazhalan (大栅栏) (about 20 minutes), take a tricycle and explore the **Eight Grand Hutong** (see p.102)—a red light district of old Beijing—for about an hour.

10.50am Take Bus 803 from Dazhalan to your next stop, the famous and awe-inspiring **Temple of Heaven** (see p.100). It takes about 15 minutes to get there. Explore this massive place where the emperor prayed to Heaven and experience the "people sights" for two good hours. Time will fly.

Afternoon

1.05pm Time for lunch, so find a restaurant outside the east gate. You'll need lots of energy for an afternoon of shopping!

2pm Close by your lunch spot, the **Pearl Market** (see p.111) is a great place to get Chinese-style gifts. Haggle ruthlessly.

5pm Phew, enough shopping. Turn left out of the market and walk 100 m along Tiantan Donglu (天坛东路) till you see the Fahuasi (法华寺) bus stop. Take Bus 723 there. About half an hour later, get off at Qianmen (前门).

5.30pm Head south to **Quanjude Restaurant** (see p.108) for the best roast duck in town. It's about 200 m south along Qianmen Dajie (前门大街) from the bus stop.

6.30pm Once you've stuffed yourself with Beijing's most famous dish, get ready to experience Beijing's most famous cultural phenomenon, **Peking Opera**. Take Bus 66 at Qianmen and get off at Hufangqiao Lukounan (虎坊桥路口南). To your right side is the **Huguang Guild Hall** (see p.110) where you can learn something about the 200-year-old art form of Peking Opera at the **Beijing Museum of Traditional Opera** (see p.105) and watch a show at 7.30pm.

7.30pm Enjoy the show. Call ahead for seats or you'll be stuck in the rafters.

8.40pm Show's over, head back to the hotel to crash.

Expenses

Niujie Mosque: RMB 10

Snacks: RMB 10

Tricycle: RMB 15

All-inclusive ticket for the Temple of Heaven: RMB 30/50

Lunch: RMB 30

Roast duck dinner: RMB 150

Peking Opera: RMB 150

Transport: RMB 5

Total: RMB 400/420 (USD 55/58)

 **Bus Details**

Major Bus Stops

These are the major bus stops in the "South." At each bus stop, there are direct routes to key destinations. **They are marked on the map on p.98.**

Tianqiao Lukoudong (天桥路口东), on Tiantan Lu (天坛路), about 400 m north of **Beijing Museum of Natural History**

To Beijing Amusement Park (北京游乐园): 6
To Beijing Railway Station (北京站): 729, 744, 20, 59, 120
To Grand View Garden (大观园): 819
To Niujie (牛街): 822, 6, 743
To Pearl Market (红桥市场): 6, 34, 35, 743, 707, 822
To Joyous Pavilion Park (陶然亭): 744, 819
To Temple of Heaven (天坛): 110, 34, 35, 822, 743, 707
To Yuanmingyuan (圆明园): 743

Beijing Amusement Park (北京游乐园), north of the park

To Drum Tower (鼓楼): 60
To Lama Temple (雍和宫): 116, 807

To Niujie (牛街): 6
To Pearl Market (红桥市场): 6, 60, 116, 807
To Qianmen (前门): 8
To Temple of Heaven (天坛): 6, 958

Muxiyuanqiao Bei (木樨园桥北), about 400 m north of Muxiyuan Qiao (木樨园桥)

To Beijing Railway Station (北京站): 729
To Beijing West Railway Station (北京西站): 854, 40
To Pearl Market (红桥市场): 707
To Summer Palace (颐和园): 826
To Temple of Heaven (天坛): 2, 17, 729, 707, 826
To Tian'anmen (天安门): 2
To Yuanmingyuan (圆明园): 826
To Zhongguancun (中关村): 732, 826

Useful Bus Routes

The following is a list of specially selected bus routes passing through the "South" area. These are not all depot-to-depot routes and many less important stops have been omitted. Sights of interest are in bold type. Bus type and times of first and last buses from the first depot are also indicated.

Suggestion: if you are unsure you have the right stop, point out the Chinese characters below for where you want to go and ask another passenger, conductor or driver for help. Many young Chinese have OK English and will be able to help.

运通102 (standard bus, 5.30am-8pm)
Dinghuisi 定慧寺-Diaoyutai Xi 钓鱼台西-Fucheng Lu 阜成路-Beijing West Railway Station 西客站-Guang'anmen Beizhan 广安门北站-**Grand View Garden 大观园**-**Temple of Heaven South Gate 天坛南门**

7 (standard bus, 5am-11pm)
Beijing Zoo 动物园-Xizhimennei 西直门内-**White Dagoba Temple 白塔寺**-Cultural

Palace of Nationalities 民族文化宫-**Liulichang 琉璃厂**-Friendship Hospital 友谊医院-Tianqiao 天桥-**Temple of Heaven West Gate 天坛西门**-Yongdingmennei 永定门内

8 (standard bus, 5am-11pm)
Beijing Amusement Park 北京游乐园-Longtanhu 龙潭湖-Beijing Tiyuguan 北京体育馆-Xingfu Dajie 幸福大街-**Tian'anmen**

Square East 天安门广场东

10 (standard bus, 5am-12am)

Beijing Railway Station East 北京站东 - **Wangfujing 王府井 -Tian'anmen East 天安门东** -Xidan Lukouxi 西单路口西 -Cultural Palace of Nationalities 民族文化宫 - **Niujie 牛街 -Niujie Mosque 牛街礼拜寺**

17 (standard bus, 5.05am-11.30pm)

Qianmen 前门 -Tianqiao 天桥 -**Temple of Heaven 天坛** -Xiannongtan 先农坛 - Muxiyuanqiao Bei 木樨园桥北

105 (trolley bus, 4.45am-11pm)

Beijing Zoo 动物园 -Xinjiekou Xi 新街口西 -Xidan Lukounan 西单路口南 - Xuanwumennei 宣武门内 -Hufangqiao Lukoudong 虎坊桥路口东-Zhushikou Xi 珠市口西 -Tianqiao 天桥

109 (trolley bus, 5am-11pm)

Guang'anmen 广安门 -Niujie Lukouxi 牛街路口西 -Xuanwumenwai 宣武门外 -**Xidan Department Store 西单商场 -Beihai Park 北海 -Forbidden City 故宫** -Meishuguan Dong 美术馆东-Chaoyangmennei 朝阳门内

116 (standard bus, 5am-12am)

Hepingli Lukounan 和平里路口南 -**Lama Temple 雍和宫 -Guozijian 国子监** -Hongqiao Lukoubei 红桥路口北-Fahuasi 法华寺-Beijing Tiyuguan 北京体育馆-**Beijing Amusement Park 北京游乐园**

120 (standard bus, 5am-12am)

Temple of Heaven South Gate 天坛南门 -Xiannongtan 先农坛 -Tianqiao 天桥 -**Dazhalan 大栅栏 -Qianmen 前门 -Tian'anmen East 天安门东 -Wangfujing 王府井** -Ritan Lu 日坛路 -Workers' Stadium 工人体育场

122 (standard bus, 5am-12am)

Beijing Railway Station East 北京站东 -Temple of Heaven South Gate 天坛南门 -Yongdingmen Dong 永定门东-Beijing South Railway Station 北京南站 -**Grand View Garden大观园-Beijing West Railway Station East 北京西客站东**

613 (standard bus, 5.30am-10pm)

Yangqiao Bei 洋桥北-**Joyous Pavilion Park North Gate 陶然亭公园北门** -Nanheng Jie 南横街 -**Niujie Lukouxi 牛街路口西** - Lianhuachi 莲花池 -Gongzhufen 公主坟

626 (standard bus, 6am-10pm)

Niujie Mosque 牛街礼拜寺 -Niujie 牛街 - Cultural Palace of Nationalities民族文化宫- **Xidan Department Store 西单商场** - Xinjiekou Bei新街口北-**Great Bell Temple 大钟寺**

707 (standard bus, 5.30am-8.30pm)

Yangqiao Dong 洋桥东 -Xiannongtan 先农坛-Tianqiao天桥-**Temple of Heaven North Gate 天坛北门** -Hongqiao Lukouxi 红桥路口西 -Fahuasi 法华寺 -Beijing Tiyuguan 北京体育馆-Agricultural Exhibition Center农展馆 -Holiday Inn Lido 丽都饭店

807 (A/C, 6am-9pm)

Beijing Amusement Park 北京游乐园 -Fahuasi法华寺-**Hongqiao Lukoubei红桥路口北 -Guozijian 国子监** -Yonghegongqiao Dong雍和宫桥东-Sino-Japanese Friendship Hospital 中日医院

819 (A/C, 5.50am-8pm)

Grand View Garden大观园-Joyous Pavilion Park North Gate 陶然亭公园北门 -Friendship Hospital 友谊医院 -**Dazhalan 大栅栏 -Qianmen 前门** -Donghuamen 东华门 - Jingshan Dongjie 景山东街 -**Drum Tower 鼓楼** -Deshengmen 德胜门

822 (A/C, 5.30am-8.30pm)

Lianhuachi莲花池 -Niujie Lukoudong牛街路口东 -Tianqiao Lukoudong 天桥路口东 - **Temple of Heaven North Gate 天坛北门** -Hongqiao Lukouxi 红桥路口西 -Fahuasi 法华寺 -Beijing Tiyuguan 北京体育馆

盧溝曉月

御筆

"The reflection of the moon at dawn from the Marco Polo Bridge" is written in those 4 little characters.

"Patriotic" Southwest

Home to the **Marco Polo Bridge** (see p.122), the **Ancient Town of Wanping** and the **Museum of the War of Chinese People's Resistance Against Japanese Aggression**, this is an area close to the hearts of Chinese people.

While the Marco Polo Bridge is famed for being praised by Marco Polo in the 13th century (hence its alias), its greater significance is for the incident here on July 7, 1937—a turning point in history—when Japan launched an attack on Beijing, firing the first shots of the eight-year-long war (1937-1945).

Lion figure on the Marco Polo Bridge.

Visible cannonball marks on the bridge and on the walls surrounding the ancient town are chilling reminders. A memorial hall here was created to honor and remember the war and all those who were part of it. Today, poignant remembrance tours are often arranged to the bridge and the memorial museum nearby.

Highlights

- **Marco Polo Bridge** 卢沟桥 An amazingly beautiful structure featuring 501 lion figures on its balustrades. **See p.122**
- **White Cloud Temple** 白云观 Come here to learn China's only home-grown religion—Taoism. The temple itself is Beijing's most authentic practicing Taoist Temple. **See p.122**
- **World Park** 世界公园 The world's most recognizable buildings are built to scale here, such as the pyramids and Capitol Hill. **See p.123**
- **Guang'anmen Dajie** 广安门大街 An east-west street abounding in restaurants. Close to Niujie (Ox Street), it also has some Muslim style restaurants. **See p.124**
- **Maliandao Tea Street** 马连道茶叶一条街 As the name says, this street has all sorts of tea and all sorts of things concerning tea, like tea wares. **See p.126**

The Ancient Town of Wanping.

Sightseeing

Tourist Attractions

❶ Marco Polo Bridge (Lugou Bridge) 卢沟桥 Lúgōuqiáo ★★★

The oldest stone arch bridge in Beijing

Hours: daily 7am-7pm (summer), 8am-5pm (winter)
Entrance: RMB 20 (for the bridge only); RMB 33 for all-inclusive ticket for the bridge, Ancient Town of Wanping (宛平城) and the Sculpture Garden in Commemoration of the Chinese People's Anti-Japanese War (中国人民抗日战争纪念雕塑园). Half price for students.
Suggested length of visit: 1 hour
Transport: Bus 310, 339, 661, 715, 748, 809, 971 to Kangzhan Diaosuyuan (抗战雕塑园)
Yongding He, Wanping, Fengtai District. (86-10-83894614/2355)
丰台区宛平永定河

✖ *200 m east of Museum of the War of Chinese People's Resistance Against Japanese Aggression (中国人民抗日战争纪念馆) is Xinhe Renju (鑫和人居86-10-83892096), offering Sichuan, Shandong food and tasty hotpot. RMB 40/person.*

✔ *With the Museum Pass you can get two free admissions to both the Museum (ticket: RMB 15) and the Sculpture Garden.*

First built in 1189 as the main route into Beijing from the south, the Lugou Bridge became known as Marco Polo Bridge following its detailed description in ***The Travels of Marco Polo***, a book popular throughout Europe.

Eleven white-marble arches carry the bridge over a 266-m span, its length guarded and decorated by **501 lion figures**. At each end stands a marble stele pavilion with intricate dragon carvings. The bridge leads to the 300-year-old town of Wanping.

❷ White Cloud Temple 白云观 Báiyúnguàn ★★

Biggest and best preserved Taoist Temple in Beijing

Hours: daily 8.30am-4.30pm
Entrance: RMB 10
Suggested length of visit: 1 hour
Transport: Bus 319, 717, 727, 特5, 特6 to White Cloud Temple (白云观)
Binhe Lu, Xibianmenwai, Xicheng District. (86-10-63463531/63443666)
西城区西便门外滨河路

✖ *Try Jiasan Guantang Baozi Restaurant (贾三灌汤包子馆 86-10-63311455), 200 m east of White Cloud Temple on Baiyunguan Jie (白云观街), famous for its Stuffed steamed buns (灌汤包子). RMB 20/person.*

This magnificent and enormous temple complex is said to be Beijing's most authentic practicing Taoist temple. Completed in 739, it has been renamed and renovated many times, and today is home to the **Chinese Taoist**

Stretch your legs and enjoy the historical view from the Marco Polo Bridge.

Association. The layout of the temple is similar to a Buddhist temple, with several courtyards and halls on a central axis. One thing worth mentioning is the bronze mule in front of the **Old Law Hall** (老律堂 Laolütang), the third hall after you enter the main gate. Legend has it that the mule can cure sickness. Touch the part of the mule in the same area where you are afflicted and you'll be healed. It's worth a try anyway, even if you don't believe.

For an afternoon truly at peace, the temple is as good as it gets. But tranquility is hard to find during Spring Festival when the temple welcomes the new year with one of the most bustling **temple fairs** in the city.

Taoism (Daoism)

Taoism is China's only homegrown religion and owes its foundation to Laozi. The great philosopher introduced thoughts about "Dao" (道, the Way or Virtue) more than 2,000 years ago in *Tao Te Ching* (*Classic of the Way and Virtue*). Today the religion is most commonly recognized by the *yin-yang* symbol, representing the balance and complementarity of opposites, which when achieved, ensures calm and harmony.

❸ Western Han Dynasty Tomb at Dabaotai 大葆台西汉墓
Dàbǎotái xihànmù ★

Best-preserved Han Dynasty tomb in China

Hours: daily 9am-4.30pm (closed on Mondays)
Entrance: free
Suggested length of visit: 1 hour
Transport: Bus 特7, 744, 967 to World Park (世界公园), or 913 to Baotai Lu (葆台路)
South of Guogongzhuang, Huaxiang, Fengtai District (600 m south of World Park). (86-10-83613073)
丰台区花乡郭公庄南 (世界公园南 600 米)

This is the final resting place of Liu Jian, grandson of a Western Han Dynasty emperor 2,000 years ago. Built completely of cypress wood (typical of tombs of the time), it would have been packed with precious objects. The relics that survived serious looting are on display in the museum, where the Han imperial burial system can be seen. A great insight into Han Dynasty times.

❹ World Park 世界公园
Shìjiè gōngyuán ★

Around the world in one day

Hours: daily 7.30am-4.30pm (Nov 1-Mar 31), 8am-5pm (Apr 1-Oct 31)
Entrance: RMB 65 for adults, RMB 35 for students
Suggested length of visit: 1 day
Transport: Bus 480, 744, 959, 967, 特7 to World Park (世界公园)
No. 158, Dabao Lu, Huaxiang, Fengtai District. (86-10-83613344) http://www.beijingworldpark.cn/ (in Chinese)
丰台区花乡大葆路 158 号

The World Park is defined by its impressive and world-renowned collection of 110 natural and man-made attractions gathered from all over the globe. Located 17 km from the heart of the city, this 46.7-ha park has been designed to reflect the five oceans, four continents and the peoples who inhabit them.

You can go around the world in one day, rather than in eighty.

🍴 Food and Entertainment

For your dining pleasure, the southwest of Beijing may not have as many choices as other parts of the city; even so it should not be totally overlooked. One locale that springs to mind is **Guang'anmen Dajie** (see below), one of Beijing's east-west thoroughfares. There are also many small eateries around the **Beijing West Railway Station** that offer good fast food as they mostly target train passengers.

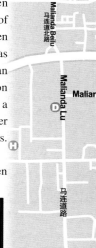
Figures made of dough.

While not many famous nightclubs call the Southwest home, you can always find a place to quench your thirst, or KTV places for singing karaoke. **World Park** (see p.123) is an interesting place, featuring architecture and décor of major world cities and tourist destinations. It is also a place where you can sample the cuisine from various countries!

The following hot spot is marked on the map on p.120.

Guang'anmen Dajie 广安门大街

During the Ming Dynasty (1368-1644), Guang'anmen (Gate of Extensive Peace) was one of the seven gates of Beijing's Outer City wall. It was originally called Guangningmen (Gate of Extensive Tranquility), but a swift name change was required because "ning" was the same character as used in an emperor's name, and therefore taboo. With the reconstruction of southwestern Beijing, the street has been developed into a food and commercial street. Close to Niujie, the Muslim quarter in "Cultural" South, it also has many cheap Muslim restaurants.

Sights nearby: Niujie Mosque (see p.103)

Transport: Bus 854, 719, 40, 732, 46, 19, 390 to Guang'anmen Bei (广安门北), then walk south for about 300 m.

Restaurant listings

Meal prices per adult

¥ under RMB 29
¥¥ RMB 30-49
¥¥¥ RMB 50-69
¥¥¥¥ RMB 70-99
¥¥¥¥¥ over RMB 100

Chinese

Jinpai Chicken Wings
金牌烤翅

Snacks ¥

Hours: 6am-10pm
Transport: Bus 109, 617 to Guang'anmen (广安门)
No. 10, Guangyi Jie, Guang'anmennei, Xuanwu District. (86-10-81647447) 宣武区广安门内广义街10号

One of the most famous BBQ chicken wing restaurants in Beijing. The delicious chicken wings will make you a return customer to this little place.

⑧ Yiduofu Restaurant
溢多福家常菜

Home-cooking dishes ¥

Hours: 10.30am-9pm
Transport: Bus 650, 45 to Tianningsi Xili (天宁寺西里)
Building 4, Tianningsi Xiaoqu, Guang'anmenwai, Xuanwu District. (86-10-63463477) 宣武区广安门外天宁寺小区4号楼

Sichuan and Beijing meet in perfect harmony. Chongqing spicy chicken (重庆辣子鸡) and Shouzhua (hand-grab) pork ribs (手抓排骨) are house specials.

⑥ Yilihe Restaurant
伊犁河美食

Xinjiang cuisine ¥

Hours: 11am-12pm
Transport: 运通102, 运通202 to Guang'anmen Beizhan (广安门北站)
No. 101, Building 3, Beibinhe Lu, Xuanwu District. (86-10-63458316) 宣武区北滨河路3号楼101号

Come here for tasty grilled lamb kebabs. Too much or too little fat can make the lamb unpalatable, but Yilihe gets it exactly right.

⑩ Ba Xiang Shi Fu
巴香食府

Sichuan cuisine
English menu, non-smoking ¥¥

Hours: 11am-2.30pm, 5pm-9.30pm
Transport: Bus 414, 609 to Maliandao Beilu (马连道北路)
No. 9, Maliandao, Guang'anmenwai, Xuanwu District (Maliandao Tea Street). (86-10-63493399) 宣武区广安门外马连道9号 (马连道茶叶一条街)

This restaurant has crazy hot food and some cool performances in traditional Sichuan style. Try the Fried crispy intestines on sizzling Yangtze rocks (三峡石爆脆肠). Yummy.

⑤ Deyuan Roast Duck Restaurant 德缘烤鸭店

Beijing cuisine ¥¥

Hours: 9.30am-2pm, 4.30pm-9pm
Transport: Bus 6, 620, 57, 822 to

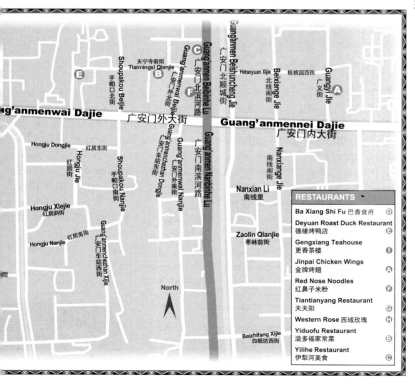

Pumpkin dipped in salted egg yolk served in Deyuan.

Daguanying (达官营)
Guanghuaxuan Xiaoqu, west of Shoupakou Qiao, Guang'anmenwai Dajie, Xuanwu District (Near Hualian Shopping Mall). (86-10-63435959) 宣武区广安门外大街手帕口桥往西广华鲜小区 (近华联商厦)
Big servings of Beijing's famous roast duck. This place gets packed! You must reserve a table or get here early; otherwise you'll be walking away with an empty stomach and full of regrets.

❻ Red Nose Noodles
红鼻子米粉
Guangxi cuisine ￥￥
Hours: 10am-10pm
Transport: Bus 运通102, 运通202 *to Guang'anmen Beizhan (*广安门北站*)*
No. A1, Beibinhe Lu, Guang'anmenwai,

Xuanwu District (close to Shenzhen Plaza). (86-10-63438367) 宣武区广安门外北滨河路甲1号 (近深圳大厦)
Healthy and delicious rice noodles from Guangxi, home to the Zhuang ethnic minority. There are more than 20 varieties of noodle dishes here with authentic seasonings.

❻ Tiantianyang Restaurant
天天阳

Sichuan, Hunan and Cantonese cuisine ￥￥
Hours: 10.30am-10pm
Transport: Bus 6, 46, 410, 719, 613, 57, 822, 特7 *to Wanzi (*湾子*)*
Maliandao, Guang'anmenwai, Xuanwu District (south of Suning Home Appliances Store). (86-10-63440228) 宣武区广安门外马连道 (苏宁电器南)
Don't miss the Scallops (扇贝), Boiled pork ribs (老汤排骨), and Boiled fish with pancake (垮炖鱼) at this respected restaurant.

❻ Western Rose 西域玫瑰
Xinjiang cuisine ￥￥

Hours: 9am-12pm
Transport: Bus 6, 46, 410, 719, 613, 57, 822, 特7 *to Wanzi (*湾子*)*
No. 1, Wanzi Jie, Xuanwu District. (86-10-63325862) 宣武区湾子街1号
Unique meat dishes given the Xinjiang treatment. The Big plate chicken (大盘鸡) and Lamb kebabs (羊肉串) are awesome. Mmm…meat.

Teahouse

❶ Gengxiang Teahouse
更香茶楼
Zhejiang cuisine ￥￥￥
Hours: 9am-10.30pm
Transport: Bus 6, 46, 410, 719, 613, 57, 822, 特7 *to Wanzi (*湾子*)*
No. A10, Maliandao, Xuanwu District. (86-10-63321938/63341946) 宣武区马连道甲10号
This teahouse features authentic Zhejiang cuisine. A nice place for a good pot of tea or other drinks and a light meal. Witness the art of tea making here.

🛒 Shopping

For shopping, there is really only one "Southwest" location that merits real attention. **Maliandao Tea Street** is where you will find "all the tea in China." From very inexpensive and delicious tea, to varieties that will leave your wallet bone dry, you will find them all here. This is also a great place to find a huge variety of teapots, cups, mugs and tea accessories. Many vendors will happily invite you in to sample. Feel free to do so, but be warned that getting out without making a purchase will be a great deal harder than getting in.

The market and supermarket listed below are marked on the map on p.120.

❺ Maliandao Tea Street
马连道茶叶一条街
All about tea
Hours: 7.30am-7pm
Transport: Bus 6, 46, 410, 719, 613, 57, 822, 特7 *to Wanzi (*湾子*); or 609 to Honglian Nanlu (*红莲南路*)*
No. 11, Maliandao Lu, Xuanwu District. (86-10-63283014) 宣武区马连道路11号
Teas from across China can be

found here, with prices ranging from cheap to super-expensive. If you are looking for a beautiful Chinese teapot, this is a good place to shop.

❻ Carrefour (Maliandao)
家乐福马连道店
Supermarket
Hours: 8.30am-10.30pm

*Transport: Bus 46, 609, 414 to Maliandao Hutong (*马连道胡同*)*
No. 11, Maliandao Lu, Xuanwu District. (86-10-63322155) 宣武区马连道路11号

Fresh produce at your fingertips at Carrefour.

Accommodation

When considering where to stay, the "Southwest" is often overlooked due to the fact that it is not close to any tourist hotspot. This can translate into some decent bargains as venues work hard to attract customers. If you are looking for budget accommodation, watch for the sign of "招待所" (cheap hotels), particularly near the **Beijing West Railway Station**. During the Olympics, more guests will find themselves staying here as the "Southwest" is home to the **Fengtai Sports Center**, an Olympic venue for softball. Very close to the sports center is the **Jufeng Hotel** (see below), a source not only of good rooms but of pretty decent food.

All the places listed below are marked on the map on p.120.

Accommodation prices per night
¥ under RMB 99
¥¥ RMB 100-199
¥¥¥ RMB 200-299
¥¥¥¥ RMB 300-399
¥¥¥¥¥ over RMB 400

Hotels (prices based on double-occupancy rooms)

Jufeng Hotel 聚丰宾馆 ¥¥

Price: RMB 162-210

Transport: Bus 811, 702, 822, 特7 to Chalukou (岔路口)

No. 61-5, Xisihuan Nanlu, Fengtai District (close to Fengtai Sports Center). (86-10-63894046) http://hotel.tw128.com/4497/hotel_introAll.asp (in Chinese) 丰台区四四环南路61-5号 (丰台体育中心附近)

Close to Fengtai Sports Center, this place has nice rooms and a great Sichuan/Cantonese restaurant. The price includes breakfast.

Beijing Railway Hotel 北京瑞尔威连锁饭店 ¥¥¥¥

3 star

Price: RMB 318-358

Transport: Bus 205, 21, 319, 387, 609, 702, 727, 802, 848 to Beijing West Railway Station (北京西站)

No. 116-2, Lianhuachi Donglu, Fengtai District. (86-10-63959988) 丰台区莲花池东路116-2号

Very close to Beijing West Railway Station, this is a nice hotel chain with non-smoking rooms.

Ⓒ Yuedu Hotel 悦都大酒店   ¥¥¥¥

3 star

Price: RMB 280-480

Transport: Bus 1, 4, 323, 300, 702, 特2 to Liuliqiao Beili (六里桥北里)

No.A1, Liuliqiao, Fengtai District. (86-10-63497722) http://www.yddjd.cn/ (in Chinese) 丰台区六里桥甲1号

Close to the Beijing West Railway Station to the north. A great place to make your temporary home.

Ⓓ Huaxia Mingzhu Hotel 华夏明珠宾馆   ¥¥¥¥

3 star

Price: RMB 380-428

Transport: Bus 122, 704, 822, 981 to Lianhuachi (莲花池)

No. 120-1, Lianhuachi Donglu, Fengtai District. (86-10-63955588) http://www.bjhxmz.com/huaxia-en/index.asp 丰台区莲花池东路120-1号

Close to China Central Television Station and White Cloud Temple and a short taxi ride from Tian'anmen Square.

Ⓔ Zhongyan Hotel 中盐饭店   ¥¥¥¥¥

3 star

Price: RMB 400-488

Transport: Bus 205, 21, 319, 387, 609, 702, 727, 802, 848 to Beijing West Railway Station (北京西站)

South Square of Beijing West Railway Station, Fengtai District. (86-10-63273366) 丰台区西客站南广场

Close to the Lianhuachi Park and the Beijing West Railway Station, it is a very well equipped hotel with 115 rooms and suites.

Ⓕ Dafang Hotel 大方酒店   ¥¥¥¥¥

4 star

Price: RMB 408-588

Transport: Bus 205, 21, 319, 387, 609, 702, 727, 802, 848 to Beijing West Railway Station (北京西站)

East of the south square of Beijing West Railway Station, Fengtai District. (86-10-63362288) 丰台区西客站南广场东侧

This 12-floor hotel is near the Beijing West Railway Station. It is a business hotel with leisure and conference facilities.

Itinerary

Itinerary D: Remembrance Tour

Morning

9am Begin your day with a visit to **White Cloud Temple** (see p.122) where you can spend an hour honing your knowledge of China's only home-grown religion—Taoism. Be sure to take some coins to throw—it's said those who can hit the bell hanging under the bridge will be granted a year's good luck—that could be a valuable penny!

10am Exit through the south gate, turn left and walk east on Baiyunguan Jie(白云观街) for about 400 m to the Tianningsi Qiaobei (天宁寺桥北) bus stop. Board Bus 662 to Kangzhan Diaosuyuan (抗战雕塑园about half an hour's journey). Allow 30 minutes to wander around **Sculpture Garden in Commemoration of the Chinese People's Anti-Japanese War**.

11.10am Exit through its east gate and walk straight for a few minutes to the end of the street, then turn left, walk for about 300 m. When you see Chengnei Jie (城内街), turn right and carry on for another 200 m until you see **Xinhe Renju Restaurant (鑫和人居)**. Spend about an hour filling your tummy with some simple but tasty Chinese food. (✔ *Restaurants are few and far between in this area so you could take a packed lunch with you as a cheaper and more convenient alternative*).

Afternoon

12.20pm Head westward from the restaurant toward **Ancient Town of Wanping**. Once there, head west along Chengnei Jie for about five minutes until you reach the **Museum of the War of Chinese People's Resistance Against Japanese Aggression** (中国人民抗日战争纪念馆). Allow half an hour to explore the hall.

1pm Leave the hall and exit the town from the west gate. Immediately outside is the **Marco Polo Bridge** (see p.122), a true architectural masterpiece. Count the stone lions and allow yourself half an hour to take some compulsory photos!

1.30pm Walk back to the Kangzhan Diaosuyuan bus stop (about 15 minutes' walk). Take Bus 309 to Wanzi (湾子) and after about half hour's travel you will see **Maliandao Tea Street** (see p.126).

2.15pm Allow about an hour to drink in this ultimate tea experience!

3.15pm End of tour.

Expenses

White Cloud Temple: RMB 10

All-inclusive ticket for Marco Polo Bridge, Wanping Town and the Sculpture Garden: RMB 33

Lunch: RMB 40

Museum of the War of Chinese People's Resistance Against Japanese Aggression: RMB 15

Transport: RMB 6

Total: RMB 104 (USD 13.5)

 **Bus Details**

Major Bus Stops

These are the major bus stops in the "Southwest." At each bus stop, there are direct routes to the key destinations. **They are marked on the map on.120.**

Lianhuachi (莲花池), southeast of the Lianhuachi Park and on Guang'an Lu (广安路)

To Grand View Garden (大观园): 53, 122

To Sculpture Garden in Commemoration of the Chinese People's Anti-Japanese War (中国人民抗日战争雕塑园): 715

To Temple of Heaven (天坛): 6, 822, 53, 122

To World Park (世界公园): 特 7

Beijing West Railway Station (北京西站), east of the railway station

To Grand View Garden (大观园): 运通102,

运通 202

To Marco Polo Bridge (卢沟桥): 661, 662, 937 支 3

To Sculpture Garden in Commemoration of the Chinese People's Anti-Japanese War (中国人民抗日战争雕塑园): 301, 661, 662, 937 支 3

To Temple of Heaven (天坛): 运通 102,

To White Cloud Temple (白云观): 特6, 727, 319, 662, 848 支

To World Park (世界公园): 937 支

To Xidan Department Store (西单商场): 47

Useful Bus Routes

The following is a list of specially selected bus routes passing through the "Southwest" area. These are not all depot-to-depot routes and many less important stops have been omitted. Sights of interest are in bold type. Bus type and times of first and last buses from the first depot are also indicated.

Suggestion: if you are unsure you have the right stop, point out the Chinese characters below for where you want to go and ask another passenger, conductor or driver for help. Many young Chinese have OK English and will be able to help.

特7 (double-decker, 5.30am-7pm)
World Park 世界公园 -Chalukou 岔路口 - Fengtai Beilu 丰台北路 -**Lianhuachi 莲花池** -Wanzi 湾子 -Xuanwumen Dong 宣武门东 -**Qianmen 前门**

53 (standard bus, 5.30am-10pm)
Beijing West Railway Station East北京西站东 -**Lianhuachi 莲花池** -Wanzi 湾子 Guang'anmen Nan 广安门南 -**Grand View Garden 大观园**-Beijing South Railway Station 北京南站 -**Temple of Heaven South Gate 天坛南门**

109 (trolley bus, 5am-11pm)

Chaoyangmennei朝阳门内-**Forbidden City 故宫**-**Beihai Park北海**-**Xidan Department Store 西单商场** -**Niujie Lukouxi 牛街路口西** -**Guang'anmennei 广安门内**

122 (standard bus, 5am-12am)
Beijing West Railway Station East北京西客站东 -**Lianhuachi 莲花池** -Wanzi 湾子 -**Grand View Garden 大观园**-Beijing South Railway Station 北京南站 -**Temple of Heaven South Gate 天坛南门**-Beijing Railway Station East 北京站东

301 (standard bus 5.30am-8.30pm)
Qianmen 前门 -Hepingmen Dong 和平门

"Wild" West

The Wild West? In Beijing? No, not "cowboys and gunfights" wild, we're talking about "wilderness" wild. The **Beijing Zoo** (see p.134) for example has hundreds of species of animals. The **Giant Pandas** are a crowd pleaser and the rare **Golden Monkeys** are often seen going wild themselves. Situated not far from the zoo, you'll find the **Beijing Planetarium** (see p.137), **Beijing Aquarium** (see p.134) and the **Paleozoological Museum of China** (see p.139) which are great spots for both adults and kids to have some fun and acquire some knowledge. The nearby **Capital Gymnasium** (being renovated for the Olympics) and **Beijing Exhibition Center** often host international concerts and Chinese acts, some are really worth checking out despite language barriers; and any challenges faced in finding them will be made up for with the experience.

Across from the exhibition center is a **public square**, which is always full of people playing, dancing, roller skating and flying kites. This is the ideal spot for people who live nearby to go a little "wild" in their spare time.

Furthermore, the most renowned **imperial waterway** (see p.154) that leads to the Summer Palace winds through the quiet, unseen wilderness in the western part of the city, and passes right behind the zoo.

Highlights

♦ **Beijing Zoo** 动物园 A great place to see animals unlikely to be found in your local zoo. Check out the pandas. **See p.134**

♦ **Capital Museum** 首都博物馆 The building itself is a great piece of art. Collections are very well sorted by theme, including jade, bronze, porcelain, painting...Don't miss the historical Beijing exhibits. **See p.137**

♦ **A boat trip in west Beijing** 京西水上游 Follow the route of Empress Dowager Cixi and see Beijing from a different angle. **See p.153**

♦ **Tianyi Market** 天意小商品批发市场 Buy something of everything at this wholesale market. The more you buy, the cheaper it gets. **See p.149**

♦ **National Library Concert Hall** 国家图书馆音乐厅 Features cheap, decent concerts. **See p.148**

Sightseeing

Tourist Attractions

❶ Beijing Zoo 北京动物园
Běijīng dòngwùyuán ★★★

China's biggest zoo

Hours: daily 7.30am-6pm (summer), 7.30am-5pm (winter)

Entrance: RMB 15 (summer), RMB 10 (winter); another 5 for pandas

Suggested length of visit: 2 hours

Transport: Bus 360, 601, 808, 105, 107, 运通105, 运通106, 特4 to Beijing Zoo (动物园)

No.173, Xizhimenwai Dajie, Xicheng District. (86-10-68314411) http://www.beijingzoo.com

西城区西直门外大街173 号

✗ *See restaurants in Beijing Zoo Area on p.140*

Originally a Ming Dynasty imperial manor, in the late Qing Dynasty it became an experimental farm with a small menagerie, called Garden of 10,000 Beasts (万牲园 Wanshengyuan), for Empress Dowager's amusement. Today, visitors can wander over Beijing Zoo's Monkey Hill, through the Panda Hall, past Lion and Tiger Hill and into the Elephant House. In its 90,000-sq-m area are over 30 halls for 20,000 animals of more than 900 species from all over the world. Exhibitions of endangered species such as Giant Panda and Golden Monkey are often on display, providing basic knowledge and awareness of the dangers facing the world's animals.

❷ Beijing Aquarium 北京海洋馆 Běijīng hǎiyángguǎn ★★

Ocean creatures perform for your pleasure

Hours: daily 9am-5pm

Entrance: RMB 100 for adults and RMB 50 for children, both including Beijing Zoo; and free for kids under 1.2 m

Suggested length of visit: 1-1.5 hours

Transport: see transport to Beijing Zoo (动物园)

No. B18, Gaoliangqiao Xiejie, Haidian District (inside the north gate of Beijing Zoo). (86-10-62176655)

A myriad of creatures ensure a wild time.

"WILD" WEST ◆ Sightseeing

Come watch the fantastic fishes.

海淀区高粱桥斜街乙 *18* 号 *(北京动物园北门内)*

Opened in 1999, this is the biggest non-coastal aquarium in the world and boasts a wealth of colorful marine life. The aquarium itself looks like a trumpet shell. One of its most exciting features is a 36-m-long **touching pool** where you can touch various cool mollusks. In the Ocean Theater, a visitors' favorite, you can watch dolphins and sea lions performing to the delight of crowds.

Commemorating the new millennium

Hours: daily 9am-5.30pm (5pm in winter)
Entrance: RMB 30 (including the World Art Museum inside)
Suggested length of visit: 1 hour
Transport: Bus 1, 4, 21, 65, 68, 320, 337, 728 or Subway Line 1 to Military Museum (军事博物馆) No. A9, Fuxing Lu, Haidian District. (86-10-68513322)
海淀区复兴路甲 *9* 号

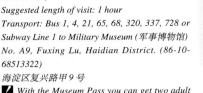 *With the Museum Pass you can get two adult tickets for half price.*

The China Millennium Monument was built to celebrate the arrival of the 21st century. Visitors can explore the sundial-shaped Main Altar, the Sacred Fire Square, Bronze Path or appreciate the superb relief sculpture symbolizing China's 56 ethnic groups. The Beijing World Art Museum inside the Main Altar hosts prestigious temporary exhibitions of Chinese and world art, ancient and modern.

❹ **Yuetan Park (Temple of the Moon)** 月坛公园
Yuètán gōngyuán ★

Pray to the cosmos

Hours: daily 6am-7.30pm

The China Millennium Monument shining toward the stars.

Try to spot the man in the moon from Yuetan Park.

Entrance: RMB 1 (closed now for renovation)
Suggested length of visit: 1 hour
Transport: Bus 13, 42, 56, 716, 823 to Yuetan Park (月坛公园)
Yuetan Beijie, Xicheng District. (86-10-68020940)
西城区月坛北街

Created in 1530, as the name indicates, Yuetan was the site where imperial sacrifices were offered to the God of the Moon. Now a quaint public park, most of its original halls are being used as offices and are not that well maintained. Fortunately, those offices will move out soon, giving way to renovation; more historical spots will be opened when the renovation is completed by 2008.

❺ Purple Bamboo Park
紫竹院 Zǐzhúyuàn ★
Famous for its bamboo

Hours: 6am-9pm
Entrance: free
Suggested length of visit: 1 hour
Transport: Bus 114, 334, 347 to Purple Bamboo Park South Gate (紫竹院南门)
No. 45, Baishiqiao, Haidian District. (86-10-68425851)
海淀区白石桥45号

Originally a reservoir, this was one of the five main water sources in the 3rd century. It was also a stop on the canal traveled by the Qing emperors to the Summer Palace. Today it has been turned into a nice free public park named after its thin purple bamboo. The dock inside still functions and you too can travel by boat to the Summer Palace.

Purple Bamboo? What next, red grass?

Museums

❻ Capital Museum
首都博物馆 ★★★

A hands-on museum
English tour guide

Hours: 9am-5pm (closed Mondays)
Entrance: RMB 30 (free for children under 1.2 m)
Suggested length of visit: 2 hours
Transport: Bus 26, 114, 319, 727, 717, 937 支到
Baiyun Lu (白云路) or Subway Line 1 to Muxidi (木
樨地)
No. 16, Fuxingmenwai Dajie. (86-10-63370491/2)
http://www.capitalmuseum.org.cn/en/index.htm
复兴门外大街16号

📝 *With the Museum Pass you can get two adult*
tickets for 20% off. 200 free admissions are given
away on Wednesdays, so better reserve by phone in
advance. English guide tours need to be reserved
three days in advance for RMB 230.

T he recently refurbished (and relocated) Capital Museum is now China's second largest, dwarfed only by the National Museum. You'll be amazed by a six-story engraved bronze cylinder as you walk in. It has beautifully displayed ceramics and jades, as well as Beijing life through the centuries and a hands-on approach that is rare in Chinese museums. Great visiting exhibitions are also hosted.

❼ Military Museum of Chinese People's Revolution
中国人民革命军事博物馆 ★★

The only comprehensive military museum in China

Hours: 8am-5pm (last entry at 4pm)
Entrance: RMB 20, RMB 10 for children and students
Suggested length of visit: 1 hour
Transport: Bus 1, 4, 21, 617, 728, 827 or Subway Line 1 to Military Museum (军事博物馆)
No. 9, Fuxing Lu, Haidian District. (86-10-
66866114) http://www.chinamil.com.cn/item/jb/ (in Chinese)
海淀区复兴路9号

W ith an exhibition of China's 5,000-year military history, this museum is a great place to satisfy your military fever. The collection includes ancient weapons, armor, chariots, modern military equipment, as well as captured weaponry. The exhibits on the War of Resistance Against Japanese Aggression (1937-1945), and the Chinese revolution led by Mao Zedong are also on display.

Guns, ammo and a lot more.

❽ Beijing Planetarium
北京天文馆 ★★

The only museum specializing in spreading astronomical knowledge in China's mainland

Hours: 10am-3pm (closed on Mon and Tues)
Entrance: New Exhibition Hall RMB 10 (5 for students), SGI Digital Universe Theater RMB 45 (35 for students), 4D Theater RMB 30 (20 for students), 3D Theater RMB 30 (20 for students), Natural Phenomena Hall RMB 15, Aerospace Exhibition RMB 15 (10 for students)
Suggested length of visit: 1 hour
Transport: see transport to Beijing Zoo (动物园) on p.134
No. 138, Xizhimen Dajie. (86-10-68352453/

"To go where no one has gone before!"

68312517) *http://www.bjp.org.cn/en/index.htm*
西直门大街138 号

🖼 *With the Museum Pass you can get two free admissions to the exhibition only.*

Beijing Planetarium consists of three parts: old facility, new facility and ancient observatory. The old facility has a planetarium, an exhibition hall, a movie/lecture hall and a public observatory. The new facility's crowning glory is the dome-like **SGI Digital Universe Theater**, where 45-minute shows project a wonderful galactic mass of stars and planets...look hard and you might even see Luke Skywalker! Other exciting facilities include 3D/4D theaters with cool effects to give visitors lifelike experience of space. The future exhibition zone and the exhibit on the sun are also big draws.

❾ Beijing Art Museum of Stone Carvings
北京石刻艺术博物馆 ★

An art world of stone carvings

Hours: daily 9am-4.30pm (closed on Mondays)
Entrance: RMB 20; RMB 10 for students
Suggested length of visit: 1 hour
Transport: Bus 319, 320, 634, 653, 716, 717, 727, 804, 827, 特4, 特6 to National Library (国家图书馆)

No. 24, Wutasicun, Baishiqiao, Xizhimenwai, Haidian District (opposite the National Library). (86-10-62173543)
海淀区西直门外白石桥五塔寺村24号(国家图书馆对面)

🖼 *Free on Wednesdays; with the Museum Pass you can get two free admissions.*

This unique and interesting museum is located within the grounds of the **Five Pagoda Temple** (五塔寺). The temple was built in the 15th century and was once an important temple outside Xizhimen attracting numerous worshippers in the Ming and Qing dynasties. This temple features intricate Buddhist carvings and unique five pagodas on one base. The pagodas suffered damage during the "cultural revolution (1966-1976)" and the earthquake centered at Tangshan in 1976, however restoration in 1979 returned it to its original shape.

The temple no longer has monks and it houses the Beijing Art Museum of Stone Carvings which displays a substantial collection of carved and inscribed stone artifacts mainly from Beijing, including memorial tablets of early Jesuit missionaries to China.

"This place rocks!"

See the modern stone-age family.

⑩ Paleozoological Museum of China 中国古动物馆 ★

Evolution of life

Hours: 9am-4.30pm (last entry at 4pm, closed on Mondays)
Entrance: RMB 20
Suggested length of visit: 1 hour
Transport: see transport to Beijing Zoo (动物园) on p.134
No. 142, Xizhimen Dajie. (86-10-68935280)
西直门大街142号
☑ *With the Museum Pass you can get one ticket for half price.*

Housing more than 200,000 vertebrate fossils, the museum is divided into four areas: Dinosaur World, Ancient Fish, Ancient Reptiles, and Mammals. Trace the origin and evolution of not only our ancestors, but those we have shared the planet with through time; from amphibians to reptiles, dinosaurs to mammals, and everything in between.

⑪ Beijing Art Museum 北京艺术博物馆 ★★

Housing nearly 70,000 artworks

Hours: daily 9am-4.30pm (closed on Mondays)
Entrance: RMB 20; RMB 10 for students
Suggested length of visit: 1 hour
Transport: Bus 300, 323, 374, 811, 944, 817 to Wanshousi (万寿寺)

Wanshousi, Xisanhuan Beilu. (86-10-68456997)
西三环北路万寿寺
☑ *With the Museum Pass you can get two free admissions. And free on Wednesdays.*

Beijing Art Museum is located in the Temple of Longevity (万寿寺 Wanshousi), an imperial temple built in 1577 during the Ming Dynasty. The museum houses nearly 70,000 pieces of precious ancient paintings, calligraphy, porcelain, jade, bronze ware, furniture, coins and imperial seals of different dynasties. The exhibitions of ceramics and artifacts of the Ming and Qing dynasties are strongly recommended.

⑫ Ethnic Museum of the Central University of Nationalities 中央民族大学民族博物馆 ★

A window on China's 56 ethnic groups

Hours: 8.30am-11.30am, 2pm-5pm (closed on Wednesdays, Friday afternoons and weekends)
Entrance: RMB 10
Suggested length of visit: 45 minutes
Transport: Bus 运通105, 运通106, 运通205 to Minzu Daxue (民族大学)
Inside the Central University of Nationalities, No. 27, Zhongguancun Nanlu. (86-10-68932760)
中关村南路27号中央民族大学内
☑ *With the Museum Pass you can get two free admissions.*

The Ethnic Museum, housed in the Central University of Nationalities, is a wonderful representation of China's eclectic mix of 56 ethnic groups. Displaying a vibrant collection of traditional dress, adornments, ornaments and handicrafts, it is a living testament to the skills and expertise handed down through the ages and still shaping China today.

🍴 Food and Entertainment

The recent development undertaken in the "West", especially the construction of the soon to be completed Subway Line 4 passing by the Beijing Zoo, has turned the area from a fairly nondescript section of town, into a lively and happening place.

The **Beijing Zoo Area** (see below) for example is one of the hottest spots for food and entertainment. The **Theater of the Beijing Exhibition Center** (see p.148) and nearby **National Library Concert Hall** (see p.148) spice things up with modern drama and ballet and cheap, decent concerts.

Drum-shaped rattle.

With a large Muslim population from Xinjiang and a growing fondness among Beijingers for this cooking style, it's hardly surprising there should be an area in west Beijing dedicated totally to Xinjiang/Muslim restaurants, viz the **Xinjiang Center** (see p.146). Not far away, the **Yuetan Area** (see p.144), where the **Temple of the Moon** is located, also offers an array of different cuisines where you're bound to find what your taste buds are searching for!

The following hot spots are marked on the map on p.132.

Beijing Zoo Area 动物园周边

Easily accessible as it is close to **Xizhimen Subway Station** and with a new subway station to emerge by 2008, the highly-populated Beijing Zoo area has attracted many restaurants and bars. Renovation of the **Capital Gymnasium** has resulted in some bars and restaurants closing, but there are still many places you can go eat, unwind, or get in touch with your inner animal, such as **Babyface** (see p.143) and **Bar Sea Sail** (see p.143). Once renovations are completed, this area will be home to some new bars and restaurants.

Sights in the area: Beijing Zoo (see p.134), Beijing Planetarium (see p.137), Palaeozoological Museum of China (see p.139) and Beijing Art Museum of Stone Carvings (see p.138)

Transport: Bus 360, 601, 808, 105, 107, 运通105, 运通106, 特4 to Beijing Zoo (动物园), then walk to your final destination.

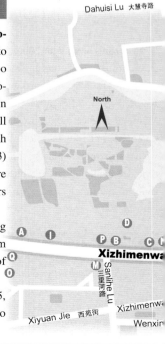

Dahuisi Lu 大慧寺路

North

Xizhimenwa

Sanlihe Lu 三里河路

Xiyuan Jie 西苑街

Xizhimenw

Wenxin

Restaurant listings

Meal prices per adult

¥ under RMB 29
¥¥ RMB 30-49
¥¥¥ RMB 50-69
¥¥¥¥ RMB 70-99
¥¥¥¥¥ over RMB 100

American

Haoshanghao
豪尚豪牛排馆

Fast food, non-smoking   ¥¥
Hours: 9am-11pm
Transport: Bus 运通104, 运通105,

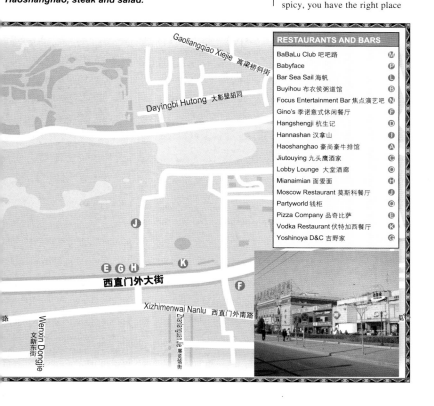

Haoshanghao, steak and salad.

运通 106 to Baishiqiao (白石桥)
No. 137, Xizhimenwai Dajie, Xicheng District (east of Carrefour Supermarket). (86-10-68313445) 西城区西直门外大街 137 号 (家乐福东)

This restaurant is famous for its low-priced steak. Includes a salad bar with the combination meal. Tie into a decent piece of beef after a draining day of sightseeing, you'll feel restored and ready for a night out.

Chinese

Ⓑ Buyihou 布衣侯粥道馆
Chinese congee   ¥

Hours: 9am-10.30pm
Transport: see transport to Beijing Zoo Area on p.140
No. 141, Xizhimenwai Dajie, Xicheng District (east of Triumph Plaza). (86-10-88383636/68314136) 西城区西直门外大街 141 号 (凯旋大厦东侧)

This restaurant serves up congee, a thick Chinese rice porridge (tastes better than it sounds!) that comes in many different flavors both sweet and savory. Hearty, traditional Chinese food that will keep your waistline slim.

Ⓒ Jiutouying 九头鹰酒家
Hubei cuisine   ¥¥

Hours: 10.30am-10.30pm
Transport: Bus 运通104, 运通105, 运通 106 to Baishiqiao (白石桥)
No. 141, Xizhimenwai Dajie, Xicheng District (close to Carrefour Supermarket). (86-10-68353919) 西城区西直门外大街 141 号 (近家乐福)

If you crave something very spicy, you have the right place

RESTAURANTS AND BARS

BaBaLu Club 吧吧路	Ⓜ
Babyface	Ⓟ
Bar Sea Sail 海帆	Ⓛ
Buyihou 布衣侯粥道馆	Ⓑ
Focus Entertainment Bar 焦点演艺吧	Ⓝ
Gino's 季诺意式休闲餐厅	Ⓕ
Hangshengji 杭生记	Ⓓ
Hannashan 汉拿山	Ⓘ
Haoshanghao 豪尚豪牛排馆	Ⓐ
Jiutouying 九头鹰酒家	Ⓒ
Lobby Lounge 大堂酒廊	Ⓞ
Mianaimian 面爱面	Ⓗ
Moscow Restaurant 莫斯科餐厅	Ⓙ
Partyworld 钱柜	Ⓠ
Pizza Company 品奇比萨	Ⓔ
Vodka Restaurant 伏特加西餐厅	Ⓚ
Yoshinoya D&C 吉野家	Ⓖ

Gaoliangqiao Xiejie 高梁桥斜街

Dayingbi Hutong 大影壁胡同

西直门外大街

Xizhimenwai Nanlu 西直门外南路

Wenxin Dongjie 文新东街

Zhanguan Jie 展览馆街

路

here. Hubei cuisine is known for being quite delicious, but really hot! You might leave here red-faced, but happy.

ⓓ Hangshengji 杭生记

Zhejiang cuisine ¥¥¥

Hours: 9.30am-9pm

Transport: see transport to Beijing Zoo Area on p.140

No. 141, Xizhimenwai Dajie, Xicheng District (west of Beijing Zoo's main gate). (86-10-88375300/0660) 西城区西直门外大街141号 (动物园正门西)

Ask local people about this restaurant and odds are they'll recommend Stewed duck (老鸭煲), the house specialty. Beautiful Hangzhou wood carvings on display.

Italian

ⓔ Pizza Company 品奇比萨

Pizza

English menu, non-smoking ¥¥¥

Hours: 10am-10.30pm

Transport: Bus运通104, 运通105, 运通106 to Baishiqiao (白石桥)

No. 137, Xizhimenwai Dajie, Xicheng District. (86-10-88371668) 西城区西直门外大街137号

Great pizza (with thick or thin crust) and delicious side dishes like onion rings, chicken wings and potato skins. Friendly, efficient service in the restaurant, or get your food to go.

ⓕ Gino's 季诺意式休闲餐厅

English menu, non-smoking ¥¥¥¥

Hours: 10am-10pm

Transport: Bus 105, 111, 27, 26, 362, 601, 634, 808 to Xizhimenwai (西直门外)

5/F, ItoYokado Department Store, No. 112, Xizhimenwai Dajie, Xicheng District. (86-10-88360991) 西城区西直门外大街112号华堂商场5层

Sample the wonderful cuisine of Italy in this nicely decorated restaurant. Polite and attentive service complements the delicious food. Their Lasagne (意大

利千层面) and Escargots (蒜香焗蜗牛) are the most popular. Get a better deal with their set menu.

Japanese

Delicious fast food from the Far East.

ⓖ Yoshinoya D&C 吉野家

Japanese fast food ¥

Hours: 9.30am-9.30pm

Transport: see transport to Beijing Zoo Area on p.140

East of Beijing Zoo's main gate, Xicheng District. (86-10-88389765) 西城区动物园正门东

This is a worldwide Japanese fast food chain specializing in tender, succulent pork, beef and chicken set meals.

ⓗ Mianaimian 面爱面

Japanese noodles ¥¥

Hours: 7.30am-10pm

Transport: see transport to Beijing Zoo Area on p.140

No. 137, Xizhimenwai Dajie, Xicheng District (east of Beijing Zoo's main gate). (86-10-68349484) 西城区西直门外大街137号(动物园正门东)

This place serves genuine Japanese noodles that lure patrons back time and again. The menu also features other favorites of China's neighbor to the east.

Korean

ⓘ Hannashan 汉拿山 ¥¥¥

Hours: 10am-10.30pm

Transport: Bus运通104, 运通105, 运通106 to Baishiqiao (白石桥)

No. B143, Xizhimenwai Dajie (near Carrefour Supermarket). (86-10-68359688) 西直门外大街乙143号

(近家乐福)

Features a wide range of barbecue items, from mushroom to ox tongue, to suit all budgets. Other Korean specialties include Stone-pot rice (石锅拌饭) and Cold noodles (冷面).

Russian

ⓙ Moscow Restaurant 莫斯科餐厅

English menu ¥¥¥¥

Hours: 11am-2 pm, 5pm-9pm

Transport: see transport to Beijing Zoo Area on p.140

West of Beijing Exhibition Center, No. 135, (86-10-68354454) 西城区西直门外大街135号北展中心西

This was the first Western restaurant allowed to open in Beijing. Try Russian standards like Borscht or Chicken Kiev, and don't forget to drink plenty of vodka.

Get the Czar treatment at Moscow Restaurant.

ⓚ Vodka Restaurant 伏特加西餐厅

English menu ¥¥¥¥

Hours: 7am-10am (breakfast), 11am-2.30pm (lunch), 5pm-10pm (dinner)

Transport: see transport to Beijing Zoo Area on p.140

Inside the Exhibition Center Hotel, No. 135, Xizhimenwai Dajie, Xicheng District. (86-10-68316633 ext. 7011) 西城区西直门外大街135号展览馆宾馆内

A fun Moscow restaurant where you can enjoy traditional Russian dance without paying through the nose. And what would a Russian meal be without vodka? Drink up!

Come sail away at Bar Sea Sail.

Bar listings

Prices for a bottle of Tsingtao beer (青岛啤酒), a favorite local beer

¥ under RMB 14

¥¥ RMB 15-24

¥¥¥ RMB 25-34

¥¥¥¥ over RMB 35

Ⓖ Bar Sea Sail 海帆

Rock, pop, live show

English menu and service　¥¥¥

Hours: 5pm-late

Entrance: free

Transport: see transport to Beijing Zoo Area on p.140

No. 141, Xizhimenwai Dajie, Xicheng District (west of Beijing Zoo). (86-10-68316187) 西城区西直门外大街141号(动物园西)

An array of performances such as singing, dancing, cross-talking and even acrobatics can be enjoyed in this show bar. Pop stars sometimes play this venue, so you might see a famous artist from China or elsewhere. Western and Chinese music mix in this classy joint.

Ⓜ BaBaLu Club 吧吧路

Live music, hip hop & house

English menu and service　¥¥¥

Hours: 8pm-2am

Entrance: free

Transport: Bus运通104, 运通105, 运通106 to Baishiqiao (白石桥)

North Building, Xiyuan Hotel, No. 1, Sanlihe Lu, Xicheng District (across from Carrefour). (86-10-88360633) 西城区三里河1号西苑饭店北配楼 (家乐福超市对面)

This is by reputation the best nightspot in west Beijing. With a funky play list and mixed clientele, it's sure to be an interesting night.

Ⓝ Focus Entertainment Bar 焦点演艺吧

Jazz; live performance　¥¥¥

Hours: 7pm-12.30am

Entrance: free

Transport: see transport to Beijing Zoo Area on p.140

300 m west of the south gate of Beijing Zoo, Xizhimenwai Dajie, Xicheng District. (13717553375 or 13261555868) 西城区西直门外大街动物园南门西300米

After you walk through a long hallway, you'll see a spacious two-floor show bar equipped with large stage and live acts every night. A varied line-up will keep you guessing just what might be next.

Ⓞ Lobby Lounge 大堂酒廊

Classical music, live piano　¥¥¥

Hours: 9am-12am

Entrance: free

Transport: Bus运通104, 运通105, 运通106 to Baishiqiao (白石桥)

No.6, Shoudutiyuguan Nanlu, Haidian District. (86-10-68492001 ext. 87) http://www.newcenturyhotel. com.cn/doce/ 海淀区首都体育馆南路6号

⬛ *15% service charge*

This classy lounge is a great spot to sit back and relax in a comfortable environment. Located within the New Century Hotel, on the pricey side, but definitely enjoyable.

Ⓟ Babyface

House, Hip-hop; DJ, live show

English menu and service　¥¥¥¥

Hours: 8.20pm-3am

Entrance: weekends, festivals and special events only

Transport: Bus运通104, 运通105, 运通106 to Baishiqiao (白石桥)

1/F, Building A, Triumph Plaza, Shoudutiyuguan Nanlu, Xicheng District. (86-10-88016848) www. faceclub.com.cn 西城区首都体育馆南路凯旋大厦A座首层

⬛ *RMB 200 will get you 6 beers.*

Post-modern décor and thumping with party-mayhem, this is your international music club. It could end up being a long night, but a good one! A multi-ethnic clientele makes for interesting encounters.

Karaoke

Ⓠ Partyworld 钱柜

Hours: 11am-2am (Mon, Tue, Thu and Sun); 11am-4am (Wed, Fri and Sat)

Beer: RMB 29/bottle, RMB 128 for 6 bottles, RMB 228 for 12.

Transport: Bus运通104, 运通105, 运通106 to Baishiqiao (白石桥)

No.168, Xizhimenwai Dajie, Xicheng District. (86-10-88576588) www. cashboxparty.com (in Chinese) 西城区西直门外大街168号

A popular alternative to the bar scene. Karaoke here provides a private room for you and your friends. There is an hourly charge for the room, which includes a free buffet dinner before 9pm. Room rates change depending on the day of the week and what time you are going.

Private KTV rooms make it easy to have fun.

Yuetan Area 月坛

Yuetan, Temple of the Moon, was where the emperor came to worship the God of the Moon. Bursting with tradition and history, this area has fought off the encroachment of bars and clubs in favor of culture and heritage handed down over the centuries. Teahouses abound in traditional splendor and elegance and restaurants offer a fabulous assortment of Chinese and Western cuisines. Be it an afternoon nibble or full-blown dining experience, visitors can find anything they're looking for (and a bit extra!).

Sights nearby: Yuetan Park (see p.135)

Transport: Bus 15 to Yuetan Beijie (月坛北街) or Bus 13, 42, 56, 716, 823 to Yuetan Park (月坛公园).

Fucheng Lu 阜成路 Fuchengmenw

Sanlihe Lu 三里河路

Yuetan Beiji

RESTAURANTS

Beijing Laobaren 北京老巴人酒楼	Ⓔ
Byone Global Food 百万庄园西餐厅	Ⓛ
Daole Japanese Restaurant 道乐	Ⓙ
Hexingyuan 合兴源东北农家菜	Ⓑ
Heyuan Renjia 禾园人家	Ⓒ
Hongmantian 洪满天	Ⓓ
Huaiyangchun 淮阳春饭店	Ⓗ
Merrylin 美林阁	Ⓘ
Wanwanfang Brazilian Barbecue 万万方巴西烤肉	Ⓐ
Xiangmeizi 湘妹子大酒楼	Ⓕ
Yongdengpu Barbecue 永登浦烧烤	Ⓚ
Yuebeilou 月北楼饭庄	Ⓖ

Yuetan Nanjie

Sanlihe Nanhengjie

Fuxingmenw

Baiyunguanjie Be

Restaurant listings

Meal prices per adult

¥ under RMB 29
¥¥ RMB 30-49
¥¥¥ RMB 50-69
¥¥¥¥ RMB 70-99
¥¥¥¥¥ over RMB 100

Brazilian

Ⓐ Wanwanfang Brazilian Barbecue 万万方巴西烤肉

Barbecue buffet ¥¥

Hours: 11am-2pm, 5pm-10pm
Transport: Bus 13, 21, 65, 68 to Sanlihe Dongkou (三里河东口)
3/F, Yindao Plaza, No. 32, Yuetan Nanjie, Xicheng District (above

Juicy BBQ served to you at your table.

McDonald's). (86-10-68511351) 西城区月坛南街32号银岛大厦3层 (麦当劳楼上)

🔲 *Monday to Friday lunchtime buffet special: for every three people eating, the fourth eats free.*

The weekday barbecue buffet is a feast for hungry eyes at a very good price. Offering a selection of meats and fresh fruit, it satisfies all taste buds. Weekend dishes tend to be slightly more diverse.

Chinese

Ⓑ Hexingyuan 合兴源东北农家菜

Northeast ¥

Hours: 11am-11pm
Transport: Bus 15 to Yuetan Beijie (月坛北街)
No. C3, Yuetan Beijie, Xicheng District. (86-10-68017518) 西城区月坛北街丙3号

Extremely reasonable prices and authentic cooking styles are top on the menu at Hexingyuan. Be

sure to try their excellent Northeast bean flour noodle (东北大拉皮).

Ⓒ Heyuan Renjia 禾园人家

Home-style dishes ¥

Hours: 6am-9.30am, 10am-12am
Transport: Bus 13, 68, 65, 21 to Sanlihe Dongkou (三里河东口)
No. 73, Yuetan Nanjie, Sanlihe, Xicheng District. (86-10-68523504) 西城区三里河月坛南街73号

🔲 *10% discount if reserved through www.qingke800.com (excluding cigarettes and drinks) (in Chinese and English).*

Big plates and small bills are certainly the theme here. We highly recommend their roast duck.

Ⓓ Hongmantian 洪满天

Xinjiang/Muslim cuisine ¥¥

Hours: 10.30am-10pm
Transport: Bus 1, 15, 52, 337, 728, 802, 937 or Subway Line 1 to Nanlishi Lu (南礼士路)
No. A44, Nanlishi Lu, Xicheng District (near Yuetan Plaza). (86-10-

Hongmantian Chinese cuisine.

68051192) 西城区南礼士路甲44号 (月坛大厦附近)

📋 *12% discount if reserved through www.ziye114.com (roast duck and drinks excluded) (in Chinese).*

For Chinese food with a difference, Hongmantian is the place. They cook up mouth-watering dishes from Xinjiang Muslim cuisine with authenticity and flair.

Beijing Laobaren
北京老巴人酒楼

Sichuan cuisine ¥¥

Hours: 10am-9.30pm
Transport: Bus 1, 15, 52, 337, 728, 802, 937 or Subway Line 1 to Nanlishi Lu (南礼士路)
No. B25, Nanlishi Lu, Xicheng District (near Nanlishilu Subway Station). (86-10-68010106) 西城区南礼士路乙25号 (南礼士路地铁站附近)

📋 *12% discount if reserved through www.eding.com.cn (seafood, drinks and dishes on special offer are excluded) (in Chinese).*

Laobaren, meaning old Sichuan folks, seems wonderfully appropriate here; traditional Sichuan dishes can be enjoyed in old-world surroundings.

Ⓕ Xiangmeizi 湘妹子大酒楼

Hunan cuisine ¥¥

Hours: 11am-11pm
Transport: Bus 13, 21, 732 to Erqijuchanglu Beikou (二七剧场路北口)
No. 19, Shehui Lu, South of Yuetan Park, Xicheng District (diagonally across from Yuetan Police Station). (86-10-68021198) 西城区月坛南社会路19号 (月坛派出所斜对面)

📋 *12% off if reserved through www.ziye114.com (in Chinese).*

In a city with so many Hunan restaurants, this one stands alone with its trademark combination of southern and northern cuisines produced by talented and inventive chefs. Their Smoked meat with pickled parsnip (萝卜干炒腊肉) is recommended.

Ⓖ Yuebeilou 月北楼饭庄

Home-style dishes ¥¥

Hours: 6am-9pm
Transport: see transport to Yuetan Area on p.144
No. 11, Yuetan Beijie, Xicheng District (right beside a bus stop). (86-10-68028355/68034083) 西城区月坛北街11号 (车站附近)

With meals to satisfy your budget and belly, Yuebeilou prides itself on its home-cooked, traditional Chinese dishes. Cheap and cheerful!

Ⓗ Huaiyangchun
淮阳春饭店

Jiangsu cuisine
English menu ¥¥¥

Hours: 9.30am-2pm, 5pm-9pm
Transport: Bus 13, 68, 65, 21 to Sanlihe Dongkou (三里河东口)
No. 10, Sanlihe Donglu, Yuetan Beijie (west of Children's Hospital). (86-10-68011117) 西城区月坛北街三里河东路10号 (儿童医院西)

Huaiyangchun is certainly the place to go for value for money. High quality food in elegant surroundings, the age-old history of the place shines through. Copy your dining neighbors and try the Lion-head meat balls (狮子头).

Ⓘ Merrylin 美林阁

Shanghai cuisine
English menu ¥¥¥¥¥

Hours: 10.50am-2pm, 4.50pm-9pm
Transport: Bus 1, 15, 52, 337, 728, 802, 937 or Subway Line 1 to Nanlishi Lu (南礼士路)
No. 2, Yuetan Beijie, Xicheng District (at the intersection of Nanlishi Lu, opposite No. 35 Middle School). (86-10-68081666/1777) 西城区月坛北街2号 (南礼士路口, 35中对面)

📋 *10% discount if reserved through www.eding.com.cn or www.qingke800.com or www.fantong.com (in Chinese).*

A businessman's favorite for a quick bite on-the-go, this restaurant is part of a Shanghai chain serving up traditional Shanghai dishes. Their Crystal shrimp (水晶虾仁) is a must-try.

Crystal shrimp at Merrylin.

Japanese

Ⓙ Daole 道乐

English menu ¥¥¥¥

Hours: 11am-11pm
Transport: Bus 395, 702 or Subway Line 1 or 2 to Fuxingmen (复兴门)
1/F, Section C, Tongtai Plaza, No. 33, Financial Street, Xicheng District (north of Parkson Shopping Mall). (86-10-88086868) 西城区金融街33号通泰大厦C段1层 (百盛购物中心北)

A great diversity of traditional colorful Japanese dishes and attentive service can be found at Daole. The standard menu is expensive, but their RMB 50 set meal is a budgeter's dream-come-true, and includes one dish, a soup, a small plate of pickles, and two bowls of rice.

Korean

Ⓚ Yongdengpu Barbecue 永登浦烧烤

Barbecue ¥¥

Hours: 11am-2pm, 5pm-10pm

Transport: Bus 68, 65, 21, 13 to Sanlihe Xikou (三里河西口)

No. 18, Nanshagou Xiaoqu, Yuetan Nanjie, Xicheng District (opposite the National Development and Reform Commission). (86-10-68578844) 西城区月坛南街南沙沟小区18号 (国家发改委对面)

🔖 *Every RMB 100 spent gets you a RMB 30 discount coupon on your next meal.*

A wide selection of meats and soups are on the menu here. With their low prices you can indulge in a starter and main course (if you can finish it all!). The ox tongue (牛舌) is a particular favorite here.

Western

Ⓛ Byone Global Food 百万庄园西餐厅

English menu ¥¥¥

Hours: 9.30am-1am

Transport: see transport to Yuetan Area on p.144

No. C10, Yuetan Beijie, Xicheng District (200 m west of Yuetan Park). (86-10-68035967) 西城区月坛北街丙10号 (月坛公园西200米)

🔖 *10% discount if reserved through www.ziye114.com (cigarettes, drinks and dishes on special excluded) (in Chinese).*

"Global" is certainly the name of the game in this motorbike-themed food bonanza. Choose from Russian, French, American, Japanese or Korean dishes to fuel your engine!

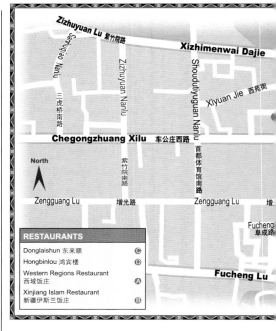

RESTAURANTS

Donglaishun 东来顺	Ⓒ
Hongbinlou 鸿宾楼	Ⓓ
Western Regions Restaurant 西域饭庄	Ⓐ
Xinjiang Islam Restaurant 新疆伊斯兰饭庄	Ⓑ

Restaurant listings

Meal prices per adult

¥ under RMB 29

¥¥ RMB 30-49

¥¥¥ RMB 50-69

¥¥¥¥ RMB 70-99

¥¥¥¥¥ over RMB 100

Chinese

Xinjiang-style fried rice.

Ⓐ Western Regions Restaurant 西域饭庄

Xinjiang cuisine ¥¥

Hours: 7am-10pm

Transport: see transport to Xinjiang Center on p.147

Inside Xinjiang Office compound, No. 7, Sanlihe Lu, Haidian District. (86-10-68332266 ext. 6613) 海淀区

三里河路7号新疆驻京办事处院内

🔖 *5% off if reserved through www.qingke800.com (excluding drinks).*

The prefered choice of Xinjiang locals. The regular queues for a table are always a good sign of quality, authenticity and value for money.

Ⓑ Xinjiang Islam Restaurant 新疆伊斯兰饭庄

Xinjiang cuisine ¥¥

Hours: 7am-9.30am, 11am-9.30pm

Transport: see transport to Xinjiang Center on p.147

Inside Xinjiang Office compound, No. 7, Sanlihe Lu, Haidian District. (86-10-68351820) 海淀区三里河路7号新疆驻京办事处院内

🔖 *5% off if reserved through www.*

Lamb and nang bread.

Left margin (map labels):
了外大街
ai Nanjie 西直门外南街
Zhanlanguan Lu 展览馆路
gzhuang Dajie 车公庄大街
展览馆路
g Dajie 百万庄大街 **D**
nwai Dajie 阜成门外大街

Xinjiang Center 新疆区

Since the establishment of the Xinjiang Office in Beijing on Sanlihe Lu (三里河路) in 1975, Uygur people native to northwest China's Xinjiang have set up shops within and nearby the compound. Consequently, the area around has became a Xinjiang center, redolent with the aroma of traditional Muslim cuisine; strong competition has resulted in great food at great prices.

However, Beijing's urbanization has not spared this area; roads and buildings have encroached and the ethnic population has diluted. Fortunately, its heart and essence have been maintained. Several good Xinjiang/Muslim restaurants still produce traditional and authentic dishes, such as Lamb kebabs (羊肉串) or Square noodles in tomato sauce (拉条子).

Sights nearby: Beijing Zoo (see p.134)

Transport: Bus 114, 118, 701, 748 to Erligou Xikou (二里沟西口), then walk eastward along Chegongzhuang Dajie (车公庄大街), when you hit an intersection, turn left and head to the Xinjiang Office.

qingke800.com (excluding drinks).
As one of the most authentic Xinjiang restaurants in Beijing, this two-story restaurant has private rooms on the first floor, and sometimes there are performances around dinner time on the second. Big plate chicken (大盘鸡) and Mutton wrapped in Nang bread (囊包肉) are big draws.

Donglaishun 东来顺
Beijing hotpot/Muslim   **¥¥¥¥**
Hours: 11am-2pm, 5pm-9.30pm
Transport: see transport to Xinjiang Center above
No. 7, Sanlihe Lu, Haidian District. (86-10-88378838) 海淀区三里河路7号
A time-honored Beijing hotpot restaurant. Its traditional coal-heated bronze pot gives special treatment to their tender mutton and beef. RMB 120 will get you a different pot—in cloisonné. It'll be a unique experience though the food tastes the same whichever pot you eat from.

Donglaishun's special cloisonné hotpot.

D Hongbinlou 鸿宾楼
Muslim
English menu   **¥¥¥¥**
Hours: 11am-2pm, 5pm-10pm
Transport: Bus 15, 26, 45, 101, 489, 65,

714, 716, 732, 814 to Baiwanzhuang Dongkou (百万庄东口)
No. 11, Zhanlanguan Lu, Xicheng District. (86-10-68992569/68994563) 西城区展览馆路11号
📋 *10% off if reserved through www. eding.com.cn (in Chinese).*
When a restaurant has been around for 150 years, you know it can't be bad! The cooking styles have been handed down from chef to chef and are now pretty much perfect. The Ox tail braised in soy sauce (红烧牛尾) is the house specialty.

Hongbinlou Muslim food.

Theaters

The theaters listed below are marked on the map on p.132.

⑱ Theater of the Beijing Exhibition Center 北京展览馆剧场
Drama, opera, ballet
Hours: 7.30pm
Price: RMB 80-880 (depending on the performance)
Transport: Bus 15, 19, 26, 107, 716, 732, 812, 特4 to Beijing Zhanlanguan (北京展览馆)
No. 135, Xizhimenwai Dajie, Xicheng District. (86-10-68354455) 西城区西直门外大街135 号
Featuring both Chinese and Western plays, opera and ballet, this Russian-style theater is part of the Beijing Exhibition Center. There's something for every culture lover at this grand building.

⑭ Mei Lanfang Grand Theater 梅兰芳大剧院
Peking Opera
Hours: 7.30pm-10pm
Transport: Bus 392, 701, 118, 107 to Chegongzhuang Xi (车公庄西) Southeast of Guanyuan Qiao, Xicheng District. (86-10-58331288/1388)西城区官园桥东南角
The theater is the first of its kind especially designed for Peking Opera performances in the capital. Named after Mei Lanfang, who has been internationally known as a great master of Peking Opera, the 3-storied building features three levels with 1,035 seats and five VIP chambers. Although designed for Peking Opera, the theater also opens its stage to other types of performances, such as dramas and musicals.

Mei Lanfang Grand Theater.

⑮ National Library Concert Hall 国家图书馆音乐厅
Concert
Hours: 7.30 pm
Price: RMB 10-480
Transport: Bus 319, 320, 634, 653, 716, 717, 727, 804, 827, 特4, 特6 to National Library (国家图书馆)
No. 33, Zhongguancun Nandajie, Haidian District. (86-10-68485462) 海淀区中关村南大街33 号
Situated within the National Library, this concert hall features cheap but quality summer concerts for kids and students.

 # Shopping

Very few foreign visitors make a trip to west Beijing to shop, but there are actually a lot of "hidden gems" worth checking out.

For example, many visitors have heard of the Beijing Zoo, but most the are unaware of the elephantine wholesale clothing market sitting on its doorstep. True, the crowds do often make one feel like being in a herd, but the prices and variety are fantastic. As the famous Pearl and Silk markets become increasingly packed by the day and prices go up, the best advice we can give is "Head West and Shop Like Beijingers!"

The markets and supermarkets listed below are marked on the map on p.132.

Tianyi Market.

The huge Zoo Clothing Market gives you everything in one spot.

⑯ Beijing Zoo Clothing Wholesale Market 北京动物园服装批发市场

A maze of clothing shops

Hours: 6am-5pm

Transport: see transport to Beijing Zoo on p.134

Xizhimenwai Dajie, Xicheng District. (86-10-88352668) 西城区西直门外大街

The business area around Beijing Zoo often makes you feel like you're in a zoo! A huge clothes trading zone, you can choose from the better decorated buildings of Dongding (东鼎), Tianle (天乐), Jinkai Lide (金开德) or, for a bit of a challenge, the louder but cheaper ones!

⑰ Guanyuan Commodities Wholesale Market 官园小商品批发市场

Cheap shopping in an excellent environment

Hours: 8.30am-7pm

Transport: Bus 107, 118, 运通106 to Guanyuan (官园)

No. A4, Chegongzhuang Dajie, Xicheng District. (86-10-51954001) 西城区车公庄大街甲4号

Compared to other markets, this is a "five-star" environment to do cheap shopping. It sells clothes predominantly, but also accessories, toys, home decorations and stationary.

⑱ Julong Clothing Wholesale Market 聚龙外贸服装批发市场

Underground shopping world

Hours: 6.30am-4.30pm

Transport: see transport to Beijing Zoo on p.134

No. 116, Xizhimenwai Dajie, Xicheng District. (86-10-68356362) 西城区西直门外大街116号

The grandfather of the Beijing Zoo clothes markets; it is generally a little less hectic than its neighbors. Don't expect super quality, but the prices are rock-bottom and it's quiet(er)!

⑲ Tianyi Market 天意小商品批发市场

One-stop shopping

Hours: 7.30am-5pm

Transport: Bus 101, 102, 103, 746, 846 to Fuwai Xikou (阜外西口)

No. 259, Fuchengmenwai Dajie, Xicheng District. (86-10-68320732) 西城区阜城门外大街259号

As a good alternative to the Pearl Market, this five-floor shoppers' paradise offers anything and everything. It's geared toward locals, so the prices are more reasonable. As always, bargain hard; vendors often up the prices for foreigners.

⑳ Tianzhaotian Wholesale Market 天照天小商品批发市场

Accessories

Hours: 7.30am-5pm

Transport: Bus 15, 19, 42, 712, 823 to Beijing Ertongyiyuan Ximen (北京儿童医院西门)

No. D9, Nanlishi Lu, Xicheng District. (86-10-68015999) 西城区南礼士路丁9号

Offering a great selection of wholesale decorations and accessories, this four-floor market is every woman's dream. Bring your husband only to help carry the bags!

㉑ Wantong New World Commodities Fair 万通新世界商品交易市场

Best located market

Hours: 9am-8.30pm

Transport: Bus 13, 19, 21, 44, 111, 121, 335, 336, 823, 921, 101, 102, 103 or Subway Line 2 to Fuchengmen (阜成门), Exit D

No. 2, Fuchengmenwai Dajie, Xicheng District. (across from Hualian Shopping Mall). (86-10-68588145) 西城区阜成门外大街2号 (华联商厦对面)

With approximately 150,000 visitors a day, this is a daunting yet fascinating place. Selling pretty much everything, it is easily accessible; Subway Line 2 Exit D will plonk you right inside!

㉒ Carrefour (Fangyuan) 家乐福方圆店

Supermarket

Hours: 8am-10.30pm

Transport: Bus 运通104, 运通105, 运通106 to Baishiqiao (白石桥)

Fangyuan Building, No. A56, Zhongguancun Nandajie, Haidian District. (86-10-88362729 ext.8000) 海淀区中关村南大街甲56号方圆大厦

A department-store-style supermarket. You can find almost any household item you need here.

Carrefour offers low prices and helpful service.

Accommodation

Many people choose to make the most of the convenience of the **Xizhimen** (西直门) area, which is blessed with everything: Xizhimen subway and light rail station, Beijing Zoo, Beijing Planetarium, wholesale market, plentiful bars and restaurants... A big drawback, however, are the crowds, noise and bad traffic. **Xizhimenwai Dajie** (西直门外大街), which runs between Beijing's West Second and West Third ring roads, is one of the busiest thoroughfares in west Beijing. It has a concentration of first-class hotels, as well as a bunch of cheap guesthouses.

For a quieter place, look further southwest. Outside the West Third Ring Road around **Wanshou Lu** (万寿路), for example, is a good choice as it is also close to Subway Line 1.

For more reasonably priced digs, look out hotels near such universities as **Beijing Jiaotong University** (北京交通大学) and **Capital Normal University** (首都师范大学).

All places listed below are marked on the map on p.132.

Accommodation prices per night
¥ under RMB 99
¥¥ RMB 100-199
¥¥¥ RMB 200-299
¥¥¥¥ RMB 300-399
¥¥¥¥¥ over RMB 400

Hotels (prices based on double-occupancy rooms)

Ⓐ Meiyuan Hotel 梅苑饭店 ¥¥¥

2 star

Price: RMB 260-280

Transport: Bus 16, 26 to Beijing Jiaotong University (北京交通大学)

No. A30, Gaoliangqiao Xiejie, Haidian District (next to Beijing Jiaotong University). (86-10-62241115)

http://www.bjmyfd.com/ (in Chinese) 海淀区高粱桥斜街甲30号 (北京交通大学旁)

Conveniently located, it offers single, double, triple rooms and suites. Its biggest draw is a two-floor **vegetarian restaurant** in the courtyard.

Ⓑ Zhongtie Wukesong Hotel 中铁五棵松饭店 ¥¥¥

2 star

Price: RMB 268

Transport: Bus 654, 748, 840, 804 to Jingouhe (金沟河)

No. 19, Xisihuan Zhonglu, Haidian District (close to PLA General Hospital). (86-10-68213355) 海淀区西四环中路19号 (解放军总医院附近)

Boasting nearly 200 single, standard, triple, or suite rooms, this well-priced hotel has lovely ambience and is also known for its seafood.

🏨	@	✕	🍷	👕	🏃	🛏

Yudu Hotel 玉都饭店   ¥¥¥

2 star

Price: RMB 258-288

Transport: Bus 334, 360, 489, 714, 804, 运通 104 to Beiwa Lu (北洼路)

No. 85, Beiwa Lu, Haidian District (close to Purple Bamboo Park). (86-10-68428882) 海淀区北洼路85 号 (紫竹院附近)

Yudu Hotel is perfect for those wanting a great dinner in the comfort of its hotel; its restaurant serves Sichuan, Hunan and Cantonese dishes, while all rooms have art deco decoration and the latest facilities.

Longxuan Hotel 龙轩宾馆   ¥¥¥

3 star

Price: RMB 258-338

Transport: Bus 489 to Zengguanglu Xikou (增光路西口)

No. 30, Zengguang Lu, Ganjiakou, Haidian District. (86-10-68321846) 海淀区甘家口增光路30 号

With 100 rooms and extremely helpful service, this new hotel is a very pleasant place to stay. A business center, desk service and free car parking are some of the amenities offered.

Yulong Hotel 裕龙大酒店   ¥¥¥¥

3 star

Price: RMB 300

Transport: Bus 27, 121, 40, 56, 368, 645, 701, 748, 850 to Xidiaoyutai (西钓鱼台)

No.40, Xidiaoyutai, Fucheng Lu, Haidian District. (86-10-68415588) 海淀区阜成路西钓鱼台40 号

Attractively situated by a canal, the warm and welcoming Yulong is ideal for business travelers. With all types of rooms and excellent in-room facilities, a wide range of leisure and entertainment options add to its attraction.

Tiantian Holiday Hotel 天天假日饭店   ¥¥¥¥

3 star

Price: RMB 398

Transport: Subway Line 1 to Wanshou Lu (万寿路)

No. 17, Wanshoulu Beikou, Haidian District (close to Chengxiang Trade Center). (86-10-68131166) http://www.ttjrhotel.com/ (in Chinese) 海淀区万寿路北口 17 号 (公主坟城乡贸易中心附近)

Offering the whole spectrum of room types including offices, guests can also take advantage of the hotel's restaurant, business center, shopping arcade and, yes, karaoke!

Accommodation prices per night
¥ under RMB 99
¥¥ RMB 100-199
¥¥¥ RMB 200-299
¥¥¥¥ RMB 300-399
¥¥¥¥¥ over RMB 400

Xinxing Hotel

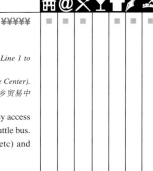

© **Xinxing Hotel** 新兴宾馆   ¥¥¥¥¥

3 star

Price: RMB 400

Transport: Bus 33, 368, 609, 631, 811, 运通 102, 运通 103 or Subway Line 1 to Gongzhufen (公主坟)

No. 17, Xisanhuan Zhonglu, Haidian District (close to Chengxiang Trade Center). (86-10-88236688) www.xinxinghotel.com 海淀区西三环中路 17 号 (城乡贸易中心附近)

This convenient and commodious hotel is perfectly located for easy access to all major sights and business zones. It is a stop for the airport shuttle bus. Geared for business (multifunction halls, conference rooms, etc) and pampering, it also has several good eating and drinking venues.

Siheyuan/Garden-style Hotels

Ⓗ **Ziyu Hotel** 紫玉饭店   ¥¥¥¥

3 star

Price: RMB 300-358

Transport: Bus 489 to Zengguanglu Xikou (增光路西口)

No. 55, Zengguang Lu, Haidian District (close to Capital Normal University). (86-10-68411188) 海淀区增光路 55 号 (首都师范大学附近)

Combining traditional and modern architectural styles, this hotel is just a 10-minute drive from Beijing Zoo or Purple Bamboo Park. A beautiful small garden adds to its appeal. Traditional *siheyuan* courtyard rooms and modern style rooms are on offer.

Itineraries

Itinerary E: "Wild" West Tour

	Expenses

Morning

8.30am Start your day with a roar at the **Beijing Zoo** (see p.134), a great day out for families, kids and animal-lovers alike. Be sure to look in on the resident Giant Pandas. 2 hours are needed here.

10.30am Make your way to the **Beijing Aquarium** (see p.134), and spend one hour in the world's largest non-coastal aquarium, its 36-m-long pool allows you to get up close to the animals—you can almost hear the seagulls!

11.30am Leave by the zoo's south gate, turn right and head west to **Hangshengji** (see p.142) for a fabulous, filling, flavorful Hangzhou-style lunch. Set aside an hour.

Beijing Aquarium: RMB 100 (including Beijing Zoo)

Afternoon

12.30pm Take a post-lunch stroll east and turn left to the rear of the Beijing Exhibition Center (about 10 minutes depending how full you are!). If the weather allows, hop on a boat to the **Purple Bamboo Park** (see p.136) and drift up the river for 20 minutes and get a duck's eye view of the city.

Lunch: RMB 50

1.30pm Take in the beauty of Purple Bamboo Park for half an hour before heading out of the south gate. Cross the road to the Purple Bamboo Park South Gate (紫竹院南门) bus stop and take Bus 114 to Muxidi Dong (木樨地东) (about 20 minutes). Once there, walk east for about 10 minutes to **Capital Museum** (see p.137) for a crash course in Beijing's history and culture—an hour and a half should do the trick!

Boat: RMB 20 (one-way trip)

Capital Museum: RMB 30

4pm Take Subway Line 1 at Muxidi (木樨地), change to Line 2 at Fuxingmen and alight at Fuchengmen Station. Exit from D and you'll see the **Wantong New World Commodities Fair** (see p.149) on the doorstep as you emerge. Its recent renovation makes it a must-see (and buy) shopping bonanza.

Transport fee: RMB 4

6pm End of tour.

Total: RMB 204 (USD 26.5)

Itinerary F: West Waterway Tour

Ever wondered how you could see a totally different side to Beijing? A side where hectic traffic, bikes and pedestrians are not an issue? Well, we strongly recommend taking to the water and hopping a boat! Take one of the city's canal routes and spend a few pleasant hours taking in the scenery from a duck's eye view. These two routes (of the four available) are chosen as providing you maximum natural beauty and minimum skyscrapers! Obviously, during winter when all waterways are solid ice there is no service.

Route 1: Beijing Exhibition Center (北京展览馆)—Kunming Lake in Summer Palace (颐和园昆明湖)

Linking the Summer Palace with Beijing proper, this imperial waterway was the chosen mode of transport for royal families traveling to their summer hideaway. Allow yourself 50 minutes to travel its 9 km course to the Summer Palace.

Along the way watch out for the following: Beijing Exhibition Center (北京展览馆), Beijing Aquarium (北京海洋馆), Beijing Zoo (北京动物园), National Library of China (国家图书馆), Purple Bamboo Park (紫竹院公园), Ziyuwan's faux-ancient architecture (紫玉湾), Wanshousi (万寿寺), Changhewan (长河湾), and Summer Palace (颐和园).

All Aboard

- **Docks:**
Beijing Exhibition Center Dock (北展码头)
Getting there: Bus Bus 15, 19, 26, 107, 716, 732, 812, 特4 to Beijing Exhibition Center (北京展览馆), turn north at KFC
Departs: once an hour between 10am-4pm.
Summer Palace South Gate (颐和园南如意门)
Getting there: Bus 374, 437, 481, 704, 952, 992 to Liulangzhuang Xikou (六郎庄西口)
Departs: once an hour between 11am-5pm
- **Prices:** single trip RMB 40; round trip RMB 70
- **Contact number:** 86-10-88363576/3577

You will need to switch boats at the Purple Bamboo Park's dock to get to the Summer Palace. If you don't wish to visit the palace, you can buy a single-trip ticket to Purple Bamboo Park for RMB 20.

Route 2: Beijing Zoo (动物园)—Jishuitan (积水潭)

This shorter (3.7 km), but equally worthwhile route provides some lovely views of the area's natural scenery, as well as the chance to embark from a royal dock. **Qihongtang** royal dock was often a rest stop for Qing Dynasty Empress Dowager Cixi and Emperor Guangxu. The whole trip takes about an hour.

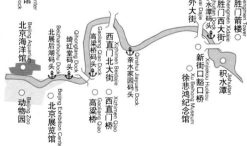

All Aboard

- **Dock:**
Qihongtang (绮红堂), west of Gaoliang Qiao (高梁桥)
Getting there: Bus 601 to Gaoliang Qiao
Departs: once an hour between 8am-9pm
- **Prices:** single trip RMB 25; round trip RMB 50
- **Contact number:** 86-10-62252110/2130

Bus Details

Major Bus Stops

These are the major bus stops in the "West." At each bus stop there are direct routes to key destinations. **They are marked on the map on p.132.**

Beijing West Railway Station (北京西站)

To Beijing Railway Station (北京站): 848 支, 848, 703, 特 2

To Beijing Zoo (动物园): 65

To Grand View Garden (大观园): 运通102, 运通 202

To Lama Temple (雍和宫): 特 2, 820

To Olympic Sports Center (奥林匹克体育中心): 特 2, 387, 702

To Purple Bamboo Park (紫竹院): 374, 437

To Qianmen (前门): 848 支, 301

To Summer Palace (颐和园): 374, 437

To Temple of Heaven (天坛): 运通102, 运通 202

To Yabao Lu (雅宝路): 特 2, 820

To Yuanmingyuan (圆明园): 320, 319, 特 6

To Zhongguancun (中关村): 特 6, 320

Beijing Zoo (动物园), in front of Beijing Zoo

To Beihai Park (北海公园): 814

To Forbidden City (故宫): 814

To Grand View Garden (大观园): 716

To Jingshan Park (景山公园): 814

To Pearl Market (红桥市场): 814

To Summer Palace (颐和园): 634, 808, 716, 332, 732

To Temple of Heaven (天坛): 105

To Weigongcun (魏公村): 特 4 , 814, 716, 634, 808, 732

To Yuanmingyuan (圆明园): 特4, 运通205, 运通 105, 814, 716, 732

To Zhongguancun (中关村): 特4, 运通205, 814, 716, 808, 732

Ganjiakou Shopping Mall (甘家口大厦), in front of Ganjiakou Shopping Mall, across the street from the Industrial and Commercial Bank of China

To Beihai Park (北海公园): 103

To Beijing West Railway Station (北京西站): 319, 320, 727, 827, 特 6

To Beijing Zoo (动物园): 102, 103

To Forbidden City (故宫): 101, 103

To Grand View Garden (大观园): 717

To Jingshan Park (景山公园): 101, 103

To Ox Street (牛街): 特 5, 717

To Summer Palace (颐和园): 特 5

To Wudaokou (五道口): 319

To Yuanmingyuan (圆明园): 特6, 717, 319, 320

To Zhongguancun (中关村): 320, 特 6, 717

Gongzhufen Nan (公主坟南), south of Gongzhufen Subway Station (公主坟地铁站), on Xisanhuan Zhonglu (西三环中路)

To Beijing West Railway Station (北京西站): 运通 102, 运通 202, 374, 52, 373, 437

To Grand View Garden (大观园): 运通102, 运通 202

To Ox Street (牛街): 57, 613

To Purple Bamboo Park (紫竹院): 968, 323, 811, 394, 374, 运通 108

To Summer Palace (颐和园): 394, 817

To Zhongguancun (中关村): 811

Useful Bus Routes

The following is a list of specially selected bus routes passing through the "West" area. These are not all depot-to-depot routes and many less important stops have been omitted. Sights of interest are in bold type. Bus type and times of first and last buses from the first depot are also indicated.

Suggestion: if you are unsure you have the right stop, point out the Chinese characters below for where you want to go and ask another passenger, conductor or driver for help. Many young Chinese have OK English and will be able to help.

运通 105 (standard bus, 6.10am-10.30pm)

Xiwai Dajie 西外大街 -**Beijing Zoo** 动物园 -Baishiqiao 白石桥 -**Weigongcun 魏公村** -**Zhongguancun** 中关村 -**Yuanmingyuan 圆明园**

运通 106 (standard bus, 5.30am-9pm)

Hangtian Qiao 航天桥 -Ganjiakou 甘家口 -**Guanyuan 官园** -**Beijing Zoo 动物园** -National Library 国家图书馆 -**Weigongcun 魏公村** -Renmin Daxue 中国人民大学 -**Zhongguancun 中关村** -Yiheyuanlu Dongkou颐和园路东口-**North Palace Gate 北宫门**

运通 103 (standard bus, 5.20am-8.30pm)

Weigongcun Lu魏公村路 -Wanshousi 万寿寺 -**Purple Bamboo Park 紫竹院** -Gongzhufen 公主坟 -Yangqiao 洋桥 -Muxiyuan Nanzhan 木樨园南站

特 5 (double-decker, 6am-8pm)

Beijing South Railway Station北京南站-Niujie Lukouxi 牛街路口西 -Guang'anmennei 广安门内 -**White Cloud Temple 白云观** -Diaoyutai 钓鱼台-Ganjiakou Shopping Mall 甘家口大厦 -**Purple Bamboo Park South Gate 紫竹院南门** -**Summer Palace North Palace Gate 颐和园北宫门**

7 (standard bus, 5am-11pm)

Beijing Zoo动物园(枢纽站)-Xizhimenwai 西直门外 -**White Dagoba Temple 白塔寺** -Cultural Palace of Nationalities民族文化宫-**Liulichang琉璃厂**-Tianqiao 天桥 -**Temple of Heaven West Gate 天坛西门**

15 (standard bus, 5am-11pm)

Tianqiao Shopping Mall 天桥商场 -Friendship Hospital友谊医院-**Liulichang琉璃厂-**

Cultural Palace of Nationalities民族文化宫-Fuxingmennei复兴门内 -**Yuetan Park月坛公园** -**Beijing Zoo 动物园(枢纽站)**

19 (standard bus, 5am-12am)

Zaolin Qianjie 枣林前街 -Guang'anmennei 广安门内 -Tianningsiqiao Bei 天宁寺桥北 -**Yuetan Park 月坛公园** -Santasi 三塔寺 -Beijing Exhibition Center 北京展览馆 -**Beijing Zoo 动物园**

102 (trolley bus, 4.50am-11pm)

Beijing South Railway Station 北京南站 -**Xidan Department Store 西单商场** -Xisi Lukounan 西四路口南 -**White Dagoba Temple 白塔寺** -Fuchengmen 阜成门 -Zhanlan Lu 展览路 -Ganjiakou Shopping Mall 甘家口大厦 -Baiwanzhuang 百万庄 -**Beijing Zoo 动物园(枢纽站)**

103 (trolley bus, 4.50am-11pm)

Beijing Railway Station West 北京站西 -Sun Dong An Plaza新东安市场-Meishuguan 美术馆 -**Forbidden City 故宫** -**Beihai Park 北海** -**White Dagoba Temple 白塔寺** -Fuchengmen 阜成门 -Ganjiakou Shopping Mall 甘家口大厦 -**Beijing Zoo 动物园(枢纽站)**

107 (trolley bus, 5am-11pm)

Beijing Zoo 动物园 -Beijing Zhanlanguan 北京展览馆 -Santasi 三塔寺 -**Guanyuan 官园** -**Beihai Park North Gate 北海北门** -**Drum Tower 鼓楼** -Dongzhimen 东直门

114 (trolley bus, 5am-11pm)

Purple Bamboo Park South Gate 紫竹院南门 -Baishiqiao Nan 白石桥南 -Sidaokou Dong 四道口东 -Baiwanzhuang 百万庄 -Ganjiakou Shopping Mall 甘家口大厦 -Diaoyutai 钓鱼台 -Baiyun Lu 白云路

118 (trolley bus, 5am-11pm)

Purple Bamboo Park South Gate 紫竹院南门 -Santasi 三塔寺 -**Guanyuan 官园** -**Beihai**

"Academic" Northwest

The northwestern part of Beijing is famous for the **university district**, a concentration of talents and facilities that make this China's academic powerhouse. No surprise then that **Peking University** and **Tsinghua University** (China's equivalents to Harvard and Yale) are located here. Not far from them is **Beijing Language and Culture University (BLCU)**, the most renowned university for foreign students to study

A painting on the Long Corridor of the Summer Palace.

Chinese. This area is also home to **Zhongguancun** (see p.176) where electronics fans can find everything from laptops to PDAs or the latest in MP4s and digital cameras.

Thanks to the large student population, the area is ripe with budget restaurants, both Chinese and foreign, and casual watering holes to quench your thirst, as well as a couple of "must-see" tourist sights such as the **Summer Palace** (see p.160) and **Yuanmingyuan** (see p.164).

Highlights

♦ **Summer Palace** 颐和园 Beijing's biggest and most impressive imperial palace garden; it's no wonder the emperors used it as a getaway. **See p.160**

♦ **Yuanmingyuan** 圆明园 Find your way through the ancient ruins in this royal garden and picture the grandeur that once stood there. **See p.164**

♦ **Great Bell Temple** 大钟寺 A museum displaying bells dating from different periods. Feast your eyes on the biggest bell in China—Yongle Bell, standing 6.75 m tall. **See p.165**

♦ **Arthur M. Sackler Museum of Art**

and Archeology at Peking University 北京大学赛克勒博物馆 Situated on the beautiful Peking University campus, it has a large collection of the university's archeological findings. **See p.166**

♦ **Zhongguancun** 中关村 A business zone dedicated to anything to do with computers. In Zhongguancun, if you can name it, they've got it! **See p.176**

♦ **Wudaokou** 五道口 Gathering spot for "local foreigners," it's one small part of Beijing where the world comes together. **See p.168**

 # Sightseeing

Tourist Attractions

❶ Summer Palace
颐和园 Yíhéyuán ★★★

Emperors' summer getaway
English audio tour

Hours: daily 6.30am-9pm (last entry at 6pm)
Entrance: RMB 30 (Apr 1-Oct 31) and RMB 20 (Nov 1-Mar 31)
Suggested length of visit: 1/2-1 day
Transport: Bus 301, 303, 330, 332, 331, 346, 394, 375, 712, 718, 726, 826, 801, 808, 817, 特5, 特6 to Summer Palace (颐和园)
No. 19, Xinjiangongmen Lu, Haidian District. (86-10-62881144) http://www.summerpalace-china.com/
海淀区新建宫门路19号

❌ *Lily Vegetarian Food (百合素食 86-10-62878726), No. 50, Kunminghu Lu (昆明湖路50号), close to the New Palace Gate (新建宫门) of the Summer Palace, RMB 65/person, a great vegetarian restaurant with a view of a lotus pond. Or try Xibei Youmiancun (西贝莜面村 010-62862150/2151) opposite the North Palace Gate (北宫门) of the Summer Palace, RMB 50/person, Chinese northwest cuisine.*

Beijing's biggest, most impressive and most visited imperial palace garden remains today as an important landmark and cultural heritage site. Its 2.97 sq km of lakes, hills, gardens and halls have been successfully restored to their former glory. It mainly consists of a lake—**Kunming Lake** (昆明湖) and a hill—**Longevity Hill** (万寿山).

Its history dates back to the Jin Dynasty in the 12th-13th century as a royal summer getaway and was called the **Garden of Clear Ripples** (清漪园 Qingyiyuan). Since then it was renovated many times, but not until Emperor Qianlong ordered a large-scale expansion in 1750 to celebrate his mother's 60th birthday did it take its present day shape.

In 1860, it was destroyed by the Anglo-

Don't be fooled by the name. The Summer Palace welcomes guests year round.

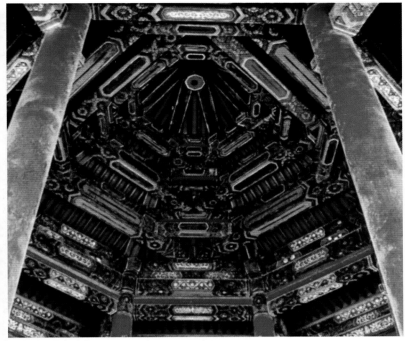

Colorfully painted ceilings remain bright to this day.

French forces. **Empress Dowager Cixi** (1835-1908) embezzled money originally designated for the Chinese navy to reconstruct the Summer Palace in 1886, a move that led to China's defeat in the **Sino-Japanese War of 1895**. In 1888, the garden was renamed Yiheyuan (Garden of Nurtured Harmony), and Cixi moved in and lived there from then on. In 1900, this garden was destroyed again by the Eight Powers Allied Army and was restored by the Qing government in 1902.

Opened as a public garden in 1924 and granted World Cultural Heritage status in 1998, the Summer Palace is one of those places you can't go home without seeing.

Imperial hills and gardens

In the 17th century the Qing rulers decided to turn the area between the city and the Western Hills (西山 Xishan) into a vast pleasure ground with "three hills and five gardens." They were **Garden of Cheerful Spring** (畅春园 Changchunyuan, located in today's Peking University), **Garden of Perfection and Brightness** (圆明园 Yuanmingyuan), **Garden of Tranquility and Brightness** (静明园 Jingmingyuan) at **Jade Spring Hill** (玉泉山 Yuquanshan), **Garden of Tranquility and Pleasure** (静宜园 Jingyiyuan) at **Fragrant Hills** (香山 Xiangshan), and **Garden of Clear Ripples** (清漪园 Qingyiyuan, the predecessor of Yiheyuan) at **Longevity Hill** (万寿山 Wanshoushan).

Marble Boat (石舫 Shifang)
Originally built in 1755, the wooden superstructure of the 36-m-long boat was severely burnt by the Anglo-French Forces in 1860; what we see today is the French-style paddleboat built in 1893.

Tower of Buddhist Incense (佛香阁 Foxiangge)
Easily spotted as the palace's tallest building, the tower stands 41 m tall and has become a symbol of the Summer Palace. The Buddha statues within preside over a magnificent view of the Kunming Lake.

West Palace Gate

Route A: about 2 hours

North Palace Gate (北宫门)-Suzhou Market Street (苏州街)-Marble Boat (石舫)-Long Corridor (长廊)-Cloud Dispelling Hall (排云殿)-Tower of Buddhist Incense (佛香阁)-Hall of Happiness and Longevity (乐寿堂)-Garden of Virtuous Harmony (德和园)-Wenchang Gallery (文昌院)-Palace of Benevolence and Longevity (仁寿殿)-East Palace Gate (东宫门)

Route B: about 2.5 hours

East Palace Gate (东宫门)-Palace of Benevolence and Longevity (仁寿殿)-Garden of Virtuous Harmony (德和园)-Wenchang Gallery (文昌院)-Hall of Jade Ripples (玉澜堂)-Hall of Happiness and Longevity (乐寿堂)-Long Corridor (长廊)-Cloud Dispelling Hall (排云殿)-Tower of Buddhist Incense (佛香阁)-Marble Boat (石舫)-South Lake Island (南湖岛) (by boat)-17-arch Bridge (十七孔桥)-Bronze Ox (铜牛)-New Palace Gate (新建宫门)

Route C: about 3 hours

North Palace Gate (北宫门)-Suzhou Market Street (苏州街)-Tower of Buddhist Incense (佛香阁)-Cloud Dispelling Hall (排云殿)-Long Corridor (长廊)-Marble Boat (石舫)-South Lake Island (南湖岛) (by boat)-17-arch Bridge (十七孔桥)-Bronze Ox (铜牛)-Wenchang Gallery (文昌院)-Hall of Jade Ripples (玉澜堂)-Hall of Happiness and Longevity (乐寿堂)-Garden of Virtuous Harmony (德和园)-Garden of Harmonious Interest (谐趣园)-Palace of Benevolence and Longevity (仁寿殿)-East Palace Gate (东宫门)

Kunming Lake

Marble Boat

Dragon King Temple

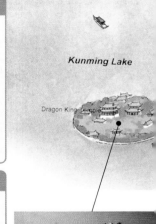

South Lake Island (南湖岛 Nanhudao)
This is the site where Empress Dowag would come and inspect the navy's dril home to many grand halls, one of which **Dragon King Temple** (龙王庙 Longwang It also has an artificial hill, which from th gives you a panoramic view of the lake a Longevity Hill.

of Wisdom (智慧海 Zhihuihai)
s architectural masterpiece was
ated without using a single beam
olumn, hence its nickname "no-
m hall." The outer walls were origi-
y plastered with small Buddhist
ptures, most of which suffered at
hands of modern day invasions.

Suzhou Market Street (苏州街 Suzhou Jie)
This 300-m-long street was originally designed to give the emperors and empresses
their very own shopping plaza. Costumed
staff, traditional shops, teahouses and restaurants add to the historic atmosphere
today.

Garden of Harmonious Interest
(谐趣园 Xiequyuan)
This "garden within a garden" was
modeled after the Pleasure Garden
(寄畅园 Jichangyuan) in southern
China after Emperor Qianlong visited there in 1751. The seasonal
blossoming of various plants ensures year-round beauty.

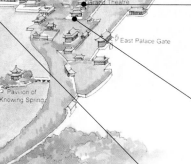

North Palace Gate
Suzhou Market Street
Back Lake
Longevity Hill
Garden of Harmonious Interest
Grand Theatre
East Palace Gate
Pavilion of Knowing Spring
Bronze Ox

Garden of Virtuous Harmony (德和园 Deheyuan)
This garden boasts China's biggest ancient theater—**Grand Theater**. Watching Peking Opera performances here was a favorite pastime of Emperor
Qianlong and, later Empress Dowager Cixi. Today
it holds regular exhibits, including the pictures and
everyday items of emperors and empresses.

**Palace of Benevolence
and Longevity** (仁寿
殿 Renshoudian)
As you enter the east
gate, you'll see this
main palace building
where Emperor
Guangxu (1871-1908)
and Empress Dowager
Cixi received their mini-
sters during their stay
here.

rch Bridge (十七孔桥
ong Qiao)
hite marble 17-arch Bridge
hes for 150 m across the
ng Lake, 544 marble lions
ng guard on its balustrades.

Bronze Ox (铜牛 Tongniu)
Sitting on the eastern bank of the
Kunming Lake and cast in 1755, it
was originally used to control the lake
flooding.

Long Corridor (长
廊 Changlang)
The longest picture
corridor in the world,
the Long Corridor, as
it is aptly known, is
728 m long. Linked
by four pavilions rep-
resenting the four
seasons, the corridor
contains ornate de-
pictions of scenery,
flowers and well-
known folktales.

❷ Yuanmingyuan
圆明园 Yuánmíngyuán ★★★

Once the most amazing royal garden in China

Hours: daily 7am-6pm (summer); 7am-5pm (winter)
Entrance: RMB 35 for an all-inclusive ticket
Suggested length of visit: 1/2 day
Transport: Bus 运通105, 运通205 to
Yuanmingyuan (圆明园); or 365, 432, 656, 717,
743, 811, 814, 特6 to Yuanmingyuan East Gate (圆
明园东门); or 319, 320, 331, 712, 716,726, 801,
825 to Yuanmingyuan South Gate (圆明园南门)
No. 28, Qinghua Xilu, Haidian District. (86-10-
62543673)
海淀区清华西路 28 号

❌ *Leave by the east gate and you will see a parking*
lot, beside it is a nice little café, MIMA (左右间咖啡
86-10-82688003), that serves good coffee and West-
ern food like pizza. RMB 50/person.

Yuanmingyuan, also known as the Old Summer Palace, lies to the east of the Summer Palace. Serving as a palace and pleasure garden for five Qing emperors, it was once the largest and most indescribably magnificent garden in 18ᵗʰ century Beijing. However, what you see now are just broken pillars and collapsed buildings that were burned and plundered by French and British troops during the 1860 Second Opium War and by the Eight-Power Allied Forces in 1900.

It is actually three separate gardens: the earliest **Garden of Perfection and Brightness** (圆明园 Yuanmingyuan) plus the later additions of **Garden of Eternal Spring** (长春园 Changchunyuan) and **Garden of Superb Spring** (绮春园 Qichunyuan, later renamed **Garden of**

Can you make your way to the center, at Yuanmingyuan's maze?

10,000 Springs万春园 Wanchunyuan). At the center is the huge manmade **Lake of Happiness** (福海 Fuhai).

To the north of the Garden of Eternal Spring there is a group of dilapidated European-style Renaissance structures which were designed by Western missionaries commissioned by Emperor Qianlong. From the ruins you can envision how impressive this garden looked in its heyday. Restoration plans for the gardens continue to be rejected due to lack of funds and its capacity to teach patriotism to youngsters. The original **Maze** however has been restored, along with the very attractive Garden of Eternal Spring. For a peek into how it would've looked had it never been destroyed, you can watch the 2006 Chinese movie, *Yuanming Yuan*, which recreates the garden in all its glory.

Today this garden provides an ideal place to enjoy a quiet picnic, for couples to get away from the crowds and for locals to exercise.

Destruction of Yuanmingyuan

To the Chinese, and the rest of the world, Yuanmingyuan remains a bitter reminder of history. After the Anglo-French armies occupied Beijing in October 1860, the British general Lord Elgin ordered the burning of the massive Yuanmingyuan complex and grounds, and the resulting fire raged for three days. Repairs were begun after the withdrawal of the troops, but in 1900, it was re-attacked by the Eight-Power Allied Forces, leaving it in total and irreparable ruin.

Yuanmingyuan ruins.

❸ Great Bell Temple
大钟寺 Dàzhōngsì ★★
Housing the largest bell in China

Hours: 8.30am-4.30pm
Entrance: RMB 10
Suggested length of visit: 1 hour
Transport: Bus 300, 626, 422, 718, 727, 特8 or Light Rail Line 13 to Dazhongsi (大钟寺)
No. A31, Beisanhuan Xilu. (86-10-62550819)
北三环西路甲31 号

With the Museum Pass, you can get two free admissions.

The temple was built in 1733 and originally named the **Temple of Awakening** (觉生寺 Jueshengsi). Because it houses the largest bell in China—**Yongle Bell**, it is popularly known as the Great Bell Temple. The bell was cast in 1406, a marvel of bronze casting technique. It stands 6.75 m tall with a diameter of 3.3 m and weighs 46.5 tons. It is engraved with 17 Buddhist scriptures (230,000 characters in all). Another impressive feature of this bell is its clear and loud sound which can be heard 50 km away on a quiet night.

The temple has now been turned into a bell museum which displays over 300

Yongle Bell, the largest bell in China, on which are carved Buddist sutras.

bells dating from different periods, in different sizes and shapes and used for different purposes. Among them, the most valuable ones are the **chime bells** (编钟 Bianzhong) of the Warring States Period (475-221 BC) and the **court bell** (朝钟 Chaozhong) during the reign period of Emperor Qianlong of the Qing Dynasty.

How was the Great Bell hung in the tower?

With great difficulty. As with the blocks of stone used to build the Forbidden City, they created an ice road and slid the bell to its new home with the help of a lot of men and oxen. When the final destination was reached, they placed the bell on top of a huge earth mound, built a frame around the bell to hang it, then removed the mound. Even the devastating earthquake of 1976 near Beijing hardly moved the bell.

Museums

❹ Arthur M. Sackler Museum of Art and Archeology at Peking University 北京大学赛克勒考古与艺术博物馆★

The first of its kind among Chinese universities

Hours: daily 9am-5pm (last entry at 4.30pm; closed for the first five days of Spring Festival)
Entrance: RMB 5
Suggested length of visit: 1 hour
Transport: Bus 运通 106, 运通 114, 运通 116 to Peking University West Gate (北大西门)
Inside the west gate of Peking University. (86-10-62751667) http://www.amsm.pku.edu.cn/en/
北京大学西校门内

⚡ *With the Museum Pass, you can get two free admissions.*

Funded by Mr. Arthur M. Sackler in 1991, this museum displays many important archeological findings, spanning 280,000 years from the Paleolithic Period to the Qing Dynasty, collected by the archeological department of Peking University. The well-presented exhibits include bronzes of the Shang Dynasty and pottery from the Tang and Song dynasties. As this museum sits on the

Find ancient artifacts without the need of digging.

The tranquil Weiming Lake.

university campus, it is highly recommended to wander along the university's beautiful **Weiming Lake** (No Name Lake 未名湖) after you visit the museum.

❻ Beijing Aviation Museum
北京航空博物馆★

China's very first aviation museum

Hours: 8.30am-12pm, 2pm-5pm (closed on Mondays)

Entrance: RMB 5, RMB 3 for students

Suggested length of visit: 1 hour

Transport: Bus 331, 375, 386, 719, 748, 810 or 944 to Beijing University of Aeronautics and Astronautics (北京航空航天大学)

No. 37, Xueyuan Lu, Haidian District. (86-10-82317513)

海淀区学院路37号

Having started out as a research and teaching center for aeronautics and aviation studies, this is China's very first aviation museum. Its two exhibition halls hold regular exhibits on the history of world aeronautics and China's achievements in aeronautic and astronautic technologies. A collection of some 30 planes including the Mig-15 fighter from the Korean War in 1950 displayed on its outdoor parking apron are worth a look.

Soviet La-11 Fighter produced in 1947.

🍴 Food and Entertainment

Abounding in universities, the northwest of Beijing has become a students' paradise that is full of gems for partying and dealing with hunger.

Here you'll find the bustling student hub of **Wudaokou** (see below), a happening place which almost matches Sanlitun, and continues to be more and more popular as it's way cheaper than Sanlitun. To the west of Wudaokou is China's "Silicon Valley"—**Zhongguancun** (see p.176). It is not just for computers; you'll find mouth-watering food from all over the world, like the American **TGI Friday's** (see p.178). Further south of Zhongguancun is **Weigongcun** (see p.172). Centered on Beijing Foreign Studies University and Central University for Nationalities, it is popular among foreign students and Chinese minorities. **Suzhou Jie** (see p.179), the northern extension of Weigongcun, is a diversity hotspot of high-class restaurants. The restaurants along this street care more about their décor than other places do, so be aware that the food here is a little pricier.

Student centers are not as animated during summer (July-August) and winter vacations (January-February) as most of the students go back to their hometowns.

The following hot spots are marked on the map on p.158.

Wudaokou 五道口

Beijing has over 40,000 foreign students all looking for somewhere to let their hair down after a long day with their noses in their books. Wudaokou, nestling amidst several universities, provides the perfect party zone. It has become, over the last decade or so, the hub of student recreational activity, and bars, eating places, clubs, boutiques and bookstores have spread like wildfire.

With the highest concentration of Korean and Japanese students in Beijing, Wudaokou abounds in Korean and Japanese restaurants, with American fast food and European cafés completing the spectrum. It's no surprise to see many restaurants here have Korean, Japanese and English on their menus.

The newly built **Huaqing Jiayuan** (华清嘉园) apartment complex is now home to many ground floor shops, restaurants and bars—a swanky and trendy area popular with wealthier international students. For a taste of student life, be it budget or luxury, Wudaoku should be your first port of call.

Sights nearby: Summer Palace (see p.160) Yuanmingyuan (see p.164), Arthur M. Sackler

Restaurant listings

Meal prices per adult	
¥	under RMB 29
¥¥	RMB 30-49
¥¥¥	RMB 50-69
¥¥¥¥	RMB 70-99
¥¥¥¥¥	over RMB 100

Chinese

Ganguoju 干锅居

Guizhou cuisine ¥¥

Hours: 11am-2pm, 5pm-10pm (weekdays), 11am-3pm, 5pm-10pm (weekends)

Transport: 运通 110 to Shuangqing Lu (双清路)

2/F, Vision International Center, No. 1, Zhongguancun Donglu, Haidian District (near Tsinghua University East Gate). (86-10-58722008) 海淀区中关

村东路1号威新国际大厦2层(清华大学东门外)

⚡ *7% off if reserved through www. qingke800.com (in English and Chinese)*

The Ganguoju chefs are masters at whipping up traditional spicy-sour Guizhou and Yunnan dishes. It can accommodate parties in its private rooms.

Guolin Home-style Restaurant 郭林家常菜

English menu, non-smoking ¥¥

Hours: 10am-2.30pm, 4.30pm-9.30pm

Transport: Bus 632, 719, 355, 419 to Jingshuyuan (静淑苑)

No. 25, Qinghua Donglu, Haidian District (opposite Golden Tower). (86-10-82377660) 海淀区清华东路25号(金码大厦对面)

This capacious restaurant offers Chinese dishes all at very good prices. Their roast duck is a big hit with all who try it.

Jingchenxuan 景晨轩食府

Sichuan cuisine ¥¥

Hours: 10am-10pm

Transport: Bus 726, 731, 331, 307 to Qinghuayuan (清华园)

No. 160, Chengfu Lu, Haidian District (opposite Tsinghua University South Gate). (86-10-62570813) 海淀区成府路160号(清华大学南门对面)

Spice up your party at this Sichuan restaurant which caters for big and boisterous groups of hungry mouths! Traditional flavor with a slight variation in the menu to suit foreign tastes.

T6 Hotpot T6 香辣火锅

Hotpot ¥¥

Hours: 11am-12am

Transport: see transport to Wudaokou below

3/F, Building 4, Huaqing Jiayuan, Chengfu Lu, Haidian District (opposite Wudaokou Light Rail Station). (86-10-82863791) 海淀区成府路华清嘉园4号楼3层(五道口城铁对面)

Zest and sizzle at Ganguoju.

Museum of Art and Archeology at Peking University (see p.166) and Beijing Aviation Museum (see p.167)

Transport: Light Rail Line 13 or Bus 331, 375, 726, 743, 825 to Wudaokou (五道口).

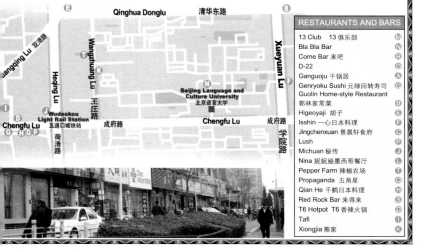

RESTAURANTS AND BARS	
13 Club 13俱乐部	Ⓜ
Bla Bla Bar	Ⓝ
Come Bar 来吧	Ⓡ
D-22	Ⓠ
Ganguoju 干锅居	Ⓐ
Genryoku Sushi 元绿回转寿司	
Guolin Home-style Restaurant 郭林家常菜	Ⓑ
Higeoyaji 胡子	Ⓔ
Isshin 一心日本料理	Ⓕ
Jingchenxuan 景晨轩食府	Ⓒ
Lush	Ⓟ
Michuan 秘传	Ⓙ
Nina 妮妮娅墨西哥餐厅	Ⓛ
Pepper Farm 辣椒农场	Ⓣ
Propaganda 五角星	Ⓞ
Qian He 千鹤日本料理	Ⓗ
Red Rock Bar 来得来	Ⓢ
T6 Hotpot T6香辣火锅	Ⓓ
Tafi	Ⓘ
Xiongjia 熊家	Ⓚ

Highly flavorful, highly spicy, this hotpot has that extra kick to it that sets it apart from the rest. The menu also features unique recipes such as Tofu-based dishes (豆腐拼盘).

Japanese

❶Higeoyaji 胡子

Japanese, Korean and Italian
English menu ¥

Hours: 10am-1am

Transport: Bus 438, 355 to Linye Daxue (林业大学)

Inside Jingyu Hotel, No. A1, Qinghua Donglu, Haidian District (near Beijing Forestry University). (86-10-82388270) 海淀区清华东路1号京裕宾馆内 (北京林业大学旁)

A mixture of Japanese, Korean and Italian cuisines, there will be something on the menu to please any craving. A pleasant and snug little restaurant, it provides for a nice evening.

❻Isshin 一心日本料理

English menu ¥¥

Hours: 11am-2pm, 5.30pm-11pm

Transport: Bus 604 to Chengfu Lukounan (成府路口南)

No. 20, Qinghua Donglu, Haidian District (opposite the east gate of Beijing Language and Culture University). (86-10-62097981) 海淀区清华东路20号 (北京语言大学东门对面)

The elegant décor belies the great, low prices in this swanky yet "studenty" Japanese restaurant. Their lovely, super-fresh sashimi is highly recommended.

Fresh rolls made to order.

The sushi bar will keep your saliva coming strong.

❼ Genryoku Sushi 元绿回转寿司

English menu ¥¥¥

Hours: 10.30am-10pm

Transport: see transport to Wudaokou on p.169

1/F, Huaqing Business Hall, Chengfu Lu, Haidian District (south of Tsinghua University East Gate, beside McDonald's). (86-10-82867858) 海淀区成府路华清商务会馆1层 (清华大学东门南, 麦当劳旁)

📅 Discounts before 5pm.

As Japanese as it gets, all the ingredients that go into their ultra-authentic dishes come straight from Japan. Their salmon sashimi is to die for.

❽ Qian He 千鹤日本料理

English menu ¥¥¥

Hours: 5pm-3am

Transport: see transport to Wudaokou on p.169

No. 12-02, Huaqing Jiayuan, Chengfu Lu, Haidian District (south of Tsinghua University East Gate). (86-10-82863668) 海淀区成府路华清嘉园12号02 (清华大学东门南)

📅 10 % off if reserved through www.qinqke800.com (excluding drinks, buffets and other dishes on special offer) (in English and Chinese)

Two buffets (RMB 68 and RMB 98) are on offer including freshly made and extremely tasty sushi, traditional dishes and some more unusual ones. The many Japanese among the clientele are a good sign.

Italian

❾ Tafi

English menu ¥

Hours: 11am-11pm

Transport: see transport to Wudaokou on p.169

1/F, Tower B, Dongsheng Mansion, No. 8, Zhongguancun Donglu, Haidian District (behind the Lotus Supermarket). (86-10-82527533) 海淀区中关村东路8号东升大厦B座一层 (易初莲花超市后)

📅 11am-2.30pm RMB 29 for lunch buffet; 2.30pm-6pm RMB 20 for afternoon tea sets

Rustic, oven-baked Italian food at reasonable prices. Not that easy to find, but worth the effort.

Korean

❿ Michuan 秘传 ¥¥

Hours: 11am-11pm

Transport: see transport to Wudaokou on p.169

No. 35, Chengfu Lu, Haidian District (north of Dongyuan Plaza). (86-10-62563749) 海淀区成府路35号 (东原大厦北侧)

Large portions of barbecued Korean meats at affordable prices. The chrome and frosted glass décor is somewhat unusual, but it works!

⓫ Xiongjia 熊家 ¥¥

Hours: 9am-12am

Transport: see transport to Wudaokou on p.169

South of Xijiao Hotel West Gate, Chengfu Lu, Haidian District. (86-10-62395521) 海淀区成府路西郊宾馆西门南侧

A chair-free zone for traditional sit-on-the-floor-Korean-style meals, the Xiongjia offers quick meals for people on the go and a great barbecue. Cheap and convenient.

Mexican

⓬ Nina 妮妮娅墨西哥餐厅 ¥¥¥¥

English menu

Hours: 11am-10pm

After the fiesta, relax with a siesta.

Transport: Bus 331, 726, 307, 726, 743 to Lanqiying (蓝旗营)
No. 252, Chengfu Lu, Haidian District. (86-10-62656588) 海淀区成府路252号

Nina's menu includes all those classic Mexican favorites including burritos, tacos and enchiladas, all with a big dollop of salsa.

Bar listings

Prices for a bottle of Tsingtao beer (青岛啤酒), a favorite local beer

¥ under RMB 14
¥¥ RMB 15-24
¥¥¥ RMB 25-34
¥¥¥¥ over RMB 35

13 Club　13俱乐部

Rock, hip hop; live bands
English menu and service　¥
Hours: 8pm-2am
Entrance: RMB 20 (special events prices may vary)
Transport: Bus 331, 726, 307, 726, 743 to Lanqiying (蓝旗营)
No. 161, Chengfu Lu, Haidian District (south of the Lanqiying bus stop). (86-10-82628077) 海淀区成府路161号 (蓝旗营车站南)

This cavernous, graffiti-filled club, pumping out rock and hip hop, is popular with the younger set. Weekends see some good live band performances.

Bla Bla Bar

Students' hangout
English menu and service　¥
Hours: 2pm-2am
Entrance: free
*Transport: Bus 726, 375, 331, 743 to Beijing Language and Culture Uni-*versity (北京语言大学)
Inside Beijing Language and Culture University, Chengfu Lu, Haidian District. (86-10-62397033) 海淀区成府路北京语言大学内

A raucous and lively bar, smack-bang at a hub of student life, offering a fun environment and cheap beer—what more could you want?

D-22

Mixed, live performance, dance
English menu and service　¥
Hours: 8pm-2am
Entrance: RMB 20 for students, RMB 30 for others
Transport: Bus 331, 726, 307, 726, 743 to Lanqiying (蓝旗营)
No. 13, Chengfu Lu, Haidian District (half-way between Wudaokou Sudway Station and Peking University East Gate). (86-10-62653177) www.d22beijing.com 海淀区成府路13号 (五道口地铁与北大东门之间)

Blaring out an impressive selection of live music bands, this American-owned bar prides itself on its music and ambience. A safe bet for a fun night out.

Lush

House, hip hop, live performance
English menu and service　¥
Hours: 24 hours
Entrance: RMB 10 (only charged on Tue and Sun after 9pm)
Transport: see transport to Wudaokou on p.169
2/F, Building 1, Huaqing Jiayuan, Chengfu Lu, Haidian District (opposite Wudaokou Light Rail Station). (86-10-82863566) 海淀区成府路华清嘉园1楼二层 (五道口城铁对面)

Cozy down with a nice hot coffee and your laptop during daylight hours, and let your hair down at night as this fantastically versatile café/pub transforms itself.

Propaganda　五角星

Hip hop, DJ, dance
English menu and service　¥
Hours: 8.30pm-5am (Tue-Sat), 8.30pm-4am (Sun-Wed)
Entrance: RMB 30 for ladies and RMB 50 for men (Wed); free for ladies and RMB 50 for men (Thu); RMB 20 for ladies and RMB 50 for men (Fri); RMB 30 (weekends) (Prices may vary on special events).
Transport: see transport to Wudaokou on p.169
100 m north of Huaqing Jiayuan, Wudaokou, Haidian District. (opposite Wudaokou Light Rail Station). (86-10-82863679/86776689) 五道口华清嘉园北100米 (五道口城铁站对面)

With two floors and its basement being a dance floor, this highly popular nightclub is standing room only on weekends. Jam-packed with students, it's a great place to get down and strut your stuff. Tequila is only RMB 5 on Friday nights.

Come Bar　来吧

Jazz
English menu and service　¥¥
Hours: 10.30am-2am
Entrance: free
Transport: Bus 331, 726, 307, 726, 743 to Lanqiying (蓝旗营)
No. 254, Chengfu Lu, Haidian District

Follow the stairs to a great evening.

Come by Come Bar.

(south of Lanqiying bus stop). (86-10-62653675) 海淀区成府路254号 (蓝旗营车站南)

🔖 *Order half a dozen beers, and snacks are on the house.*

Offering a young and breezy atmosphere this is a favorite student haunt. Chill out in the comfy booths with an ice cold drink (or two!)

ⓢ Red Rock Bar 来得来

Korean style

English menu and service ¥¥

Hours: 4pm-5am

Entrance: free

Transport: see transport to Wudaokou on p.169

North of the east gate of Huaqing Jiayuan, Wudaokou, Haidian District. (86-10-82863665) 海淀区五道口华清嘉园东门以北

Open until the birds start chirping outside, the Red Rock Bar caters for serious night owls in search of greasy food to line the stomach and cheap beer to fill it.

ⓣ Pepper Farm 辣椒农场

Jazz, R&B

English menu and service ¥¥

Hours: 7pm-4am

Entrance: free

Transport: see transport to Wudaokou on p.169

North of Xijiao Hotel, No. 1, Wangzhuang Lu, Wudaokou, Haidian District. (86-10-82372963) 海淀区五道口王庄路1号西郊宾馆北侧

For a boisterous night out, Pepper Farm won't disappoint. Colorful (and lethal) cocktails are flipped and thrown around as talented bartenders whip up some mean concoctions.

Weigongcun 魏公村

Weigongcun, host to several universities (e.g. Foreign Studies University and Central University for Nationalities), used to be concentrated with Chinese Xinjiang Uygur people. Though it has long lost its Xinjiang flavor, you can still find some nice Xinjiang restaurants and other great foods of regional cuisines. A selection of bars and cafés has created a young, trendy scene where good coffee and an arty ambience are the main attraction. **Sculpting in Time** (see p.175) is a particular favorite.

Transport: Bus 332, 320, 716, 808, 814, 特4 to Weigongcun (魏公村).

Restaurant listings

Meal prices per adult

¥	under RMB 29
¥¥	RMB 30-49
¥¥¥	RMB 50-69
¥¥¥¥	RMB 70-99
¥¥¥¥¥	over RMB 100

Chinese

Ⓐ Baoqin Dai Restaurant 宝琴傣味餐馆

Yunnan Dai ethnic cuisine ¥¥

Hours: 11am-2.30pm, 5am-9.30pm

Transport: see transport to Weigongcun above

No. 2, Minzu Daxue Beilu, Weigongcun, Haidian District. (86-10-68483189) 魏公村民族大学北路2号

A top Yunnan restaurant with rock bottom prices. Traditional and authentic, this is Dai food cooked as it should be.

Ⓑ Golden Peacock Dehong Dai Restaurant 金孔雀德宏傣家风味餐厅

Yunnan Dai ethnic cuisine ¥¥

Hours: 11am-9.30pm

Transport: see transport to

Fried potato balls at Baoqin.

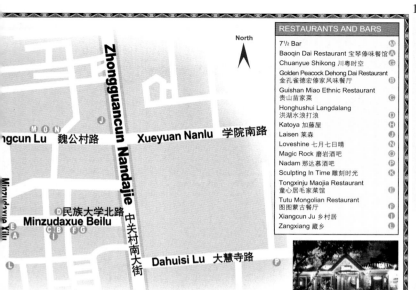

North

RESTAURANTS AND BARS

7½ Bar	Ⓜ
Baoqin Dai Restaurant 宝琴傣味餐馆	Ⓐ
Chuanyue Shikong 川粤时空	Ⓖ
Golden Peacock Dehong Dai Restaurant 金孔雀德宏傣家风味餐厅	Ⓑ
Guishan Miao Ethnic Restaurant 贵山苗家菜	Ⓒ
Honghushui Langdalang 洪湖水浪打浪	Ⓓ
Katoya 加藤屋	Ⓗ
Laisen 莱森	Ⓙ
Loveshine 七月七日晴	Ⓝ
Magic Rock 磨岩酒吧	Ⓞ
Nadam 那达慕酒吧	Ⓟ
Sculpting In Time 雕刻时光	Ⓚ
Tongxinju Maojia Restaurant 童心居毛家菜馆	Ⓔ
Tutu Mongolian Restaurant 图图蒙古餐厅	Ⓕ
Xiangcun Ju 乡村居	Ⓘ
Zangxiang 藏乡	Ⓛ

Weigongcun on p.172
No. 16, Minzu Daxue Beilu, Weigongcun, Haidian District (across from Webok House). (86-10-68932030) 海淀区魏公村民族大学北路 16 号 (韦伯豪对面)

To be sure of a table, book ahead or arrive early; this place is wildly and deservedly popular amongst locals, students and foreigners alike for its ethnic Yunnan dishes.

Guishan Miao Ethnic Restaurant 贵山苗家菜

Yunnan and Guizhou cuisines ¥¥
Hours: 9am-10pm
Transport: see transport to Weigongcun on p.172
Building 14, Minzu Daxue Beilu, Weigongcun, Haidian District (outside the west gate of Central University of Nationalities). (86-10-68421881) 海淀区魏公村民族大学北路 14 号楼 (民族大学西门外)

Frequented by Yunnan and Guizhou students in search of home-style dishes, the food is authentically prepared and served. The Sour soup fish (酸汤鱼) should top the "must-try" list.

Honghushui Langdalang. Good eats!

Ⓓ ## Honghushui Langdalang 洪湖水浪打浪

Hubei cuisine ¥¥
Hours: 10am-10pm
Transport: see transport to Weigongcun on p.172
B1, Building 8, Webok House, No. 1, Weigongcun Lu, Haidian District. (86-10-88571566) 海淀魏公村路1号韦伯豪家园8号楼地下一层

As if plucked straight from a street in Hubei Province, this restaurant offers Hubei foods, Hubei ingredients and even Hubei chefs and staff! Hoobay! Hoobay!

Ancient style mixed with modern flavor. Tongxinju.

❻ Tongxinju Maojia Restaurant 童心居毛家菜馆

Hunan cuisine ¥¥

Hours: 10.30am-12pm
Transport: Bus 320, 716, 808, 特4 to Central University for Nationalities (中央民族大学)
No. 26, Minzudaxue Lu, Weigongcun (near the west gate of Central University for Minorities). (86-10-68439049) 魏公村民族大学路26号(民族大学西门附近)

This incredibly spicy cooking style from Chairman Mao's native Hunan has taken the capital by storm. Fruits are often served as a necessary antidote to the super-spicy dishes. Red-cooked pork (红烧肉), Mao's favorite, and Pickled duck (酱板鸭) are the must-trys.

❻ Tutu Mongolian Restaurant 图图蒙古餐厅

Mongolian cuisine ¥¥

Hours: 11am-2pm, 5pm-9.30pm
Transport: see transport to Weigongcun on p.172
No. 16, Minzu Daxue Beilu, Haidian District (near People's Education Press). (86-10-68468500) 海淀区魏公村民族大学北路16号(人民教育出版社附近)

Good value, hearty Mongolian fare, popular amongst local students. Despite the initial impression, it is actually a very pleasant and spacious restaurant inside.

❻ Chuanyue Shikong 川粤时空

Sichuan and Cantonese cuisines ¥¥¥

Hours: 11am-10pm
Transport: see transport to Weigongcun on p.172
No. 8, Weigongcun Lu, Haidian District (opposite the south gate of Webok House). (86-10-88512313) 海淀区魏公村路8号(韦伯豪南门对面)

Blending Sichuan and Cantonese dishes, two of China's most popular cuisines, is a sure recipe for success, as Chuanyue Shikong proves.

Japanese

❼ Katoya 加藤屋 ¥¥

Hours: 11am-11pm
Transport: see transport to Weigongcun on p.172
No. 304, Weigongcun, Haidian District (walk 300 m north from the west gate of Central University of Nationalities, then head west down the hutong). (86-10-68481766) 魏公村304号(民族大学西门北三百米路西胡同内)

The dishes served at Katoya are like mini pieces of art—colorful and original but paying tribute to their Japanese origins. Katoya's prices are more than fair and their rice dishes are simply superb.

Korean

❶ Xiangcun Ju 乡村居 ¥¥

Hours: 10am-10.30pm
Transport: see transport to Weigongcun on p.172
Building 14, Minzu Daxue Beilu, Weigongcun, Haidian District (diagonally opposite the south gate of Webok House). (86-10-68470318) 海淀区魏公村民族大学北路14号楼(韦伯豪南门斜对面)

Targeting the student budget, this Korean restaurant offers great value for money. They have lots of soups, seafood and cold noodles—all typical dishes.

Bar listings

Prices for a bottle of Tsingtao beer (青岛啤酒), a favorite local beer
¥ under RMB 14
¥¥ RMB 15-24
¥¥¥ RMB 25-34
¥¥¥¥ over RMB 35

❶ Laisen 莱森 ¥

Light music, live performance

Hours: 5pm-3am
Entrance: free
Transport: see transport to Weigongcun on p.172
No. 16, Minzu Daxue Beilu, Weigongcun, Haidian District (opposite the Technology Plaza). (86-10-68468200) 海淀区魏公村民族大学北路16号(理工科技大厦对面)

Beer is RMB 12 per bottle if you buy a dozen.

A Westerner's favorite, it's decorated in an "olde-worlde" pub

Xiangcun Ju Korean serves it well.

On a scale from 1-8, it's 7½!

style with wooden furniture. If you're looking for a taste of the familiar, this is a good bet.

Sculpting In Time
雕刻时光

Light music ¥

Hours: 9am-1am

Entrance: free

Transport: see transport to Weigongcun on p.172

No. 7, Weigongcun Lu, Haidian District (outside the south gate of Beijing Institute of Technology). (86-10-68946825) 海淀区魏公村路7号 (北京理工大学南门)

Popular with students from all over the world, this relaxed and cozy café is a bookworms' dream. It is stuffed with hundreds of books and CDs, contributing to its laid-back atmosphere.

Zangxiang 藏乡

Tibetan style, live performance ¥

Hours: 1pm-1am

Entrance: free

Transport: Bus 320, 716, 808, 特4 to Central University for Nationalities (中央民族大学)

Opposite the west gate of Central University of Nationalities, Weigongcun, Haidian District. (86-10-68715102) 海淀区魏公村中央民族大学西门对面

🗝 *Buy a dozen beers, get one free.*

Zangxiang specializes in all things Tibetan. From the food and décor, to the live singing and dancing, this is an unusual and enjoyable evening's entertainment.

ⓜ 7½ Bar

Pop music, live performance ¥¥

Hours: 2.30pm-2.30am

Entrance: free

Transport: see transport to Weigongcun on p.172

No. 3, Weigongcun Lu, Haidian District (near the Technology Plaza). (86-10-68946711) 海淀区魏公村路3号 (近理工大厦)

With live performances and a swanky, elegant ambience, this is the place to see and be seen. Trendy in a way only Parisians can achieve, it is French through and through.

ⓝ Loveshine 七月七日晴

French music ¥¥

Hours: 11am-2am

Entrance: free

Transport: see transport to Weigongcun on p.172

No. 3, Weigongcun Lu, Haidian District. (86-10-68451137) 海淀区魏公村路3号

🗝 *Buy a dozen beers get two free.*

The perfect hideaway for love-birds wanting to spend a quiet and romantic evening together, Love Shine caters to all things mushy!

ⓞ Magic Rock 磨岩酒吧 ¥¥

Pop music, R&B; live performance

Hours: 7pm-2am

Entrance: free

Transport: see transport to Weigongcun on p.172

No. 3, Weigongcun Lu, Haidian District. (86-10-68451142) 海淀区魏公村路3号

A lively and chilled out atmosphere. The unusual camping and climbing décor may puzzle you; the explanation lies in its being the regular haunt of the West Side climbing club.

ⓟ Nadam 那达慕酒吧 ¥¥

Mongolian style, live performance

Hours: 7pm-2am

Entrance: free

Transport: Bus 26 to Dahuisi (大慧寺)

No. 18, Dahuisi Lu, Haidian District (by the Dahuisi bus stop). (86-10-62126698) 海淀区大慧寺路18号 (大慧寺车站旁)

🗝 *Beer is RMB 15 each if you buy 6 or more bottles.*

For the full Mongolian drinking and dancing experience, Nadam is a lot of raucous fun. Traditional singing and dancing is performed every night—certainly an unusual evening can be spent here.

Hang out with the crew at Magic Rock.

Zhongguancun 中关村

Zhongguancun is Beijing's answer to Silicon Valley. With a rapidly expanding high-tech industry, it is predicted to become China's biggest technological center.

Plans have been made to develop this area to its fullest with bio-tech, medicine, energy-saving technology and IT businesses. Its proximity to Tsinghua and Peking universities and their interest in its research potential make this a likely outcome. Already, with high-tech business and investors well-established, the area has attracted many nice restaurants to open up.

Sights nearby: Summer Palace (see p.160) and Yuanmingyuan (see p.164)

Transport: Bus 307, 302, 320, 365, 运通105, 运通106 to Zhongguancun (中关村).

RESTAURANTS

Back to Lijiang 回到丽江云南特色餐厅	Ⓓ
Banana Leaf 蕉叶	Ⓘ
Caprio Western Restaurant 卡布里奥西菜馆	Ⓙ
CARNAVAL 戈拿旺巴西烤肉	Ⓐ
Chuanjun Bense 川军本色	Ⓔ
Courtyard 四合院风味菜馆	Ⓕ
Dinghao Restaurant 鼎好大酒楼	Ⓑ
Pier Restaurant & Bar 蓝顿港西餐厅	Ⓚ
Shuxiang Zhulin 蜀乡竹林风味酒楼	Ⓖ
TGI Friday's 星期五餐厅	Ⓛ
Tokugawa 德川家日本料理	Ⓗ
Xiao Saozi 小嫂子	Ⓒ

Fourth Haidian Bei
海淀北一
Haidian Daj
Suzhou Jie 苏州街
Dan
Haidian 海淀
Third
Third Ring Road
三环路
Weigc

Restaurant listings

Meal prices per adult
¥ under RMB 29
¥¥ RMB 30-49
¥¥¥ RMB 50-69
¥¥¥¥ RMB 70-99
¥¥¥¥¥ over RMB 100

Brazillian

Ⓐ **CARNAVAL** 戈拿旺巴西烤肉 ¥¥¥

Hours: 11.30am-2pm, 5.30am-9.30pm
Transport: Bus 386, 725, 826 to Zhichunli (知春里)
Building 13, Zhichun Dongli, Kexueyuan Nanlu, Haidian District (opposite Shuang'an Department Store). (86-10-82133026) 海淀区科

Loads of meat at CARNAVAL.

学院南路知春东里13号楼(双安商场对面)

A mouth-watering buffet (RMB 48 for lunch, RMB 58 for dinner) displaying an array of barbecued meats, this is not for vegetarians! A funky saxophonist puts on a good show and provides a relaxed atmosphere.

Chinese

Ⓑ **Dinghao Restaurant** 鼎好大酒楼

Cantonese cuisine ¥
Hours: 11am-11pm
Transport: see transport to Zhongguancun above
5/F, Top Electronic City,

Dinghao Restaurant.

ziye114.com (excluding drinks, seafood and other discounted dishes) (in Chinese)

Its yummy snacks for people on the go are cheap and filling. It also offers a neat view over the area.

Ⓒ Xiao Saozi 小嫂子

Beijing cuisine ¥

Hours: 9.30am-2pm, 4.30pm-3am
Transport: Bus 384 to Shuangyushu Park (双榆树公园)
No. 25, Shuangyushu Beili, Haidian District (north of Modern Plaza). (86-10-62650866) 海淀区双榆树北里25号 (当代商场北)

This novel restaurant has made use of an old opera theater and now provides for a dramatic evening of hearty local cuisine.

Ⓓ Back to Lijiang 回到丽江 云南特色餐厅

Yunnan cuisine ¥¥

Hours: 11am-9.30pm
Transport: Bus 367, 727, 619, 827 to Hongmincun (红民村)
No. 43, Beisanhuan Xilu, Haidian District (100 m west of Lianxiang Qiao, near Shuang'an Department Store). (86-10-62131899) 海淀区北三环西路43号 (联想桥西100米,双安商场附近)

✒ 12% off if reserved through www. qingke800.com (excluding seafood and drinks) (in English and Chinese)

Traditional Yunnan dishes such as Noodle soup with ham, egg, chicken and vegetables (过桥米线), Pineapple rice (菠萝饭) and

Potato balls (土豆球) are the house specialties.

Fight for your right to tasty food! — Chuanjun Bense

Ⓔ Chuanjun Bense 川军本色

Sichuan cuisine ¥¥

Hours: 11am-11pm
Transport: Bus 367, 727, 619, 827 to Hongmincun (红民村)
No. A30, Beisanhuan Xilu, Haidian District (near Shuang'an Department Store). (86-10-68400286) 海淀区北三环西路甲30号 (双安商场附近)

✒ Receive a RMB 20 coupon for every RMB 100 spent.

Choose from the first floor hotpot or second floor Sichuan menu; both are equally good. The service is as impeccable as the staff's military-style uniforms!

Ⓕ Courtyard 四合院风味菜馆

Xinjiang Muslim cuisine ¥¥

Hours: 9am-10pm
Transport: Bus 320, 运通105 to Renmin Daxue (人民大学)
No. 53, Shuangyushu Beili, Haidian District (close to Shuang'an Department Store). (86-10-62572176) 海淀区双榆树北里53号 (双安商场附近)

Full of loyal patrons, this is a favorite with locals. The Lamb shank (羊羯子 Yangjiezi) is by far their most popular dish, and worth shelling out that bit extra for.

Ⓖ Shuxiang Zhulin 蜀乡竹林风味酒楼

Sichuan cuisine ¥¥

Hours: 11am-10.30pm
Transport: Bus 332, 320, 808 to Na-

Zhongguancun, Haidian District (west of Hilon Plaza). (86-10-82699258) 海淀区中关村鼎好电子商城5层 (海龙大厦西)

✒ 12% off if reserved through www.

Treat yourself to the sweet Pineapple Rice at Back to Lijiang.

tional Library (国家图书馆) Building C, No. 48, Zhongguancun Nandajie, Haidian District (opposite National Library). (86-10-62175995) 海淀区中关村南大街48号C座(国家图书馆对面)

Small, cheap portions mean you can try and test different dishes to your heart's content. Their Mashed potato dish (土豆泥) is delicious; be sure to give it a try.

Japanese

 Tokugawa 德川家日本料理

English menu ¥¥¥

Hours: 11.30am-2pm, 5.30pm-9.30pm Transport: Bus 26, 727 to Zhongguo Nongkeyuan (中国农科院) 2/F, Pan-Pacific Plaza, No. A12, Zhongguancun Nandajie, Haidian District (opposite the east gate of Beijing Institute of Technology). (86-10-62109096) 海淀区中关村南大街甲12号赛太大厦2层(北京理工大学东门对面)

The buffet is great value for money. At just RMB 68 you will go home stuffed to the gills. The regular menu is also very appealing and diverse.

Thai

❶ Banana Leaf 蕉叶

English menu ¥¥¥¥

Hours: 11am-2.30pm, 5.30pm-10pm (first floor); 11am-11pm (second floor) Transport: see transport to Zhongguancun on p.176 2/F, Commerce District, Finance Center, Zhongguancun Plaza, Haidian District (opposite Zhongguancun Shopping Center). (86-10-59863666) www.bananaleaf.com.cn 海淀区中关村广场金融中心商业二层(中关村购物中心)

🔑 *Half price for the buffet on the first floor and 12% off for meals on the second floor if you come here on your birthdays.*

Authentic Thai food is served in this lavishly decorated restaurant, a branch of China's largest Thai restaurant chain. The first floor

Creative and exotic. The Banana Leaf.

offers a seafood buffet at RMB 88 or 108. On the second floor its Thai staff will sing for you or invite you to dance with them after the meal.

Western

❿ Caprio Western Restaurant 卡布里奥西菜馆

English menu ¥¥¥¥

Hours: 9.30am-2pm, 5pm-9.30pm Transport: Bus 466 to Zhongguancun Nanlu Dongkou (中关村南路东口) 1/F, Tower A, Rongke Information Center, Kexueyuan Nanlu, Zhongguancun, Haidian District. (86-10-82861553) 海淀区中关村科学院南路融科咨询中心A座1层

🔑 *10% off if reserved through www. qingke800.com (excluding set meals, drinks and other discounted dishes) (in Chinese and English).*

A rather unusual restaurant where the West meets Beijing! Offering Western-style hotpot, and Mediterranean influenced dishes, you get the best of both worlds.

ⓚ Pier Restaurant & Bar 蓝顿港西餐厅

French

English menu ¥¥¥¥

Hours: 9am-10.30pm Transport: Bus 26, 727 to Zhongguo Nongkeyuan (中国农科院) 1/F, Pan-Pacific Plaza, No. A12, Zhongguancun Nandajie, Haidian District (opposite the east gate of Beijing Institute of Technology). (86-10-62109988) 海淀区中关村南大街甲12号赛太大厦1层(北京理工大学东门对面)

🔑 *12% off if reserved through www. qingke800.com (in Chinese and English) or www.ziye114.com (in Chinese) (excluding set meals and other discounted dishes).*

Crack open a nice bottle of wine and let the live piano music wash over you as you unwind and enjoy some good French food.

ⓛ TGI Friday's 星期五餐厅

American

English menu ¥¥¥¥

Hours: 11am-12am Transport: Bus 320, 运通105 to Renmin Daxue (人民大学) 1/F, south of Friendship Hotel, No. 1, Zhongguancun Nandajie, Haidian District. (86-10-68498738) 海淀区中关村南大街1号友谊宾馆南侧一层

🔑 *Put your name card in their lottery box, you might win their lucky draw which is a small TGI's Three-for-all (三式组合) appetizer platter.*

The internationally popular TGI's whacks out all those greasy American classics from burgers to Mexican (as well as dangerously delicious selection of desserts!). Decked out diner-style, it is a fun place to spend the evening, however not the place to go when on a budget.

TGI Friday's, a Western gem in the East.

Suzhou Jie 苏州街

Don't mix it up with the Suzhou Jie in the Summer Palace. This is another magnet for food, a north-south parallel to Zhongguancun, but further west. The restaurants found here can sometimes be polar opposites of each other, some being posh and expensive, while others are very casual "hole-in-the-walls."

Alternatively, if you're after some literary desserts, then **Haidian Book City** and **Zhongguancun Book Building** around the corner will satisfy your hunger!

Transport: take Bus 26, 302, 394 to Beijing Dizhenju (北京市地震局) or 725, 386, 304 to Haidian Nanlu (海淀南路), then walk to your final destination.

RESTAURANTS	
Jinbaiwan 金百万沸腾 180 度	Ⓐ
Meilu Village 美炉村	Ⓑ
Paradise Island 桃源岛餐吧	Ⓒ
Weilan Western Restaurant 维兰西餐厅	Ⓓ

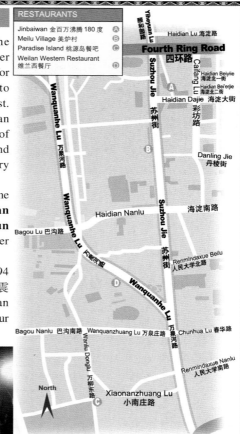

Restaurant listings

Meal prices per adult

¥ under RMB 29
¥¥ RMB 30-49
¥¥¥ RMB 50-69
¥¥¥¥ RMB 70-99
¥¥¥¥¥ over RMB 100

Chinese

Jinbaiwan
金百万沸腾 180 度

Sichuan cuisine   ¥¥
Hours: 11am-10pm
Transport: Bus 26, 302, 394 to Beijing Dizhenju (北京市地震局)

Jinbaiwan
No. 35, Haidian Dajie, Haidian District (near Haidian Book City). (86-10-82620008/0009) 海淀区海淀大街 35 号 (海淀图书城附近)

✒ *10% off if reserved through www. qingke800.com (excluding seafood and drinks) (in Chinese and English).*

If your taste buds crave something fishy, then this Sichuan restaurant will happily satisfy them.

Spicy crab (香辣蟹), fish dishes and Mouth-watering frog (馋嘴蛙) will add a bounce to your step! Ask about discounts for big groups.

Ⓑ Meilu Village 美炉村

Jiangxi cuisine   ¥¥¥
Hours: 10.30am-10.30pm
Transport: Bus 26, 302, 394 to Beijing Dizhenju (北京市地震局)
No. 11, Suzhou Jie, Haidian District (opposite Digital China Building). (86-10-62538883) 海淀区苏州街 11 号 (神州数码大厦对面)

✒ *10% off if reserved through www. qingke800.com (in Chinese and English) or www.ziye114.com (in*

Meilu Village does fowl right.

Chinese) (excluding seafood and drinks).

For a true taste of Jiangxi cuisine and culture, you shouldn't miss this traditional restaurant. One of few Jiangxi restaurants in Beijing, it prides itself on the authenticity of its chicken and duck dishes.

Western

ⓒ **Paradise Island** 桃源岛餐吧　　　　　　¥¥
Hours: 10am-1am

Transport: Bus 365,运通 101, 394 to Changchunqiao Lu (长春桥路)
Xinqidian Jiayuan, No. 5, Changchunqiao Lu, Haidian District (200 m west of Suzhou Qiao). (86-10-82563364) 海淀区长春桥路5号新起点嘉园 (苏州桥西200 米)

🗹 *12% off if reserved through www. qingke800.com (excluding drinks) (in Chinese and English).*

Paradise Island offers diners an unusual array of dishes cooked from organic produce. Healthy, nutritious and extremely tasty, this restaurant will allow you to experience the outdoors, indoors.

ⓓ **Weilan Western Restaurant** 维兰西餐厅
English menu　　　　　¥¥¥¥
Hours: 10am-10pm
Transport: 374, 968 to Daoxiangyuan (稻香园)
No. 75, Wanquanhe Lu, Suzhou Qiao. (86-10-82535055) 苏州桥万泉河路 75 号

🗹 *10% off if reserved through www. qingke800.com (in Chinese and English).*

For a special evening take your loved one to Weilan Restaurant. Gaze into each other's eyes over candlelight and one of their Western-style dishes. You certainly get what you pay for.

Comfy sofa at Weilan.

🛒 Shopping

An abundance of universities and students in the northwest translates into some cheap shopping. **Zhongguancun** (see p.181) is where you'll find every manner of electronic device in one convenient location. For great deals on the latest fashions you can go to **Wudaokou Clothing Market** (see p.181), and bring your bargaining resolve and stamina (the market is big). If what you seek isn't clothing or electronics (heck, even if it is), there's every chance you'll find it at the **Golden Five-star Wholesale Market** (see p.181). This vast warehouse of vendor stalls features everything from office supplies to plumbing accessories.

The following markets and supermarkets are marked on the map on p.158.

Golden Five-star Wholesale Market
金五星百货批发城

One-stop shopping

Hours: 8.15am-6pm

Transport: Bus 601, 123, 650 to Jinwuxing Baihuocheng (金五星百货城)

Xueyuan Nanlu, Haidian District (north of Mingguang Market). (86-10-62226829) 海淀区学院南路 (明光市场北侧)

To describe the produce of this market is an impossible task. Put simply—absolutely everything and anything under one roof! This market is extremely popular with Beijing locals; you may well be the only foreign face there.

Wudaokou Clothing Market 五道口服装市场

Garments and accessories

Hours: 9am-7pm

Transport: Bus 26, 331, 375, 604, 719, 748, 836 to Chengfu Lukounan (成府路口南)

No. 261, Beisihuan Zhonglu, Haidian District (northeast of Xueyuan Qiao). (86-10-62396347) 海淀区北四环中路 261 号 (学院桥东北角)

Filled to the brim with every type, shape and color of garments, bags, shoes, etc, it's a giant Aladdin's Cave of the fashion world.

A booth in Wudaokou Clothing Market.

⑧ Zhongguancun 中关村

Electronics

Transport: Bus 运通105, 运通106 to Zhongguancun (中关村)

Zhongguancun Dajie, Haidian District. 海淀区中关村大街

In Zhongguancun area, you will find everything computer oriented at reasonable prices you could possibly wish for. There are many big electronics buildings, just name a few: Top Electronics City Plaza (鼎好电子商城 86-10-82698269, 9am-9pm), Hilon Plaza (海龙大厦, 86-10-82663883, 9am-8pm). If your Mandarin isn't up to scratch then we recommend taking along an interpreter if you plan to do more than window shop at this electronics Mecca.

⑨ Carrefour 家乐福

Supermarket

Hours: 8.30am-10.30pm

Transport: Bus 302, 801, 特4 to Haidian Huangzhuang Nan (海淀黄庄南)

Zhongguancun Plaza, Haidian District. (86-10-51721517) 海淀区中关村广场

⑩ Walmart 沃尔玛

Supermarket

Hours: 7am-10pm

Transport: 386, 725, 735, 804, 851, 944 to Zhichun Lu (知春路)

B1-2/F, No. A48, Zhichun Lu, Haidian District. (86-10-58733666 or free call at 8009901122) 海淀区知春路甲48号地下1层，地上1，2层

Zhongguancun electronics heaven!

Accommodation

With accommodation choices to suit almost every budget, and the convenience factor of being close to many tourist destinations, shopping hotspots, AND nightlife action, it makes sense to at least consider the "Northwest." For budget travelers, you can find many nice and cheap hotels along **Xueyuan (University) Lu** (学院路), a reference to the nearby universities. If you're willing to pay a little more, **Zhongguancun Dajie** (中关村大街), a parallel to Xueyuan Lu but further west, won't disappoint you. For example, the mammoth **Friendship Hotel** (see p.185) with a vast Asian garden is a great choice, which has been a hit with foreign guests for years.

Be aware that around university admission time from August to September it's hard to get a room, with anxious parents settling their precious offspring into university life.

All places listed below are marked on the map on p.158.

Accommodation prices per night
¥ under RMB 99
¥¥ RMB 100-199
¥¥¥ RMB 200-299
¥¥¥¥ RMB 300-399
¥¥¥¥¥ over RMB 400

Hotels (prices based on double-occupancy rooms)	🏨	@	✕	🍸	👕	🏃
Ⓐ Yunhong Hotel 运鸿宾馆 ¥¥	▪	▪				

2 star

Price: RMB 180
Transport: Bus 16, 726 to Zhixin Beili (志新北里)
No.16, Zhixin Lu, Haidian District. (86-10-82381166) www. yunhonghotel.com (in Chinese) 海淀区志新路16号

The newly decorated Yunhong Hotel is located amidst several university campuses, surrounded by good public transport connections. Comfortable and relaxed, it is an affordable and pleasant option.

Ⓑ Beiti Hotel 北体宾馆 ¥¥	▪		▪		▪	

Price: RMB 180-210
Transport: Bus 743,特4 to Beijing Sports University (北京体育大学)
Yuanmingyuan Donglu, Haidian District (inside Beijing Sports University). (86-10-62989000) 海淀区圆明园东路 (北京体育大学内)

Great value for money, this comfortable economy hotel aims mainly at foreign visitors, with a good selection of amenities.

Beilin Hotel 北林宾馆

2 star

Price: RMB 200-246

Transport: Bus 438, 355, 749 to Beijing Linye Daxue (北京林业大学)

No. 35-2, Qinghua Donglu, Haidian District (inside Beijing Forestry University). (86-10-62338046) 海淀区清华东路35-2号 (北京林业大学内)

The Beilin Hotel offers rooms ranging from single to luxury apartments, all fully equipped with the creature comforts that make such a difference.

Jingyu Hotel 京裕宾馆

2 star

Price: RMB 200-270

Transport: Bus 438, 355, 749 to Beijing Linye Daxue (北京林业大学)

No. A1, Qinghua Donglu, Haidian District. (86-10-62393058) 海淀区清华东路甲1号

Another fabulous budget hotel, Jingyu offers the whole array of room facilities, and spoils guests for choice with standard, double, triple, deluxe or superior room options.

Zhongguancun Hotel 中关村酒店

1 star

Price: RMB 268

Transport: Bus 运通 105, 运通 106 to Zhongguancun (中关村)

No. 19, Haidian Lu, Haidian District (50 m west of Peking University South Gate). (86-10-62565577) 海淀区海淀路19号 (北大南门西50米)

Offering single and double rooms, this budget abode is clean and well equipped. Guests can take advantage of the self-catering kitchen, washing machine and free hot drinks! There's a Korean and Chinese restaurant on-site.

Shengtang Hotel 盛唐饭店

2 star

Price: RMB 280-300

Transport: Bus 374, 651, 704, 634 to Wanquanhe Lu (万泉河路)

No. 2, Wanggongfen, Wanquanzhuang, Haidian District (close to the west gate of Renmin University of China). (86-10-62564433) 海淀区万泉庄王公坟2号 (人民大学西门附近)

A popular choice with foreign visitors, this hotel is neat and tidy, with clean, comfortable rooms and extremely obliging staff. Tours can be arranged through the front desk, in advance or impromptu!

Qinghuayuan Hotel 清华园宾馆

3 star

Price: RMB 260-382

Transport: Bus 331, 375 or Light Rail Line 13 to Wudaokou (五道口)

No.45-1, Chengfu Lu, Haidian District (near Wudaokou Light Rail Station). (86-10-62573355) www.tsinghuahotel.com 海淀区成府路45-1号 (五道口城铁站附近)

Ideally located in the heart of the Wudaokou area, just a few steps away from Propaganda. A range of elegant, modern, nicely decorated rooms come complete with all mod cons to ensure a comfortable stay.

ⓗ Wudaokou Hotel 五道口宾馆

2 star

Price: RMB 280-358

Transport: Bus 331, 375 or Light Rail Line 13 to Wudaokou (五道口)

No. 23, Chengfu Lu, Haidian District. (near Beijing Language and Culture University). (86-10-62316688) 海淀区成府路23号(北京语言大学附近)

The towering Wudaokou Hotel offers 130 rooms as well as a whole host of services and activities. Located in the Wudaokou area, it is close to food and entertainment spots.

ⓘ Dayuan Hotel 达园宾馆

3 star

Price: RMB 280-400

Transport: Bus 375, 331, 726, 运通106 to Yiheyuanlu Dongkou (颐和园路东口)

No.1, Fuyuanmen, Haidian District. (86-10-62561115) 海淀区福缘门1号

Close to Yuanmingyuan and Summer Palace, the Dayuan Hotel is conveniently located and offers single, double or triple rooms as well as bigger luxury apartments, all with efficient and modern facilities.

ⓙ Longdu Hotel 龙都宾馆

2 star

Price: RMB 330-388

Transport: Bus 634, 367, 361 to Wanquanzhuang (万泉庄)

No. 400, Xiaonanzhuang, Haidian District. (86-10-62542277) www.bjlongdu.cn 海淀区小南庄400号

Full to the brim with great facilities and close to many sights in the "Northwest," the spacious Longdu Hotel has an impressive range of rooms and suites.

ⓚ Jimen Hotel 蓟门饭店

2 star

Price: RMB 380

Transport: Bus 836, 398 to Jimen Qiao (蓟门桥)

No. 3, Xitucheng Lu, Haidian District (close to Beijing Film Academy). (86-10-62012211) 海淀区西土城路3号(北京电影学院附近)

The long-established Jimen Hotel has been a foreigners' favorite. They have recently redecorated over half of the 300 pleasant and spacious rooms.

ⓛ Resource Yanyuan Hotel 资源燕园宾馆

3 star

Price: RMB 380

Transport: Bus 运通106, 运通110 to Haidian (海淀)

No.1, Yiheyuan Lu, Haidian District (close to southwest gate of Peking University, opposite the Silicon Valley Computer City). (86-10-62757199) 海淀区颐和园路1号 (北京大学西南门, 硅谷电脑城对面)

Set in the grounds of the Zhongguancun Science Park, this well-equipped and well-decorated hotel has a nice atmosphere and plenty of facilities to add to the pleasures of your stay.

Accommodation prices per night
¥ under RMB 99
¥¥ RMB 100-199
¥¥¥ RMB 200-299
¥¥¥¥ RMB 300-399
¥¥¥¥¥ over RMB 400

Beiwai Hotel

🏛 @ ✗ 🍸 👕 🏃 ⛰

Ⓜ **Beiwai Hotel 北外宾馆** ¥¥¥¥

3 star

Price: RMB 398

Transport: Bus 634, 849 to Weigongcunlu Xikou (魏公村路西口)

No.19, Xisanhuan Beilu, Haidian District (inside Beijing Foreign Studies University).

(86-10-88812255) 海淀区西三环北路 19 号 (北京外国语大学内)

Located on the campus of Beijing Foreign Studies University, the hotel offers 112 standard or luxury rooms—so wonderfully cozy you won't want to get out of bed! They also offer bike rental and free Internet.

Ⓝ **Yiquan Villa Hotel 颐泉山庄宾馆** ¥¥¥¥¥

3 star

Price: RMB 322-460

Transport: Bus 375, 特 4 to Heishanhu (黑山扈)

No.1, Yangchang, Heishanhu, Haidian District (close to the former No. 309 Hospital).

(86-10-62895533) 海淀区黑山扈羊场 1 号 (原三 0 九医院附近)

Guests are spoilt for choice with all the activities on offer, ranging from a bowling alley and swimming pool to a dance hall and billiards room, and even a playroom for the little ones. Good location for visiting Beijing's suburban sites.

Siheyuan/Garden-style Hotel

🏛 @ ✗ 🍸 👕 🏃 ⛰

Ⓞ **Friendship Hotel 友谊宾馆** ¥¥¥¥¥

4 star

Price: RMB 438-518

Transport: Bus 26, 727 to Zhongguo Nongkeyuan (中国农科院)

No.1, Zhongguancun Nandajie, Haidian District. (86-10-68498888) http://www.

bjfriendshiphotel.com/ 海淀区中关村南大街 1 号

This absolutely vast expanse of beautiful gardens is the largest garden-style hotel in Asia, covering a whopping 335,000 sq m. Traditional and elegant, it combines serenity and tranquility with modern facilities and amenities. There are 1,700 rooms, suites, apartments and offices.

Itinerary

Itinerary G: University Bicycle Tour

Tsinghua University 清华大学—**Peking University** 北京大学—**Renmin University of China** 人民大学—**Beijing Film Academy** 北京电影学院—**Beijing University of Aeronautics and Astronautics** 北京航空航天大学—**Beijing Language and Culture University** 北京语言大学

This bicycle tour takes you to visit the best of the best in Beijing's universities. Some of China's greatest minds have once called these institutions home. Beautiful architecture and intellectual history abound.

| | **Expenses** |

Morning

Begin at **Tsinghua University** west gate, where you can rent a bicycle for RMB 2 per hour (or RMB 12 per day) with a 200 RMB deposit. Pick up a Tsinghua map for RMB 4 (Chinese only) and hit the campus through the gate. Spend about an hour and a half, then exit out the west gate.

Bicycle rental: RMB 12

Proceed south along Zhongguancun Beidajie (中关村北大街), take a right at the intersection of Zhongguancun Beidajie and Chengfu Lu (成府路) you'll see the east gate of **Peking University**. Spend another hour and a half there.

Map: RMB 4

Try having lunch in one of campus cafeterias; ask a student for directions.

Lunch: RMB 20

Afternoon

Leave via the east gate and head south along Zhongguancun Dajie (中关村大街). Opposite Modern Plaza (当代商场) is the east gate of **Renmin University of China**. About 45 minutes is enough here.

Leave Renmin University, ride south and make a left at Sitong Qiao (四通桥); continue along Beisanhuan Xilu (北三环西路) till you encounter Jimen Qiao (蓟门桥). Go left, head north five minutes, and you'll see **Beijing Film Academy** to your right. Half an hour is enough for this campus.

Leave by the same gate, go along Xueyuan Lu (学院路). Cross the first overpass you see and you'll find the gate of **Beijing University of Aeronautics and Astronautics**. Wander around in its aviation museum for about an hour, then get back on Xueyuan Lu.

Beijing Aviation Museum: RMB 5

Proceed north. At the intersection of Xueyuan Lu and Chengfu Lu (成府路) you'll see a McDonald's on your left. Head that way, ride for a couple of minutes and you'll arrive at the south gate of **Beijing Language and Culture University (BLCU)**. Get tanked up at **Bla Bla Bar** (see p.171) on campus.

Tour ends here. The bike can be returned the next day.

Total: RMB 41 (USD 5.6)

Tsinghua University (清华大学)
It is formerly a Qing Dynasty imperial garden—**Qinghuayuan** (清华园). This garden has been the home of this illustrious university since 1911. The best spots to view are the former residence of Emperor Xianfeng, **Jinchunyuan** (近春园); the beautiful lake-fronted **Ziqing Pavilion** (自清亭); and the symbol of Tsinghua, the **Second Campus Gate** (二校门).

Beijing Language and Culture University (北京语言大学)
Since 1962, this has been the only university in China specializing in teaching Chinese to foreigners. Its 9,000 foreign students represent a multitude of ethnicities, resulting in the school's reputation as a "mini-UN." There's good, inexpensive food in its dining halls or head to **Bla Bla Bar** for a few pints.

Peking University (北京大学)
Among the oldest and most respected universities in all of China, this school was set up in 1898 in what was the imperial garden of the Ming and Qing dynasties. Don't miss the **Weiming Lake** (未名湖); **Shaoyuan** (勺园), famous Ming painter Mi Wanzhong's (1570-1631) garden; and the **Arthur M. Sackler Museum of Art and Archeology** (see p.166).

…enmin University of China (人民大学)
…is famous research university was formed …1937. The garden **Baijiayuan** (百家园) is …orth a wander. Featured here is a well-known …**nglish Corner**" inside the garden's east …te. Lots of students, including those from …her universities, gather to polish their Eng-…h and meet people on Friday nights.

…jing University of Aeronautics and Astronautics (北京航空航天大学)
…ina's very first institute of aeronautical and astronautic engineering was …ablished in 1952. One of its key features is the **Beijing Aviation Museum** (see p.167), where you can see the recorded history of China's …ationship with flight.

Beijing Film Academy (北京电影学院)
This is where the future stars of film and television come to study. Formed in 1950, it's the biggest film academy in all of Asia.

Bus Details

Major Bus Stops

These are the major bus stops in the "Northwest." At each bus stop there are direct routes to key destinations. **They are marked on the map on p.158.**

Summer Palace (颐和园), southwest of Yuanmingyuan

To Beijing Zoo (动物园): 332, 732, 808
To Fragrant Hill (香山): 737, 331
To Ox Street (牛街): 特 5
To Temple of Heaven (天坛): 826
To Wudaokou (五道口): 331, 726
To Yuanmingyuan (圆明园): 801, 331, 726, 737, 826
To Zhongguancun (中关村): 332, 826, 732

Wudaokou (五道口), close to Wudaokou Light Rail Station

To Fragrant Hill (香山): 726
To Pearl Market (红桥市场): 743
To Qianmen (前门): 726
To Summer Palace (颐和园): 331, 726
To Temple of Heaven (天坛): 743
To Yuanmingyuan (圆明园): 331, 726
To Zhongguancun (中关村): 731, 307

Xiyuan (西苑), between Summer Palace and Yuanmingyuan

To Beijing West Railway Station (北京西站): 特 6, 320

To Beijing Zoo (动物园): 634, 332, 732, 716, 808
To Drum Tower (鼓楼): 834
To Fragrant Hill (香山): 331, 634, 737
To Ox Street (牛街): 特 5
To Summer Palace (颐和园): 726, 732, 817, 826, 394, 737
To Temple of Heaven (天坛): 826
To Wudaokou (五道口): 331, 726, 825
To Yuanmingyuan (圆明园): 432
To Zhongguancun (中关村): 826, 834, 716, 801

Zhongguancun Nan (中关村南), in front of Hilon Plaza (海龙大厦) on Zhongguancun Nandajie (中关村南大街)

To Beijing West Railway Station (北京西站): 特 6
To Beijing Zoo (动物园): 808, 732, 716, 332, 特 4
To Grand View Garden (大观园): 717
To Ox Street (牛街): 717
To Summer Palace (颐和园): 718, 332, 726, 826, 732, 808, 716
To Wudaokou (五道口): 731, 307
To Yuanmingyuan (圆明园): 320, 365, 717, 811, 716, 801, 特 4, 特 6

Useful Bus Routes

The following is a list of specially selected bus routes passing through the "Northwest" area. These are not all depot-to-depot routes and many less important stops have been omitted. Sights of interest are in bold type. Bus type and times of first and last buses from the first depot are also indicated.

Suggestion: if you are unsure you have the right stop, point out the Chinese characters below for where you want to go and ask another passenger, conductor or driver for help. Many young Chinese have OK English and will be able to help.

运通106 (standard bus, 6.15am-9pm)
North Palace Gate 北宫门 -Yiheyuanlu Dongkou 颐和园路东口 -Peking University West Gate 北大西门 -**Zhongguancun 中关村** -Renmin Daxue 人民大学 -**Weigongcun 魏公村** -Baishiqiao 白石桥 -**Beijing Zoo 动物园** -Xizhimen 西直门 -**Guanyuan 官园** -Ganjiakou 甘家口

331路 (standard bus, 5.10am-11pm)
Xinjiekou Huokou 新街口豁口 -Chengfu Lukounan 成府路口南 -Beijing Language and Culture University 北京语言大学 -**Wudaokou 五道口** -**Yuanmingyuan South Gate 圆明园南门** -**Summer Palace 颐和园** -**Beijing Botanical Garden South Gate 北京**

Online ordering
internationally will
be ready soon! In the
meantime, to order
Streetwise Guide Beijing,
please email:
streetwiseguide@flp.com.cn.
Free delivery anywhere within
Beijing's Fourth Ring Road.
Orders from other parts of
China can be made with
additional postal
charges. Readers in North
America can purchase online
at **www.chinabooks.com**.

WHAT READERS SAY

"...The maps and pictures are far superior to any other guide book I have ever used–it's simply all you need!"
—Dianne Maddrell
(Canada, Receptionist)

"...Visiting China for the first time, thanks to this book I used the local subway and buses my entire stay, seeing Beijing through local eyes! The insights provided could only have been written by those with strong appreciation of Chinese history and culture, rare in most guidebooks. I look forward to *Streetwise Shanghai*!"
—Chio, Siew Chin
(Singapore, MBA)

"I highly recommend it to anyone planning to visit Beijing, with so many detailed & useful maps it'd be impossible to get lost using this guide!"
—Patience Manyanhaire
(Zimbabwe, Teacher in Beijing)

"My children are very fussy about food, but this book provides cool & useful information on so many great places to eat (& visit), so for once I won't have to worry. Thanks so much!"
—Kathy Clark
(an Australian mom living in Beijing)

"Olympic" North

The northern part of Beijing is home to Yayuncun (**Asian Games Village**) and the major venues of the **2008 Olympic Games**. It is also an extensive newly rising business and residential area. Since hosting the 11th Asian Games in 1990, northern Beijing has become more and more popular, and not just for sports. When the Olympic flame is lit, Beijing will be in the global spotlight again, and its northern area will be the focus of the spotlight.

To present to the world a splendid Olympics, swathes of the city are being remodeled, new buildings are rising every day and new subway lines scooped out. The new **Olympic Subway Line**, expected to be operational in 2008, will lead you directly into the heart of the **Olympic Park** (see p.192), making the "North" easily accessible.

Nini (the swallow)

Nevertheless, the city's historic past is still with us. In northern Beijing you will find the **Temple of the Earth** (see p.194) and one of the eight finest sights in ancient Beijing— **Yuan Dadu City Wall Site Park** (see p.194).

While sports still continues to be the major theme, the **Chinese Ethnic Culture Park** (see p.192), **China Science & Technology Museum** (see p.196) and **Yanhuang Art Museum** (see p.196) add more than a dash of culture and art.

Highlights

- **Chinese Ethnic Culture Park** 中华民族园 Come here for a glimpse of China's 56 ethnic groups, their culture, architecture, costume and customs and all within the Fourth Ring Road! **See p.192**
- **Olympic Park** 奥林匹克公园 Home to 10 Olympic venues, this will become Beijing's biggest park after the Games. **See p.192**
- **China Science & Technology Museum** 中国科技馆 An absolutely great opportunity for the kid in all of us to explore first hand those won-

ders of science. Perfect for families. **See p.196**
- **Yayuncun Area** 亚运村周边 Sports, drinks, and shopping galore. **See p.198**
- **China Puppet Theater** 中国木偶剧院 Stages traditional Chinese shadow puppet shows and acrobatics. Great entertainment for both children and adults. **See p.205**
- **Dadu Bar Street** 大都酒吧街 The only bar street inside a park in Beijing. Have a great time walking from bar to bar trying their different atmospheres. **See p.202**

Sightseeing

Tourist Attractions

❶ Chinese Ethnic Culture Park 中华民族园
Zhōnghuá mínzúyuán ★★

A living museum of China's ethnic diversity

Hours: 8.30am-4.50pm (winter), 8am-6pm (summer) (the southern park is closed in winter)
Entrance: RMB 60 for one park; all-inclusive ticket RMB 90 for two parks
Suggested length of visit: 3 hours
Transport: Bus 645, 113 to Minzuyuan Lu (民族园路)
No.1, Minzuyuan Lu, Chaoyang District. (86-10-6206/3647) http: //www.emuseum.org.cn/etext/eindex.htm
朝阳区民族园路 1 号
🔲 *With the Museum Pass you can get two tickets for half price.*

To fully understand China, you need to know its different ethnic groups. There are 56 of them, each with particular traditions, celebrations, costumes, and customs, and all are unique.

Sitting at the very south end of the Olympic Park, this culture park consists of two large main sections, divided up into smaller "ethnic" groups. Here, visitors can see well-preserved crafts, enjoy ethnic food, take part in traditional festivals (the Dai **Water-splashing Festival** for example), and experience the living environments of different peoples, from Mongolians in the north, to the Miao in the southwest of China.

Staged presentations include singing, dancing, farming, and traditional crafts in this celebration of ethnic diversity.

❷ Olympic Park 奥林匹克公园
Àolínpǐkè gōngyuán ★★★

Main venue for the 2008 Games, and an iconic architecture

Entrance: free
Suggested length of visit: 3 hours
Transport: Bus 466 to Beichen Donglu Beikou (北辰东路北口)
Datunxiang and Walixiang, Chaoyang District.
朝阳区大屯乡与洼里乡
🔲 *No vehicles are allowed in the Olympic venue area. You may need to take a shuttle bus or walk.*

Beijing's 2008 Olympic Park (Olympic Green) is home to **10 Olympic venues**, the Olympic Forest

56 native ethnicities all rolled into one park.

Park, the Chinese Ethnic Culture Park, the Olympic Village, the Media Center, the Olympic Sports Center and the National Conference Center. The park is designed to unite modern and historic Beijing, drawing on the city's culture, life and energy, so that it will serve the city well in the future.

The **Olympic Forest Park** occupies the northern area, while to the south, is the **Olympic Sports Center** and the **Chinese Ethnic Culture Park**. Post-Olympic plans see this area morphing from China's greatest sporting achievement, to Beijing's biggest multi-functioning business, residential and entertainment zone yet, along with great access to the rest of the city and a massive array of entertainment, food and drink venues.

❸ West Yellow Lamasery
西黄寺 Xīhuángsì ★★

Hours: re-opens by 2008 Olympics

Huangsi Lu, Andingmenwai, Chaoyang District.
朝阳区安定门外黄寺路

This lamasery, built in 1652, is little known to most Beijingers, let alone foreign visitors.

It was a temple of the Yellow Sect of Lamaism, whose monks were so referred to because of their yellow robes and hats. After the **Sixth Panchen Lama** (1738-1780) died in the temple while visiting Emperor Qianlong, the emperor ordered a memorial **stupa** built in his honor, combining Indian, Tibetan and central China styles, and this is the biggest feature of this lamasery today.

There were once two Yellow Sect lamaseries in Beijing—east and west—but only this west one survived. The temple also houses the **China Tibetan-Language Academy of Buddhism** where Tibetan and Mongolian high monks study Tibetan Buddhism. It is currently under renovation and will re-open by the 2008 Olympics.

The West Yellow Lamasery was the former accommodation for visiting emissaries sent by the Dalai Lama and the Panchen Lama.

The large square altar represents the Earth.

❹ Temple of the Earth
地坛公园 Dìtán gōngyuán ★

The place where emperors worshipped the God of Earth

Hours: 6am-9pm
Entrance: RMB 2
Suggested length of visit: 1 hour
Transport: Bus 104, 108, 328, 407, 643, 758, 850, 特 2 to Temple of the Earth West Gate (地坛西门)
East side of Andingmenwai Dajie, Dongcheng District. (86-10-64214657)
东城区安定门外大街路东

As we mentioned before, Beijing has a symmetrical layout. There is the Temple of Heaven, so there is the Temple of the Earth.

This is the place where emperors of the Ming and Qing dynasties worshipped the God of Earth. Built in 1530, this sacred place is second in size only to the Temple of Heaven, making it huge indeed. This holy ground was made open to the public in 1984, and has been a popular tourist attraction and a public park since.

The **temple fair** held here during Spring Festival brings lots of fun, but it can be a surprisingly quiet and tranquil place at other times.

❺ Yuan Dadu City Wall Site Park
元大都城墙遗址公园 Yuándàdū chéngqiáng yízhǐ gōngyuán ★

Home to one of the "eight finest sights of ancient Beijing"

Hours: 24 hours
Entrance: free
Suggested length of visit: 1/2 hour
Transport: Bus 113, 21, 380, 702, 839 to Anzhen Xili (安贞西里)
Xiaoguan, Andingmenwai, Chaoyang District. (86-10-64222821)
朝阳区安定门外小关

Once one of the eight finest sights of ancient Beijing, it's now a public park. In the park is the east-west **Earthen Wall**, which dates back to 1267 and is the remains of the Yuan city wall.

A corner of Yuan Dadu City Wall Site Park.

The eight finest sights of ancient Beijing

Way back in the early Jin Dynasty (12th century), a decision was made to nominate the city's eight finest sights based on their beauty and poetic quality. Later, during the 15th century, Ming Emperor Yongle became the first to commission a guide-book of the capital, in which these eight sites were described in detail. The sites were again honored when Qing Emperor Qianlong had a stele erected at each site, all but one of which remain today (listed below), hidden amidst modern Beijing.

No.	Finest Sights	Present Location
1	The spring clouds on Jade Island (琼岛春荫 Qiongdao Chunyin)	The Jade Island resides in the center of Beihai Park, and is home to the White Dagoba.
2	The autumn breeze over Taiye Pond (太液秋风 Taiye Qiufeng)	Beihai and Zhongnanhai lakes. Zhongnanhai is not open to the public.
3	Dense trees veiled in mist at Jimen Gate (蓟门烟树 Jimen Yanshu)	Jimen Gate is near the remains of Yuan Dadu City Wall, today posing between the North Third Ring Road and North Fourth Ring Road near Jimen Qiao (蓟门桥).
4	The reflection of the moon at dawn from the Marco Polo Bridge (卢沟晓月 Lugou Xiaoyue)	The Marco Polo Bridge is in southwest Beijing, stretching across the Yongding River. While the stele still remains, the chance of admiring the reflection has dried up along with the river.
5	The snow on the Western Hills on a clear day (西山晴雪 Xishan Qingxue)	In the Fragrant Hill Park.
6	The Jade Spring gushing out (玉泉趵突 Yuquan Baotu)	The spring can be found on the Jade Spring Hill, roughly one km west of the Summer Palace.
7	Shades of green at the Juyong Pass (居庸叠翠 Juyong Diecui)	On the Great Wall approximately four km from the Juyong Pass.
8	Sunset at the Golden Terrace (金台夕照 Jintai Xizhao)	The terrace, now long gone, was sited near today's Ritan Park. It was originally set up by King Zhao in the 3rd century, and atop laid gold in an attempt to attract talented people to serve the state.

Museums

❻ China Science & Technology Museum 中国科技馆 ★★

The only national comprehensive sci-tech museum in China

Hours: 9am-4.30pm (closed on Mondays but open during national holidays)
Entrance: Exhibition hall A: RMB 30 for adults;
Exhibition hall B: RMB 30 for adults;
Exhibition hall C: RMB 20 for adults
Suggested length of visit: 1.5-2 hours
Transport: Bus 300, 302, 367, 380, 387, 422, 702, 718, 725, 731, 735, 801, 825, 831, 835, 967, 特8 or 运通101, 运通104 to China Science & Technology Museum (中国科技馆)
No 1, Beisanhuan Zhonglu, Xicheng District. (86-10-6237 1177 ext. 2109) http://www.cstm.org.cn/index.html
西城区北三环中路 1 号

 One of China's main vehicles of public education in science and technology. Of its three exhibition halls, Hall A has permanent exhibitions of modern science, ancient Chinese technology and science for children. Hall B houses one of the biggest astro-vision theaters in the world, while Hall C houses temporary exhibitions.

Art fans and non-fans alike can enjoy the Yanhuang Art Museum.

❼ Yanhuang Art Museum 炎黄艺术馆 ★

The first privately funded art museum in China

Hours: 9am-4pm (closed on Mondays)
Entrance: RMB 10
Suggested length of visit: 1-1.5 hours
Transport: Bus 108, 328, 387, 408, 758, 850, 985, 特 2 to Yanhuang Art Museum (炎黄艺术馆)
No. 9, Huizhong Lu, Yayuncun, Chaoyang District. (86-10-64910909/2902)
朝阳区亚运村慧中路 9 号

🅿 *With the Museum Pass you can get two free admissions.*

Given life by its sponsor, the celebrated Chinese painter Huang Zhou (1925-1997), this museum has continued to grow thanks to donations from art lovers from around the world. Collected here are ancient Chinese paintings, calligraphy, cultural relics as well as contemporary paintings and ancient pottery.

Have fun learning and playing at the China Science & Technology Museum.

Compare your hand to the writer Ba Jin's on the doors to the museum below.

❽ National Museum of Modern Chinese Literature 中国现代文学馆 ★

Preserving the works of modern Chinese writers

Hours: 9am-4.30pm (closed on Mondays)
Entrance: RMB 20
Suggested length of visit: 1 hour
Transport: Bus 119, 409, 422 to Zhongguo Xiandai Wenxueguan (中国现代文学馆)
No. 45, Wenxueguan Lu, Shaoyaoju Beili, Chaoyang District. (86-10-84619054) http://www.wxg.org.cn/index.aspx 朝阳区芍药居北里文学馆路 45 号

Free on the first Sunday of every month and the first three days of the week-long May Day and National Day holidays.

Museum, library and archive all in one, literary works from the 20th

century are displayed here; other exhibits include reproductions of the homes of the most respected writers of the 20th century.

❾ Museum of Chinese Medicine 中医药博物馆 ★

The secrets of Chinese medicine revealed

Hours: 8.30am-4.30pm (Mon, Wed and Fri, except festivals and holidays)
Entrance: RMB 10, half price for students
Suggested length of visit: 1 hour
Transport: 运通104 to Hepingjie Beikou (和平街北口)
Inside Beijing University of Chinese Medicine, No. 11, Beisanhuan Donglu, Chaoyang District. (86-10-64286845/6835)
朝阳区北三环东路11号北京中医药大学内

With the Museum Pass you can get one free ticket.

Thanks to generous donations, the Museum of Chinese Medicine was finally created in 1990 and is today a mighty building housing all things related to the ancient and ever-popular art of Chinese medicine. Two main halls display medicine samples as well as the history behind this age-old traditional healing technique.

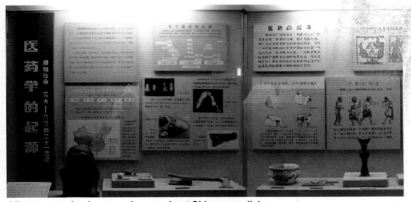

All you wanted to know, and more, about Chinese medicine.

Food and Entertainment

It's very easy to find a restaurant almost anywhere in the North, but if you want to try some special food in a nice environment, a visit to the **Yayuncun Area** (see below) is recommended. If you are searching for something more in the line of bars, **Dadu Bar Street** (see p.202) between the North Third and Fourth ring roads is a new rising star that mostly offers places for people to relax, talk, drink and enjoy a nice show.

If live entertainment piques your interest, check out the **China Puppet Theater** (see p.205) where acrobats (and of course, puppets) delight audiences of all ages!

Ain't no child's play.

The following hot spots are marked on the map on p.190.

Yayuncun Area 亚运村周边地区

By the Yayuncun area, we refer to the Olympic Sports Center, the Asian Games Village and a large residential area nearby. This is one of Beijing's most dynamic and fastest developing city sectors. You can smell the development here as the countdown for the 2008 Olympics ticks by. One obvious result is the growing number of restaurants. Two places, **Datun Lu** (大屯路) and **Huizhong Lu** (惠忠路), have the densest concentration of restaurants in this area. The restaurants here are renowned for their spaciousness, high-quality food, excellent service, even though big bills can be included too.

Sights nearby: Chinese Ethnic Culture Park (see p.192).

Transport: Bus 386, 656, 737, 753, 804, 827, 939, 运通 113 to Yayuncun (亚运村) or 407 to Olympic Sports Center West Gate (奥体西门)

Kehui Xilu 科荟西路

Beichen Donglu 北辰东路

Anli Lu 安立路

Datun Lu 大屯路

Huizhong

Beichen Donglu 北辰东路 Huizhong Lu 惠忠路

Anli Lu 安立路

Beisihuan Zhonglu 北四环中

Beichen Xilu 北辰西路

Minzuyuan Lu 民族园路

Beichen Lu 北辰路

Anding Lu 安定路

Xiaoguan Lu 小关路

Beitucheng Donglu 北土城东路   Beitucher

Jian'an Donglu 建安东路   Jian'a

Restaurant listings

Meal prices per adult	
¥	under RMB 29
¥¥	RMB 30-49
¥¥¥	RMB 50-69
¥¥¥¥	RMB 70-99
¥¥¥¥¥	over RMB 100

Brazilian

Ⓐ Bavarian BBQ 巴伐利亚中西自助餐厅　　¥¥

Hours: 11am-11pm (weekends); 11am-2pm, 5pm-10pm (week days)
Transport: Bus 108, 643, 984, 124, 419 to Anhuiqiao Bei (安惠桥北)
Building 4, Huizhong Lu, Yayuncun,

Bavarian's huge BBQ skewers!

Chaoyang District. (86-10-86251111) 朝阳区亚运村慧忠路 1 区 4 号楼
Cheap Brazilian barbecue buffet. It has free beer 11am-2pm, and half price beer 5-10 pm. Curry chicken wings and roast beef are recommended.

Ⓑ Brazilian Churrascos 巴西烤肉

BBQ
English menu　　　　　¥¥¥¥¥
Hours: 11.30am-2.30pm, 5.30pm-10pm
Transport: Bus 运通 113 to Beichen Lu (北辰路)
1/F, Crowne Plaza, No. 8, Beisihuan Zhonglu, Chaoyang District. (86-10-84982288 ext. 6178) 朝阳区北四环中路 8 号五洲皇冠假日酒店 1 层
The RMB 138 buffet (excluding 15 % service fee) with its unlimited salads and soups should pacify any vegetarian friends at this meat-eaters' heaven. The chicken, beef and lamb, charcoal-grilled to perfection, are all mouth-watering.

Chinese

Ⓒ Aiyao Hunan Restaurant 爱遥湘菜馆

Hunan cuisine　　　　　¥¥
Hours: 10am-10pm
Transport: Bus 108, 643, 984, 124, 419 to Anhuiqiao Bei (安慧桥北) or 运通 113 to Anhui Qiao (安慧桥)
Building 24, Anhuili-1, Yayuncun, Chaoyang District (east of Yayuncun post office). (86-10-64972413) 朝阳区亚运村安慧里 1 区 24 号楼 (亚运村邮局东)

📋 *12 % off if reserved through www.ziye114.com (in Chinese)*

Enjoy spicy Hunan dishes like Stir-fried Chinese bacon (湖南腊肉), Cumin ribs (孜然寸骨) and Spicy shrimp (香辣河虾).

Toad served up hot in Aiyao!

Ⓓ Huangjihuang 黄记煌

Beijing cuisine　　　　　¥¥
Hours: 9am-11pm
Transport: Bus 108, 328, 387, 408, 758, 850, 985, 特2 to Yanhuang Art Museum (炎黄艺术馆)

Xindian Lu 辛店路

Lize Xijie 利泽西街

North

Xiaoying Beilu 小营北路
Yuhui Beilu 育慧北路
Xiaoying Lu 小营路
Yuhui Donglu 育慧东路
...huan Zhonglu 北四环中路
Huixin Donglie 惠新东街
Wenxueguan Lu 文学馆路
Yinghuayuan Dongjie 迎春园东街

RESTAURANTS AND BARS

Aiyao Hunan Restaurant 爱遥湘菜馆	Ⓒ
Ancient Tea-horse Road Bar & Restaurant 茶马驿站酒店	Ⓟ
Bavarian BBQ 巴伐利亚中西自助餐厅	Ⓐ
Brazilian Churrascos 巴西烤肉	Ⓑ
Caprio 卡布里奥西餐厅	Ⓚ
Carburetor 卡布瑞特音乐酒吧	Ⓣ
Flower House Coffee Bar 花舍咖啡酒吧	Ⓓ
Galaxy Bar 银河酒廊	Ⓠ
Huangjihuang 黄记煌	Ⓓ
Jiangzhitian 江织田日本料理	Ⓛ
Meizhou Dongpo Restaurant 眉州东坡酒楼	Ⓘ
Milo Coffee 米萝咖啡	Ⓔ
Music Club 音乐俱乐部	Ⓡ
Nameless Highland 无名高地酒吧	Ⓢ
Northeast Tiger 东北虎	Ⓕ
Red Lotus 红莲烤鸭店	Ⓞ
Sanhe BBQ 三和烤肉	Ⓜ
Seoul City 首尔城	Ⓝ
Taizhongtai 泰中泰泰式新潮料理	Ⓞ
Yijiayao 彝家肴	Ⓙ
Yiwanju Old Beijing Noodles 一碗居老北京炸酱面	Ⓗ

Building 5, Anyuan, Anhui Beili, Yayuncun, Chaoyang District (near Sunshine Square). (86-10-64898620) 朝阳区亚运村安慧北里安园 5 号楼 *(近阳光广场)*

🎁 *Free drink with purchase of the combination pot (组合锅).*

Famous for its Savory fish with sauce (鲶鱼锅). Boil vegetables in the flavorful soup after all the fish is gone.

❺ Milo Coffee 米萝咖啡
Coffee, refreshment
English menu, non-smoking ¥¥
Hours: 8.30am-1am
Transport: Bus 430, 758, 984 to Huizhong Beili (慧忠北里) or 380, 406, 408, 415 to Huizhongli (慧忠里)
No.406, Huizhong Beili, Yayuncun, Chaoyang District (near Beichen Shopping Center). (86-10-64868448) 朝阳区亚运村慧忠北里406号 *(近北辰购物中心)*

This Taiwan-style café features the island's cuisine and refreshments. A great place that's open late, where you can relax with friends or talk business in a pleasant setting.

Gives other coffee stars a run for their bucks.

❻ Northeast Tiger 东北虎
Northeast cuisine ¥¥
Hours: 11am-11pm
Transport: Bus 108, 643, 984, 124, 419 to Anhuiqiao Bei (安慧桥北)
Building 1, Anhuili-2, Chaoyang District (near Beichen Shopping Center). (86-10-64985015) 朝阳区安慧里2区 *1 号楼 (北辰购物中心附近)*

Put a tiger in your tank with delicious northeastern dishes like Roast pork joint (酱大棒骨) and Eggplant with sauce (酱茄子).

❻ Red Lotus 红莲烤鸭店
Beijing cuisine ¥¥
Hours: 11am-10.30pm
Transport: Bus 124, 108 to Datun Nan (大屯南)
Building 111, Huizhong Beili, Chaoyang District (near Huahui Plaza). (86-10-64808411) 朝阳区慧 忠北里 111 号楼 *(近华汇大厦)*

Famous for succulent roast duck, this place offers great prices and a nice array of dishes. Take your family, arrange a banquet or hold a meeting here.

❼ Yiwanju Old Beijing Noodles
一碗居老北京炸酱面
Beijing cuisine ¥¥
Hours: 11am-9.30pm
Transport: Bus 运通113 to Anhui Qiao (安慧桥)
Building 5, Anhuili-4, Yayuncun, Chaoyang District. (86-10-64911258) 朝阳区安慧里4区 5 号楼
Beijing's famous Minced pork sauce noodle (炸酱面) should be eaten here, the best spot in the whole city.

And you will be welcomed by the waiters' "loud" warm greetings.

❽ Meizhou Dongpo Restaurant 眉州东坡酒楼
Sichuan cuisine
English menu ¥¥¥
Hours: 11am-5am
Transport: Bus 430, 758, 984 to Huizhong Beili (慧忠北里) or 380, 406, 408, 415 to Huizhongli (慧忠里)
Building 111, Huizhong Beili, Chaoyang District (near Beichen Shopping Center). (86-10-64800776/0775) 朝阳区慧忠北里111号楼 *(近北辰购物中心)*

Traditional, delicious snacks (under RMB 5) are available all day, complementing a wide variety of typical Sichuan dishes at this great spot for lovers of spicy fare.

❾ Yijiayao 彝家肴
Yi ethnic cuisine

English menu ¥¥¥
Hours: 11am-3.30pm, 5pm-10.30pm
Transport: Bus 108, 643, 984, 124, 419 or 运通 113 to Anhui Qiao (安慧桥)
No. 14, Anhuili, Yayuncun, Chaoyang District. (86-10-64947188) 朝阳区亚运村安慧里 14 号

This place looks like a bar, but is in fact an authentic Yi ethnic restaurant; clean and highly recommended. The house specialty Cold-water fish (冷水鱼) should not be missed.

Italian

❿ Caprio 卡布里奥西餐厅
English menu, non-smoking ¥¥¥¥
Hours: 10am-9pm
Transport: Bus 124, 108, 850, 803, 425 to Datun (大屯)
2/F, Fifth Avenue Shopping Mall, Huizhong Beili, Yayuncun, Chaoyang District. (86-10-64809830) 朝阳区亚运村惠忠北里第五大道商厦2层

🎁 *10 % off if reserved through www.fantong.com (in Chinese).*

Long on history, long on quality, this restaurant's Seafood pizza (海鲜比萨), BBQ chicken bonanza (幸运烧烤) and Ranch-style chicken (农庄烤鸡) are superb, amongst others.

Japanese

ⓛ Jiangzhitian
江织田日本料理
English menu ¥¥¥¥
Hours: 11am-11.30pm
Transport: Bus 108, 643, 984, 124,

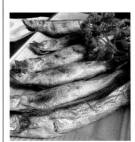

Sink your teeth into these little swimmers.

419 to Anhuiqiao Bei (安慧桥北) Building 1, Anhuili-1, Yayuncun, Chaoyang District (near Beichen Shopping Center). (86-10-64948070/8071) 朝阳区亚运村安慧里1区1号楼(北辰购物中心附近)

A sushi restaurant with a price-scaled buffet menu starting at RMB 70, this place offers a good bang for the buck. The varied menu should suit any Japanese food fan.

Korean

Sanhe BBQ 三和烤肉

BBQ ¥¥

Hours: 10am-10pm
Transport: Bus 119, 125, 361, 379, 406, 602, 713, 807 to University of International Business and Economics (对外贸易大学)
Building 16, Huixin Dongjie, Chaoyang District (opposite the west gate of University Of International Business and Economics). (86-10-64936286)
朝阳区惠新东街16号楼 (对外经济贸易大学西门对面)

Grilled but not greasy, this place features Grilled beef (烤牛肉) and Chicken wings (烤鸡翅) with sides of nice Korean pickles.

Seoul City 首尔城

BBQ
English menu ¥¥

Hours: 9am-11pm
Transport: Bus 119, 125, 361, 379, 406, 602, 713, 807 to University of International Business and Economics (对外贸易大学)
1/F, Huiqiao Hotel, No. 19, Huixin Dongjie, Chaoyang District. (86-10-64918811 ext. 1772)朝阳区惠新东街19号侨饭店1层

Genuine Korean style in Beijing,

Seoul City, haha. Do you get it?

this restaurant stands out from the crowd, serving grilled beef or lamb, with a nice selection of vegetables.

Thai

Taizhongtai 泰中泰泰式新潮料理

English menu, non-smoking ¥¥¥
Hours: 10am-10pm
Transport: Bus 108, 643, 984, 124, 419 to Anhuiqiao Bei (安慧桥北) or 运通 113 to Anhui Qiao (安慧桥) Building 1, Anhuili-1, Yayuncun, Chaoyang District (near Beichen Shopping Center). (86-10-64924680 /4682) 朝阳区亚运村安慧里1区1号楼 (北辰购物中心附近)

Nice Thai-style dishes adapted to suit Chinese taste buds. The result is a fusion worth the visit. House specials are Pineapple and seafood fried rice (菠萝海鲜炒饭), Spicy chicken (椒麻鸡) and Curry vegetables (黄咖喱焗时蔬).

Bar listings

Prices for a bottle of Tsingtao beer (青岛啤酒), a favorite local beer

¥	under RMB 14
¥¥	RMB 15-24
¥¥¥	RMB 25-34
¥¥¥¥	over RMB 35

Ancient Tea-horse Road Bar & Restaurant 茶马驿站酒吧

Chinese ancient ethnic music ¥¥
English menu & service
Hours: 10am-2am
Entrance: free
Transport: Bus 839,113, 645 to Minzuyuan Lu (民族园路) No.1, Minzuyuan Lu, Chaoyang District. (86-10-62361973) 朝阳区民族园路1号

Traditional Chinese decoration in this "ancient" bar can make you feel like you are back in time, particularly when sam-

pling the Tibetan barley wine (青稞酒).

Galaxy Bar 银河酒廊

Light music
English menu & service ¥¥
Hours: 9am-1am
Entrance: free
Transport: Bus 108, 328, 387, 408, 758, 850, 985, 特2 to Yanhuang Art Museum (炎黄艺术馆)
International Celebrity Grand Hotel, No. 99, Anli Lu, Chaoyang District. (86-10-58651166 ext. 6144) 朝阳区安立路99号名人国际大酒店内

A relaxing place in elegant, regal style. Soothing piano music helps you relax in this cathedral-dome-shaped bar.

Relax at Galaxy Bar.

Music Club 音乐俱乐部

Pop music, live band
English menu & service ¥¥
Hours: 5pm-3am
Entrance: free
Transport: Bus 406, 983, 944, 740, 804, 827, 836 to Anhuili (安慧里)
Building 1, Anhuili-4, Yayuncun, Chaoyang District. (86-10-64913308) 朝阳区亚运村安慧里4区1号楼

From Thursday through Saturday, all kinds of live music rock the Music Club, but the rest of the time it's a good place to chill out and discuss music.

Nameless Highland 无名高地酒吧

Live performance
English menu and service ¥¥
Hours: 8pm-2am
Entrance: free
Transport: Bus 464 to Anhuili Wuqu (安慧里五区)
Building 14, Anhuili-1, Yayuncun,

Chaoyang District (50 m south of Bus 387 terminal). (86-10-64891613) 朝阳区亚运村安慧里1区14号楼 (387 总站南50米)

With military-style decoration this cutting-edge bar provides a great ambiance to enjoy music by established and new artists.

❶ Carburetor
卡布瑞特音乐酒吧

Jazz, live performance
English menu and service ¥¥¥
Hours: 9pm-4am
Entrance: free
Transport: Bus 407 to Olympic Sports Center West Gate (奥体西门)
West Gate of Olympic Sports Center, No.1, Anding Lu, Chaoyang District. (86-10-64910228) 朝阳区安定路1号奥体中心西门

This bar is owned by a car club, and car enthusiasts congregate here. The beer garden lets you relax in the open air. "Silver bullet" is the house special drink.

❶ Flower House Coffee Bar
花舍咖啡酒吧

Light music, classics
English menu and service ¥¥¥
Hours: 9am-3am
Entrance: free
Transport: 387, 702, 713, 858 to Xiuyuan (秀园)
1/F, No. 28, Yiyuan, Yayuncun, Chaoyang District (east of Sunshine Square). (86-10-64959139) 朝阳区亚运村逸园28号1层 (阳光广场东)
🔖 *25% off on Chinese food after 10pm.*

Comfortable and quiet, a perfect spot for a nice chat or business lunch. A stream flows through the hall, adding a touch of nature.

Get more than just coffee at Flower House Coffee Bar.

Dadu Bar Street 大都酒吧街

Situated in the Yuan Dadu City Wall Site Park, this bar street was developed by the city government in September 2004. Still quite new compared to the Sanlitun and Houhai bar areas, it is also not as busy. Flanking a canal, it boasts some 40 bars and a bunch of nice restaurants. Most buildings here have huge beams and columns, which remind people of the Long Corridor in the Summer Palace. While many other bar areas are overloaded with foreign visitors, this is a great alternative for enjoying quieter Chinese-style nightlife.

Sights nearby: Yuan Dadu City Wall Site Park (see p.194), Chinese Ethnic Culture Park (see p.192)

Transport: Bus 113, 21, 380, 702, 839 to Anzhen Xili (安贞西里) or 422, 361, 713, 119, 62, 379, 406, 807 to Sino-Japanese Friendship Hospital (中日医院).

Restaurant listings

Meal prices per adult
¥ under RMB 29
¥¥ RMB 30-49
¥¥¥ RMB 50-69
¥¥¥¥ RMB 70-99
¥¥¥¥¥ over RMB 100

Chinese

Ⓐ Zhimahua 芝麻花

Home-style ¥
Hours: 8am-10pm
Transport: Bus 55, 210, 305, 315 , 727, 804, 949 to Qijia Huozi (祁家豁子)
Qijia Huozi, Jiande Qiao, Haidian District. (86-10-62007022) 海淀区建德桥祁家豁子

Cheap, delicious home-style food featuring Baked bean curd threads (拌豆腐丝), Mutton pot (罐焖羊肉), and Guizhou chicken (贵州鸡).

Ⓑ Laobian Dumplings
老边饺子馆

Dumplings ¥¥

Hours: 11am-10.30pm
Transport: Bus 21, 113, 645, 849 to Beitucheng Xilu Dongkou (北土城西路东口)
No. 179, Beitucheng Xilu, Haidian District. (86-10-62352308) 海淀区北土城西路179号

Dumplings are a delicious staple of Chinese cuisine, and this famous restaurant gives you a chance to sample many different kinds. Other traditional northeast cuisine is offered as well.

Ⓒ Shizhongtang 食盅汤

Sichuan cuisine ¥¥
Hours: 9am-12am

The house specialty, Spicy Chicken Pot.

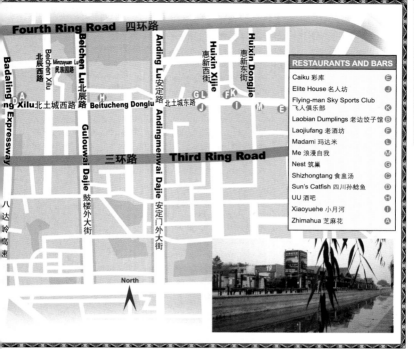

RESTAURANTS AND BARS	
Caiku 彩库	Ⓔ
Elite House 名人坊	Ⓙ
Flying-man Sky Sports Club 飞人俱乐部	Ⓚ
Laobian Dumplings 老边饺子馆	Ⓑ
Laojiufang 老酒坊	Ⓕ
Madami 玛达米	Ⓛ
Me 浪漫自我	Ⓜ
Nest 筑巢	Ⓖ
Shizhongtang 食盅汤	Ⓒ
Sun's Catfish 四川孙鲶鱼	Ⓓ
UU 酒吧	Ⓗ
Xiaoyuehe 小月河	Ⓘ
Zhimahua 芝麻花	Ⓐ

Transport: Bus 21, 113, 645, 849 to Beitucheng Xilu Dongkou (北土城西路东口)

No. 177, Beitucheng Xilu, Haidian District. (86-10-62036867) 海淀区北土城西路 177 号

Fill up here with large portions of cheap, delicious food. The house specials are the "Pot" (锅) dishes served boiling hot with chicken, beef or vegetables. Chicken pot is highly recommended.

Sun's Catfish 四川孙鲶鱼
Sichuan cuisine   ¥¥¥

Hours: 10.30am-10.30pm
Transport: Bus 21, 113, 645, 849 to Beitucheng Xilu Dongkou (北土城西路东口)
Beitucheng Xilu, Haidian District (east of Mudanyuan). (86-10-62386604) 海淀区北土城西路 (牡丹园东)

Come get your catfish! This restaurant has three methods of preparing this river dweller: spicy (麻辣), traditional (家常) and with sour cabbage (酸菜).

Bar listings

Prices for a bottle of Tsingtao beer (青岛啤酒), a favorite local beer
¥   under RMB 14
¥¥   RMB 15-24
¥¥¥   RMB 25-34
¥¥¥¥   over RMB 35

Ⓔ Caiku 彩库
Live music   ¥¥
Hours: 1.30pm-2am

Entrance: free
Transport: Bus 422, 361, 713, 119, 62, 379, 406, 807 to Sino-Japanese Friendship Hospital (中日医院)
No.7, East Dadu Bar Street, Chaoyang District. (86-10-84614500) 朝阳区大都酒吧街东街 7 号

A very colorful and almost bizarre interior sets this bar apart from the rest. First-class bands and dancers perform in this wildly decorated place. Come drink with the beasts.

Get the party on at Caiku.

F Laojiufang 老酒坊

Light music ¥¥

Hours: 4pm-1am

Entrance: free

Transport: Bus 422, 361, 713, 119, 62, 379, 406, 807 to Sino-Japanese Friendship Hospital (中日医院)

No.3, West Dadu Bar Street, Chaoyang District. (86-10-84614287) 朝阳区大都酒吧街西街3号

Step back in time to an ancient Chinese tavern in our own modern world. Try some traditional Chinese wine or sample a healthy Chinese dish from their menu.

G Nest 筑巢

R&B, jazz, rock

English menu and service ¥¥

Hours: 6.30pm-3am

Entrance: free

Transport: Bus 422, 361, 713, 119, 62, 379, 406, 807 to Sino-Japanese Friendship Hospital (中日医院)

No.14, East Dadu Bar Street, Chaoyang District. (86-10-84614690) 朝阳区大都酒吧街东街14号

If you're a darts fan, you've hit the bull's-eye with this place. Relax in this famous bar and work on your game, while socializing and enjoying some good rock music.

H UU 酒吧

English menu and service ¥¥

Hours: 5pm-2am

Entrance: free

Transport: Bus 422, 361, 713, 119, 62, 379, 406, 807 to Sino-Japanese Friendship Hospital (中日医院)

No. 19, West Dadu Bar Street,

Chaoyang District. (86-10-84616637) 朝阳区大都酒吧街西街19号

Postmodern décor with crystal art and roses, plus a live band and great Italian and French food. Take in dinner, a show and a few drinks for good measure.

I Xiaoyuehe 小月河

Light music

English menu and service ¥¥

Hours: 7pm-2am

Entrance: free

Transport: Bus 422, 361, 713, 119, 62, 379, 406, 807 to Sino-Japanese Friendship Hospital (中日医院)

No. 9, West Dadu Bar Street, Chaoyang District. (86-10-84614699) 朝阳区大都酒吧街西街9号

This riverside bar is a good place to meet that special someone. The bar's name (meaning "small moon river") is a clue to its romantic aspirations.

J Elite House 名人坊

R&B

English menu and service ¥¥¥

Hours: 6pm-2am

Entrance: free

Transport: Bus 422, 361, 713, 119, 62, 379, 406, 807 to Sino-Japanese Friendship Hospital (中日医院)

No. 11, Yuan Dadu City Wall Site Park, Chaoyang District (north of the Sino-Japanese Friendship Hospital). (86-10-84614336) 朝阳区元大都城墙遗址公园11号 (中日医院北侧)

You might get to brush elbows with the rich and famous at this bar. Rest assured, you'll be given A-list celebrity treatment here

from the top-notch bartenders and bands.

K Flying-man Sky Sports Club 飞人俱乐部

Pop music ¥¥¥

Hours: 7pm-2am

Entrance: free

Transport: Bus 422, 361, 713, 119, 62, 379, 406, 807 to Sino-Japanese Friendship Hospital (中日医院)

No. 5, East Dadu Bar Street, Chaoyang District. (86-10-84616573) 朝阳区大都酒吧街东街5号

Come in and fly through a few drinks at this glider lover's drinking hole. Founded by flight enthusiasts, there's a real glider above your head to add to the sky-high décor.

L Madami 玛达米

Traditional ethnic music ¥¥¥

Hours: 12pm-2am

Entrance: free

Transport: Bus 422, 361, 713, 119, 62, 379, 406, 807 to Sino-Japanese Friendship Hospital (中日医院)

No. 13, East Dadu Bar Street, Chaoyang District. (86-10-84614399) 朝阳区大都酒吧街东街13号

This bar is interesting because of its Mosuo ethnic minority theme. Culture meets the bar scene with live performances you won't see elsewhere! Ethnic dance performances are staged as well.

M Me 浪漫自我

House, disco, DJ

English menu and service ¥¥¥

Hours: 8pm-2am

Entrance: free

Transport: Bus 422, 361, 713, 119, 62, 379, 406, 807 to Sino-Japanese Friendship Hospital (中日医院)

No.15, East Dadu Bar Street, Chaoyang District. (86-10-84614370/4662) 朝阳区大都酒吧街东街15号

This bar is designed to give patrons a place for self-expression under its flashing neon lights. "Bust a move" in this dance bar that also has live performances of house and hip hop. Show the world, "this is ME."

The comfy belly of the Elite House.

Theaters

The theaters listed below are marked on the map on p.190.

Guo'an Theater.

China Puppet Theater
中国木偶剧院
Shadow puppet shows, acrobatics
Hours: varied play schedule
Price: RMB 20-80
Transport: Bus 104, 108, 117, 387, 426, 850, 特2, 运通101 to Anzhenli (安贞里)
No. A1, Anhua Xili, Chaoyang District. (86-10-64243698) 朝阳区安华西里甲1号
Traditional stories come to life in

the form of shadow and hand puppets. Suitable for kids or adults, the shows also feature acrobatics. Call for event information.

Beijing Theater 北京剧场
Ballet, opera, classical
Hours: 7.30pm
Price: RMB 80-880
Transport: Bus 386, 656, 737, 753, 804, 827, 939, 运通113 to Yayuncun (亚运村)

No.10, Anhuili-3, Yayuncun, Chaoyang District. (86-10-6491228/0516) 朝阳区亚运村安慧里3区10号

Guo'an Theater
国安剧院
Dance, opera, ballet
Hours: according to performance
Price: RMB 80-580
Transport: Bus 16, 726, 815, 851 to Mudanyuan Bei (牡丹园北)
No. A16, Huayuan Donglu, Haidian District. (86-10-62026328) 海淀区花园东路甲16号

Star Live
星光现场音乐厅
Musicals
Hours: 7.30pm
Price: RMB 100-1000
Transport: Subway Line 2 to Yonghegong (雍和宫)
Upstairs of Tango Club, No. 79, Hepingli Xijie, Dongcheng District (50 m north of Yonghegong Qiao). (86-10-64255166/64264436) 东城区和平里西街79号糖果楼上星光现场 (雍和宫桥北50米)

China Puppet Theater is not just for kids.

 # Shopping

Xinjiekou Clothing Street 新街口服装街
Clothes
Hours: 10am-8pm (weekdays), 10am-8.30pm (weekends)
Transport: Bus 22, 47, 726, 826, 409 to Xinjiekou Bei (新街口北)
Xinjiekou Nandajie/Beidajie, Xicheng District. 西城区新街口南大街/北大街
This hip clothing street is where fashionable young women can

shop till they drop. It deserves the reputation as a good place to find something unique, yet cheap. Long and lively, it's perfect to spend an afternoon hunting for that just-right addition to your wardrobe.

Here are some shops worth checking out:
Cao Shi (曹氏 66150568) No. 56, Xinjiekou Beidajie, west-

ern-style women's woolens and interesting Chinese designs.
Xiyinli (吸引力 66510413) No. 52, Xinjiekou Beidajie, has various T-shirts.
A-you (阿尤 66163006) No. 108, Xinjiekou Beidajie, another highlight for Chinese ethnic designs.

Accommodation

Chinese people believe that "North" has better *fengshui* than other directions, which makes the north of Beijing the hottest residential area. Since the **Olympic Park** (see p.192) made its home here, real estate developers have been betting that all this development will continue to raise land prices, and so they continue to raise apartments, shopping malls and office buildings. Hotels also continue to spring up to suit all budgets. The **Yayuncun Area**, embracing two of Beijing's most important sports centers—Beijing Olympic Sports Center and Asian Games Village, is of course one of the hottest places to bunk down. It is, however, also one of the most expensive areas and there are few hostels.

For the budget-conscious, **Andingmenwai Dajie** (安定门外大街) and **Gulouwai Dajie** (鼓楼外大街) have more choices. They are also closer to the center of Beijing and easily accessed by Subway Line 2 (the Loop Line).

When you're coming for sport events, especially if you are planning for the 2008 Olympic Games, make sure to reserve rooms several months earlier to get the best deal.

The places listed below are marked on the map on p.190.

Accommodation prices per night
¥ under RMB 99
¥¥ RMB 100-199
¥¥¥ RMB 200-299
¥¥¥¥ RMB 300-399
¥¥¥¥¥ over RMB 400

Hotels (prices based on double-occupancy rooms)

Ⓐ Longhe Hotel 隆和宾馆   ¥¥

2 star

Price: RMB 150-198

Transport: Bus 104, 108, 119, 113, 358, 328, 803, 407 to Jiangzhaikou (蒋宅口)

No. 78, Jiangzhaikou, Andingmenwai Dajie, Dongcheng District. (86-10-51697500) 东城区安外大街蒋宅口 78 号

With nearly 100 rooms, this hotel enjoys an ideal location, only five minutes' drive from the Asian Games Village.

Ⓑ Daizong Hotel 岱宗大酒店   ¥¥¥

3 star

Price: RMB 198-280

Transport: Bus 602, 702 to Xiaoying Beilu (小营北路)

No. 19, Xiaoying Beilu, Chaoyang District. (86-10-64898808) 朝阳区小营北路 19 号

This hotel is run by the Shandong provincial government, so it must be well equipped and comfortable.

Haoyishe Hotel 好意舍酒店 ¥¥¥

3 star

Price: RMB 209-299

Transport: Bus 108, 643, 984, 124, 419 to Anhuiqiao Bei (安惠桥北)

No.21, Anhuili-3, Chaoyang District. (86-10-64892775) 朝阳区安慧里3区21号

Designed to meet the needs of young travelers, this low priced hotel is clean and comfortable. You can rent bikes here.

Fleet Hotel 福丽特酒店 ¥¥¥

3 star

Price: RMB 240-298

Transport: Bus 300, 367, 387, 718, 801, 825 to Madianqiao Dong (马甸桥东)

No.23, Huangsi Dajie, Xicheng District. (86-10-82087112) 西城区黄寺大街23号

Easily accessible and close to North Third Ring Road. Over 70 double rooms are very well equipped and very reasonably priced.

Diamond Lanbaoyuan Hotel 钻石蓝宝苑宾馆 ¥¥¥

3 star

Price: RMB 260-298

Transport: Bus 117, 300, 302, 731, 735, 749, 825, 954 to Anzhenqiao Dong (安贞桥东)

No.1, Shenggu Zhonglu, Andingmenwai Dajie, Dongcheng District. (86-10-64415533) 东城区安外大街胜古中路1号

Equipped with modern facilities, this moderately-priced hotel offers spacious and comfortable rooms for tourists and business guests.

Capital Sunshine Hotel 都市阳光酒店 ¥¥¥

3 star

Price: RMB 268-288

Transport: Bus 117, 367, 407, 422, 718, 725, 735, 特8 to Heping Xiqiao (和平西桥)

No.3, Heping Xijie, Chaoyang District. (86-10-51309600) 朝阳区和平西街3号

More than half of the guest rooms are equipped with comfortable double beds. Perfect for families and business travelers.

Jinggangwan Hotel 京港湾宾馆 ¥¥¥¥

3 star

Price: RMB 288-368

Transport: Bus 运通104 to Hepingjie Beikou (和平街北口)

No. 11, Beisanhuan Donglu, Chaoyang District. (86-10-64286432) 朝阳区北三环东路11号

Quiet and comfortable and in the grounds of Beijing University of Chinese Medicine, this is a convenient spot to call your temporary home. Internet is RMB 20 per day.

Aoya Hotel

❶ Yungang Hotel 云冈商务酒店 ¥¥¥¥

4 star

Price: RMB 280-448

Transport: Bus 运通 113 to Jianxiang Qiao (健翔桥)

No.68, Huayan Beili, Yayuncun, Chaoyang District (southeast of Jianxiang Qiao). (86-10-82846968) 朝阳区亚运村华严北里 68 号 (健翔桥东南角)

Located to the west of the Olympic Sports Center and the Chinese Ethnic Culture Park, it boasts nice business rooms. Its restaurant offers excellent Shanxi food.

❷ Aoya Hotel 奥亚酒店 ¥¥¥¥

3 star

Price: RMB 318-398

Transport: Bus 358, 602, 713, 751 to Beiyuanlu Datun (北苑路大屯)

No. 169, Beiyuan Lu, Chaoyang District. (86-10-64892299) 朝阳区北苑路 169 号

Five minutes' walk to the Olympic Park, it has 152 rooms of different types. All well equipped.

❸ Yayuncun Hotel 亚运村宾馆 ¥¥¥¥

Price: RMB 360-460

Transport: Bus 108, 643, 984, 124, 419 to Anhuiqiao Bei (安惠桥北)

No.8, Beichen Donglu, Chaoyang District. (86-10-64991188) 朝阳区北辰东路 8 号

Nearly 400 well-equipped rooms at various prices available, from single rooms all the way to luxury suites. International TV channels.

❹ Best Orient Hotel 金梧桐宾馆 ¥¥¥¥¥

4 star

Price: RMB 400-450

Transport: Bus 702 to Jiamingyuan (嘉铭园)

No. 5, Jiaming-1, Beiyuan Lu, Chaoyang District. (86-10-84858822) www.kingwutong.com 朝阳区北苑路嘉铭 1 区 5 号

Located in the Olympic Sports area of Beijing, this hotel features several kinds of well-equipped rooms in Chinese and Western styles and extras like an exercise center.

Long Wise Hotel 龙强大酒店　　　　　¥¥¥¥¥

3 star

Price: RMB 398-560

Transport: Bus 387, 特2, Trolley bus 108 to Olympic Sports Center East Gate (奥体东门)

No.1, Anyuanli, Andingmenwai, Chaoyang District. (86-10-64917666) 朝阳区安定门外安苑里1号

Well-appointed hotel within walking distance of the Olympic Sports Center. Its restaurant provides delicious Cantonese and Sichuan food.

Huiyuan Service Apartment 汇园国际公寓　　¥¥¥¥¥

Price: RMB 400-620

Transport: Bus 108, 328, 643, 984, 124, 419 to Anhuiqiao Bei (安惠桥北)

No.8, Anli Lu, Andingmenwai, Chaoyang District. (86-10-64991555) http://www.huiyuangongyu.com.cn/ 朝阳区安定门外安立路8号

Located inside the Asian Games Village, this hotel has spacious apartment-style rooms all equipped with modern facilities. A large selection of international TV channels makes you feel at home.

Itinerary

Itinerary H: Sports Tour

Morning

8am Start your day at the **Temple of the Earth** (see p.194). Enjoy the local people doing all kinds of morning exercise for half an hour, and maybe learn a few movements of Taijiquan (called Tai Chi in the West). Then explore the historical remains like the **Altar of the Earth** for about half an hour.

9am Exit from the west gate of the temple, walk to Andingmenwai Dajie (安定门外大街), then turn left. Walk for about 200 m, you'll see the Temple of the Earth West Gate (地坛西门) bus stop on the east side of the street. Take Bus 113 and in about 15 minutes you'll arrive at the east gate of the **China Science & Technology Museum** (see p.196). Have some fun and learn some ancient and modern Chinese technology for about an hour. The Astro-vision Theater, one of the biggest in the world, is worth a look.

Expenses

Temple of the Earth: RMB 2

China Science & Technology Museum: RMB 80

10.30am Exit from the east gate and your next destination is the **Chinese Ethnic Culture Park** (see p.192), taking Bus 113 and getting off at Minzuyuan Lu (民族园路). (About 15 minutes by bus)

10.45am Explore the multi-ethnic culture of China in this beautiful park for about two hours. If it's summer, you can experience the Dai Water-splashing Festival where people splash or pour water over each other; or join in their bamboo dance. Eat snacks in the park for lunch.

Chinese Ethnic
Culture Park:
RMB 90

Afternoon

1pm Exit the park and walk east along Minzuyuan Lu until you cross Beichen Lu (北辰路). You'll see the west gate of the **National Olympic Sports Center** (国家奥林匹克中心). Three Olympic venues—Olympic Sports Center Stadium, Olympic Sports Center Gym and Ying Tung Natatorium—are situated inside. Explore these places to get an idea of the Beijing Olympics. 45 minutes should be enough.

2pm Exit from the north gate and cross the street; to your right is the block of **Asian Games Village** which was built for the 11th Asian Games in 1990. Walking along Beichen Donglu (北辰东路), view the group of buildings (including the International Convention Center and the Continental Grand Hotel) that were the working and living areas for the media, Asian Games Committee, and athletes during the Asian Games. Today they've been transformed into office buildings, apartments or hotels. In the center of the buildings is a beautiful semicircular park, where you can rest your feet. One hour is enough to spend in this block.

3pm Across Beichen Donglu is the **Olympic Park** (see p.192), the most important place for the Beijing Olympics and the best place to learn about the Olympics. You'll need about two hours here. First have a look at the amazing architectural masterpiece—the **National Stadium (Bird's Nest)** and take a picture there. Then walk west from there to see the **National Aquatics Center (Watercube)**, another Olympic venue. Then walk north along the road to check the following venues—**Olympic Indoor Stadium** and the **Fencing Hall**. Continue north to the **Olympic Forest Park** (complete by the end of 2007), the biggest park in Beijing.

Transport:
RMB 2

5pm End of the tour.

Total: RMB 174 (USD 23.8)

Bus Details

Major Bus Stops

These are the major bus stops in the "North." At each bus stop there are direct routes to key destinations. **They are marked on the map on p.190.**

Anzhenli (安贞里), close to Anzhen Qiao (安贞桥)

To Beihai Park (北海公园): 850
To Beijing West Railway Station (北京西站): 特2
To China Science & Technology Museum (中国科技馆): 运通101, 运通104
To Drum Tower (鼓楼): 124
To Forbidden City (故宫): 124
To Jingshan Park (景山公园): 124
To Lama Temple (雍和宫): 117, 特2
To Temple of Heaven (天坛): 803

Beitaipingqiao Xi (北太平桥西), west of Beitaiping Qiao (北太平桥)

To Beijing West Railway Station (北京西站): 387, 702, 727
To Chaoyang Park (朝阳公园): 731, 831

To Fragrant Hill (香山): 331
To Summer Palace (颐和园): 718, 801, 331
To Wudaokou (五道口): 331
To Yuanmingyuan (圆明园): 801, 331
To Zhongguancun (中关村): 801

Yayuncun (亚运村), on Beisihuan Zhonglu (北四环中路), north of the Olympic Sports Center

To Beijing West Railway Station (北京西站): 827
To Grand View Garden (大观园): 939
To Summer Palace (颐和园): 737
To Fragrant Hill (香山): 737
To Wudaokou (五道口): 656
To Yuanmingyuan (圆明园): 656
To Zhongguancun (中关村): 737, 运通113, 983 支, 740 外

Useful Bus Routes

The following is a list of specially selected bus routes passing through the "North" area. These are not all depot-to-depot routes and many less important stops have been omitted. Sights of interest are in bold type. Bus type and times of first and last buses from the first depot are also indicated.

Suggestion: if you are unsure you have the right stop, point out the Chinese characters below for where you want to go and ask another passenger, conductor or driver for help. Many young Chinese have OK English and will be able to help.

运通104 (standard bus, 5.45am-9.30pm)
Holiday Inn Lido 丽都饭店 -Anzhen Qiao 安贞桥 -**China Science & Technology Museum** 中国科技馆 -Xinjiekou Huokou 新街口豁口 -Xiwai Dajie 西外大街 -

Beijing Zoo动物园-**Purple Bamboo Park** 紫竹院

特2 (double-decker, 5.30am-7.30pm)
Beijing West Railway Station 北京西站 -**Qianmen East**前门东-Beijingzhankou Dong

北京站口东 - **Y a b a o   L u** 雅宝路 - Yonghegongqiao Dong 雍和宫桥东 - Gulouwai Dajie Beizhan 鼓楼外大街北站 - Anzhen Xili 安贞里 - **Olympic Sports Center East Gate** 奥体东门 - **Yanhuang Art Museum** 炎黄艺术馆

21 (standard bus, 5am-11pm)

Beijing West Railway Station 北京西站 - **Military Museum** 军事博物馆 - Yuetan Stadium 月坛体育场 - Xizhimen Nan 西直门南 - **China Science & Technology Museum East Gate** 中国科技馆东门

108 (trolley bus, 5am-11pm)

Meishuguan Bei 美术馆北 - Dafosi 大佛寺 - Andingmennei 安定门内 - **Temple of the Earth West Gate** 地坛西门 - **Olympic Sports Center East Gate** 奥体东门 - **Yanhuang Art Museum** 炎黄艺术馆

119 (standard bus, 5am-11pm)

Temple of the Earth West Gate 地坛西门 - Jiangzhaikou 蒋宅口 - Huixin Xijie 惠新西街 - **National Museum of Modern Chinese Literature** 中国现代文学馆 - Shaoyaoju 芍药居

124 (standard bus, 6am-10pm)

Yanhuang Art Museum 炎黄艺术馆 - **Olympic Sports Center East Gate** 奥体东门 - **Temple of the Earth West Gate** 地坛西门 - **Drum Tower** 鼓楼 - Jingshan Dongjie 景山东街 - **Jingshan Park East Gate** 景山东门 - **Forbidden City** 故宫 - **Beihai Park** 北海

328 (standard bus, 5.30am-10.30pm)

Andingmen 安定门 - **Temple of the Earth West Gate** 地坛西门 - Jiangzhaikou 蒋宅口 - Anzhenqiao Bei 安贞桥北 - **Olympic Sports Center East Gate** 奥体东门 - Anhuiqiao Bei 安慧桥北 - **Yanhuang Art Museum** 炎黄艺术馆

367 (standard bus, 5.30am-10pm)

Jimenqiao Dong 蓟门桥东 - Beitaipingqiao Xi 北太平桥西 - **China Science & Technology Museum** 中国科技馆 - Anzhenqiao Xi 安贞桥西 - Xibahe 西坝河 - International Exhibition Center 国际展览中心

380 (standard bus, 6am-10pm)

Deshengmen 德胜门 - Gulouwai Dajie Beizhan 鼓楼外大街北站 - **Olympic Sports Center East Gate** 奥体东门 - Anhuiqiao Bei 安慧桥北 - **Yanhuang Art Museum** 炎黄艺术馆 - Huizhongli 惠中里

387 (standard bus, 5.30am-11pm)

Beijing West Railway Station 北京西站 - Xizhimen Nan 西直门南 - **China Science & Technology Museum** 中国科技馆 - Anzhenli 安贞里 - **Olympic Sports Center East Gate** 奥体东门 - **Yanhuang Art Museum** 炎黄艺术馆

407 (standard bus, 6am-10.30pm)

Andingmen 安定门 - Temple of the Earth West Gate 地坛西门 - **Chinese Ethnic Culture Park** 中华民族园 - **Olympic Sports Center West Gate** 奥体西门 - Beichenqiao Xi 北辰桥西 - Qinghe 清河

409 (standard bus, 5.30am-8.30pm)

Fuchengmennei 阜成门内 - **White Dagoba Temple** 白塔寺 - Deshengmen 德胜门 - **China Science & Technology Museum East Gate** 中国科技馆东门 - Beitucheng Donglu 北土城东路 - **Olympic Sports Center East Gate** 奥体东门 - **National Museum of Modern Chinese Literature** 中国现代文学馆

731 (standard bus, 5.30am-8pm)

Chaoyang Park 朝阳公园 - Liangma Qiao 亮马桥 - Sanyuan Qiao 三元桥 - Anzhenqiao Dong 安贞桥东 - **China Science & Technology Museum** 中国科技馆 - Zhongguancun Nan 中关村南 - Zhongguanyuan 中关园 - Qinghuayuan 清华园 - **Wudaokou** 五道口

737 (standard bus, 5.40am-7.30pm)

Fragrant Hill 香山 -Wofosi 卧佛寺 -**Summer Palace** 颐和园 -Xiyuan 西苑 -**Yuanmingyuan South Gate** 圆明园南门 -Tsinghua University West Gate 清华大学西门 -Zhongguanyuan 中关园 -**Yayuncun 亚运村**

801 (standard bus, 5.50am-8pm)

Sanyuan Qiao 三元桥 -Anzhenqiao Xi 安贞桥西 -**China Science & Technology Museum 中国科技馆** -Madianqiao Dong 马甸桥东 -Beitaipingqiao Xi北太平桥西-Zhongguanyuan 中关园-**Yuanmingyuan South Gate圆明园南门** -**Summer Palace 颐和园**

819 (A/C, 5.30am-8pm)

Jingchanglu Huilongguan 京昌路回龙观 -Deshengmen 德胜门 -**Drum Tower 鼓楼** -Di'anmennei地安门内-Jingshan Dongjie景山东街-**Donghuamen 东华门** -**Qianmen 前门**-**Dazhalan大栅栏**-Friendship Hospital友谊医院 -**Grand View Garden 大观园**

825 (A/C, 5.30am-10.30pm)

Agricultural Exhibition Center农业展览馆-Liangma Qiao 亮马桥 -**China Science & Technology Museum 中国科技馆** -Beijing Language and Culture University 北京语言大学 -**Wudaokou 五道口** -Zhongguanyuan Beizhan 中关园北站 -Tsinghua University West Gate 清华大学西门 -**Yuanmingyuan South Gate 圆明园南门**

849 (A/C, 5.30am-8.30pm)

Yanhuang Art Museum 炎黄艺术馆 -Olympic Sports Center East Gate 奥体东门 -Mudanyuan 牡丹园 -Beijing Normal University South Gate 北京师范大学南门 -Mingguangcun 明光村 -Wanshousi 万寿寺

984 (standard bus, 6am-8pm)

Chaoyang Park 朝阳公园 -Agricultural Exhibition Center 农业展览馆 -Liangma Qiao 亮马桥 -Sanyuan Qiao 三元桥 -**Yanhuang Art Museum 炎黄艺术馆**

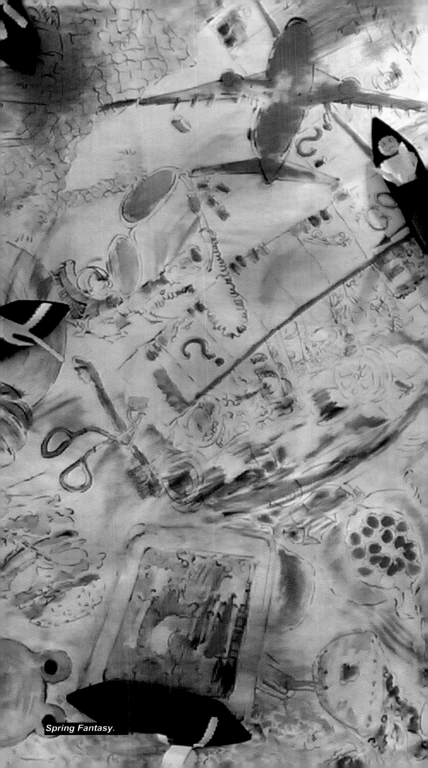

Spring Fantasy.

"Arty" Northeast

Construction, change and evolution are everywhere in Beijing and so the "Northeast" is no exception. State-of-the-art and high-tech items of every description can be found at **Beijing Electronic City Science and Technology Park** (北京电子城科技园) at Jiuxianqiao and Wangjing. It is part of the Zhongguancun Science Park (中关村科技园区) and boasts 555 high-tech enterprises. 16 of the global top 500 enterprises have invested, or set up headquarters in the Park, including Siemens.

However, what makes the Northeast of special value is the ongoing development of another kind. Art and artists have also staked their claim on the Northeast and (as one would expect) have done it in style! Art galleries, studios, workshops, supply outlets, book sellers and related businesses are opening almost daily here. It makes no difference if you have only a casual and a more sophisticated love of art (sculpture, painting, ceramics, performance art and more!). 798, also known as the **Dashanzi Art**

Sculpture—Future Woman.

District, (see p.220) is a real "must-see." Launched in 2005, the **East End Art** area (see website: http://www.eastendart.net/EN/eastendart.htm) is another emerging art district worth exploring. Many of the original artists from Dashanzi relocated here after that area became more popular (and thus expensive). With an intention of being more workspace and less commercially oriented, you'll find up-and-coming, talented, contemporary Chinese artists many of whom are willing to let you watch them as they work.

Time spent wandering through the artist havens in the Northeast will leave you feeling a deeper connection with both the ancient and modern interpretations of China's long history and current merging onto the world's stage. Watching many artists as they do their work in open workshop/studio combined spaces is a real treat and a chance to appreciate the hard work and vision that goes into their creations. When you're ready for a respite, a visit to any of the small, wonderful and extremely art-themed cafés, bistros, or restaurants will complete your introduction.

Highlights

♦ **Dashanzi Art District** 大山子艺术区 A ferment of contemporary art creativity, and connoisseurs' paradise, with many artists beginning to command high prices on the international market. Artists from around the world display their works here. Even if you have no idea what you are looking at, it is definitely worth a

look. **See p.220**

♦ **Liangma Antique Market** 亮马古玩收藏品市场 The goods at this market come from private collections. **See p.233**

♦ **Lady's Street**女人街 Lose yourself in a maze of clothing shops, bars and restaurants on Lady's Street. **See p.230, p.233**

🍴🎸 Food and Entertainment

From an area of rural farm land and factory space, to a thriving center of entertainment, shopping, accommodation, dining and world-class residential neighborhoods in less than 20 years, this is Beijing's Northeast. Getting it all started was the **Holiday Inn Lido** built in 1984; its arrival also brought the first of what would ultimately be many first-class food and entertainment establishments to open in the Northeast (some located in the hotel itself). The famous philosophy of "if you build it, they will come" indeed worked for the Northeast, and many businesses to suit all tastes, lifestyles and budgets have opened and continue to spring up in the area.

The nearby and densely populated **Wangjing** (see p.217) residential area was started in the early 1990s and like most of Beijing, they're still

The fun tiger pillow from northern China.

adding to it today! As such, new restaurants, theaters, nightclubs and related recreational areas continuously flow into this area. Mentioned in other spots in our book, the **Dashanzi Art District** (see p.220) is likewise packed with a plethora of interesting and mysterious places to make the most of your trip to Beijing. Nightclub enthusiasts, shoppers, eaters, and fans of imbibing, will find an endless source of fun and frivolity waiting for them at **Lady's Street** (see p.230).

Not to be forgotten, fans of live performances would do well to check out the **Century Theater** (see p.232) where ballet, opera and classical music are all on the bill. The Northeast is a destination that warrants time on your itinerary during your stay in Beijing.

The following hot spots are marked on the map on p.214.

"What if the Terracotta Warriors were women, or even pregnant?!"

Wangjing Area 望京区

Resting on the edge of the super built-up parts of the city, but still within easy access is the Wangjing area. Drawn by its humongous shopping center, Chinese and foreign visitors are spoilt for choice when it comes to retail, food and fun. Convenient to the airport and the Olympics Center, it is also within easy reach of Sanlitun Bar Street, Lido Area and downtown Beijing.

Need a bit of a break from things Chinese? Western-style shops abound alongside some extremely popular restaurants and bars. **Victor's Place and Curry House** (see p.218) pulls off a double, as a combined Italian and Indian restaurant, serving up carbonaras and curry alike! If you want to stick with Chinese food, there are some good hotpot restaurants around—**Donglaishun** (see p.218) is a local favorite.

Transport: Bus 402, 418, 813, 909 to Wangjing Huayuan (望京花园)

RESTAURANTS AND BARS

Black Horse Football Bar 黑马足球酒吧	Ⓚ
Blue Lake Bar 蓝湖酒吧	Ⓛ
Donglaishun 东来顺	Ⓒ
Guxiang Shanchuan 故乡山川	Ⓗ
Jihouniao 季候鸟咖啡 & 吧	Ⓜ
Little Italy 小意大利	Ⓘ
Obisco 阿根廷烤肉	Ⓐ
Tanzhou Restaurant 潭州酒楼	Ⓑ
Tongda Ecosystem Park 同达生态园	Ⓕ
Verandah 长廊西餐厅	Ⓙ
Victor's Place and Curry House 天竺阁	Ⓖ
Yintan Restaurant 银滩酒楼	Ⓔ
Yuelu Shanwu 岳麓山屋	Ⓓ

Restaurant listings

Meal prices per adult

¥	under RMB 29
¥¥	RMB 30-49
¥¥¥	RMB 50-69
¥¥¥¥	RMB 70-99
¥¥¥¥¥	over RMB 100

Argentinean

Ⓐ Obisco 阿根廷烤肉 ¥¥¥¥¥
English menu
Hours: 11am-2.30pm, 5.30pm-10pm (Mon-Thur); 11am-10pm (Fri-Sun)
Transport: Bus 415 to Jingshun Lukou (京顺路口)
No.1, Laiguangying Donglu,

Crispy roasted lamb ribs.

Chaoyang District (No. 4 Exit of Airport Expressway, look for a giant obelisk). (86-10-84701666) 朝阳区来广营东路1号(机场高速4号出口京顺路右边)

Argentina is famed for its first-class meats and Oblisco most certainly doesn't let the side down (side of beef that is!). Refined and elegant, it has a great list of wines imported from the motherland, and steaks cooked to perfection.

Chinese

Ⓑ Tanzhou Restaurant
潭州酒楼
Hunan cuisine
English menu　　¥¥

Hours: 10am-10pm
Transport: Bus 361, 420, 614, 701, 752, 运通 101, 运通 104 to Huajiadi Beili (花家地北里)
Building 1, Huajiadi Beili, Chaoyang District. (86-10-64734418) 朝阳区花家地北里1号楼

To complete the full Hunan experience, Tanzhou hires only Hunan waitresses; great food at low prices served by those who would know!

Ⓒ Donglaishun 东来顺
Hotpot
English menu　　¥¥¥

Hours: 9am-2pm, 5pm-9.30pm
Transport: Bus 361, 409, 416, 422, 470, 623, 627, 657, 710, 827, 939, 944 运通 201, 运通 113, 运通 110 to Nanhu Dongyuan (南湖东园)
Building 221, Nanhu Dongyuan, Wangjing, Chaoyang District. (86-10-64756804/05) 朝阳区望京南湖东园221号楼
See write-up on p.147.

Thinly shaved beef perfect for hotpot.

Yuelu Shanwu specializes in spicy Hunan food.

Ⓓ Yuelu Shanwu 岳麓山屋
Hunan cuisine
English menu　　¥¥¥

Hours: 10.30am-2.30pm, 5pm-11pm
Transport: Bus 运通 111, 运通 113, 409, 421, 422, 629, 630, 657 to Wangjing Huayuan (望京花园)
Building 101, Wangjing Huayuan, Guangshun Beidajie, Chaoyang District. (86-10-84713613) 朝阳区广顺北大街望京花园101号楼

Beautifully decorated in traditional Chinese décor reminiscent of days gone by, Yuelu prepares exquisite Hunan-style dishes.

Ⓔ Yintan Restaurant
银滩酒楼
Hotpot
English menu　　¥¥¥¥

Hours: 11am-10pm
Transport: Bus 361, 409, 627, 710, 827, 944, 运通113, 运通110 to Nanhu Dongyuan (南湖东园)
2/F, Building 117, Nanhu Xiyuan, Wangjing, Chaoyang District. (86-10-64704958) 朝阳区望京南湖西园117楼2层

A bit pricier than other hotpot eateries, but certainly as good, Yintan is a pleasant place to make the most of being in Beijing and enjoy a Beijing hotpot.

Ⓕ Tongda Ecosystem Park
同达生态园
Northeast cuisine
English menu　　¥¥¥¥¥

Hours: 10am-10pm
Transport: Bus 415, 991 to Mananli (马南里)
No. 99, Laiguangying Donglu, Chaoyang District (Beigao Exit off the Airport Expressway). (86-10-64319099/9299) 朝阳区来广营东路99号(机场高速北皋出口上京顺路)

Elaborate piles of rocks and a thick blanket of plants and flowers will make you feel like you're eating dinner in a Costa Rican jungle. Housed in a massive, two-floored, greenhouse, the Tongda Ecosystem Park is an experience in itself—the food isn't bad either!

Enjoy your meal in the wild of Tongda.

Indian

Ⓖ Victor's Place and Curry House 天竺阁
English menu　　¥¥¥

Hours: 10.30am-2.30pm, 4.30pm-10.30pm
Transport: Bus 415, 710 to Laiguangying Donglu (来广营东路)
No. 8, Laiguangying Donglu,

Chaoyang District (near Western Academy of Beijing). (86-10-84701306/1308) 朝阳区来广营东路 8 号 *(京西学校旁边)*

Predominantly a take-away joint, it does have a few tables where you can choose from Indian or Italian dishes. From curry to carbonara, the menu is eclectic.

Korean

Guxiang Shanchuan
故乡山川

English menu ¥¥¥

Hours: 9am-2am

Transport: Bus 运通 104, 运通101 to Wangjing Xincheng (望京新城)

1/F, Building 423, Wangjing Xincheng, Chaoyang District (beside KFC). (86-10-64709292) 朝阳区望京新城 423 楼 1 层 *(肯德基旁边)*

Cook your own succulent fatty meats on a piping hot skillet—from pan to mouth, literally!

Western

Little Italy 小意大利

Italian

English menu ¥¥¥

Hours: 11.30am-2.30pm, 5pm-10.30pm

Transport: Bus 415, 710 to Laiguangying Donglu (来广营东路)

No. 8, Laiguangying Donglu, Chaoyang District (next to Western Academy of Beijing). (86-10-84702962/2967) 朝阳区来广营东路 8 号 *(京西学校旁边)*

Straight from mama's kitchen, Little Italy offers a big variety of classic pizza and pasta dishes as well as those all-important desserts.

Verandah 长廊西餐厅

English menu ¥¥¥¥

Hours: 9am-9.30pm

Transport: Bus 415, 991 to Mananli (马南里)

No. 8, Laiguangying Donglu, Chaoyang District (50m west of Western Academy of Beijing). (86-10-84703821) 朝阳区来广营东路 8 号 *(京西学校西 50 米)*

Treat yourself at Verandah.

Verandah does a good job at getting a balanced cross-section of European foods. From Italian pizzas to French and Greek-style seafood, meats and salads, it most surely has something for everyone.

Bar listings

Prices for a bottle of Tsingtao beer (青岛啤酒), a favorite local beer

¥	under RMB 14
¥¥	RMB 15-24
¥¥¥	RMB 25-34
¥¥¥¥	over RMB 35

Black Horse Football Bar
黑马足球酒吧

Pop/ live music

English menu and service ¥¥

Hours: 2pm-2am

Entrance: free

Transport: Bus 420, 991 to Wangjingjie Xikou (望京街西口)

B1, Building 322, Wangjing Xiyuan-3, Chaoyang District. (86-10-84716903) 朝阳区望京西园3区322 号楼地下1层

As expected, the Black Horse Football Bar is a strong favorite with football fans of whatever nationality. Many a noisy, passionate and exciting evening can be spent watching live games!

Blue Lake Bar
蓝湖酒吧

Light music

English menu and service ¥¥

Hours: 1pm-2am

Entrance: free

Transport: Bus 976, 404 to Daxiyang Xincheng Dongmen (大西洋新城 东门)

1/F, Building 420, Wangjing Xincheng-4, Chaoyang District. (86-10-84712562) 朝阳区望京新城4区420 栋1层

With gentle, soft decoration, this is the prefect place to whisper sweet nothings to a loved one. They have an extensive wine and beer menu to help things along!

Jihouniao
季候鸟咖啡 & 吧

Light music

English menu and service ¥¥

Hours: 10am-12am

Entrance: free

Transport: Bus 471, 623, 827 to Huajiadi Nanjie (花家地南街)

Building 5, Huajiadi Nanjie, Chaoyang District. (86-10-84725541) 朝阳区花 家地南街5 号楼

One of Beijing's few pet-friendly bars; the huge outdoor area is full of dog-lovers enjoying the sunshine, a cool beer and the company of man's best friend.

Come on over, Rover. Have a drink at Jihouniao.

Dashanzi Art District 大山子艺术区

The Dashanzi Art District started life a world away from today's contemporary art scene, as a Bauhau-style industrial zone designed by East Germany back in 1959. At the heart is the 798 Factory, which is actually a series of converted warehouses off Jiuxianqiao Lu (酒仙桥路). Since 2001, art, music, fashion, design, photography and architecture studios have been booming here. With some 200 art organizations in this area, it is now a maelstrom of imagination, flamboyance and risk-taking creativity.

Transport: Bus 401, 402, 405, 955, 973, 991 to Dashanzi Lukounan (大山子路口南).

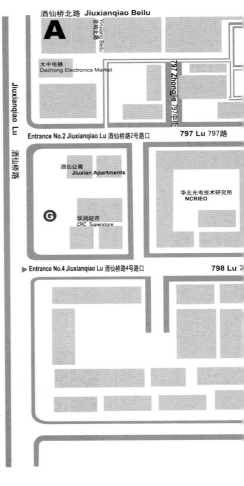

North

GALLERIES, ART SPACES AND ARTIST STUDIOS	
3818 Cool Gallery 3818 库画廊	ⓐ
798 Photo Gallery 百年印象摄影画廊	ⓑ
798 Space 时态空间	ⓝ
China Art Seasons 季节画廊	ⓒ
Chinese Contemporary Gallery 中国当代画廊	ⓓ
Chinese" 的 "China Art Office 李明铸办公室	ⓢ
Contrasts Gallery 对比窗艺廊	ⓔ
East West Art Space 东成西就艺术空间	ⓞ
Galleria Continua 常青画廊	ⓕ
Hart Center of Art 哈特艺术沙龙	ⓟ
High Land Gallery 高地画廊	ⓠ
OffiCina 意中艺术工作室	ⓘ
Rain Gallery 雨画廊	ⓗ
Red Gate Gallery 红门画廊	ⓘ
Red Star Gallery 红星画廊	ⓙ
Representational Art gallery 具象画廊	ⓚ
Timezone 8 Editions 东八时区空间	ⓠ
White Space 空白空间	ⓛ
Yan Club 仁艺术空间	ⓡ
Yufine Art Institution 禹风艺术	ⓜ
Zhuangtang Village Sculpture Art Studio 庄塘村雕塑工作室	ⓤ

RESTAURANTS AND BARS	
As One 爱心旺	Ⓓ
At Café 爱意特	Ⓐ
Liaogezhi 料阁子	Ⓔ
Old Factory 老工厂	Ⓕ
Café Pause 闲着也是闲着	Ⓑ
Tianxiayan 天下盐	Ⓒ
Vibes Art Space 微波释艺术交流中心	Ⓖ

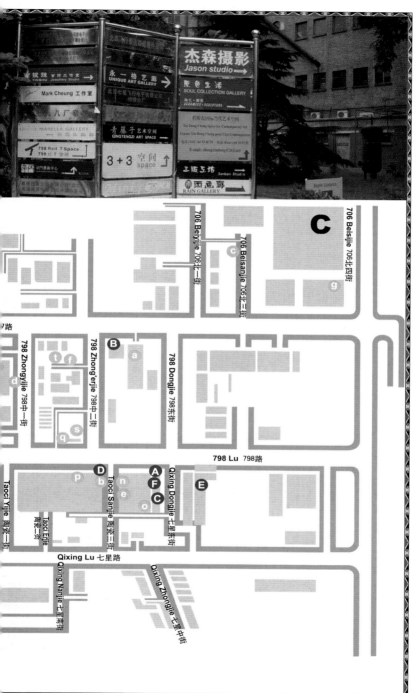

3818 Cool Gallery.

Galleries

ⓐ 3818 Cool Gallery
3818 库画廊
Tel: 86-10-86882525/84566664
Fax: 86-10-84566664
Email: gallery3818@126.com
Web: www.3818coolgallery.com
Providing a platform for Chinese artists of all ages to display and promote their contemporary works, it encourages national and international communication and exchange. It has various galleries and a coffee shop inside.

ⓑ 798 Photo Gallery
百年印象摄影画廊
Tel: 86-10-64381784
Fax: 86-10-64375284
Email: 798@798photogallery.cn
Web: www.798photogallery.cn
China's first gallery dedicated solely to photography, 798 Photo Gallery discovers, collects and exhibits outstanding photographic works, providing a platform for cultural and commercial exchange.

ⓒ China Art Seasons
季节画廊
Tel/fax: 86-10-64311900
Web: www.artseasons.com.sg
Promoting Chinese and Southeast Asian contemporary art, this gallery also delves into and encourages experimental art. It is the first Singapore-owned gallery to make the move to China.

ⓓ Chinese Contemporary Gallery 中国当代画廊
Tel: 86-10-84562421 or 13521492101
Email: Beijing@chinesecontemporary.com
Web: www.chinesecontemporary.com
This long-established gallery was opened in 1996 and specializes in Chinese avant-garde styles. All its contributing artists work in China.

ⓔ Contrasts Gallery
对比窗艺廊
Tel/fax: 86-10-64321369
Web: www.contrastsgallery.com
China's first gallery dedicated exclusively to Chinese contemporary design, it displays both art and design.

ⓕ Galleria Continua
常青画廊
Tel: 86-10-64361005
Fax: 86-10-64364464
Email: Beijing@galleriacontinua.com
Web: www.galleriacontinua.com
Galleria Continua's new space in Beijing's 798, displays and promotes Western contemporary art to the Chinese market.

ⓖ High Land Gallery
高地画廊
Tel: 86-10-64377177/83770077
Email: 798highland@sina.com, gallery@vip.sina.com
Web: www.highlandgallery.cn
High Land Gallery prides itself on its academic roots and well-established expertise in collecting, exhibiting and exchanging carefully chosen artistic works.

ⓗ Rain Gallery 雨画廊
Tel/fax: 86-10-64323274
Email: raingallery798@yahoo.com.cn
Specializing in all things beautiful, Rain Gallery concentrates on items of beauty, Chinese contemporary works and pieces of extremely high caliber.

ⓘ Red Gate Gallery
红门画廊
Tel: 86-10-64381005
Email: redgate798@aer.net.cn
Web: www.redgategallery.com
One of the most interesting places in 798, it is set in an enormous Ming Dynasty watchtower. Exhibiting contemporary pieces by

Rain Gallery.

Chinese artists, the Red Gate Gallery has been around since 1991.

▶ Red Star Gallery
红星画廊
Tel: 86-10-84599234/64370781
Fax: 86-10-64370781
Email: redstar@chinaredstargallery.com
Web: www.chinaredstargallery.com
Aiming to unite Chinese and Western modern art styles through exchange and co-operation, Red Star Gallery has played a key role in promoting modern art in China.

Human cast at Red Star Gallery.

ⓚ Representational Art Gallery 具象画廊
Tel: 86-10-51374021
Email: wgw_2006@163.com
Displaying a fine selection of oil paintings and sculptural pieces from well-known and accomplished Chinese artists, this gallery is contemporary in its ideals and styles.

ⓛ White Space 空白空间
Tel: 86-10-84562054
Fax: 86-10-84562749
Web: www.alexanderochs-galleries.de
Email: info@whitespace-beijing.com
A recent addition to the 798 scene, White Space was founded in 2004 to connect German and Chinese artistic styles.

ⓜ Yufine Art Institution
禹风艺术
Tel: 86-10-51305590
Performing the role of intermediary, this gallery/agency represents up-and-coming young artists. It deals predominantly with sculptures, pottery and paintings.

Art spaces

ⓝ 798 Space 时态空间
Tel: 86-10-64376248/64384862
Email: info@798space.com
Web: www.798space.com
Chic, trendy and oozing avant-garde, this commodious center hosts cultural, artistic and commercial events. It can easily accommodate 1,000 people.

ⓞ East West Art Space
东成西就艺术空间
Tel: 86-10-84573595/94
Mobile: 13601225198
Fax: 86-10-84573595/94
Email: tea_hong@eastwest-ad.com, eastwest@vip.163.com
This great space is perfect for a whole host of activities up to 150 people. Exhibitions, parties, dances or performances are often held, as well as Latin dance classes and carnival festivals.

ⓟ Hart Center of Art
哈特艺术沙龙
Tel/fax: 86-10-64353570
Email: info@hart.com.cn
Web: www.hart.com.cn
Providing Chinese artists with a platform to reach the international arts community, the Hart Center of Art is a multi-disciplinary gallery dealing with a varied range of artistic styles.

ⓠ Timezone 8 Editions
东八时区空间
Tel: 86-10-84560336/84599332
Fax: 86-10-64311226
Email: info@timezone8.com
Timezone 8 Editions provides a prefect backdrop for gatherings of the art community, where book launches, talks and exhibitions are often hosted. Its great café prides itself on imported coffees, Chinese teas and delicate pastries. It also has a rather delicious menu of healthy food: salads, pastas and sandwiches.

ⓡ Yan Club 仁艺术中心
Tel: 86-10-84573506
Web: www.yanclub.com

Yan Club.

Email: events@yanclub.com

A popular place for parties, events, concerts and exhibitions. It has over 1,000 sq m of space which can house 500 guests.

Artist studio

❂ Chinese" 的 "China Art Office 李明铸办公室
Tel: 86-10-69590408
Mobile: 13693367860
Email: chauchau-m@hotmail.com
The self-assigned goal of "study hard, work hard and contribute to the development of 798" appears to be realized within this well-respected office.

❶ OffiCina
意中艺术工作室
Tel: 86-10-64361191
Fax: 86-10-64351324
Email: info@officinaltd.com
Web: www.officinaltd.com
With strong and active links between China and Europe, OffiCina is an Italian venture whose aims are to provide an international center for exchange and exhibition.

❼ Zhuangtang Village Sculpture Art Studio
庄塘村雕塑工作室
Tel: 86-10-64311756
Email: ZhuangTangCun@163.com
The works on display aim to reflect rural poverty among China's post-reform farmers.

Restaurant listings

Meal prices per adult
¥ under RMB 29
¥¥ RMB 30-49
¥¥¥ RMB 50-69
¥¥¥¥ RMB 70-99
¥¥¥¥¥ over RMB 100

Café

Ⓐ At Café 爱意特
Italian music, jazz
English menu and service ¥¥
Hours: 11am-12am
Transport: see transport to Dashanzi on p.220
798 Factory, Courtyard 4, Jiuxianqiao Lu, Chaoyang District. (86-10-64387264) 朝阳区酒仙桥路4号院 798 工厂
Laid back and chilled out, At

Take a break in Café Pause.

Café is a wonderfully lazy place to sip hot coffee, tea or taste carefully prepared pastas, listen to jazz and chat with friends. The unusual decoration may be the first talking point!

Ⓑ Café Pause
闲着也是闲着
English menu ¥¥
Hours: 10am-9pm
Transport: see transport to Dashanzi on p.220
798 Factory, Courtyard 2, Jiuxianqiao Lu, Chaoyang District. (86-10-64316214) 朝阳区酒仙桥路2号院 798 工厂
With furnishings to please both the mind and the behind, this is a lovely little place to enjoy a cappuccino and reflect on the meaning of life!

Chinese

Ⓒ Tianxiayan 天下盐
Sichuan cuisine
English menu ¥¥¥
Hours: 11am-11pm
Transport: see transport to Dashanzi on p.220
798 Factory, Courtyard 4, Jiuxianqiao Lu, Chaoyang District. (86-10-64323577) 朝阳区酒仙桥路4号院 798 工厂
Carving its own in the arty atmosphere of the area, this warehouse restaurant specializes in authen-

OffiCina.

tic Sichuan dishes, which are good. Very, very good.

Japanese

As One 爱心旺

English menu ¥¥¥

Hours: 11.30am-11pm

Transport: see transport to Dashanzi on p.220

East of the 798 Factory gate, Courtyard 4, Jiuxianqiao, Chaoyang District. (86-10-84560437) 朝阳区酒仙桥4号院798工厂入口东侧

For great value for money, "do lunch" at As One. Their set specials are fantastic and seriously filling. By the way, if you have difficulty finding the place, it's the luminous yellow building!

Bar listings

Prices for a bottle of Tsingtao beer (青岛啤酒), a favorite local beer

¥ under RMB 14

¥¥ RMB 15-24

¥¥¥ RMB 25-34

¥¥¥¥ over RMB 35

Liaogezhi 料阁子

English menu and service ¥

Hours: 10am-10pm

Entrance: free

Transport: see transport to Dashanzi on p.220

798 Factory, Courtyard 4, Jiuxianqiao Lu, Chaoyang District. (86-10-64317908) 朝阳区酒仙桥路4号院798工厂

This minimalist French bar and restaurant is fresh and pleasant. A music-free zone, its hushed, private feel gives it a certain "je ne sais quoi."

Old Factory 老工厂

Jazz

English menu and service ¥¥

Hours: 10.30am-9pm

Entrance: free

Transport: see transport to Dashanzi on p.220

798 Factory, Courtyard 4, Jiuxianqiao Lu, Chaoyang District. (86-10-64376248) 朝阳区酒仙桥路4号院798工厂

Following the arty theme of the area to which it owes its existence, Old Factory is plastered with impressive and unusual works of art. A great place to come and reflect upon life and art!

Vibes Art Space 微波释艺术交流中心

Live music

Vibes Art Space.

English menu and service ¥¥¥

Hours: 11am-midnight

Entrance: free

Transport: see transport to Dashanzi on p.220

798 Factory, Courtyard 4, Jiuxianqiao Lu, Chaoyang District. (86-10-64378082) 朝阳区酒仙桥路4号院798工厂

Making the most of its big warehouse location, Vibes Art Space often hosts theme evenings including film showings, live music or parties.

Try something different for a change at Liaogezi.

Lido Area 丽都区

Looking for somewhere to unwind with a glass of something imported and a greasy dinner? You'll find it in the Lido area, sitting by the Airport Expressway, with the Holiday Inn Lido at its center. This area is a perfect spot for expats wanting a taste of home comforts all within easy staggering distance of each other after a few pints! If you're missing the green hills (or the lean mean burgers), this is the place to head for. Cafés, bars, pubs and restaurants all cater to the Western palate.

Transport: Bus 408, 416, 420, 701, 707, 752, 934, 运通 101, 运通 104, 运通 107 to Holiday Inn Lido (丽都饭店). Then walk to your final destination.

Futong Dongdajie 芙蓉东大街

RESTAURANTS AND BARS	
Café del Mar 海润天缘	Ⓜ
Eudora Station 亿多瑞站	Ⓡ
Frank's Place 法兰克	Ⓟ
Kong House Bar & Restaurant 空	Ⓝ
Lemon Leaf 柠檬叶子	Ⓚ
Lido Deli 熟食店	Ⓖ
Mimi's Roast Duck 咪咪香烤鸭店	Ⓔ
NHU	Ⓞ
Nyonya Kitchen 娘惹厨房	Ⓙ
Pure Lotus Vegetarian 净心莲	Ⓛ
Qinyuan Restaurant 沁园餐厅	Ⓕ
Rumi 入迷	Ⓘ
Taj Pavilion 泰姬楼印度餐厅	Ⓗ
Texas Bar and Grill 德克萨斯扒房	Ⓐ
The Cellar at Trio	Ⓓ
Trio's Park Grill	Ⓑ
Wanlefu 万乐福烤鸡	Ⓒ
Yaodianzi 四川么店子	Ⓓ

Xiaoyun Lu 霄云路 Ⓚ

Restaurant listings

Meal prices per adult

¥	under RMB 29
¥¥	RMB 30-49
¥¥¥	RMB 50-69
¥¥¥¥	RMB 70-99
¥¥¥¥¥	over RMB 100

Tasty home-cooked food.

American

Ⓐ Texas Bar and Grill 德克萨斯扒房

English menu　　　　¥¥¥

Hours: 11.30am-2pm, 5.30pm-10.30pm

Transport: see transport to Lido Area above

1/F, Holiday Inn Lido, No. 6, Jiangtai Lu, Chaoyang District. (86-10-64376688 ext. 1849) 朝阳区将台路6号丽都饭店1层

Don your spurs, holster those pistols and chow down Texan style in this Tex-Mex favorite. With saloon-style surroundings you'll find yourself drawling your accent and over the menu.

BBQ

Ⓑ Trio's Park Grill

English menu　　　　¥¥¥¥¥

Hours: 8am-2am

Transport: see transport to Lido Area above

West of Rosedale Hotel, Jiangtai Xilu, Chaoyang District. (86-10-64378399) 朝阳区将台西路珀丽酒店西侧

As live jazz music drifts from the

Strap on the feed bag at Qinyuan.

A great little Sichuan restaurant serving up what the cuisine is famous for; spicy food, in big quantities at low prices! The Dandanmian noodles (担担面) should be top on the list.

❺ Mimi's Roast Duck 咪咪香烤鸭店

English menu   **¥¥¥**

Hours: 10am-12am
Transport: see transport to Lido Area on p.226
No. 5, Hairun International Apartment, Chaoyang District. (86-10-51358353) 朝阳区海润国际公寓底商5号

Ignore the somewhat dated décor and concentrate on your plate and you won't be disappointed. Reasonably priced and extremely tasty, the whole roast duck and beef rolls are a must.

❻ Qinyuan Restaurant 沁园餐厅

Cafeteria
English menu   **¥¥¥¥**

Hours: 24 hours
Transport: see transport to Lido Area on p.226
Holiday Inn Lido, No. 6, Jiangtai Lu, Chaoyang District. (86-10-64376688 ext. 1971) 朝阳区将台路6号丽都饭店

All you can eat (but not drink) for RMB 90 is a pretty good deal for those with a big appetite, and even better if you get there early when it is buy one get one free! The outdoor barbecue emits some great smells that will get those juices flowing.

---

piano strings, sink your teeth into a juicy steak or flaming lobster fresh off the grill. A well-stocked wine list is a welcome addition too.

Chinese

● Wanlefu 万乐福烤鸡

Roast chicken
English menu   **¥**

Hours: 11.30am-2pm, 4.30pm-9pm
Transport: see transport to Lido Area on p.226
East entrance of Holiday Inn Lido, Chaoyang District. (86-10-64380290) 朝阳区丽都饭店东门

A popular local joint, it is cheap and cheerful, though probably not for the chickens that make their specialty; roasted Asian style chicken.

⒟ Yaodianzi 四川幺店子

Sichuan cuisine
English menu   **¥¥**

Hours: 10.30am-11pm
Transport: see transport to Lido Area on p.226
No. 311, Gaojiayuan, Jiangtai Lu, Chaoyang District (opposite Holiday Inn Lido). (86-10-64341534) 朝阳区将台路高家园311号 (丽都饭店对面)

Classy and inexpensive at Yaodianzi.

Get those Western rarities at Lido Deli.

Deli

Ⓖ Lido Deli 熟食店

English menu ¥¥

Hours: 7am-9pm
Transport: see transport to Lido Area on p.226
Holiday Inn Lido, No. 6, Jiangtai Lu, Chaoyang District. (86-10-64376688 ext. 1542) 朝阳区将台路6号丽都饭店

Craving some of life's little luxuries? The Lido Deli stocks an eye-popping, mouth-watering, budget-busting selection of sausages, smoked salmon, pâtés and world renowned caviar.

Indian

Ⓗ Taj Pavilion

泰姬楼印度餐厅

English menu ¥¥¥¥¥

Hours: 11am-2.30pm, 6pm-10.30pm
Transport: see transport to Lido Area on p.226
3/F, Holiday Inn Lido, No. 6, Jiangtai Lu, Chaoyang District. (86-10-64367678/64376688 ext. 3811) 朝阳区将台路6号丽都饭店缤纷廊3层

Curries cooked in authentic Indian spices in authentic Indian surroundings. Friendly staff and management ensure your meal goes as smoothly as their korma!

Persian

Ⓘ Rumi 入迷

English menu ¥¥¥¥

Hours: 11am-10pm (Sun-Thur), 11am-11pm (Fri and Sat)
Transport: Bus 405, 707, 752 to Wuligou (五里沟)
No. 29, Wuligou, Xiaoyun Lu, Chaoyang District (opposite King's Garden Villas). (86-10-84543838) 朝阳区霄云路五里沟29号 (京润水上花园对面)

Beijing's only Persian restaurant, Rumi certainly doesn't relax in its rivalless status with respect to quality and service. Elegant and comfortable, its kebabs are legendary, as is its fab dessert list!

Southeast Asian

Ⓙ Nyonya Kitchen

娘惹厨房

English menu ¥¥¥

Hours: 11am-9.30pm
Transport: see transport to Lido Area on p.226
Beside Gaojiayuan Middle School, Chaoyang District (opposite Holiday Inn Lido). (86-10-64337377) 朝阳区高家园中学旁边 (丽都饭店对面)

Fresh from Malaysia, this is local cuisine at its best. For the novice to Southeast Asian food, the owners are on stand-by to explain and demonstrate the processes and ingredients behind the steaming foods they serve.

Thai

Ⓚ Lemon Leaf 柠檬叶子

English menu ¥¥¥

Hours: 11am-1am
Transport: Bus 405, 707, 752 to Wuligou (五里沟)
No. 15, Xiaoyun Lu, Chaoyang District. (86-10-64625505) 朝阳区霄云路15号

Hot, hot hotpot! Try Thai spices cooked in one of their eight differently flavored broths for a well-

Mouth-tingling Thai.

priced, sweaty meal.

Vegetarian

Pure Lotus Vegetarian
净心莲

English menu   ¥¥¥¥
Hours: 11am-11pm
Transport: see transport to Lido Area on p.226
3/F, Holiday Inn Lido, No. 6, Jiangtai Lu, Chaoyang District. (86-10-64376688 ext. 3812) 朝阳区将台路6号丽都饭店3层

For some ecclesiastical veggies, the Pure Lotus Vegetarian will serve you an imaginative array of filling, meat-less dishes in a restaurant run wholly by monks. A bit on the pricey side, you'd better start praying against temptation!

The Pure Lotus veggie roll. Yum!

Bar listings

Prices for a bottle of Tsingtao beer (青岛啤酒), a favorite local beer

¥   under RMB 14
¥¥   RMB 15-24
¥¥¥   RMB 25-34
¥¥¥¥   over RMB 35

Café del Mar 海润天缘
Pop music
English menu and service   ¥
Hours: 9am-3pm
Entrance: free
Transport: see transport to Lido Area on p.226
No. A2, Jiangtai Lu, Chaoyang District. (86-10-51357028) 朝阳区将台路甲2号

Boasting an amazing range of drinks from teas to cocktails, there is also an abundance of great

Café del Mar.

eateries. Choose from Chinese, Western or the new Japanese restaurants while enjoying the spectacular view.

Kong House Bar & Restaurant 空
Light music
English menu and service   ¥¥
Hours: 10am-2am (closed on Mondays)
Entrance: free
Transport: Bus 405, 421 to Fangyuanli (芳园里)
No. 6, Fangyuan Xili, Xiaoyun Lu, Chaoyang District. (86-10-64321157) 朝阳区宵云路芳园西里6号

This elegant and classy joint doubles as a restaurant and bar. Enjoy lavish cocktails and superb food served in a sumptuous atmosphere. Private rooms, a roomy dance floor and huge roof terrace are the icing on the cake.

NHU
Electronic music, house, fusion
English menu and service   ¥¥
Hours: 6pm-2am (closed on Mondays)
Entrance: free
Transport: see transport to Lido Area on p.226
No. 6, Fangyuan Xili, Chaoyang District (south gate of Lido Park). (86-10-64356762) 朝阳区芳园西路6号 (丽都花园南门)

Often hosting live DJs, this sophisticated venue can be enjoyed from the roof terrace or executive VIP lounge. The big dance floor is ringed with posh, behind-friendly sofas.

Frank's Place 法兰克
Light music, R&B, rock music
English menu and service   ¥¥

Hours: 9am-late
Entrance: free
Transport: Bus 752 to Fangyuanli Xizhan (芳园里西站)
B1 of Trio, west of Rosedale Hotel, Jiangtai Xilu, Chaoyang District. (86-10-64378399 ext. 213) 朝阳区将台西路珀丽酒店西侧 Trio 地下 1 层

Fun and funky, Frank's Place is a sports-themed pub with some great draught lagers and good old English pub grub. If you can find a seat on the terrace in summer, it's the perfect place to try some of them.

The Cellar at Trio
English menu and service   ¥¥
Hours: 6pm-10pm
Entrance: free
Transport: Bus 752 to Fangyuanli Xizhan (芳园里西站)
B1 of Trio, west of Rosedale Hotel, Jiangtai Xilu, Chaoyang District. (86-10-64378399) 朝阳区将台西路珀丽酒店西侧 Trio 地下 1 层

Boasting an impressive list of international wines, the Cellar basement will appeal to vintage connoisseurs. The outdoor summer barbecues and a mouth-watering menu are pretty appealing too!

Eudora Station 亿多瑞站
Light music, Latin, rock, R&B
English menu and service   ¥¥¥
Hours: 9am-2am
Entrance: free
Transport: see transport to Lido Area on p.226
No. 6, Fangyuan Xilu, Chaoyang District. (86-10-64378331) 朝阳区芳园西路6号

With a restaurant on the first floor and wine bar on the second, you can happily spend a pleasant evening in the simple yet sturdy Eudora Station.

Eudora Station.

Lady's Street 女人街

It may be one of the newest additions to Beijing's fashion scene, but with over 700 stalls to chose from and growing all the time, **Tianze Lu** (天泽路 commonly known as **Lady's Street**) is a real Mecca for shopaholics, bargain hunters and glamour girls of all shapes and budgets. You can easily use up an entire day wandering around the clothes market and for a change of pace, you can make your way through the humid and fragrant flower market and any of the numerous nearby boutiques selling everything from trinkets to house wares.

After a day of shopping, what better way for resting weary feet than a visit to the east side of the women's emporium, where shoppers can meet up with the guys in their group who have no doubt taken refuge at either **Liyumen Gourmet Street** (鲤鱼门美食街) or **Super Bar Street** (星吧路). Start the evening's festivities at any of Liyumen's dozens of restaurants (from Chinese to African and everything in between) and end your day with celebratory drinks at any of a number of cozy, or jumping, nightclubs along the Super Bar Street. The entire area is becoming increasingly more popular, and so the pond flanked nightclubs are frequently host to Chinese pop stars, keep your eyes open and cameras ready!

Transport: Bus 特3 to Qicai Dashijie (七彩大世界) or 659, 707, 752 to Laitaihuahui (莱太花卉).

North

Airport Expr 首都机场

Tianze

Laitai Flo
莱花卉市

Restaurant listings

Meal prices per adult

¥ under RMB 29
¥¥ RMB 30-49
¥¥¥ RMB 50-69
¥¥¥¥ RMB 70-99
¥¥¥¥¥ over RMB 100

African

Ⓐ **Pili Pili** 比力必利
African
English menu　　　　¥¥¥¥¥
Hours:11am-1am
Transport: see transport to Lady's Street above
Super Bar Street, Laitai, Chaoyang District. (86-10-84483372/4332)
朝阳区莱太星吧路

As if straight from the grasslands of Kenya, you can almost hear the elephants trumpeting in this funky African hut-style restaurant—Beijing's one and only.

This and more at Xi Mi Hun Zhen Cun.

Chinese

Ⓑ **Xi Mi Hun Zhen Cun**
西迷魂阵村
Guizhou cuisine
English menu　　　　¥¥
Hours: 11am-11.30pm
Transport: see transport to Lady's Street above
No. 26, Tianze Lu, Chaoyang District. (86-10-84545539) 朝阳区天泽路26号

Serengeti specialties.

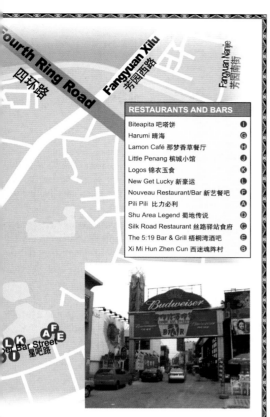

RESTAURANTS AND BARS

Biteapita 吧嗒饼	❶
Harumi 晴海	❻
Lamon Café 那梦香草餐厅	❸
Little Penang 槟城小馆	❿
Logos 锦衣玉食	❹
New Get Lucky 新豪运	❼
Nouveau Restaurant/Bar 新艺餐吧	❻
Pili Pili 比力必利	❹
Shu Area Legend 蜀地传说	❶
Silk Road Restaurant 丝路驿站食府	❸
The 5:19 Bar & Grill 梧桐湾酒吧	❸
Xi Mi Hun Zhen Cun 西迷魂阵村	❸

Quiet and comfortable, this Guizhou restaurant goes against the grain and provides eaters with plenty of elbow space. Housed on two floors and decorated with comfort in mind, it is highly recommended.

Silk Road Restaurant
丝路驿站食府

Xinjiang cuisine
English menu ¥¥¥

Hours: 11am-Late
Transport: see transport to Lady's Street on p.230
Qicai Beilu, Chaoyang District (south of Laitai Flower Market). (86-10-64656565/64676467) 朝阳区七彩北路 (莱太花卉市场南侧)

This all-singing, all-dancing restaurant is a commodious and pleasant place to try some food from Xinjiang. Their mutton kebabs are great.

Shu Area Legend
蜀地传说

Sichuan cuisine
English menu ¥¥¥

Hours: 10am-2am
Transport: see transport to Lady's Street on p.230
Super Bar Street, Chaoyang District.

Shu Area Legend.

(86-10-84543276) 朝阳区星吧路

Made famous by its Chinese actor owner, the blockbusting dish here is most certainly the Spicy fish cooked Sichuan-style (辣子鱼).

European

❸ The 5:19 Bar & Grill
梧桐湾酒吧

English menu ¥¥¥

Hours: 4pm-late (Mon-Fri); 11am-late (Sat-Sun)
Transport: see transport to Lady's Street on p.230
No. 26, Super Bar Street, Chaoyang District (next to Pili Pili). (86-10-84480896) 朝阳区星吧路 26 号 (Pili Pili 非洲餐厅旁)

A mixture of Western and Middle Eastern foods, this is a great place to grab a big bite or small snack. They have a good selection of sandwiches and hummus.

Fusion

❻ Nouveau Restaurant/Bar
新艺餐吧

English menu ¥¥¥¥

Hours: 11am-12am
Transport: see transport to Lady's Street on p.230
No. 20, Super Bar Street, Chaoyang District. (86-10-64607158) 朝阳区星吧路 20 号

Serving a fishy fusion of Asian cuisines, this is a quaint, elegant little place to dine or to relish a calming gulp of something cold.

Japanese

❻ Harumi 晴海

English menu ¥¥¥¥

Hours: 11.30am-2pm, 5.30pm-10pm
Transport: see transport to Lady's
Street on p.230
No. 31, Lady's Street, Chaoyang
District. (86-10-84480546) 朝阳区女
人街31号

The increasingly popular Japanese barbecue is performed to perfection at Harumi. Enjoy grilled Japanese specialties within the garden-style surroundings.

Mediterranean

ⓗ Lamon Café
那梦香草餐厅

English menu ¥¥¥
Hours: 10am-midnight
Transport: see transport to Lady's
Street on p.230
B6-B7, Liyumen Gourmet Street,
Chaoyang District. (86-10-64656681)
朝阳区鲤鱼门美食街B6-B7

The chefs at the upstairs-downstairs Lamon Café are specialists in fresh seafood dishes Mediterranean-style. With a closed-in garden area or views of the lake from the top floor, the surroundings aren't half bad either.

Middle Eastern

ⓞ Biteapita 吧嗒饼
Middle Eastern
English menu ¥¥¥
Hours: 10am-10pm; 10am-11pm (Fri
and Sat)
Transport: see transport to Lady's
Street on p.230
No. A30, Tianze Lu, Chaoyang District
(in front of the New Get Lucky Bar).
(86-10-64672961) 朝阳区天泽路甲
30号(新豪运吧前)

A fond favorite with Israelis (and Israeli-owned) they serve a mean falafel. Loud and busy, the chatter flies as freely as the pitas.

Southeast Asian

ⓞ Little Penang 槟城小馆
English menu ¥¥¥
Hours: 11am-11pm
Transport: see transport to Lady's
Street on p.230

No. 32, Tianze Lu, Chaoyang District
(close to Super Bar Street). (86-10-
64620004) 朝阳区天泽路32号(近
星吧路)

Offering a menu packed with traditional Southeast Asian dishes, notably those of Malaysia and Hong Kong, Little Penang is a cosmopolitan and trendy, yet inexpensive, place to dine.

Bar listings

Prices for a bottle of
Tsingtao beer (青岛啤酒),
a favorite local beer
¥   under RMB 14
¥¥   RMB 15-24
¥¥¥   RMB 25-34
¥¥¥¥   over RMB 35

ⓚ Logos 锦衣玉食
Local rock, live music
English menu and service ¥¥¥
Hours: 6pm-2am
Entrance: free
Transport: see transport to Lady's
Street on p.230
No. 2, Super Bar Street, Chaoyang
District. (86-10-84480880) 朝阳区星
吧路2号

While the sheepskin rugs, dramatic décor and geometric furnishings are a bit much for some, Logos' lakeside position and rock singer owner ensure a steady flow of customers.

ⓛ New Get Lucky 新豪运
Live music
English menu and service ¥¥¥
Hours: 4pm-2am
Entrance: RMB 30 (weekends only)
Transport: see transport to Lady's
Street on p.230
No. A1, Super Bar Street, Chaoyang
District. (86-10-84483339) 朝阳区星
吧路甲1号

New Get Lucky has chosen to leave the Cordon Bleu to others and offers a yummy selection of beers and greasy finger foods. They often have live music events.

Theaters

The theater listed below is marked on the map on p.214.

ⓞ Century Theater 21st
二十一世纪剧院
Classical, orchestra
Hours: according to program
Price: RMB 80-1800
Transport: Bus 413, 420, 701, 710
Anjialou (安家楼)
No. 40, Liangmaqiao Lu, Chaoyang
District. (86-10-64686708) 朝阳区亮
马桥路40号

This double-tiered theater is a fusion of Japanese and Chinese architectural styles; the result is unusual and attractive.

The ultra-modern Logos.

🛒 Shopping

With a population of over 200,000, Wangjing, in the Northeast, is the largest residential area in Asia (and that's really saying something!). As you would expect then, the area is rife with shopping centers and malls. Worth mentioning to our female readers (or anyone with a special lady on their gift list) is the aptly named **Lady's Street** (see below). However if foreign labels and/or designs are an important consideration in your fashion choices, a visit to the **Jia Yi Fashion Square** (see below) should "suit" you just fine! For the collectables type of shoppers, or those seeking potentially valuable and older items of interest, fret not as the **Liangma Antique Market** (see below) contains everything for almost every budget. Grab your wallets and brush up on your bargaining skills and venture into the shopping excitement of the Northeast.

The markets listed below are marked on the map on p.214.

Join the trend and visit Jiayi Fashion Square.

❷ Jiayi Fashion Square 佳亿时尚广场
Clothing, jewelry
Hours: 10am-9pm
Transport: Bus 413, 418, 813 to Xiaoliangmaqiao Xizhan (小亮马桥西站)
No. A3, Xinyuan Nanlu, Chaoyang District. (86-10-84511810) 朝阳区新源南路甲3号

A little pricier than other fashion markets, it does offer a different selection of fashions with styles from Italy, Japan and Singapore gracing the shelves.

❸ Lady's Street 女人街
Clothing
Hours: 10am-8pm

Transport: see p.230
Tianze Lu, Chaoyang District (500 m east of Lufthansa Center). (86-10-64626636) 朝阳区天泽路（燕莎友谊商城往东500米)

With over 700 boutiques this is a shopping Mecca. From clothes to shoes to accessories you can find all ranges, styles and quality.

Lady's Street is the spot to shop, ladies.

Leave your man at home and allow at least half a day to get round!

❹ Liangma Antique Market 亮马古玩收藏品市场
Antiques
Hours: 9.30am-6pm
Transport: Bus 413, 420, 701, 710 to Anjialou (安家楼)
No. 27, Liangmaqiao Lu, Chaoyang District. (86-10-64621625) 朝阳区亮马桥路27号

One of several, the Liangma Antique Market sports over 200 stalls selling a fascinating display of antiques, handicrafts and second-hand books. An interesting place to look around, even if you're not in the market for anything!

❺ Carrefour 家乐福
Supermarket
Hours: 8.30am-10.30pm
Transport: Bus 18, 300, 302, 367, 404, 419, 718, 725, 731, 801, 825, 967 to Jing'anzhuang (静安庄)
No. B6, Beisanhuan Donglu, Chaoyang District. (86-10-84601013) 朝阳区北三环东路乙6号

They have a good selection of cheese here for those in need of a fix.

Accommodation

With close proximity to the Beijing Capital Airport, it comes as no surprise that many first-class hotels have chosen to settle in the Northeast. In fact the **Airport Expressway** (机场高速), **Xiaoyun Lu** (霄云路) and **Liangmaqiao Lu** (亮马桥路) have the highest concentration of expensive international hotels, including the Holiday Inn Lido, the Kempinski Hotel and the Hilton (thrown in for good measure). The arrival of the 2008 Olympic Games will also see the **Airport Subway Line** (see p.312) open from Dongzhimen, and following the successful Hong Kong model will have baggage and ticket check-in available at the subway station itself.

It is also of little surprise that all of this makes the Northeast one of the most expensive places to stay during a trip to Beijing. However, near the **International Exhibition Center** (国际展览中心) and also near the Grand Dragon Hotel (close to East Third Ring Road) there are some cheaper hotels and hostels. It is strongly recommended that you book such rooms well in advance, as they do tend to go quickly (particularly during exhibition and international events *think Olympics*).

Another emerging option is appealing to those looking for a "home away from home" and can be found in what is being called **"mobile home" hotels** (no, they don't come on wheels). These recently developed home-style hotels are apartments of local Beijing folk who rent them out, fully equipped and comfortably furnished, saving you at least 40% over quality hotels of similar comfort. For more information on this type of unique lodging, visit their website (you can even reserve a room) at: **http://www.mohotel.com/en/**

All the places listed below are marked on the map on p.214.

Accommodation prices per night
¥ under RMB 99
¥¥ RMB 100-199
¥¥¥ RMB 200-299
¥¥¥¥ RMB 300-399
¥¥¥¥¥ over RMB 400

Hotels (prices based on double-occupancy rooms)		🏨	@	✕	🍸	🍴	🛒	🏠
Ⓐ **Julong Guangdian Hotel** 巨龙光电宾馆 2 star **English service** *Price: RMB 230-260* *Transport: Bus 402, 988 to Dashanzi (大山子)* *No.3, Jiuxianqiao Lu, Chaoyang District. (86-10-64315551) 朝阳区酒仙桥路 3 号* This delicately designed hotel has 64 rooms decorated in a fusion of modern and ancient Chinese styles.	¥¥¥	■	■	■		■	■	
Ⓑ **Hailun Hotel** 海伦宾馆 3 star *Price: RMB 240-280* *Transport: Bus 401, 955, 991 to Jiuxianqiao (酒仙桥)*	¥¥¥	■	■			■	■	

No.18, Jiangtai Xilu, Chaoyang District (close to Guobin Building). (86-10- 64330888) 朝阳区将台西路 18 号 (国宾大厦附近)
A bargain priced hotel stocked to the hilt with amenities: business center, conference room, laundry, parking, restaurant, tennis court…phew!

Yisida Hotel 益思达宾馆 ¥¥¥
2 star
Price: RMB 280
Transport: Bus 110, 606 to Liufang Beijie (柳芳北街)
Liufang Beijie, Chaoyang District. (86-10-64636655) 朝阳区柳芳北街
Great business services are provided, with fax, copying and typing services as well as secretarial options, and three commodious conference rooms. The rooms aren't half bad either!

Jiali Hotel 佳丽饭店 ¥¥¥
2 star
English service
Price: RMB 288
Transport: Bus 401, 955, 991 to Jiuxianqiao (酒仙桥)
No. B21, Jiuxianqiao Lu, Chaoyang District. (86-10-64363399) 朝阳区酒仙桥路乙 21 号
Clean, comfortable and convenient are the three "C"s to describe Jiali Hotel. Guests from all of its 49 rooms are invited to join in the lively karaoke downstairs!

Utels International Youth Hostel 万里路国际青年酒店 ¥¥¥
Price: RMB 238-298
Transport: Bus 300, 718, 725, 运通 104 to Xibahe (西坝河)
No.23, Xibahe Xili, Chaoyang District. (86-10-51391166) http://www.chinayha.com/ chinayhaE/indexe2.html 朝阳区西坝河西里 23 号
Many business features are on offer, in addition to its Chinese restaurant. A good budget option.

Guozhan Hotel 国展宾馆 ¥¥¥
2 star
English service
Price: RMB 268-350
Transport: Bus 特 8, 300, 801 to Jing'anzhuang (静安庄)
No.10, Jing'an Xijie, Chaoyang District (close to the International Exhibition Center). (86-10-64639922) www.bj-guozhanhotel.com 朝阳区静安西街 10 号 (国际展览中心附近)
With an international ambiance and carefully considered room facilities (Internet access and refrigerator in all rooms), the hotel seems to have got the formula just right.

Accommodation prices per night
¥ under RMB 99
¥¥ RMB 100-199
¥¥¥ RMB 200-299
¥¥¥¥ RMB 300-399
¥¥¥¥¥ over RMB 400

Comfortel Hotel

⑥ Ziyingge Hotel 紫英阁宾馆 ¥¥¥¥
3 star
Price: RMB 288-360
Transport: Bus 361, 701, 运通 101, 运通 107 to Huajiadi-Beili (花家地北里)
No.3, Huajiadi Donglu, Chaoyang District (close to Siemens Beijing Branch). (86-10-64720431) 朝阳区花家地东路 3 号 (西门子公司附近)
With restaurants offering Chinese or Western food, guests are spoilt for choice. Ticket booking and a business center are also available.

⑪ Comfortel Hotel 康菲特酒店 ¥¥¥¥
3 star
Price: RMB 300
Transport: Bus 特8, 300, 801 to Jing'anzhuang (静安庄)
No. 45, Jing'anli, Chaoyang District (close to the International Exhibition Center). (86-10-64612288) 朝阳区静安里 45 号 (国际展览中心附近)
The well-located Comfortel is what its name implies, a comfortable, European-style hotel. Easy airport access makes it a very convenient choice.

① Jing An Hotel 静安宾馆 ¥¥¥¥
3 star
Price: RMB 320-410
Transport: Bus 110, 104 快 to Jing'anli (静安里)
Xiangheyuan Zhongli, Zuojiazhuang, Dongzhimenwai, Chaoyang District (close to Jing'an Market). (86-10-64677177) 朝阳区东直门外左家庄香河园中里 (静安市场附近)
In addition to agreeable rooms and a comprehensive selection of business facilities, its restaurant and cocktail bar are nice extras for a well-deserved unwind!

① Minggong Hotel 明宫宾馆 ¥¥¥¥¥
3 star
Price: RMB 468, 488
Transport: Bus 300, 718, 725, 运通 104 to Xibahe (西坝河)
No.16, Xibahe Xili, Chaoyang District (close to Dazhong Home Appliances). (86-10-64273355) 朝阳区西坝河西里 16 号 (大中电器附近)
One of their 200 rooms (from single to triple and deluxe) will surely suit you. Well located near the International Exhibition Center.

⑯ Yuanfang Hotel 远方饭店 ¥¥¥¥¥
3 star
Price: RMB 470
Transport: Bus 300, 718, 725, 运通 104 to Xibahe (西坝河)
No.22, Guangximen Beili, Chaoyang District. (86-10-64225588) 朝阳区光熙门北里 22 号
With nearly 200 guest rooms, this hotel benefits from a great location near Subway Line 13 and the International Exhibition Center. Above standard for this price.

Itinerary

Itinerary I: Modern Art Tour

Morning

9am Take Bus 401, 402, 973, 991 to Dashanzi Lukounan (大山子路口南). Start your day at **Dashanzi Art District** (see p.220) where art galleries, studios and eateries abound. You may find 3 hours not enough for taking in all you want here, as there is much to see and do.

Afternoon

12pm From your morning explorations, you will have come across many choices for where to have your lunch. Restaurants, cafes, bistros and coffee bars can be found in abundance here. Spend a leisurely hour enjoying the atmosphere and rest up for your afternoon.

1pm Exit Dashanzi and head west to Jiuxianqiao Lu (酒仙桥路) and take Bus 402 at the stop called Dashanzi Lukounan (大山子路口南) on the east side of the road, get off at Caochangdi (草场地). Here you'll find the **East End Arts**, located just five km north of the Dashanzi Art District. This is a relatively new artist community, with many of its resident artists formerly based in Dashanzi. Rising popularity, and therefore costs, caused many of the founding artists from Dashanzi to relocate, many of them to East End Arts. Its stated purpose is to provide more art studios and galleries, in a less commercial environment. Enjoy two hours making your way through the variety of workspaces.

3pm Take Subway Line 1 to Dawang Lu (大望路), leave through Exit B, then take Bus "930支1" at Bawangfen Dong (八王坟东) to **Songzhuang** (宋庄) (see p.23). Then you can take a private motorcycle taxi there (just a few RMB) to one of the sites in this village. Your first impression of this village may not be good—shabby unpaved roads, garbage everywhere and simple houses. But upon closer look, you'll find some interesting artists who call themselves "villagers." The original farmers, influenced by the artists who came to the area, call themselves "artists," perhaps a strange mix, but it works. Offer to take their picture and they will happily "strike a pose." Songzhuang Village is a "melting pot" of art and people. Take some time and walk around, enjoying the canal and natural scenery here, amidst the tranquility you may just come to understand why these artists wanted to quit their modern life and live here.

5pm End of the day.

 **Bus Details**

Major Bus Stops

These are the major bus stops in the "Northeast." At each bus stop, there are direct routes to the key destinations. **They are marked on the map on p.214.**

Sanyuan Qiao (三元桥), close to Sanyuan Qiao

To Chaoyang Park (朝阳公园): 731, 831
To China Science & Technology Museum (中国科技馆): 967, 731, 954
To Dashanzi (大山子): 916, 923, 935
To Olympic Sports Center (奥林匹克体育中心): 985
To Wudaokou (五道口): 731, 825
To Yuanmingyuan (圆明园): 825

To Zhongguancun (中关村): 731, 302

Holiday Inn Lido (丽都饭店), in front of the hotel, on Jiangtai Lu (蒋台路)

To Beijing Zoo (动物园): 运通 104
To China Science & Technology Museum (中国科技馆): 967, 运通 104
To Pearl Market (红桥市场): 707
To Temple of Heaven (天坛): 707
To World Park (世界公园): 967
To Zhongguancun (中关村): 983 支

Useful Bus Routes

The following is a list of specially selected bus routes passing through the "Northeast" area. These are not all depot-to-depot routes and many less important stops have been omitted. Sights of interest are in bold type. Bus type and times of first and last buses from the first depot are also indicated.

Suggestion: if you are unsure you have the right stop, point out the Chinese characters below for where you want to go and ask another passenger, conductor or driver for help. Many young Chinese have OK English and will be able to help.

运通 104 (standard bus, 5.45am-9.30pm)

Wangjing New City 望京新城 -Holiday Inn Lido 丽都饭店 -Sanyuan Qiao 三元桥 -Xibahe 西坝河 -**China Science & Technology Museum 中国科技馆** -Beijing Normal University 师范大学 -Xinjiekou Huokou 新街口豁口 -**Beijing Zoo 动物园** -Baishiqiao 白石桥 -**Purple Bamboo Park 紫竹院**

运通 107 (standard bus, 5.30am-8.30pm)

Wangjing New City 望京新城-Wangjing Lu 望京路-Holiday Inn Lido 丽都饭店 -Jiuxian Qiao 酒仙桥-Lufthansa Friendship Shopping Center 燕莎友谊商城 -Liangma Qiao 亮马桥 -Agricultural Exhibition Center 农展馆 -

Panjiayuan 潘家园

401 路 (standard bus, 5am-11pm)

Dongzhimenwai 东直门外-Zuojiazhuang 左家庄 -Sanyuan Qiao 三元桥 -Holiday Inn Lido (on Jingshun Lu) 京顺路丽都饭店 -Dashanzi Lukounan 大山子路口南 -Wangyefen 王爷坟 -Jiuxian Qiao 酒仙桥

403路 (standard bus, 5.05am-11.05pm)

Dashanzi Lukoudong 大山子路口东 -Holiday Inn Lido (on Jingshun Lu) 京顺路丽都饭店 -Siyuanqiao Dong 四元桥东 -Sanyuan Qiao 三元桥 -Xingfu Sancun 幸福三村 -**Workers' Stadium 工人体育场** -Beijing Railway Station East 北京站东

404 路 (standard bus, 5am-11pm)

Dongzhimenwai 东直门外-Sanyuan Qiao 三元桥-Holiday Inn Lido (on Jingshun Lu) 京顺路饭都饭店-Wangjing Huayuan Xiqu 望京花园西区-Laiguangying 来广营

408 路 (standard bus, 5.30am-10pm)

Yanhuang Art Museum 炎黄艺术馆-Anhuiqiao Bei 安慧桥北-Wangjingqiao Xi 望京桥西-Holiday Inn Lido 丽都饭店-Jiuxian Qiao 酒仙桥

413 路 (standard bus, 5.30am-9.30pm)

Nanshiliju 南十里居-Jiuxianqiao Shopping Mall 酒仙桥商场-**Chaoyang Park North Gate 朝阳公园北门**-Anjialou 安家楼-Yanshaqiao Dong 燕莎桥东-Chunxiu Lu 春秀路-Dongzhimen 东直门

418 路 (standard bus, 5.30am-9.30pm)

Caochangdi 草场地-Wangjing Park 望京公园-Dashanzi Lukoudong 大山子路口东-Jiuxian Qiao 酒仙桥-**Chaoyang Park North Gate 朝阳公园北门**-Anjialou 安家楼-Chunxiu Lu 春秀路-Dongzhimen 东直门

606 路 (standard bus, 6am-9.30pm)

Wangjingqiao Bei 望京桥北-Xibahe 西坝河-Guangximen Beili 光熙门北里-International Exhibition Center 国际展览中心-Liufang Beijie 柳芳北街-Dongtucheng Lu 东土城路-Beixiaojie Huokou 北小街豁口-Yonghegongqiao Dong 雍和宫桥东

614 路 (standard bus, 5.30am-8.30pm)

Wangjing Science & Technology Park 望京科技创业园-Wangjing Huayuan 望京花园-Sanyuan Qiao 三元桥-Zuojiazhuang 左家庄-Chunxiu Lu 春秀路-Dongzhimen 东直门

623 路 (standard bus, 6am-8.15pm)

Dongzhimen 东直门-Sanyuan Qiao 三元桥-Wangjingqiao Dong 望京桥东-Nanhu Nanlu 南湖南路-Wangjing Huayuan 望京花园-Wangjing Science & Technology Park 望京科技创业园

701路 (standard bus, 5.45am-8pm)

Beihai Park North Gate 北海北门-Di'anmen Dong 地安门东-Dongsishitiao 东四十条-**Workers' Stadium 工人体育场**-**Sanlitun 三里屯**-Agricultural Exhibition Center 农业展览馆-Jiuxian Qiao 酒仙桥-Holiday Inn Lido 丽都饭店

707路 (standard bus, 5.30am-8.30pm)

Temple of Heaven North Gate 天坛北门-Agricultural Exhibition Center 农业展览馆-Holiday Inn Lido 丽都饭店-Huajiadi Beili 花家地北里-Wangjing Huayuan Xiqu 望京花园西区

801路 (standard bus, 5.50am-8pm)

Agricultural Exhibition Center 农业展览馆-Sanyuan Qiao 三元桥-Xibahe 西坝河-Anzhenqiao Xi 安贞桥西-**China Science & Technology Museum 中国科技馆**-**Zhongguancun Nan 中关村南**-Zhongguanyuan 中关园-**Yuanmingyuan South Gate 圆明园南门**-**Summer Palace 颐和园**

813路 (standard bus, 5.50am-8.30pm)

Workers' Stadium 工人体育场-Xingfu Sancun 幸福三村-Yanshaqiao Xi 燕莎桥西-Jiuxian Qiao 酒仙桥-Dashanzi Lukoudong 大山子路口东-Caihong Lu 彩虹路-Caochangdi 草场地

955路 (standard bus, 6.30am-9pm)

Dongzhimenwai 东直门外-Xinyuan Nanlu Xikou 新源南路西口-Yanshaqiao Dong 燕莎桥东-Anjialou 安家楼-Jiuxian Qiao 酒仙桥-Jiangtai Lukoubei 将台路口北-Dashanzi Lukounan 大山子路口南

966路 (standard bus, 6.30am-8.30pm)

Dongzhimen 东直门-International Exhibition Center 国际展览中心-Wangjingqiao Nan 望京桥南-Nanhu Xili 南湖西里-Wangjing Huayuan Xiqu 望京花园西区-Guangshunqiao Nan 广顺桥南

Commerce, commerce and more commerce. The Int'l Finance Center.

"Modern" East

I f any area can be considered home to "business" in Beijing, it is the "East."

This is where the **Central Business District (CBD)** is located and it's also the densest residential area of foreign expats. From the famous **Sanlitun Bar Street** (see p.248), to embassies of almost all foreign governments. It is like "foreign town" in China.

Every type of business, shop, housing, hotel and restaurant can also be found. Under rapid and ongoing construction, the CBD is slated to continue its expansion. Considering that almost everywhere in China is under construction, stating that the CBD is one of the areas undergoing the most dynamic and intense changes is really saying something!

Given the frenetic pace of redevelopment and new businesses, despite our efforts to ensure information is as up-to-date as possible, there will be instances where a business, bar or restaurant, is no more.

Highlights

◆ **Temple of the God of Mount Tai** 东岳庙 Dedicated to Mount Tai, one of the five sacred mountains in China, this is still a practicing place of Taoist worship. **See p.243**

◆ **Sanlitun Bar Street** 三里屯酒吧街 Whatever type of bar you are looking for, it is here. Additionally this area is full of some of the best restaurants in Beijing. **See p.248**

◆ **Chaoyang Theater** 朝阳剧场 Acrobats on the flying trapeze, eat your heart out! You pale in comparison to what goes on here! **See p.259**

◆ **Silk Street** 秀水 Yes, they have silk, but that is just the tip of the iceberg. You can come here and find almost anything you are looking for. **See p.260**

The China World Trade Center.

Sightseeing

Tourist Attractions

❶ Chaoyang Park 朝阳公园
Cháoyáng gōngyuán ★

The most dynamic public park in the east part of Beijing

Hours: park 6.30am-8.30pm, amusements open from 8am-6pm
Entrance: RMB 5 (amusements have separate ticket prices)
Suggested length of visit: 1-2 hours
Transport: Bus 117, 302, 703, 710, 815, 985 to Chaoyang Park (朝阳公园) or 419, 852, 985 to Chaoyang Park West Gate (朝阳公园西门)
No.1, Nongzhanguan Nanlu, Chaoyang District. (86-10-65065409)
朝阳区农展馆南路1号

C haoyang Park, intentionally created to be Beijing's largest public park, is certainly that. In a city as vast as this, Chaoyang offers locals and visitors the chance to see plenty of greenery, take a long walk around the lake, enjoy sculptures, bungee jumping, amusements, a swimming pool, or to simply relax. The park is accessible from north, south, east and west gates.

❷ Ritan Park 日坛公园
Rìtán gōngyuán ★

An altar where emperors worshipped the sun

Hours: 6am-9pm
Entrance: free
Suggested length of visit: 1 hour
Transport: Bus 639, 640 to Ritan Park (日坛公园)
No. 6, Ritan Lu, Jianguomenwai, Chaoyang District. (86-10-85616301)
朝阳区建国门外日坛路6号

R itan (Temple of the Sun) is part of an elite group of Beijing parks. Forming the five major spots where Chinese emperors worshipped the gods, Ritan and its three counterparts (Temple of the Earth, Temple of the Moon and Temple of Heaven) stretch across the city surrounding their central marker, the Altar of Land and Grain.

Constructed in 1530, Ritan was an altar where emperors performed annual rites to the sun. Today it serves local people (including the diplomatic community), with such things as a teahouse, rock-

There is something fun happening anytime at Chaoyang Park.

climbing wall, foot-powered mono rail, kites, fishponds and a bonsai market.

❸ Temple of the God of Mount Tai 东岳庙 Dōngyuèmiào ★

Folk museum and Taoist temple

Hours: 8.30am-4.30pm
Entrance: RMB 10
Suggested length of visit: 1 hour
Transport: Bus 109, 110, 112, 750, 813 to Shenlu Jie (神路街)
No.141,Chaoyangmenwai Dajie Zhongduan, Chaoyang District. (86-10- 65510151)
朝阳门外大街中段141号

📝 With the Museum Pass you can get two free admissions.

Dating back more than 600 years, this temple is still a practicing place of Taoist worship, being the biggest temple of the Zhengyi Sect of Taoism in north China. It is also the place of worship for the God of Mount Tai, one of China's five sacred mountains. The over 3,000 statues of gods in different gestures and expressions are the biggest draw of this temple.

Home to the **Beijing Folk Museum**, it holds regular cultural activities during traditional Chinese festivals, such as Spring Festival and Mid-autumn Festival.

Temple of the God of Mount Tai.

Museums

❹ Poly Art Museum 保利博物馆 ★

Hours: daily 9.30am-4.30pm (closed on Sundays and state holidays)
Entrance: RMB 50
Suggested length of visit: 1 hour
Transport: Bus 115, 118 or Subway Line 2 to Dongsishitiao (东四十条)
2/F, Poly Plaza, No. 14, Dongzhimen Nandajie. (86-10-65001188 ext. 3250)
东直门南大街14号保利大厦2层

This small but perfectly formed museum displays some beautiful national treasures including ancient bronzes, Buddha statues and stone carvings, and shows many pieces retrieved from abroad. Be sure to seek out the three-ox-head goblets of the Shang Dynasty, exquisite.

❺ Beijing Jintai Art Museum 北京金台艺术馆

Hours: 10am-4pm
Entrance: free (but it costs RMB 5 to enter the Chaoyang Park)
Suggested length of visit: 1/2 hour
Transport: see transport to Chaoyang Park on p.242
Inside Chaoyang Park West Gate. (86-10-65019441)
http://www.jintaimuseum.org/
朝阳公园西门内

The museum aims to bring to life China's ancient folk art and cultural heritage, while introducing into China an eclectic mix of arts from abroad. The adjacent sculpture park of eminent foreign celebrities is worth wandering through.

⨝ Food and Entertainment

The East is arguably one of the most famous spots for having fun. Any foreigner who has been in Beijing longer than a weekend will know where to find **Sanlitun** (see p.248), **Chaoyang Park** (see p.254), or the **Workers' Stadium** (see below). But fame comes at a price, so expect to pay more in this part of town.

For live performances, jump, roll, tumble or swing your way over to the **Chaoyang Theater** (see p.259), one of the two places in the East for acrobatic shows that will delight and amaze you.

The following hot spots are marked on the map on p.240.

Swallow Kite.

Around the Workers' Stadium
工体周围

The Workers' Stadium is a colossal building; you can't fail to find it. Constructed as a monument to China's sporting heritage, it is now a venue for sports and entertainment events. It is ringed with a selection of sports and health shops, with some teahouses thrown in for good measure!

If you're tired just thinking about all that sport, then several acclaimed restaurants will do the trick. The **Outback Steakhouse** (see p.245) is a long-standing favorite, and serves a mean rump steak, while the **Green T. House** (see p.246) couldn't be more in contrast, serving delicate Asian-fusion cuisine within the surroundings of an art gallery. If it is arts rather than sports that float your boat, then be sure to visit the **Beijing Art Now Gallery (BANG)** which houses some nationally acclaimed artists' pieces. Completing the whole experience, one mustn't forget **Vics** (see p.247) and **Babyface** (see p.247)—the area's pumping nightspots!

Transport: Bus 110, 113, 118, 406, 701, 758, 813, 823 to Workers' Stadium (工人体育场); or Subway Line 2 to Dongsishitiao (东四十条), then walk along Gongrentiyuchang Beilu (工人体育场北路) to Workers' Stadium.

North

Shizipo Jie 十字坡街

Xinzhongjie Sitiao 新中街四条

Xinzhongjie Ertiao 新中街二条

Xinzhongjie Yitiao 新中街一条

Gongrentiyuchang B

Xinzhong Jie 新中街

Workers' Gymnasium
工人体育馆

Restaurant listings

Meal prices per adult

¥ under RMB 29
¥¥ RMB 30-49
¥¥¥ RMB 50-69
¥¥¥¥ RMB 70-99
¥¥¥¥¥ over RMB 100

American

Ⓐ Outback Steakhouse
澳拜客

English menu ¥¥¥¥¥
Hours: 5pm-11pm (Mon-Fri), 11am-10.30pm (Sat-Sun)
Transport: see transport to Workers' Stadium on p.244
Inside Workers' Stadium North Gate,

American owned, Australian themed.

Chaoyang District. (86-10-65066608) 朝阳区工人体育场北门内东侧
American-style grill restaurant

gives you big chunks of meat with the appropriate side dishes. The big deep-fried onion is their specialty appetizer.

Chinese

Ⓑ Anytime Café 狮子山下
Cantonese cuisine
English menu ¥¥
Hours: 10am-1pm
Transport: Bus 113, 115, 406, 416, 701, 734 to Sanlitun (三里屯)
No. 4, Gongti Beilu, Chaoyang District (close to Yashow Market). (86-10-65863948) 朝阳区工体北路4号 (近雅秀市场旁)

You can sample the incredibly vast cuisine of Guangdong by day and party with the KTV

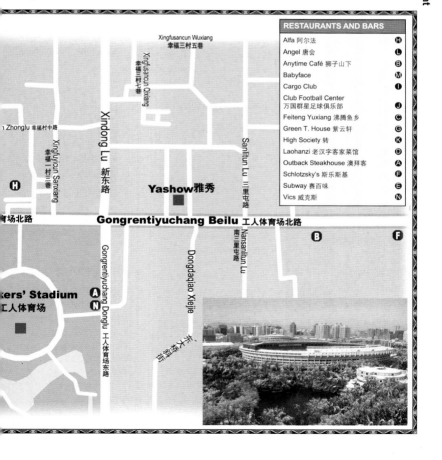

RESTAURANTS AND BARS	
Alfa 阿尔法	Ⓗ
Angel 唐会	Ⓛ
Anytime Café 狮子山下	Ⓑ
Babyface	Ⓜ
Cargo Club	Ⓘ
Club Football Center 万国群星足球俱乐部	Ⓙ
Feiteng Yuxiang 沸腾鱼乡	Ⓒ
Green T. House 紫云轩	Ⓖ
High Society 转	Ⓚ
Laohanzi 老汉字客家菜馆	Ⓓ
Outback Steakhouse 澳拜客	Ⓐ
Schlotzsky's 斯乐斯基	Ⓕ
Subway 赛百味	Ⓔ
Vics 威克斯	Ⓝ

Anytime Café also provides your libations.

crowd at night in this super cool Cantonese joint. Guangdong is legendary for its culinary diversity.

❻ Feiteng Yuxiang 沸腾鱼乡

Sichuan cuisine

English menu   ¥¥¥¥

Hours: 11am-2.30pm, 4pm-10pm (Mon); 11am-2.30pm, 4pm-10.30pm (Tues-Sun)
Transport: see transport to Workers' Stadium on p.244
Chunxiu Lu, No. 1, Gongti Beilu, Chaoyang District. (86-10-64153764)
朝阳区工体北路1号春秀路

Leave your nice shirts at home, strap on a bib and chow down at this Sichuan place where you can get the best Hot boiled fish (水煮鱼) in all of Beijing.

Feiteng Yuxiang.

❼ Laohanzi 老汉字客家菜馆

Hakka

English menu   ¥¥¥¥¥

Hours: 11am-2pm, 5pm-11pm

Transport: see transport to Workers' Stadium on p.244
1/F, Just Make Plaza, No. 57, Xingfucun Zhonglu, Chaoyang District. (86-10-64177720) 朝阳区幸福村中路57号杰座大厦1层

With savory dishes like Three cup duck (三杯鸭) and Sizzling perch (纸包鲈鱼), this place is the perfect introduction to the Chinese minority Hakka cuisine. You won't be disappointed with the quality.

Deli & Sandwich

❺ Subway 赛百味

English menu   ¥¥

Hours: 10am-10pm
Transport: see transport to Workers' Stadium on p.244
Opposite Workers' Gymnasium North Gate, Chaoyang District. (86-10-64169480) 朝阳区工人体育馆北门对面

Famous international sandwich shop gives you what you've been missing, foot long or six-inch sandwiches with all the trimmings and sauces. Just ask for double cheese or meat.

❻ Schlotzsky's 斯乐斯基

English menu   ¥¥¥

Hours: 8am-9pm (Mon-Fri), 11am-7pm (Sat and Sun)
Transport: Bus 113, 115, 117, 701, 958 to Changhongqiao Xi (长虹桥西) No. 102, 1/F, Pacific Century Place, No. A2, Gongti Beilu, Chaoyang District. (86-10-65393922) 朝阳

区工体北路甲2号盈科中心1层102号

Straight out of Texas, this sandwich shop has its own baked bread, fresh from the oven. Texans are passionate about their food, so rest assured it's delicious.

Fusion

❼ Green T. House 紫云轩

English menu   ¥¥¥¥

Hours: 12pm-3pm, 6pm-12am
Transport: Bus 115, 118, 406, 758 to Workers' Gymnasium (工人体育馆) No. 6, Gongti Xilu, Chaoyang District. (86-10-65528310/11) 朝阳区工体西路6号

This tripped-out teahouse restaurant will delight your senses and perhaps even make you a bit giddy. Interesting and fun décor and great food make this a relaxing afternoon or evening locale.

Let Green T. House tease all your senses.

Bar listings

Prices for a bottle of Tsingtao beer (青岛啤酒), a favorite local beer

¥ under RMB 14
¥¥ RMB 15-24
¥¥¥ RMB 25-34
¥¥¥¥ over RMB 35

❽ Alfa 阿尔法

Disco

English menu and service   ¥¥

A hot dance spot. Alfa.

Hours: 4pm-2am
Entrance: free
Transport: see transport to Workers'
Stadium on p.244
No. 6, Xingfu Yicun, Chaoyang
District. (in the lane opposite Work-
ers' Stadium North Gate). (86-10-
64130086) 朝阳区幸福一村6号 (工
体北门对面胡同)

This is a crazy bar with lots of fun events like 80s nights. You can also pop upstairs for a bite to eat at La Mission. Never a dull moment here.

Cargo Club

Rock, pop; live bands
English menu and service   ¥¥
Hours: 7.30pm-late
Entrance: free (Mon-Thurs), RMB 50
(Fri-Sun)
Transport: see transport to Workers'
Stadium on p.244
No. 6, Gongti Xilu, Chaoyang District.
(86-10-65516898/78) 朝阳区工体西
路6号

Party people who miss the 80s can go back in time on the dance floor. Great visuals including an enormous LED wall in synch with the beat.

Club Football Center
万国群星足球俱乐部

Pop, rock
English menu and service   ¥¥
Hours: 11am-11pm
Entrance: free
Transport: Bus 117, 413, 416, 418,
*623, 815 to Chunxiu Lu (*春秀路*)*
Red House Hotel, No. 10, Chunxiu
Lu, Chaoyang District. (86-10-
64167786) 朝阳区春秀路10号瑞秀
宾馆

A sports bar of the true vein that shows plenty of live soccer games as well as basketball and American football. Football, pool and darts are on hand if you want to get up.

High Society 转

Jazz
English menu and service   ¥¥
Hours: 11.30am-2am
Entrance: free
Transport: Bus 117, 413, 416, 418,
*623, 815 to Chunxiu Lu (*春秀路*)*
1/F, Just Make Plaza, No. 55, Xingfu
Zhongjie, Chaoyang District. (86-10-
64179780) 朝阳区幸福中街55号杰
座大厦首层

Relaxation is the goal of this bar. Jazz plays on a small stage and delicate and aromatic wines complement a superb menu. Ceramic art works are on display.

Angel 唐会

Disco, rock, hip hop
English menu and service   ¥¥¥
Hours: 8.30pm-late
Entrance: RMB 50+ (Fri/Sat)
Transport: see transport to Workers'
Stadium on p.244
No. 6, Gongti Xilu, Chaoyang District
(between Gongti 100 Bowling Alley
and Bellagio). (86-10-65528888) 朝
阳区工体西路6号 (工体一百保龄球
馆和鹿港小镇之间)

A bigger, better clone of next-door Babyface, this place is well serviced by a large staff and has big private rooms with DJ decks for private parties.

Babyface

Disco, rock, hip hop
English menu and service   ¥¥¥
Hours: 8.30pm-late
Entrance: RMB 50+ (Fri/Sat)
Transport: see transport to Workers'
Stadium on p.244
No. 6, Gongti Xilu, Chaoyang District
(next to Gongti 100 Bowling Alley).
(86-10-65519081) 朝阳区工体西路6
号 (工体一百保龄球馆旁)

Pretentious place filled with money flashers, yet still immensely popular. After debuting in Guangzhou, this is now a famous club in China.

Vics 威克斯

Hip hop
English menu and service   ¥¥¥
Hours: 8.30pm-late
Entrance: RMB 30 (Sun-Thurs), RMB
50 (Fri-Sat)
Transport: see transport to Workers'
Stadium on p.244
Inside Workers' Stadium North Gate,
Chaoyang District. (86-10-65936215)
朝阳区工体北门内

This place is always packed, a great place to go with a few friends for a fun night. Mix of R&B and hip hop, some trance. New "relaxation zone" now open.

High class, high fashion, and high times at Angel.

Sanlitun Bar Street 三里屯酒吧街

H ow to describe Sanlitun? A whole host of opposing adjectives spring to mind, and in truth, most are apt.

Sanlitun is an area of contrasts, frequented by expats and foreign visitors. With a top-notch selection of Western and Asian restaurants, you will find anything your taste buds are looking for. Turn off one of the leafy, tree-lined streets fringed with guarded foreign embassies however, and you will find yourself on bar street, which is anything but guarded—a hubbub of nightlife and entertainment that continues into the wee hours.

Early bar street residents such as **Aperitivo** (see p.253), **Bar Blu** (see p.252) or **Kai Club** (see p.252) are still strong favorites where karaoke blares out. If it's something a little more subdued you're after (firstly avoid Bar Street!), head for the chilled out roof-top cafés and gardens of bars such as **The Tree** (see p.253), which offers Mediterranean-style sidewalk tables, perfect for a quiet sip of something cool.

A little "home away from home," Sanlitun offers a taste of something you know, while never letting you forget you're in China!

Transport: Bus 113, 115, 406, 416, 701, 758 to Sanlitun (三里屯)

RESTAURANTS AND BARS

Alameda
Aperitivo 意式餐吧
Bar Blu 蓝吧
Beer Mania 麦霓啤酒吧
Bookworm 书虫综合餐吧
Brown's Pub 红磨坊
Cheers Café
Downtown Café & Bar 骉姿园
Fish Nation 鱼邦三里屯店
Flo Prestige 福楼
Gesangmedo 格桑梅朵
Javayangon 印甸苑
Jazz Ya 爵士屋
Kai Club 开
Kiosk
Le Petit Gourmand 小美食家
Le Petit Paris 小巴黎
Middle 8th Restaurant 中八楼
Old Town Roses 老镇玫瑰西餐厅
Poachers Inn 友谊青年吧
Qu Na'r 去那儿
The Bund
The Tree 树酒吧
Top Club and Lounge
Yunnan Yinxiang 云南印象

Chunxiu Lu 春秀路

Gongrentiyuchang Xilu 工人体育场西路

Workers' S
工人体育

Restaurant listings

Meal prices per adult

¥ under RMB 29
¥¥ RMB 30-49
¥¥¥ RMB 50-69
¥¥¥¥ RMB 70-99
¥¥¥¥¥ over RMB 100

Brazilian

Ⓐ Alameda

English menu   ¥¥¥¥

Hours: noon-3pm, 5pm-10.30pm (Mon-Sat)

Transport: see transport to Sanlitun above

Sanlitun Beijie, Chaoyang District (beside Nali Shopping Complex). (86-10-64178084) 朝阳区三里屯北街(那里秀色服装市场旁边)

Hungry for charbroiled meat on a skewer? The Brazilians do it better than most. Said to be one of the best restaurants in town, the food here is fresh and there's

Liangmahe Nanlu 亮马河南路 **D**

North

Sanlitun Dongliujie 三里屯东六街

Sanlitun Dongwujie 三里屯东五街

Xindong Lu 新东路

Sanlitun Beixiaojie 三里屯北小街

Sanlitun Lu 三里屯路

M

Sanlitun Xiwujie 三里屯西五街

Sanlitun Dongjie 三里屯东街

Dongzhimenwai Dajie 东直门外大街

D

Dongsanhuan Lu 东三环路

K

Xindong Lu 新东路

J

Sanlitun Lu 三里屯路

Sanlitun Zhongjie 三里屯中街

Sanlitun Dongsijie 三里屯东四街

Xingfusancun Wuxiang 幸福三村五巷

Sanlitun Dongsanjie 三里屯东三街

Xingfusancun Sixiang 幸福三村四巷

C E

3.3 Clothing Market 三点三服饰大厦

N T O U
G

B

L V
W X
P S

三里屯路

Y F A

Yashow 雅秀

Gongrentiyuchang Beilu 工人体育场北路

R

H

Dongdaqiao Xiejie 东大桥斜街

Nansanlitun Lu 南三里屯路

Q

Gongrentiyuchang Dongli

---

plenty of space for you and all your hungry friends.

Chinese

B Middle 8ᵗʰ Restaurant
中八楼
Yunnan cuisine
English menu ¥¥¥

Middle 8ᵗʰ Restaurant.

Hours: 11am-12.30am
Transport: Bus 113, 115, 117, 701,
958 to Changhongqiao Xi (长虹桥西)
Building 8, Sanlitun Beijie, Chaoyang
District. (86-10-64130629) 朝阳区三
里屯北街8号楼

Featuring food from the green, beautiful and ethnically diverse southern province, this restaurant exhibits just how delicious Yunnan cuisine can be. Specialties are Kung-Pow mushrooms (宫爆蘑菇) and Rice wine (米酒).

ⓓ Qu Na'r 去那儿
Zhejiang cuisine
English menu　　　　　¥¥¥
Hours: 4pm-11am
Transport: Bus 402, 405, 701, 801, 825, 984 to Agricultural Exhibition Center (农业展览馆)
No. 16, Dongsanhuan Beilu, Chaoyang District (in the lane behind the sign "Lapopo"). (86-10-65081597)朝阳区东三环北路16号(辣婆婆牌子后面巷内)

Arty place with home cooking. Opened by Chinese art guru Ai Weiwei, this place has received positive reviews. Funky wines available like the plum and red bayberry.

ⓓ Gesangmedo 格桑梅朵
Tibetan
English menu　　　　　¥¥¥¥
Hours: 9.30am-2pm, 5pm-11pm
Transport: Bus 117, 120, 823 to Xingfusancun (幸福三村)
Southwest corner of the intersection of Xindong Lu, Dongzhimenwai Dajie,
Chaoyang District (opposite Canadian Embassy). (86-10-64179269) 朝阳区东直门外大街新东路路口西南角(加拿大使馆对面)

You can feast on buttery yak at this interesting, unique Tibetan spot and stick around to watch the exciting nightly performance at 9.

ⓔ Yunnan Yinxiang 云南印象
Yunnan cuisine
English menu　　　　　¥¥¥¥
Hours: 10.30am-10.30pm
Transport: Bus 402, 405, 701, 801, 825, 984 to Agricultural Exhibition Center (农业展览馆)
No. 16, Dongsanhuan Beilu, Chaoyang District (in the lane behind the sign "Lapopo"). (86-10-85951277)朝阳区东三环北路16号(辣婆婆牌子后面巷内)

Yunnan food is a step outside the box when it comes to Chinese cuisine. This is an unpredictable restaurant as the menu is constantly changing.

Deli & Sandwich

ⓕ Kiosk
English menu　　　　　¥¥¥

Hours: 11am-9pm
Transport: Bus 117, 120, 823 to Xingfusancun (幸福三村)
Nali Mall, Sanlitun Beijie, Chaoyang District (in front of Jazz Ya). (86-10-64132461) 朝阳区三里屯北街那里秀色服装市场 (Jazz Ya 的前面)

Sandwiches, burgers and sausages served up Serbian style in a little shop with outdoor seating. There's a coffee shop nearby that will give you refuge when the weather gets nasty.

English

ⓖ Fish Nation 鱼邦三里屯店
English menu　　　　　¥¥¥
Hours: 11am-2am (weekdays), 11am-4am (weekends)
Transport: Bus 117, 120, 823 to Xingfusancun (幸福三村)
Sanlitun Beijie, Chaoyang District (close to Poachers Inn). (86-10-64150119) 朝阳区三里屯北街 (友谊青年酒吧附近)

Fish 'n' Chips? It's here with massive fish fillets and thick-cut chips. Add a Belgian beer and some Asian specials like squid and tempura prawns and you've got a winner.

A mouthful of yak and an eyeful of dancers at Gesangmedo.

Bookworm — A haven for lovers of quality reading, eating and relaxing!

European

ⓘ Bookworm
书虫综合餐吧

English menu ¥¥

Hours: 9am-2am

Transport: Bus 113, 115, 117, 701, 958 to Changhongqiao Xi (长虹桥西) Building 4, Nansanlitun Lu, Chaoyang District. (86-10-65869507) 朝阳区南三里屯路4号楼

Book lovers with an appetite could find no better spot to have a light or big meal. Sandwiches, pastas, and larger meals are on the menu along with over 40 different wines.

ⓘ Old Town Roses
老镇玫瑰西餐厅

English menu ¥¥¥¥¥

Hours: 10am-1am

Transport: Bus 110, 623, 823 to Xinyuanli (新源里)

Old Town Roses.

No. 1, Sanlitun, Chaoyang District (south of the Liangma River). (86-10-64612689) 朝阳区三里屯1号(亮马河南)

All pretentiousness is set aside in this simple European restaurant designed in simple wood beams and furniture. Enjoy a pizza, pasta or steak in a relaxed environment.

French

ⓞ Le Petit Paris 小巴黎

English menu ¥¥¥

Hours: 9am-9pm

Transport: Bus 117, 120, 823 to Xingfusancun (幸福三村)

No. 29, Sanlitun Beijie, Chaoyang District (opposite the French School). (86-10-64169381) 朝阳区三里屯北街29号(法国学校对面)

Specializing in sandwiches and other delights at good prices, you can relax outside in their lush green patio. In cold months, the DVD room is a great place to relax.

ⓚ Flo Prestige 福楼

English menu ¥¥¥¥¥

Hours: 11am-2.30pm, 6pm-11pm

Transport: Bus 402, 405, 701, 801, 825, 984 to Agricultural Exhibition Center (农业展览馆)

2/F, Rainbow Plaza, No. 16, Dongsanhuan Beilu, Chaoyang District (close to the Great Wall Hotel). (86-10-65955135) 朝阳区东三环北路16号隆博广场2层(近长城饭店)

Featuring an online menu, this French restaurant even provides take-out and delivery. All the best of authentic French food, with the convenience of home or office delivery.

ⓛ Le Petit Gourmand
小美食家

English menu ¥¥¥¥¥

Hours: 10.30am-12am

Transport: see transport to Sanlitun on p.248

3/F, Tongli Studio, Sanlitun, Chaoyang District. (86-10-64176095) 朝阳区三里屯同里3层

French food done American-style, this place has a massive 9,000 volume library and wireless Internet. Sample the crepes or couscous. Comfortable and welcoming, you can lose yourself here.

Pick a book to read with dinner at Le Petit Gourmand.

Indonesian and Burmese

ⓜ Javayangon 印甸苑

English menu and service ¥¥¥

Hours: 11.30am-2.30pm, 4,30pm-10.30pm

Transport: Bus 117, 120, 823 to Xingfusancun (幸福三村)

Xiwu Jie, Sanlitun, Chaoyang District (behind German Embassy). (86-10-84517489) 朝阳区三里屯西五街(德国大使馆后面)

RMB 118 set meal for two-three people; RMB 228 set meal for four-five people.

In Beijing this is the only place you can get real Burmese and Indonesian food. It's situated in a natural outdoor environment amongst trees.

MODERN' EAST · Food and Entertainment

Bar listings

Prices for a bottle of Tsingtao beer (青岛啤酒), a favorite local beer

¥ under RMB 14
¥¥ RMB 15-24
¥¥¥ RMB 25-34
¥¥¥¥ over RMB 35

ⓃKai Club 开
House, indie rock, break beats & old school
English menu and service ¥
Hours: 11am-2am (Mon-Fri), 11am-4am (Sat-Sun)
Entrance: free
Transport: see transport to Sanlitun on p.248
Sanlitun Beijie, Chaoyang District (around the corner from Poachers Inn). (86-10-64166254) 朝阳区三里屯北街 (从友谊青年吧拐弯)

It's party time at this place where the young and beautiful hang out. Lots of different music and reasonable drink prices ensure it's packed on the weekend.

ⓄPoachers Inn 友谊青年吧
R&B, hip hop
English service ¥
Hours: 8.30pm-late
Entrance: free (Fri-Sat)
Transport: see transport to Sanlitun on p.248
No. 43, Sanlitun Beijie, Chaoyang District. (86-10-64172632 ext. 8506) 朝阳区三里屯北街43号

With wide-open space, this is the place that nearly every traveler to Beijing who likes to party has been to. Playing popular music, it's hard not to have a good, rowdy time here.

The party always starts at Bar Blu.

ⓅBar Blu 蓝吧
Jazz, light music
English menu and service ¥¥
Hours: 4pm-4am
Entrance: free
Transport: Bus 117, 120, 823 to Xingfusancun (幸福三村)
4/F, Tongli Studio, Sanlitun Beijie, Chaoyang District. (86-10-64174124) 朝阳区三里屯北街同里4层

This lively bar is a happening spot every night of the week: Wednesday is quiz night for example. Two live DJs, a pool table and a fun atmosphere ensure a good time.

ⓆBeer Mania 麦霆啤酒吧
Light music
English menu and service ¥¥
Hours: 2pm-2am
Entrance: free
Transport: see transport to Sanlitun on p.248
1/F, Taiyue Fang, Sanlitun Nanlu, Chaoyang District. (86-10-65850786) 朝阳区三里屯南路太乐房1层

Aptly named, this place has a crazily huge selection of Belgian beer for lovers of man's real best friend. Cozy and cramped, you can have your own mini-October fest any night of the week.

ⓇBrown's Pub 红磨坊
Light music
English menu and service ¥¥
Hours: 11am-2am (Mon-Thurs); 11am-4am (Fri-Sun)
Entrance: free
Transport: Bus 113, 115, 117, 701, 958 to Changhongqiao Xi (长虹桥西) Sanlitun Nanlu, Chaoyang District (above Loft). (86-10-65912717/65923692) 朝阳区三里屯南路 (藏酷楼上)

With a selection of 500 shooters, you can get your drink on every weekend for months and never have the same one twice. Beijing's alcohol university, so to speak.

ⓈCheers Café
Pop, rock; live bands
English menu and service ¥¥
Hours: 6.30pm-late
Entrance: free
Transport: see transport to Sanlitun

"I like beer! I'm going to Beer Mania!"

on p.248

2/F, Tongli Studio, Sanlitun Beijie, Chaoyang District. (86-10-13520446062) 朝阳区三里屯北街同里2楼

This bar has great live music and a comfortable, cozy atmosphere. Grab a couple of music loving friends and make an evening of it.

◗ The Bund
Rock & pop
English menu and service   **¥¥**
Hours: 10am-2am
Entrance: free
Transport: see transport to Sanlitun on p.248
1/F, Building 7, Sanlitun Beijie, Chaoyang District (behind 3.3 Clothing Market). (86-10-64178288) 朝阳区三里屯北街7号楼1层 (三点三大厦后面)

A new bar that offers the dubious motto of "load up." Anyway, it's got potential and good music well into the small hours. Maybe you can get "loaded" here.

◗ The Tree 树酒吧
Live music
English menu & service   **¥¥**
Hours: 11am-2am
Entrance: free
Transport: see transport to Sanlitun on p.248
No. 43, Sanlitun Beijie, Chaoyang District (behind Poachers Inn). (86-10-64151954) 朝阳区三里屯北街43号 (友谊青年吧后面)

Famous in most circles for their great pizza, this is a great place to go with a group of friends or by

The Tree has become synonymous with great pizza.

For a splash of everything, come to Downtown.

yourself to meet new people. Either way makes it a stop on your itinerary.

◗ Top Club and Lounge
House & electronic
English menu and service   **¥¥**
Hours: 6pm-2am
Entrance: free
Transport: see transport to Sanlitun on p.248
4/F, Tongli Studio, Sanlitun Beijie, Chaoyang District. (86-10-64131019) 朝阳区三里屯北街同里4层

There's no hip hop here, just electronic, house and trance. Comfortable place to relax with sofas and a rooftop patio or you can hit the dance floor.

◗ Aperitivo 意式餐吧
Light music
English menu and service   **¥¥¥**
Hours: 10am-2am
Entrance: free
Transport: see transport to Sanlitun on p.248
No. 43, Sanlitun Beijie Nanlu, Chaoyang District (next to Tongli Studio). (86-10-64177793) 朝阳区三里屯北街南路43号 (同里旁边)

Popular with the European crowd, this place has a nice patio and an Italian touch to its drink menu. Have another cocktail and stay late.

❸ Downtown Café & Bar
骊姿园
Pop, hip hop
English menu and service   **¥¥¥**
Hours: 11am-2am
Entrance: free
Transport: see transport to Sanlitun on p.248
No. 26, Sanlitun Beijie, Chaoyang District. (86-10-64152100) 朝阳区三里屯北街26号

This place is open all day for those blessed occasions where you can spend the afternoon in a bar. DVDs shown in the day, belly dancers at night and great food all the time.

❾ Jazz Ya 爵士屋
Jazz, Japanese music
English menu and service   **¥¥¥**
Hours: 11.30am-2am
Entrance: free
Beer: Heiniken RMB 25, draft beet 15
Transport: see transport to Sanlitun on p.248
No. 18, Sanlitun Beijie, Chaoyang District (inside the hutong next to 44 Bar). (86-10-64151227) 朝阳区三里屯北街18号 (44号酒吧旁胡同内)

Japanese people hang out at this place styled like their homeland's diners. Japanese pop music is in heavy rotation, but expect to hear some jazz too.

Around Chaoyang Park
朝阳公园周围

Chaoyang Park is one of Beijing's newest kids on the block in regards to food and fun! Now holding claim to being the city's largest green area, the park, with an amusement area and big boating lake, is a little rural world of its own. But walk a few minutes to the edge of the park, namely the West Gate, and it is a different story. Restaurants of every type imaginable have popped up, with bars and nightclubs not far behind! The **Goose and Duck Pub** (see p.255), a well-known expat hang-out, is a good landmark to get your bearings (perhaps before a few beers!). **The World of Suzie Wong** (see p.255), a great lounge bar, and too many good restaurants to name are all within sight.

Transport: Bus 117, 302, 703, 710, 815, 985 to Chaoyang Park (朝阳公园) or 419, 852, 985 to Chaoyang Park West Gate (朝阳公园西门)

Liangmaqiao
亮马桥路

Nongzhanguan Bei
农展馆北路

Third Ring Road 三环路

F

Nongzhanguan N
农展馆南路

Restaurant listings

Meal prices per adult
¥ under RMB 29
¥¥ RMB 30-49
¥¥¥ RMB 50-69
¥¥¥¥ RMB 70-99
¥¥¥¥¥ over RMB 100

Chinese

A An Die An Niang
俺爹俺娘
Shandong cuisine
English menu　　　¥¥
Hours: 10am-3am
Transport: Bus 419, 710, 752, 985 to Jingyuan (景园)
Chaoyang Park West Gate, Chaoyang District. (86-10-65910231) 朝阳区朝阳公园西门

Huge *baozi* (steamed bun with pork or vegetable filling), delicious rice congees and a homey feeling make this Shandong res-

taurant a great place to fill up. Scenic and central location at Chaoyang Park.

B Ri Chang 日昌茶餐厅
Cantonese cuisine
English menu　　　¥¥
Hours: 24 hours
Transport: Bus 419, 710, 752, 985 to Jingyuan (景园)
Chaoyang Park West Gate, Chaoyang District. (86-10-65931078) 朝阳区朝阳公园西门

There's no better place to be on a cold day in Beijing than in a steam-

ing hotpot restaurant. Also sample Cantonese clay pot dishes at this comfortable spot.

Fusion

C Huangjihuang
黄记煌三汁焖锅
English menu　　　¥¥
Hours: 10am-5am
Transport: Bus 419, 710, 752, 985 to Jingyuan (景园)
Chaoyang Park West Gate, Chaoyang District. (86-10-65021649/65005128) 朝阳区朝阳公园西门

Get your spice fix at Huangjihuang.

RESTAURANTS AND BARS

An Die An Niang 俺爹俺娘	Ⓐ
Black Sun Bar 黑太阳	Ⓔ
CD Jazz Café 森帝爵士	Ⓕ
Goose and Duck Pub 鹅和鸭	Ⓖ
Huangjihuang 黄记煌三汁焖锅	Ⓒ
Ri Chang 日昌荼餐厅	Ⓑ
Souk 苏克会馆	Ⓓ
The World of Suzie Wong 苏西黄	Ⓗ

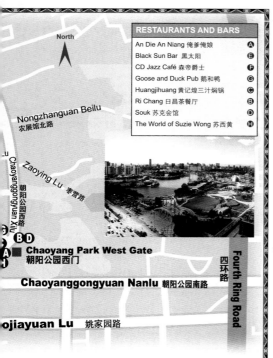

North

Nongzhanguan Beilu
农展馆北路

Zaoying Lu
枣营路

朝阳公园西路
Chaoyanggongyuan Xilu

ⒷⒹ
ⒶⒸ
Chaoyang Park West Gate
朝阳公园西门

Chaoyanggongyuan Nanlu 朝阳公园南路

ojiayuan Lu 姚家园路

四环路 Fourth Ring Road

This place specializes in hotpot, and like KFC they've got their own secret recipe that gives their food a taste like no other. Can you figure out what the secret ingredients are?

Middle Eastern / Mediterranean

Ⓓ Souk 苏克会馆

English menu ¥¥¥¥

Hours: 5pm-1am

Transport: Bus 419, 710, 752, 985 to Jingyuan (景园)

Chaoyang Park West Gate, Chaoyang District (tucked behind Annie's). (86-10-65067309) 朝阳区朝阳公园西门 (安妮餐厅后面)

Relax in soothing Chaoyang Park and dig into a nice selection of Middle Eastern and Mediterranean food. Looks like a stately African home from the outside.

Bar listings

Prices for a bottle of Tsingtao beer (青岛啤酒), a favorite local beer

¥ under RMB 14

¥¥ RMB 15-24

¥¥¥ RMB 25-34

¥¥¥¥ over RMB 35

Ⓔ Black Sun Bar 黑太阳

Rock, pop, hip hop

English menu and service ¥¥

Hours: 5.30pm-2am

Entrance: free

Transport: Bus 419, 710, 752, 958 to Jingyuan (景园)

Chaoyang Park West Gate, Chaoyang District. (86-10-65936909) 朝阳区朝阳公园西门

This born-again version of a well-equipped bar has low prices and lots to do. Play pool, shoot darts, have a football match or just chill on the patio.

Ⓕ CD Jazz Café 森帝爵士

Jazz

English menu and service ¥¥

Hours: 3pm-late

Entrance: free

Transport: Bus 402, 405, 701, 984 to Agricultural Exhibition Center (农业展览馆)

300 m south of Agricultural Exhibition Center, East Third Ring Road, Chaoyang District. (86-10-65068288) 朝阳区东三环农展馆往南 300 米

Live jazz performances provide the entertainment at this bar, formerly the DC Café and Tree Lounge. Take advantage of the convenient location and late hours.

Ⓖ Goose and Duck Pub 鹅和鸭

Pop, hip hop, rock

English menu and service ¥¥

Hours: 24 hours

Entrance: free

Transport: Bus 419, 710, 752, 958 to Jingyuan (景园)

Chaoyang Park West Gate, No. 1, Bihuju Nanlu, Chaoyang District. (86-10-65381691) 朝阳区碧湖居南路 1 号朝阳公园西门

This 24-hour sports bar has two pool tables, darts and even shuffle board. Watch a game on the big screen and enjoy two for one drinks from 4 to 8pm, plus a huge Western menu.

Ⓗ The World of Suzie Wong 苏西黄

Pop, jazz

English menu and service ¥¥¥¥

Hours: 7pm-late

Entrance: RMB 30 (Wed ladies' night), RMB 50 (Fri-Sat)

Transport: see transport to Chaoyang Park on p.254

Chaoyang Park West Gate, Chaoyang District. (86-10-65003377) 朝阳区朝阳公园西门

Step back to the days of yore, when opium dens still operated in Shanghai. Grab a Ming bed and get drinking, opium is illegal now! Come early to beat the pack.

Jianguomenwai Dajie
建国门外大街

D ue to government efforts, the area around Jianguomenwai Dajie is being turned into a flourishing central business district (CBD), where financial and service industries proliferate. As companies relocate faster than buildings can go up, it is growing daily, with an approximate five million sq m of offices accounting for 50% of the area's space.

As anticipated, as people, buildings and business increase by the second, so does the number of restaurants, bars and entertainment venues. If techno music makes your heart race, then **Banana** (see p.259) will probably give

you a heart attack, while **Grandma's Kitchen** (see below) offers great Western food needed to line your stomach before hitting the bars. To add that bit more spice to your evening, **Peter's Tex-Mex Grill** (see p.258) will certainly oblige!

Restaurant listings

Meal prices per adult
¥ under RMB 29
¥¥ RMB 30-49
¥¥¥ RMB 50-69
¥¥¥¥ RMB 70-99
¥¥¥¥¥ over RMB 100

American

Ⓐ Sizzler 时时乐
English menu   ¥¥¥
Hours: 11am-10.30pm
Transport: Subway Line 1 to

Sizzler's amazing hospitality abounds.

Jianguomen (建国门), Exit B
No. 21 Jianguomenwai Dajie, Chaoyang District (next to St. Regis Hotel). (86-10-65320475) 朝阳区建国门外大街21号 (国际俱乐部饭店旁边)

You can stuff yourself at the salad bar. Fill your plate as many times as you want, but make sure to leave room for the steak or ribs at the American BBQ experts.

Ⓑ Grandma's Kitchen
祖母的厨房
English menu   ¥¥¥¥
Hours: 7.30am-11pm

Food from across the Americas. Grandma's Kitchen.

Transport: Subway Line 1 to Guomao (国贸), Exit C
No. 0103, Building B, SOHO, No. 39, Dongsanhuan Zhonglu, Chaoyang District. (86-10-58693055/3056) 朝阳区东三环中路39号建外SOHO B座0103号

If you love gravy, you are going to be a happy camper in this restaurant. Traditional American meals served with the savory sauce of the gods. Sandwiches and desserts too!

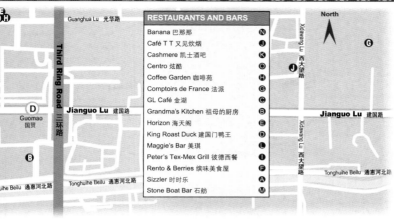

RESTAURANTS AND BARS	
Banana 巴那那	Ⓝ
Café T T 又见炊烟	Ⓙ
Cashmere 凯士酒吧	Ⓚ
Centro 炫酷	Ⓞ
Coffee Garden 咖啡苑	Ⓗ
Comptoirs de France 法派	Ⓖ
GL Café 金湖	Ⓒ
Grandma's Kitchen 祖母的厨房	Ⓑ
Horizon 海天阁	Ⓔ
King Roast Duck 建国门鸭王	Ⓓ
Maggie's Bar 美琪	Ⓛ
Peter's Tex-Mex Grill 彼德西餐	Ⓘ
Rento & Berries 缤味美食屋	Ⓕ
Sizzler 时时乐	Ⓐ
Stone Boat Bar 石舫	Ⓜ

So lose the tie, drop the briefcase and let your hair down, everyone else will!

Transport: Subway Line 1 to Jianguomen (建国门), then walk to your final destination.

Chinese

● GL Café 金湖
Cantonese cuisine
English menu ¥¥¥
Hours: 24 hours
Transport: Subway Line 1 to Jianguomen (建国门)
No. 21, Jianguomenwai Dajie, Chaoyang District (beside St. Regis Hotel). (86-10-65328282) 朝阳区建国门外大街21号(国际俱乐部饭店旁边)

Great for a drunken hunger in the middle of the night, this Hong Kong food is set in a huge cafeteria. Since it never closes, you can show up at any time for a snack or meal.

● King Roast Duck
建国门鸭王
Peking duck
English menu ¥¥¥
Hours: 10am-9.30pm
Transport: Subway Line 1 to Jianguomen (建国门), Exit B

No. 24, Jianguomenwai Dajie, Chaoyang District (east of MacDonald's). (86-10-65156908) 朝阳区建国门外大街24号(麦当劳东边)

Succulent Peking duck is served with paper-thin wraps and a sauce so delicious you'll want to drink it. Anyway you slice it, you can't go wrong with this famous dish.

● Horizon 海天阁
Cantonese dim sum
English menu ¥¥¥¥

Hours: 11.30am-2.30pm; 5.30pm-10pm
Transport: Bus 974 to Guanghua Lu (光华路)
1/F, Kerry Center Hotel, No. 1, Guanghua Lu, Chaoyang District. (86-10-65618833 ext. 41) 朝阳区光华路1号嘉里中心饭店1层

A broad spectrum of the vast and varied Cantonese cuisine can be sampled here. Drop by in the afternoon only to enjoy the dim sum.

Have "sum" dim sum at Horizon.

Coffee Garden.

Deli

ⓕ Rento & Berries
缤味美食屋

English menu ¥¥

Hours: 7am-11pm (Mon-Fri), 8am-7pm (Sat-Sun)

Transport: Bus 974 to Guanghua Lu (光华路)

1/F, Kerry Center, No. 1, Guanghua Lu, Chaoyang District. (86-10-65618833 ext. 45) 朝阳区光华路1号嘉里中心饭店1层

📋 *Free delivery within 500 m of Kerry Center.*

A bakery, café and deli-takeout joint in one. Diverse menu in a fresh atmosphere, you'll want to check out the daytime specials.

Dessert

ⓖ Comptoirs de France
法派

French bakery
English menu ¥¥¥¥¥

Hours: 10am-10pm

Transport: Subway Line 1 to Dawang Lu (大望路), Exit A

Room 102, Building 15, China Central Place, No. 89, Jianguo Lu, Chaoyang District. (86-10-65305480) 朝阳区建国路89号华贸中心15号楼102

Located at the famous China Central Place, this is Beijing's newest French bakery. Decorated in classic French style with au-

thentic breads, cakes and chocolates that won't disappoint.

European

ⓗ Coffee Garden 咖啡苑

English menu ¥¥¥¥

Hours: 6am-11pm

Transport: Bus 974 to Guanghua Lu (光华路)

Kerry Center Hotel, No. 1, Guanghua Lu, Chaoyang District. (86-10-65618833 ext. 40) 朝阳区光华路1号嘉里中心饭店

This place is known for its fresh fare, prepared in an open kitchen, where you can watch your meal grow from ingredients into a tasty masterpiece.

Mexican/Tex-Mex

ⓘ Peter's Tex-Mex Grill
彼德西餐

English menu ¥¥¥

Hours: 7.30am-11.30pm

Transport: Subway Line 1 to Jianguomen (建国门), Exit B

No. 88A, International Club, No. 21, Jianguomenwai Dajie, Chaoyang

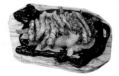

Tex-Mex specialty, Fajita.

District. (86-10-85322449) 朝阳区建国门外大街21号国际俱乐部甲88号

Don't mess with Texas! Tex-Mex food like fajitas and burritos borrow a lot from Mexican cuisine, meaning it's spicy and sensational. If you've never tried it, you are missing out.

Bar listings

Prices for a bottle of Tsingtao beer (青岛啤酒), a favorite local beer

¥	under RMB 14
¥¥	RMB 15-24
¥¥¥	RMB 25-34
¥¥¥¥	over RMB 35

ⓙ Café T T 又见炊烟

Light music
English menu and service ¥¥

Hours: 8am-1am

Entrance: free

Transport: Bus 4, 402, 648, 848 to Bawangfen Dong

S120, Blue Castle International Apartment, No. 3, Xidawang Lu, Chaoyang District. (86-10-85997488) 朝阳区西大望路3号蓝堡国际公寓南区底商S120

With a good library of travel books in Chinese, this place is great for your local friends, but there's also a nice collection of Lonely Planet guides for you to read up on the country you're drinking in.

ⓚ Cashmere 凯士酒吧

Pop
English menu and service ¥¥

Hours: 2pm-12am

Entrance: free

Transport: Bus 208, 750, 810, 820, 44, 特2 to Yabao Lu (雅宝路)

No. 44, Guanghua Lu, Chaoyang District (behind John Bull Pub). (86-10-65035050) 朝阳区光华路44号 (尊伯英式后面)

Super slick cigar bar complete with leather couches and a shining wooden floor, you'll feel like Tony Soprano as you kick back here and enjoy a few drinks.

● Maggie's Bar 美琪
Rock, pop
English menu and service ¥¥
Hours: 7.30pm-late
Entrance: free
Transport: Bus 639, 640 to Ritan Park (日坛公园)
Ritan Park South Gate, Chaoyang District. (86-10-85628142/8143) 朝阳区日坛公园南门

Maggie's is a long established club for good music and partying. Known as a bit of a pick-up joint.

⑩ Stone Boat Bar 石舫
Light music
English menu and service ¥¥
Hours: 10am-11pm
Entrance: free
Transport: Bus 974 to Guanghua Lu (光华路)
By the lake in Ritan Park, Chaoyang District. (86-10-65019986) 朝阳区日坛公园内湖边

This bar is right on the shore of a lake, courtesy of Ritan Park. A really nice environment that's green and near the water, you can drink in peace here.

⑪ Banana 巴那那
Light music
English menu and service ¥¥¥
Hours: 8.30pm-4.30am
Entrance: RMB 20 (weekdays), RMB 30 (weekends)
Transport: Bus 1, 9, 403, 802, 120 to Ritan Lu (日坛路) or Subway Line 1 to Jianguomen (建国门站), Exit B

The hip and fresh "Banana."

1/F, Scitech Hotel, No. 22, Jianguomenwai Dajie, Chaoyang District. (86-10-65283636) 朝阳区建国门外大街22号赛特饭店1层
A dance club with Chinese style, cage dancing and a throbbing dance floor. You can escape upstairs to the Spicy Lounge to check out world famous DJs live.

● Centro 炫酷
Jazz
English menu and service ¥¥¥¥
Hours: 24 hours
Entrance: free
Transport: Bus 207, 640, 639 to Guanghua Zhonglu (光华中路) or Subway Line 1 to Guomao (国贸)
1/F, Kerry Center Hotel, No. 1, Guanghua Lu, Chaoyang District. (86-10-65618833) 朝阳区光华路1号嘉里中心饭店1层

This spot is done out to perfection, neither too much nor too little in classy décor. Featuring a bar that never seems to end and plenty of room to relax and take care of that favorite cocktail.

Centro.

Theaters

The theaters listed below are marked on the map on p.240.

The high-quality Universal Theater.

❻ Chaoyang Theater
朝阳剧场
Acrobatics
Hours: 5.15 or 7.15pm (call to check)
Price: RMB 180-380
Transport: Bus 113, 402, 405, 707 to Hujialou Bei (呼家楼北)
No. 36, Dongsanhuan Beilu, Chaoyang District. (86-10-65072421) http://www.bjcyjc.com/ 朝阳区东三环北路36号

Come and be amazed by the acrobatic feats performed here by brave Chinese using bikes, seesaws, catapults and other props. Enough agility to make your jaw drop.

❼ Universal Theater
天地剧场
Acrobatics & dance
Hours: 6.30pm
Price: RMB 100-300
Transport: Bus 44, 820, 858 to Dongsishitiaoqiao Nan (东四十条桥南) or Subway Line 2 to Dongsishitiao (东四十条)
No. 10, Dongzhimen Nandajie, Chaoyang District. (86-10-64169893/64157775 ext. 102) 朝阳区东直门南大街10号
Highly skilled and nearly flawless in execution, the stunts you'll see here will take your breath away. This is an art form that has a distinctly extreme edge.

🛒 **Shopping**

Practically anywhere in China when it comes to shopping, you need to be ready to bargain. This is especially true in the "Modern" East where the savvy merchants have a steady supply of naive foreigners to whom to peddle their wares. Still, you'll want to hit the **Silk Street** (see below) where all manner (and sizes) of clothes and cloth can be found. Great bargains on trinkets galore can be found at **Laofanjie** (see below) while the **Gaobeidian Antique Furniture Market** (see below) is where Ming and Qing Dynasty style furniture, pottery and the like abound!

The markets listed below are marked on the map on p.240.

❽ 3.3 Clothing Market 三点三服饰大厦

Clothing

Hours: 9am-7pm

Transport: Bus 117, 120, 823 to Xingfusancun (幸福三村)

No. 33, Sanlitun Beijie, Chaoyang District. (86-10-64173333) 朝阳区三里屯北街33号

A great new place to stock up on clothing; it's huge and located in Sanlitun. There are a lot of original designs here you won't find elsewhere.

❾ Gaobeidian Antique Furniture Market 高碑店古旧家具市场

Antique furniture

Hours: 8am-5pm

Transport: Bus 363, 725 or Batong Subway Line to Gaobeidian (高碑店)

No. 551, Gaobeidian, Chaoyang District. (86-10-85761701) 朝阳区高碑店551号

Ming and Qing Dynasty style furniture is the main attraction at this vast market. Also on offer are antique decorations and ceramics as well as old- and modern-style woodcrafts.

❿ Laofanjie (Alien Street Market) 老番街市场

Clothing

Hours: 9.30am-5pm

Transport: Bus 101, 109, 110, 112, 420, 750, 813, 846, 858 to Chaoyangmenwai (朝阳门外)

Chaoyangmenwai Dajie, Chaoyang District (close to Yijingyuan International Apartment). (86-10-85614649) 朝阳区朝阳门外大街 (靠近怡景园涉外公寓)

This is known as the new Russian market, located near the ruins of the old one. Definitely dubious but a worthwhile spot to get watches and cool clocks. This place has two stories: the first floor where you can find shoes, knock-off sunglasses and watches, and other stuff like toys. Second floor, you can find everything associated with clothes. And you'll most likely find your size of shoes.

⓫ Silk Street 秀水

Clothes, silk, sundries

Hours: 9am-9pm

Transport: Bus 1, 4, 37 to Yong'anli Lukouxi (永安里路口西) or Subway Line 1 to Yong'anli (永安里)

No. 8, Xiushui Dongjie, Chaoyang District. (86-10-51698800) http://www.xiushui.com.cn/English.asp 朝阳区秀水东街8号

Everyone's favorite dodgy mar-

Silk Street is the ruthless bargainers' home away from home.

ket is the place to get almost anything as well as clothes and silk. Bargain hard, especially as a foreigner.

⓬ Yabao Lu 雅宝路

Clothing, shoes, jewelry, watches

Hours: 9am-9pm

Transport: Bus 44, 208, 750, 810, 820, 特2 to Yabao Lu (雅宝路)

Chaoyangmenwai Dajie, Chaoyang District. (86-10-885622741) 朝阳区朝阳门外大街

Of every three dollars Russian merchants spend in Beijing, two will go to the businesses along Yabao Lu. This road is filled with everything imaginable in the realm of home/clothing (including furs) and kids stuff. Catch a look at the mind-boggling assortment.

⓭ Yashow Clothing Market 雅秀服装市场

Clothing, shoes

Hours: 9.30am-9pm

Transport: Bus 115, 113, 406, 701, 416 to Sanlitun (三里屯)

No. 58, Gongti Beilu, Chaoyang District. (86-10-64168945) 朝阳区工体北路58号

This Silk Street clone is near the embassy zone. You can get all the name brands of clothing and shoes here, but don't expect them to be genuine. Sellers are marginally less pushy than at the Silk Street, however, bargain, bargain, bargain!

Accommodation

Y ou won't be close to major tourist sites should you choose to stay in the East, but you'll find yourself "in the thick of the action" for nightspots and clubbing. Smack dab in the middle of Sanlitun for example is the **Eastern Inn Hotel** (see p.262). If you are in the mood for a bit more relaxation, enjoy the **Yuan Yuan Hot-spring Hotel** (see p.263) where (as the name implies) you will find a great hot spring to soak and unwind. The **Home Inn Hotel** (see p.262) chain has a number of locations in the area, all well equipped and catering for budget-conscious visitors.

Accommodation prices per night	
¥	under RMB 99
¥¥	RMB 100-199
¥¥¥	RMB 200-299
¥¥¥¥	RMB 300-399
¥¥¥¥¥	over RMB 400

Dorms/Hostels

Ⓐ Zhaolong Youth Hostel 兆龙青年旅舍 ¥

Price: RMB 60/bed (one room has 6 beds), RMB 70/bed (4 beds)
Transport: Bus 402, 405, 701, 984 to Agricultural Exhibition Center (农展馆)
No. 2, Gongti Beilu, Chaoyang District (by the Pacific Shopping Mall). (86-10-65972299) 朝阳区工体北路2号 (太平洋百货旁边)

Offering 1-, 2-, 4- and 6-bed rooms, this is a fantastic budget option. With efficient air conditioning, heating and lockers, it is comfortable and clean. The hostel is attached to the Zhaolong Hotel. ¥¥¥¥¥ (All services)

Ⓑ Friendship Hostel 友谊青年酒店 ¥

Price: RMB 70/bed
Transport: Bus 113, 115, 406, 416, 701, 758, 834 to Sanlitun (三里屯)
No. 43, Sanlitun Beijie, Chaoyang District. (86-10-64172632 ext. 8506) 朝阳区三里屯北街43号

Attached to Poachers Inn, this is the ideal spot for party animal travelers. You won't ever have a boring night in this area.

Hotels (prices based on double-occupancy rooms)

Ⓒ Jintailante Hotel 金泰蓝特宾馆 ¥¥

2 star
Price: RMB 168
Transport: Bus 37, 52, 705 to Guangmingqiao Dong (光明桥东)
No. 9, Guanghe Nanli Ertiao, Chaoyang District (near Jinsong Community). (86-10-67747088) http://www.lantehotel.com/jianjie.htm 朝阳区广和南里二条9号 (劲松家园附近)

You can choose from dormitory to deluxe rooms, all of which are nicely decorated and spacious, with en-suite bathrooms. Service in the hotel is top-notch and you will be well looked after.

Accommodation prices per night
¥ under RMB 99
¥¥ RMB 100-199
¥¥¥ RMB 200-299
¥¥¥¥ RMB 300-399
¥¥¥¥¥ over RMB 400

Ⓓ Home Inn Hotel (Chaoyang Park) ¥¥¥
如家快捷酒店 (朝阳公园店)

Price: RMB 239

Transport: Bus 117, 302, 703, 710, 815, 985 to Chaoyang Park (朝阳公园) or 302, 703, 758, 831 to Dougezhuang Lukouxi (豆各庄路口西)

No. 105, Shifoying Dongli, Chaoyang District. (86-10-85833388)

http://www.homeinns.com/program/index.aspx 朝阳区石佛营东里 105 号

Targeting independent travelers trying to keep within a budget, this is a good choice for those who want friendly service, clean rooms and value for money. It is an extremely popular economy choice.

Ⓔ Home Inn Hotel (Guomao) 如家快捷酒店 (国贸店) ¥¥¥

Price: RMB 239

Transport: Bus 300 or Subway Line 1 to Guomao (国贸)

No. 20, Baiziwan Lu, Chaoyang District (close to Fuli City). (86-10-87771155) 朝阳区百子湾路20号(富丽城附近)

Ⓕ Home Inn Hotel (Nongzhanguan) ¥¥¥
如家快捷酒店 (农展馆店)

Price: RMB 299

Transport: Bus 302, 701, 758 to Liangma Qiao (亮马桥)

No. A5, Nongzhanguan Beilu, Chaoyang District (close to Great Wall Hotel). (86-10-65954488) 朝阳区农展馆北路甲5号(长城饭店附近)

Ⓖ Home Inn Hotel (Tuanjiehu) ¥¥¥
如家快捷酒店 (团结湖店)

Price: RMB 299

Transport: Bus 43, 731 to Tuanjiehu (团结湖)

No. 17, Tuanjiehu Lu, Chaoyang District (close to Zhaolong Hotel). (86-10-85982266) 朝阳区团结湖路17号(兆龙饭店附近)

Ⓗ Eastern Inn Hotel 逸羽连锁酒店 ¥¥¥

Price: RMB 288

Transport: Bus 43, 110, 118 to Chaoyang Hospital (朝阳医院)

No. 6, Baijiazhuang Lu, Chaoyang District (east of Chaoyang Hospital). (86-10-65085005) 朝阳区白家庄路6号(朝阳医院东侧)

If it's location you're after, then it doesn't get much better than Eastern Inn, which is close to the Sanlitun area. Banks, Bar Street, restaurants, supermarkets and cafés are all within walking distance.

	🏨	@	✕	🍸	🍶	👞	🛏	🛋

Yuan Yuan Hot-spring Hotel 元远温泉宾馆 ¥¥¥

2 star

Price: RMB 288

Transport: Bus 115, 718 to Tuanjiehu Beikou (团结湖北口)

No. 9, Tuanjiehu Lu, Chaoyang District (close to Jingkelong Supermarket). (86-10-65825553) http://www.998e.com/balehotel.asp?baleid=2428 朝阳区团结湖路9号 (京客隆超市附近)

Yuan Yuan Hot-spring Hotel is exactly that; it offers guests a wonderful hot spring where they can soak their tiredness away. The rooms are comfortable and pleasant too!

Jianguomen Hotel 建国门饭店 ¥¥¥

2 star

Price: RMB 270-298

Transport: Bus 1, 4, 9, 120 to Ritan Lu (日坛路)

No. 12, Jianhua Nanlu, Jianguomenwai, Chaoyang District (close to Guiyou Shopping Mall). (86-10-65685577) 朝阳区建外大街建华南路12号(近贵友商场)

Within easy walking distance to World Trade Center, the Jianguomen Hotel caters mainly for foreign visitors. It is mid-sized, so the service is personal and attentive.

Liuhe Hotel 六合饭店 ¥¥¥¥

2 star

Price: RMB 368

Transport: Bus 110, 113, 118, 406, 701, 758, 813, 823 to Workers' Stadium (工人体育场)

No. 1, Chunxiu Lu, Gongti Beilu, Chaoyang District. (86-10-64157766) 朝阳区工体北路春秀路1号

Located within easy walking distance of Workers' Stadium, this mid-sized hotel offers good value for money and all those little extra comforts.

Tuanjiehu Super 8 Hotel 团结湖速8酒店 ¥¥¥¥

Price: RMB 398

Transport: Bus 117, 731, 834 to Tuanjiehu (团结湖)

No. 10, Beitoutiao, Tuanjiehu Beilu, Chaoyang District (close to Zhaolong Hotel). (86-10-65821008) 朝阳区团结湖北路头条10号(兆龙饭店附近)

Well-planned facilities accommodate business and leisure travelers equally; a business center, free Internet, a meeting room, laundry service and Chinese restaurant will make a stay more enjoyable.

Jingduyuan Hotel 京都苑宾馆 ¥¥¥¥¥

3 star

Price: RMB 580

Transport: Subway Line 1 or 2 to Jianguomen (建国门)

No. 8, Jianguomen Nandajie, Chaoyang District. (86-10-65291166) www.jdyhotel.net 朝阳区建国门南大街8号

The rooms offer an extra level of comfort, with cushioned window seats, en-suite bathrooms and warm décor. The restaurant downstairs cooks up a wide selection of Chinese food.

Itinerary

Itinerary J: Weekend Pub Crawl Tour

This weekend tour is our guide to a "fun-packed, let-your-hair-down, beer-swilling trip" around the most pumping, lively and popular drinking holes in the east of the city. Throw caution to the wind and who knows what (or who!) awaits you...!

Friday Night

8pm After-dinner Drink: Bookworm (see p.251)
What better way to kick off your weekend fun than an energizing coffee, or great glass of wine? Head over to the Bookworm where you'll find all you need to get ready to rock!

10pm Get the Party Started: Kai Club (see p.252)
Head north from the Bookworm to Kai Club where you can buy your first round of drinks and make the most of their low prices! Cocktails are RMB10 and shots RMB 5. A cosy, two-story bar where you are bound to bump into some real characters.

12am Late-night Munchies: Fish Nation (see p.250)
If you've worked up an appetite or simply need something to soak up the alcohol, Fish Nation's huge portions of English fish 'n' chips will give you that much needed carbohydrate boost to keep you going all night!

1am Big Party: Poachers Inn (see p.252)
For a late night party, Poachers Inn is one of the area's most popular hangouts. You most certainly won't be the only foreigner in the joint—cheap drinks and a buzzing atmosphere ensure its continued popularity.

Saturday Night

9pm After-dinner Drink: Club Football Center (see p.247)
The ever lively Club Football Center is the sports hub of the area. Showing soccer and basketball games on big screens and offering darts boards, competition really is the name of the game. Undoubtedly, the big winner is the cheap drinks!

11pm Get the Party Started: Babyface (see p.247)
For a rowdy knees-up Babyface will happily oblige, so head on over to strut your stuff and do your thing on the dance floor!

2am Party Continues: Vics (see p.247)
For the real night owls (and you know who you are!), Vics should just be warming up by 2am. Open until 6 in the morning, this is your evening's last, but by no means least, port of call.

Sunday Night

9pm After-dinner Drink: Black Sun Bar (see p.255)
The Black Sun Bar has always held a special place in the hearts of Beijing's expats (probably something to do with their astoundingly cheap shots!). Pool, darts and a nice patio are on offer to keep you thoroughly entertained!

11pm Get the Party Started: The World of Suzie Wong (see p.255)
Get your glad rags on and head to Suzie Wong! Either stake your claim on a section of their somewhat small dance floor or head upstairs to enjoy your drinks with a nice view of the area.

2am Still Partying: Goose and Duck Pub (see p.255)
For the seasoned party animal the Goose and Duck is one of the city's few 24-hour sports pubs. Late-night munchies like Shepherds Pie will do the trick if you're famished!

Bus Details

Major Bus Stops

These are the major bus stops in the "East." At each bus stop there are direct routes to key destinations. **They are marked on the map on p.240.**

Chaoyanggongyuanqiao Dong (朝阳公园桥东), east of Chaoyanggongyuan Qiao (朝阳公园桥)

To Sanlitun (三里屯): 406, 834
To Beijing Amusement Park (北京游乐园): 750
To Beijing Railway Station (北京站): 703, 729
To Summer Palace (颐和园): 834
To Yabao Lu (雅宝路): 750
To Yuanmingyuan (圆明园): 834
To Zhongguancun (中关村): 302, 834

Jianguomen Nan (建国门南), about 400 m south of Jianguomen Subway Station

To Beijing Railway Station (北京站): 52
To Beijing West Railway Station (北京西站): 特2, 820 内
To Chaoyang Park (朝阳公园): 750
To Grand View Garden (大观园): 122
To Lama Temple (雍和宫): 800 外
To Temple of Heaven (天坛): 122
To Yabao Lu (雅宝路): 750, 800 外, 820 外

Sanlitun (三里屯), close to Sanlitun Bar Street

To Beihai Park (北海公园): 701
To Chaoyang Park (朝阳公园): 406, 431, 834, 758
To Summer Palace (颐和园): 834
To Yuanmingyuan (圆明园): 834

Workers' Stadium (工人体育场), in front of the Workers' Stadium

To Beijing Railway Station (北京站): 703, 120
To Beijing West Railway Station (北京西站): 703, 823
To Summer Palace (颐和园): 834
To Yuanmingyuan (圆明园): 834
To Beihai Park (北海公园): 701, 823, 118
To Zhongguancun (中关村): 834

Ritan Lu (日坛路), on Jianguomenwai Dajie (建国门外大街)

To Tian'anmen Square (天安门): 1, 126, 120, 728, 802
To Beijing Railway Station (北京站): 126, 120, 728, 802
To Beijing West Railway Station (北京西站): 9, 802
To Wangfujing (王府井): 120, 126, 703, 802

Useful Bus Routes

The following is a list of specially selected bus routes passing through the "East." These are not all depot-to-depot routes and many less important stops have been omitted. Sights of interest are in bold type. Bus type and times of first and last buses from the first depot are also indicated.

Suggestion: if you are unsure you have the right stop, point out the Chinese characters below for where you want to go and ask another passenger, conductor or driver for help. Many young Chinese have OK English and will be able to help.

特 2 (double-decker, 6am-8pm)

Yanhuang Art Museum 炎黄艺术馆 - Olympic Sports Center East Gate 奥体东门 -Anzhenli 安贞里 -Temple of the Earth West Gate 地坛西门 -Yonghegongqiao Dong 雍和宫桥东 -Yabao Lu 雅宝路 - Qianmen East 前门东 -Beijing West Railway Station 北京西站

31 (standard bus, 5am-10.20pm)

Houfengqiao Nan (Beijing Happy Valley) 厚棒桥南(北京欢乐谷)-Baiziwan 百子湾 - Bawangfen Bei 八王坟北 -Hongmiao Lukoubei 红庙路口北 -Tuanjiehu 团结湖 - Chaoyang Park 朝阳公园

43 (standard bus, 5.10am-11pm)

Tuanjiehu 团结湖 -Baijiazhuang 白家庄 - Chaoyang Hospital 朝阳医院 -Fangcaodi 芳草地 -Ritan Lu 日坛路 -Jianguomen Nan 建国门南 -Wujianlou 五间楼

113 (standard bus, 5am-11pm)

Minzuyuan Lu 民族园路 -Temple of the Earth West Gate 地坛西门 -Dongsishitiao 东四十条 -Workers' Stadium 工人体育场 -Sanlitun 三里屯 -Changhongqiao Xi 长虹桥西 -Baijiazhuang 白家庄 -Dabeiyao 大北窑

115 (trolley bus, 5am-11pm)

Donghuangchenggen Beikou 东黄城根北口 -Dongsishitiao 东四十条 -Workers' Stadium 工人体育场 -Sanlitun 三里屯 - Changhongqiao Xi 长虹桥西 -Tuanjiehu Park 团结湖公园 -Hongmiao Lukouxi 红庙路口西 -Dongbalizhuang 东八里庄 -Qingnianlu Nankou 青年路南口

118 (trolley bus, 5am-11pm)

Hongmiao Lukouxi 红庙路口西 -Workers' Stadium 工人体育场 -Dongsishitiao 东四十条 -Luoguxiang 锣鼓巷 -Beihai Park North Gate 北海北门 -Guanyuan 官园 -Purple Bamboo Park South Gate 紫竹院南门

117 (standard bus, 6am-10pm)

Wuluju 五路居 -Anzhenli 安贞里 -Anzhenqiao Dong 安贞桥东 -Hepingli Shopping Mall 和平里商场 -Temple of the Earth East Gate 地坛东门 -Lama Temple 雍和宫 -Dongzhimen 东直门 -Xingfu Sancun 幸福三村 -Workers' Stadium 工人体育场 -Tuanjiehu 团结湖 - Chaoyang Park 朝阳公园

120 (standard bus, 5am-12am)

Temple of Heaven South Gate 天坛南门 - Tianqiao 天桥 -Dazhalan 大栅栏 -Qianmen 前门 -Tian'anmen East 天安门东 - Wangfujing 王府井 -Beijingzhankou Dong 北京站口东 -Ritan Lu 日坛路 -Fangcaodi 芳草地 -Workers' Stadium 工人体育场 - Xingfu Sancun 幸福三村

122 (standard bus, 5am-12am)

Beijing Railway Station East 北京站东 - Jianguomen Nan 建国门南 -Temple of Heaven South Gate 天坛南门 -Grand View Garden 大观园 -Lianhuachi 莲花池 -Beijing West Railway Station East 北京西站东

302 (standard bus, 5.30am-11pm)

China Science & Technology Park 中国科技馆 -Sanyuan Qiao 三元桥 -Liangma Qiao 亮马桥 -Tuanjiehu 团结湖 -Chaoyang Park 朝阳公园 -Xinzhuang 辛庄

350 (standard bus, 5.30am-10.20pm)

Dongdaqiao 东大桥 -Baijiazhuang 白家庄 - Changhonqiao Dong 长虹桥东 -Tuanjiehu 团结湖 -Chaoyang Park 朝阳公园 -Dougezhuang Lukoudong 豆各庄路口东 -Caogezhuang 曹各庄

403 (standard bus, 5am-11pm)

Beijing Railway Station East 北京站东 -Ritan Lu 日坛路 -Yonganli Lukoubei 永安里路北 -Chaoyang Hospital 朝阳医院 -Workers' Stadium 工人体育场 -Xingfu Sancun 幸福三村 -Sanyuan Qiao 三元桥

406 (standard bus, 5.30am-10pm)

Yanhuang Art Museum 炎黄艺术馆 - Workers' Stadium 工人体育场 -Sanlitun 三里屯 -Changhongqiao Dong 长虹桥东 - Tuanjiehu 团结湖 -Chaoyang Park 朝阳公园 -Olympic Park North Gate 奥林匹克公园北门

416 (standard bus, 5.30am-10pm)

Laiguangying 来广营 -Liangma Qiao 亮马桥 -Agricultural Exhibition Center 农展馆 -**Sanlitun 三里屯** - **Workers' Stadium 工人体育场** -Dongzhimen 东直门

431 (standard bus, 6am-9.40pm)

Workers' Stadium 工人体育场 -**Sanlitun 三里屯** -Changhongqiao Dong 长虹桥东 -Tuanjiehu 团结湖 -**Chaoyang Park 朝阳公园** -Dandian 单店

701 (standard bus, 5.30am-10pm)

Holiday Inn Lido 丽都饭店 -Jiuxian Qiao 酒仙桥 -Liangma Qiao 亮马桥 -Agricultural Exhibition Center 农业展览馆 -**Sanlitun 三里屯** -**Workers' Stadium 体育场** -Dongsishitiao 东四十条 -**Beihai Park North Gate 北海北门**

731 (standard bus, 5.30am-8.30pm)

Wudaokou 五道口 -Zhongguancun Bei 中关村北 -Madianqiao Dong 马甸桥东 -**China Science & Technology Museum 中国科技馆** -Anzhenqiao Xi 安贞桥西 -Xibahe 西坝河 -Sanyuan Qiao 三元桥 -Liangma Qiao 亮马桥 -Tuanjiehu 团结湖 -**Chaoyang Park 朝阳公园**

750 (standard bus, 5.30am-8.30pm)

Beijing Amusement Park 北京游乐园 -Guangqumen 广渠门 -**Yabao Lu 雅宝路** -Chaoyangmenwai 朝阳门外 -Tuanjiehu 团结湖 -**Chaoyang Park 朝阳公园**

758 (standard bus, 5.30am-8.30pm)

Yanhuang Art Museum 炎黄艺术馆 -**Olympic Sports Center East Gate 奥体东门** -**Temple of the Earth West Gate 地坛西门** -Dongsishitiao 东四十条 -**Workers' Stadium 工人体育场** -**Sanlitun 三里屯** -Tuanjiehu 团结湖 -**Chaoyang Park 朝阳公园**

800 外 (A/C, 6am-8pm)

Caihuying Qiao 菜户营桥 - **Grand View Garden 大观园** - **Temple of Heaven South Gate 天坛南门** -**Panjiayuan 潘家园** -Guangming Qiao 光明桥 -Guangqumen Qiao 广渠门桥 -Jianguomen Nan 建国门南- Yabao Lu 雅宝路 -Chaoyangmen Nan 朝阳门南 -Dongzhimen Bei 东直门北 -Caihuying Qiao 菜户营桥

800 内 (A/C, 6am-8pm)

Zuo'an Lu 左安路 -**Temple of Heaven South Gate 天坛南门** -**Grand View Garden 大观园** -Dongzhimen Bei 东直门北 -Chaoyangmen Nan 朝阳门南 -**Yabao Lu 雅宝路** -Jianguomen Nan 建国门南 -Guangming Qiao 光明桥 -Zuo'an Lu 左安路

815 (A/C, 5.50am-8pm)

Erlizhuang 二里庄 -Dongzhimen 东直门 -Xingfusancun Bei 幸福三村北 -Agricultural Exhibition Center 农业展览馆 -Tuanjiehu 团结湖 -**Chaoyang Park 朝阳公园** -Hongmiao Lukoubei 红庙路口北

823 (A/C, 6am-9pm)

Dongzhimenwai 东直门外 -Xinyuanli 新源里 -Xingfu Sancun 幸福三村 -**Workers' Stadium 工人体育场** -Dongsishitiao 东四十条 -Luoguxiang 锣鼓巷 -**Beihai Park North Gate 北海北门** -**White Dagoba Temple 白塔寺** -**Yuetan Park 月坛公园** -Beijing West Railway Station 北京西站

831 (A/C, 5am-8pm)

China Science & Technology Museum 中国科技馆 -Anzhenqiao Xi 安贞桥西 -Xibahe 西坝河 -Sanyuan Qiao 三元桥 -Liangma Qiao 亮马桥 -Tuanjiehu 团结湖 -**Chaoyang Park 朝阳公园**

834 (A/C, 5.30am-8pm)

Chaoyang Park 朝阳公园 -Tuanjiehu 团结湖 -**Sanlitun 三里屯** -**Workers' Stadium 工人体育场** -Dongsishitiao 东四十条 -Luoguxiang 锣鼓巷 -**Drum Tower 鼓楼** -**Yuanmingyuan South Gate 圆明园南门**

984 (standard bus, 5.20am-7.30pm)

Yanhuang Art Museum 炎黄艺术馆 -Sanyuan Qiao 三元桥 -Agricultural Exhibition Center 农业展览馆 -Tuanjiehu 团结湖 -**Chaoyang Park 朝阳公园** -Sihuizhan 四惠站

Panjiayuan Antique Market, the mother of all antique markets.

"Antiques" Southeast

Unlike the other parts of Beijing, the "Southeast" doesn't have the same historical or cultural pizzazz. When speaking of it, the first thing that springs to Beijingers' minds are the two huge markets to shop for antiques or antiqued stuff—the **Panjiayuan Antique Market** (the Dirt Market, see p.273) and the **Beijing Curio City** (see p.273).

It was not so long ago in the Southeast of the city (1992, to be precise) that small

Wood carving

traders came together, setting up stands, or spreading their wares on the ground by the road. Stunning finds were made by collectors and from those humble beginnings have grown these two giant hubs of antiques, arts and crafts, second-hand goods and related articles.

But with the newly opened **Happy Valley Amusement Park** (see p.270) this area is showing new promise to provide other attractions beyond shopping.

Highlights

♦ **Happy Valley** 欢乐谷 Said to be the happiest place in China and featuring many exciting rides, it is fun and thrilling for both kids and adults. **See p.270**

♦ **Fangzhuang** 方庄 A huge residential area in the southeast of Beijing. Restaurants of different regional and international cuisines all compete to set up shop here. **See p.271**

♦ **Panjiayuan Antique Market** 潘家园 旧货市场 Originally a flea market, it is now Beijing's most famous antique market. **See p.273**

♦ **Beijing Curio City** 北京古玩城 Boasts to be Asia's largest antiques exchange center. **See p.273**

Sightseeing

❶ Happy Valley
欢乐谷 Huānlègǔ ★★
Beijing's first major thrill-seeking theme park

Hours: 10am-5pm (winter); 9am-7pm (summer)
Entrance: RMB 100 (winter) and RMB 160 (summer)
for adults; free for kids under 1.2 m; half price for
kids between 1.2 m-1.4 m; 20% off for students.
Suggested length of visit: 1 day
Transport: Subway Line 1 to Dawang Lu (大望路),
then take Bus 31 to Houfengqiao Nan (厚俸桥南)
Xiaowuji Beilu, Dongsihuan, Chaoyang District.
(86-10-67383333) http://bj.happyvalley.com.cn/
park/index.asp
朝阳区东四环小武基北路

Rivaling Disneyland, Happy Valley is the country's biggest theme park. Since opening in July 2006, it has already welcomed hundreds of thousands of visitors. The park consists of six imaginative and colorful themed areas: Firth Forest (峡湾森林), Atlantis (亚特兰蒂斯), Lost Maya (失落玛雅), Aegean Port (爱琴港), Shangri-La (香格里拉) and Ant Kingdom (蚂蚁王国). 120 attractions (such as the ever-popular Maya Disaster) enthrall kids and big kids alike! The park also features many exciting rides such as huge roller coasters, water rides, reverse bungee chairs and more!

Hold on to your wallet when riding.

🛒 Shopping

Think of the Southeast and one kind of shopping springs to mind, namely antiques. So, if you are an "antique buff," or just have a casual interest, you should find time to visit this part of Beijing. The largest antique exchange in not only China, but all of Asia, is **Beijing Curio City** (see below) which often hosts exhibitions and auctions. You can easily spend the better part of a day visiting this vast market. Not to be outdone, with over 4, 000 stalls of its own, the **Panjiayuan Antique Market** (see below) is another great find for antiques, collectables and second-hand books.

The following markets are marked on the map on p.268.

See anything you like at Panjiayuan?

Beijing Curio City
北京古玩城
Antiques

Hours: 9.30am-6.30pm
Transport: Bus 300, 28, 特8 to Panjiayuan (潘家园)
No. 21, Dongsanhuan Nanlu, Chaoyang District. (86-10-67747711)
朝阳区东三环南路21号

Proudly standing as Asia's largest antique exchange center, it often hosts exhibitions and auctions. Over 1,000 types of antiques pass through the doors, ranging from paintings, calligraphy to jewelry and jade items. Of particular interest is the furniture section to the rear of the building where some very good reconditioned pieces can be picked up at surprisingly good prices.

❸ Panjiayuan Antique Market 潘家园旧货市场

Antiques, art, furniture, jewelry
Hours: 8.30am-6pm (Mon-Fri), 4.30am-6pm (Sat & Sun)
Transport: Bus 51 to Huawei Nanlu Dongkou (华威南路东口)
No. 18, Huaweili, Panjiayuan Lu, Chaoyang District. (86-10-67752405)
朝阳区潘家园路华威里18号

This is Beijing's most famous antique market, growing from its humble beginnings as a flea market in the early 1990's. All manner of antiques are on sale among the thousands of market stalls. Paintings, calligraphy, ceramics, jade, furniture, coins, army surplus, "cultural revolution" memorabilia, Buddhist artefacts and much, much more. If you're not an expert, simply wandering around the 4,000 plus stalls is just as much fun!

The market is specially animated on weekends when the permanent stalls and shops are joined by vendors setting out their wares on the ground. Get there early.

❹ Carrefour 家乐福

Supermarket
Hours: 8.30am-10.30pm
Transport: Bus 23 to Zhujiang Dijing (珠江帝景)
No. 31, Guangqu Lu, Chaoyang District. (86-10-51909508) 朝阳区广渠路31号

Accommodation

When it comes to finding a good place to stay, there are fewer choices in the Southeast as it is far away from most of Beijing's tourist sites. Still, finding comfort and economy is not a "mission impossible." Business travelers would find **Jinsong** (劲松) a good area to stay—CBD, Panjiayuan and Curio City are all within an easy taxi ride—albeit the accommodation is a bit pricier.

The fast development of Panjiayuan and Beijing Curio City has helped the accommodation business in the area to expand. Today antique lovers will easily find hotels that suit to all budgets, with most choosing the **Beijing Curio City Hotel** (as it is attached to the Curio City).

All places listed below are marked on the map on p.268.

Accommodation prices per night
¥ under RMB 99
¥¥ RMB 100-199
¥¥¥ RMB 200-299
¥¥¥¥ RMB 300-399
¥¥¥¥¥ over RMB 400

Hotels (prices based on double-occupancy rooms)

❶ Huatai Hotel 华泰饭店 ¥¥¥

3 star

Price: RMB 280
Transport: Bus 运通107, 974 to Jinsong Dongkou (劲松东口)
South of Jinsong Dongkou, Chaoyang District. (86-10-67716688) 朝阳区劲松东口南侧

Less than 10 minutes' drive from Panjiayuan Market, Beijing Curio City and Longtanhu Park (龙潭湖公园) this hotel is well equipped and offers comfy rooms at decent prices.

❷ Beijing Curio City Hotel 北京古玩城宾馆 ¥¥¥¥

3 star

Price: RMB 298-398
Transport: Bus 36, 368, 800 内, 802 to Zuo'an Lu (左安路) or 运通107, 434, 800 外 to Panjiayuan (潘家园)
No. 21, Dongsanhuan Nanlu, Chaoyang District. (86-10-67747711) 朝阳区东三环南路21号

Connecting to the Curio City, the hotel offers elegant and classically old-fashioned décor, and combines accommodation and shopping in one building. Rooms are on the sixth and seventh floors and the rest are curio shops.

Itinerary

Itinerary K: Weekend Treasure-hunting Tour (Two Days)
Day 1

Morning

9am Start your tour at **Liulichang** (see p.112) on Saturday, a short walk south of Hepingmen (和平门) Subway Station. With a long history as a shopping location, the east-west Liulichang is lined with stores selling genuine and replica antiques, paintings, woodprints, calligraphy scrolls, etc. The buildings are all in traditional Chinese style, worth checking out. **Rongbaozhai** (荣宝斋), one of the most famous and oldest stores (over 300 years), is a good place to buy the "four treasures of the study" and calligraphy scrolls.

11am Move on from Liulichang, take Bus 15 at the Liulichang stop on Nanxinhua Jie (南新华街) and get off at the Friendship Hospital (友谊医院), then transfer to Bus 34 to another antique spot—**Panjiayuan** (see p.273). It's about 30 minutes' drive. Buy a little antique Buddha or jade bracelet—but be warned that very few are genuine, so watch out and bargain hard! Two hours is enough in this market.

Afternoon

1.30pm Lunch at any of the small restaurants outside the market, 45 minutes.

2.15pm Walk east from Panjiayuan Market. When you see a bridge (潘家园桥Panjiayuan Qiao) turn right (south) and walk for about five minutes and you'll see the **Beijing Curio City** (see p.273), the largest antique exchange center in Asia. Spend an hour in its front section. Then check the furniture section to the rear of the building, where you can also buy small antiques like jewelry boxes and carved wall hangings. Spend another hour here.

4.30pm End of tour.

Day 2

9am Take the Batong Subway Line east to Gaobeidian (高碑店). Exit and take a private motorcycle taxi (just a few RMB) to **Gaobeidian Antique Furniture Market** (see p.260), another interesting place for fans of antique-style furniture. There are so many shops that you'll need at least three hours if you really want to buy something.

12.30pm End of tour.

 # Bus Details

Major Bus Stops

These are the major bus stops in the "Southeast." At each bus stop, there are direct routes to the key destinations. **They are marked on the map on p.268.**

Fangzhuangqiao Xi (方庄桥西), west of Fangzhuang Qiao

To Agricultural Exhibition Center (农展馆): 627

To Beihai Park (北海): 812

To Beijing Zoo (北京动物园): 812, 732

To China Science & Technology Museum (中国科技馆): 954, 957 支, 特 8 外

To Forbidden City (故宫): 812

To Panjiayuan Market (潘家园市场): 627, 757, 368

To Qianmen (前门): 723, 826

To Summer Palace (颐和园): 826, 732

To Temple of Heaven (天坛): 826

To Yuanmingyuan (圆明园): 826

Panjiayuanqiao Xi (潘家园桥西), west of Panjiayuan Qiao and in front of the Panjiayuan Market

To Temple of Heaven (天坛): 34

To Tian'anmen Square (天安门广场), Wangfujing (王府井), Military Museum (军事博物馆) and Beijing West Railway Station (北京西站): 802

Zuo'anmenwai (左安门外), 300 m south of Zuo'anmen Qiao

To Beijing Amusement Park (北京游乐园): 12, 750, 807

To Grand View Garden (大观园): 122, 特3, 800 内

To Tian'anmen (天安门): 37

To Temple of Heaven (天坛): 122, 特3, 800 内

To Wangfujing (王府井): 807, 37

To Zhongshan Park (中山公园): 37

Useful Bus Routes

The following is a list of specially selected bus routes passing through the "Southeast" area. These are not all depot-to-depot routes and many less important stops have been omitted. Sights of interest are in bold type. Bus type and times of first and last buses from the first depot are also indicated.

Suggestion: if you are unsure you have the right stop, point out the Chinese characters below for where you want to go and ask another passenger, conductor or driver for help. Many young Chinese have OK English and will be able to help.

运通 107 (standard bus, 5.30am-8.30pm)

Majiapu Xiaoqu 马家堡小区 -Muxiuyuan 木樨园 -Fangzhuang Qiao 方庄桥 -Chengshousi 成寿寺 -**Panjiayuan 潘家园** -Jinsong Dongkou 劲松东口 -Agricultural Exhibition Center 农展馆 -Liangma Qiao 亮马桥 -Lufthansa Center 燕莎友谊商城 -Jiuxian Qiao 酒仙桥-Holiday Inn Lido 丽都饭店 -Wangjing Lu 望京路

特 3 (double-decker, 6.40am-8.30pm)

Qicai World 七彩大世界 -Lufthansa Center 燕莎友谊商城 -Liangma Qiao 亮马桥 -Agricultural Exhibition Center 农展馆 -Jinsongqiao Bei 劲松桥北 -Zuo'anmenwai 左安门外 -**Temple of Heaven South Gate 天坛南门**- Beijing South Railway Station 北京南站

28 (standard bus, 5am-11pm)

Dongdaqiao 东大桥 -Fangcaodi 芳草地 -Shuangjing Qiao双井桥 -Jinsongqiao Nan劲松桥南 -Panjiayuan Qiao 潘家园桥 -Shilihe 十里河

34 (standard bus, 5.50am-10.20pm)

Friendship Hospital 友谊医院 -**Temple of Heaven North Gate 天坛北门** -Fahuasi 法华寺 - Panjiayuanqiao Xi 潘家园桥西

37 (standard bus, 6am-10pm)

Fangzhuang Beikou 方庄北口 -Fangchengyuan 芳城园 -Beijingzhankou Dong 北京站口东 -**Wangfujing 王府井** -**Tian'anmen East 天安门东** -Xidan Lukoudong 西单路口东 -Cultural Palace of Nationalities 民族文化宫

122 (standard bus, 5am-12pm)

Beijing West Railway Station East北京西站东 -**Lianhuachi 莲花池** -**Grand View Garden 大观园** -Beijing South Railway Station 北京南站 -**Temple of Heaven South Gate 天坛南门** -Fangchengyuan 芳城园 -Beijing Railway Station East 北京站东

300 外 (standard bus, 5.30am-10pm)

Panjiayuanqiao Bei潘家园桥北 -**China Science & Technology Museum 中国科技馆** -Zizhu Qiao 紫竹桥 -Fangzhuangqiao Xi 方庄桥西

368 (standard bus, 5am-8.30pm)

Zuo'an Lu 左安路 -Panjiayuan Qiao 潘家园桥 -Fangzhuangqiao Xi 方庄桥西 -Gongzhufen 公主坟 -Yuyuantan Park West Gate 玉渊潭西门

627 (standard bus, 5.30am-7pm)

Sanyingmen 三营门-Fangzhuangqiao Xi 方庄桥西 -Panjiayuan Qiao 潘家园桥 -Agricultural Exhibition Center 农展馆

741 (standard bus, 5.40am-10pm)

Beijing West Railway Station 北京西站 -Tianningsiqiao Bei 天宁寺桥北 -Guang'anmennei 广安门内 Beijing South Railway Station 北京南站 -Fangzhuang Nankou 方庄南口 -Fangchengyuan 芳城园 -Zuo'anmenwai 左安门外

757 (double-decker, 5.20am-7.30pm)

Chaoyang Park North Gate 朝阳公园北门 -Panjiayuan Qiao 潘家园桥 -Fangzhuangqiao Xi 方庄桥西 -Muxiyuanqiao Dong 木樨园桥东-Yangqiao Xi 洋桥西

800 外 (A/C, 6am-8pm)

Grand View Garden 大观园-Beijing South Railway Station 北京南站 -**Temple of Heaven South Gate 天坛南门** -Fangchengyuan 芳城园 -Zuo'anmenwai 左安门外 -**Panjiayuan 潘家园** -Yabao Lu 雅宝路 -Yonghegongqiao Xi 雍和宫桥西

802 (A/C, 6am-9pm)

Beijing West Railway Station 北京西站 -Gongzhufen Dong 公主坟东 -**Military Museum 军事博物馆** -**Tian'anmen East 天安门东** -**Wangfujing 王府井** -Panjiayuanqiao Xi 潘家园桥西

954 (standard bus, 5am-7.30pm)

Fangzhuangqiao Xi 方庄桥西 -Panjiayuanqiao Bei 潘家园桥北 -Shuangjingqiao Bei 双井桥北-Sanyuan Qiao 三元桥-**China Science & Technology Museum 中国科技馆**

974 (standard bus, 5am-8.30pm)

Dongzhimenwai 东直门外 -Agricultural Exhibition Center 农展馆 -Shuangjing Qiao 双井桥 -Panjiayuan Qiao 潘家园桥 -Capital Library 首都图书馆

During the Qin Dynasty, about 70% of China's population worked on the first 3,000 miles of the Great Wall.

Beyond the Fifth Ring Road

With so much to see and do, you could understandably use all your time in the city without venturing farther afield. That would be a pity, because much of what makes Beijing a truly international magnet exists beyond the Fifth Ring Road. Who would want to come to China and not walk on the **Great Wall** (see p.280)?

Ancient bronze vessel.

You can walk many different sections of this truly great construction, depending on the time available and sense of adventure.

It is beyond the Fifth Ring Road too that you may find mountains, caves, forests, temples and tombs, as well as rural life, all of it worth visiting. Hike up **Fragrant Hills** (or ride a cable car if you prefer) (see p.289), view centuries-old courtyards at **Cuandixia Village** (see p.293), or spend some time in reflection at the **Temple of Ordination Altar** (see p.292). You'll find fewer cars, fresher air, home-grown food and rich cultural experiences awaiting you. A variety of transportation options get you from the city and into the countryside, so be sure to plan for at least one trip to visit what lies waiting for you "Beyond the Fifth Ring Road!"

Albeit much fewer and lower in quality than in the city, restaurants can be found around most of these sites. Even so we strongly recommend that you take some packed food/snacks and plenty of water.

Highlights

- **Great Wall** 长城 The Great Wall, being one of the seven medieval wonders of the world, has always been a favorite destination of people worldwide. **See p.280**

- **Fragrant Hills Park** 香山公园 Known for its red maple tree leaves—take a hike up here to see a different side of Beijing. **See p.289**

- **Ming Tombs** 明十三陵 A final resting place fit for 13 emperors! **See p.286**

- **Museum of Peking Man Site at Zhoukoudian** 周口店遗址博物馆 Home to the Peking Man, and a great place to learn something new, even if you aren't an anthropologist. **See p.294**

- **Temple of Pool and Wild Mulberry** 潭柘寺 A temple that is older than Beijing. The 75 stupas nearby are an amazing site. **See p.292**

- **Cuandixia Village** 爨底下村 Hidden in the mountains for a couple of hundred years, this village draws large crowds because of its well preserved Ming and Qing courtyard architecture. **See p.293**

The Great Wall 长城 ★★★

The Great Wall of China is one of the world's most famous pieces of masonry, stretching for a staggering 6,200 km across rugged, sharp mountain ridges. It has easily become one of the wonders of the world and made its way onto the World Cultural Heritage list in 1987. From its beginning near the sea at Shanhaiguan Pass, Hebei Province, it snakes and weaves its way westward to end at Jiayuguan Pass in Gangsu Province. The Chinese saying, "You are not a real man until you have climbed the Great Wall" is corroborated by millions of visitors every year who come to experience first-hand this amazing ancient defense work.

A common misconception is that the Great Wall was built as a single continuous construction. It is in fact a series of defensive walls, each with a different date and history. The walls were first constructed by various feudatory states during the Spring and Autumn Period (770-476 BC) and Warring States Period (475-221 BC) to defend their territories. After conquering all the rival states, the First Emperor of the Qin Dynasty (221-206 BC), and of all China, ordered the linking of existing walls to form a 5,000-

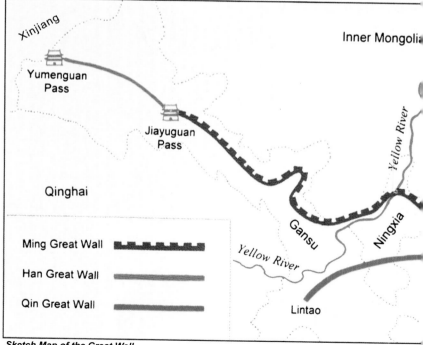

Sketch Map of the Great Wall

km continuous line of defense around his new united realm from attack by northern nomadic Xiongnu. Later dynasties, from Han to Ming, continued to rebuild and add to the wall, strengthening and extending it to 6,200 km.

Most of what remains today is Ming Dynasty in date. Those classic "Great Wall" features—walls, passes, watchtowers, castles and fortresses—can all be attributed to this phase of construction. Today it is possible to visit some beautifully preserved (and equally beautifully unpreserved) sections, the best well-known being the Badaling section. Its classic, well-preserved features plus its proximity to Beijing and easy access (by expressway and a cable car once you get there) has made it the most visited section. From east to west, the Shanhaiguan Pass, Jinshanling, Simatai, Mutianyu and Jiayuguan Pass sections are also frequented by big numbers of visitors.

Other, lesser-known areas of this 700-year-old wall have, unsurprisingly, felt the test of time and fallen into ruins. In an attempt to preserve their structure (and hikers' limbs) these "wild walls" as they are known locally, have been made off-limits to walkers, although enforcement is often lax. However, there are some legal hikes you can do if you fancy getting off the "beaten wall." Information can be found at **www.wildwall.com**.

Hotels and restaurants can be found at the foot of any section of the Wall, and most hotels offer cheap food. In winter, however, they are usually closed.

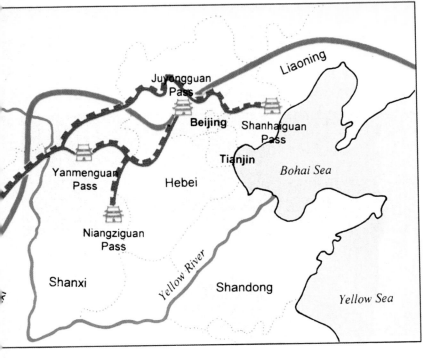

❶ Badaling Great Wall
八达岭长城

Opens earliest to tourists

Hours: 7.30am-7.30pm
Entrance: RMB 45 or 40 (off-season), half price for students
Suggested length of visit: 2 hours
*Transport: Bus 919快 at Deshengmen (德胜门) to Badaling (八达岭) or official tour bus at Tian'anmen Square (see p.315). **About two hours' journey.***
Yanqing County. (86-10-69121383, 69121737) http://badaling.gov.cn/
延庆县内

❌ 🏠 *Badaling Hotel (八达岭饭店, 86-10-69121657) inside the gate of ticket office. Meals RMB 20/person; rooms RMB 50/bed. Or Jinyuanlong Hotel (金源隆大酒店, 13716692560) opposite the Badaling bus stop. Meals RMB 20-30/person; rooms RMB 120/night.*

📝 *Badaling is the busiest section of the Great Wall, and the closest to the Beijing. If time allows, head out to one of the other sections to avoid the crowds.*

Badaling is the best-preserved, most well-trodden section of the Great Wall, and it became a very important military strategic site during the Spring and Autumn Period and the Warring States Period. Its bricks have seen the footsteps of over 370 world leaders. Made of huge bar stones weighing hundreds of kilos each, the top is paved with bricks, making it easily traversable.

Nearby, the **Great Wall Museum** winds up the day nicely.

❷ Juyongguan Great Wall
居庸关长城

A very important strategic pass

Hours: 8.30am-4.30pm (winter), 7.30am-5.30pm (summer)
Entrance: RMB 45, half price for students
Suggested length of visit: 1 hour
*Transport: Bus 919 慢 at Deshengmen (德胜门) or official tour bus at Tian'anmen Square to Juyongguan (居庸关) (see p.315). **About one hour's journey.***
20 km north of Changping County. (86-10-69771665)
昌平县城以北 20 公里
❌ 🏠 *See the Badaling Great Wall.*

About 20 km south of Badaling is the most recently restored section of the Wall, Juyongguan Pass. Less crowded, it was one of the three most important strategic passes along the Great Wall. As it is on the way to Badaling, it is convenient to visit both on the same trip.

Badaling is popular for tourists, as it is closest to Beijing.

Picturesque and over-grown Simatai.

❸ Simatai Great Wall
司马台长城

Dangerous, but definitely worth a trip

Hours: 6am-7pm (winter), 5am-8.30pm (summer)
Entrance: RMB 40; half price for students; free for children under 1.2 m
Suggested length of visit: 3-4 hours
Transport: Bus 970 or 980 at Dongzhimen Long-distance Bus Station (东直门长途汽车站) to Miyun Bus Station (密云汽车站), then transfer a bus to Simatai (司马台). Or take official tour bus from Tian'anmen Square around 6.30am-8.30am on weekends (see p.315). ***About 3 hours' journey.***
Simatai Village, Gubeikou, Miyun County. (86-10-69031051)
http://www.simatai-greatwall.net/english.asp
密云县古北口镇司马台村
❌ ♨ *Great Wall Hotel (长城山庄, 86-10-69035159), features Sima Restaurant (司马饭庄) and traditional siheyuan courtyard houses. Meals RMB 40-50/person; double rooms RMB 240/night.*

Unlike elsewhere, Simatai has received little or no restoration, making it a favorite "authentic" Ming section to visit. Crumbling and in a state of disrepair, it looks as it should after 500 years of life. It lies on a very steep mountain, and it's said that from its 986-m-high **Watching-Beijing Tower** (望京楼 Wangjinglou), people can see the lights of Beijing at night and the White Dagoba in Beihai Park by day.

Though not an easy passage, those up for the challenge will reap the rewards. Taking a cable car is always an easy-on-the-feet alternative. Very close to the Jinshanling section.

❹ Jinshanling Great Wall
金山岭长城

Concentration of watchtowers and beacon towers

Hours: 8am-5pm
Entrance: RMB 30
Suggested length of visit: 2-3 hours; 4 hours if you walk to Simatai Great Wall
Transport: take a Chengde-bound bus (RMB 15) at Dongzhimen (东直门) to Jinshanling Scenic Area (金山岭景区), then transfer to a mini-bus to the destination. ***About 3 hours' journey.***
On the border between Beijing's Miyun County and Hebei Province's Luanping County. (86-10-84024627/4628, 86-314-8830222)
http://www.jinshanlinggreatwall.com/
北京市密云县与河北省滦平县交界处
❌ ♨ *Jinshan Hotel (金山宾馆, 86-10-84024627), inside the gate of ticket office. Meals RMB 50/person; rooms RMB 200/night.*

Named after the mountain on which it stands, this Ming wall is second only to Badaling in terms of preservation. However, it is far less crowded and great to explore, and boasts the greatest number of watch and beacon towers anywhere along the wall. At 700 m, it provides some spectacular photo opportunities. **Camping overnight** here is legal.

❺ Jiankou Great Wall
箭扣长城

Photographers' favorite section

Hours: 24 hours
Entrance: RMB 10
Suggested length of visit: 3-4 hours
Transport: Bus 916, 936 at Dongzhimen Long-distance Bus Station (东直门长途汽车站) to Huairou Bus Station (怀柔汽车站), then change a mini-bus to Jiankou. **About 2.5 hours' journey.**
28 km northwest of Huairou District. (86-10-61611674)
怀柔区城西北28公里

❌ 🚌 *Zhaoshi Village House (赵氏山居, 86-10-61611762, http://www.jkwall.com/dispbbs.asp? boardid=3&id=27), a hotel highly recommended by photographers. It also has bus service (RMB 70, they can pick you up at the Huairou Bus Station). Meals RMB 20/person; rooms RMB 80/night.*

📝 *There is only one way to the Jiankou Great Wall and you should come back along the same way.*

Connecting with the Mutianyu and Huanghuacheng sections, Jiankou is probably the most authentic and dangerous part of the Great Wall in Beijing. Sadly, this also means it's the most endangered.

Built during the Ming Dynasty, it possesses some stunning hikes and photo opportunities, notably the wall's highest point and the **"Sky Stairs"** (天梯) which are almost (but not quite!) unclimbable.

❻ Mutianyu Great Wall
慕田峪长城

The largest-scale and highest-quality section of the Great Wall

Hours: 7am-5pm
Entrance: RMB 40, half price for students
Suggested length of visit: 1.5-2 hours
Transport: Bus 916 at Dongzhimen Long-distance Bus Station (东直门长途汽车站) to Huairou International Conference Center (怀柔国际会议中心),
and change to a mini-bus to Mutianyu. **About 1.5 hours' journey.**
Beisanduhe, Huairou District. (86-10-61626873/ 6505, 60626022)
http://www.mutianyugreatwall.com/banner.html
怀柔区北三渡河

❌ 🚌 *Take a mini-bus at Huairou International Conference Center to Xinying Roundabout (辛营环岛) which is about 1 km west of Mutianyu. There are many cheap hotels around. Rooms RMB 80/ night.*

Rebuilt in 1569, Mutianyu is loved for its unusual fortifications. The Mutianyu Pass consists of three connected watchtowers, with a big one in the center and two on the sides.

Mutianyu Greall Wall.

Jiuyanlou Great Wall Watchtower.

❼ Huanghuacheng Great Wall
黄花城长城

Hikers' favorite section

Hours: 8am-5pm (winter),7am-6pm (summer)
Entrance: RMB 25, half price for students
Suggested length of visit: 3 hours
*Transport: Bus 916 at Dongzhimen Long-distance Bus Station (东直门长途汽车站) to Huairou International Conference Center (怀柔国际会议中心), and change to a mini-bus to Huanghuacheng, or take official tour bus at Tian'anmen Square to Huanghuacheng (see p.315). **About 1.5 hours' journey.***

Chengguan Town, Huairou District.
怀柔城关镇

❌ 🛏️ *Xiaohong Yilufa (晓红一路发, 86-10-61651393), meals RMB 20/person; rooms RMB 10/bed, RMB 50-80/room. Take a mini-bus at Huairou International Conference Center to Xishuiyu (西水峪).*

Connected with Mutianyu, this section of the Wall by a reservoir is a hikers' favorite, as it has never been restored. The **Yaoziyu Fort** (鹞子峪城堡) is one of the best-preserved forts, covering 7,257 sq m.

❽ Jiuyanlou Great Wall
九眼楼长城

The Great Wall's largest watchtower

Hours: 24 hours
Entrance: RMB 20, students RMB 10
Suggested length of visit: 3-4 hours
Transport: Bus 919快 at Deshengmen (德胜门) to Yanqing Bus Station (延庆汽车站), change a bus to Sihai (四海), then take a mini-bus to Jiuyanlou.
About 3.5 hours' journey.

1 km southeast of Shiyao Village, Sihai, southeast of the county proper of Yanqing. (86-10-60187367/7019)
延庆县城东南部四海古镇石窑村东南1千米

❌ 🛏️ *The ticket office (九眼楼售票处, 86-10-60187367) can arrange accommodation: meals RMB 20/person; rooms RMB 20/bed. Or Zhaochunhua's Hotel (赵春华农家院, 86-10-60187157), RMB 50/person (including accommodation, breakfast, lunch and dinner).*

Built in 1543, this section of the Wall is home to the largest watchtower, measuring 7.8 m high and 13 m wide. Nicknamed by the locals "nine holes tower," it contains the greatest number of crenels of any tower along the entire Great Wall...nine.

Do-able Day Trips

❾ Ming Tombs
明十三陵 Míng shísānlíng ★★★
13 Ming emperors' mausoleums

Suggested length of visit: half day
Transport: Bus 345 快 from Deshengmen Xi (德胜门西) to Changping Dongguan (昌平东关), and then transfer to bus 314 to the final destination.
About 2 hours' journey.
http://www.mingtombs.com.cn/cn/lswh/cbw.asp
Jundushan, Changping District.
昌平区军都山

The Ming Tombs are the best and most extensive display of imperial tombs in China, covering 120 sq km. The final resting place of 13 of the 16 Ming emperors, 23 empresses and a multitude of concubines, princes and princesses, they are a clear and fascinating reflection of the strict hierarchy of life being perpetuated after death. Among them, only three—Changling, Dingling and Zhaoling—are open to the public. Changling is the most opulent and Dingling is the only underground palace open to public today. Strictly, following *fengshui* principles, each of the Ming tombs lies against a hill to the north.

There are three Ming emperors who were not buried here. They are the dynasty's founder Zhu Yuanzhang whose tomb is in Nanjing, the second emperor whose tomb whereabouts is still unknown, and the seventh who was dethroned and buried near Fragrant Hill.

Dingling 定陵
Hours: 8.30 am-6pm
Entrance: RMB 60 (Apr 1-Oct 31), RMB 45 (Nov 1-Mar 31), half price for students. (86-10-60761424)
❌ *Dingling Restaurant (定陵餐厅, 86-10-60761432), north of the Dingling Museum. About RMB 30-50/person.*
Tomb of the 13th Emperor Wanli and his two empresses, Dingling is the only fully excavated underground palace tomb, a labyrinthine complex of great halls. The coffins of the emperor and his empresses can be found in the largest hall at the rear. The Dingling Museum houses some enchanting pieces: the Phoenix and Dragon Crowns (genuine) worn by the emperor and his empresses, the emperor's Ceremonial Dress (replica) and Hundred-children Gown (replica).

Zhaoling 昭陵
Hours: 8am-5.30pm
Entrance: RMB 30 (Apr 1-Oct 31), RMB 20 (Nov 1-Mar 31), half price for students. (86-10-60761435)
While lacking the "wow factor" of Dingling and Changling, Zhaoling was built for Emperor Longqing and his three empresses.

Changling 长陵
Hours: 8am-5.30pm
Entrance: RMB 45 (Apr 1-Oct 31), RMB 30 (Nov 1-Mar 31), half price for students. (86-10-60761334)
✗ *Ming Changling Restaurant (明长陵餐厅, 86-10-60761061), east of the Changling Square. About RMB 20/person.*
Far outdoing his predecessors and successors, Emperor Yongle was the proud builder of not only the Forbidden City but also of the largest of the Ming Tombs, Changling. The ground structure, Ling'en Hall (陵恩殿), the same size as the Hall of Supreme Harmony in the Forbidden City, is open to the public, showing off impressive marble floors and sandalwood columns.

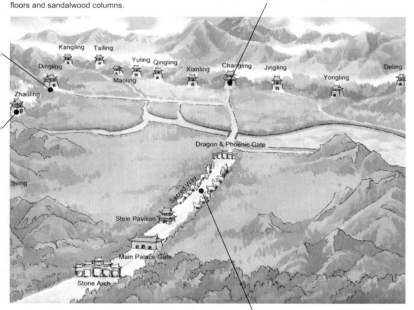

Sacred Way 神路
Hours: 8.30am-6pm
Entrance: RMB 30 (Apr 1-Oct 31), RMB 20 (Nov 1-Mar 31). (86-10-89749383)
The Sacred Way, a 7-km-long path leading to the Ming Tombs, begins with the biggest and perfectly preserved archway in China. Made of marble and erected in 1540, the archway is a demonstration of the triumphs of Chinese architecture at the time. The most impressive is a collection of 24 stone animals and 12 stone civil and military officials guarding on both sides along the way.

Why was a tomb so important to the emperor?

Grave designation in Chinese society was a complex and strict process, from the highest-ranking emperors' mausoleums (*ling* 陵) to the common people's graves (*fen* 坟) and everything in between. A strong belief in the power of *fengshui* to protect their dynasty meant that an emperor had hardly ascended the throne before he started construction on his own tomb.

The 13 Imperial Tombs of the Ming Dynasty

Tomb	Emperor	Reign title	Reign period
Changling	Zhu Di	Yongle	1402-1424
Xianling	Zhu Gaochi	Hongxi	1424-1425
Jingling	Zhu Zhanji	Xuande	1425-1435
Yuling	Zhu Qizhen	Zhengtong	1435-1449
		Tianshun	1457-1464
Maoling	Zhu Jianshen	Chenghua	1464-1487
Tailing	Zhu Youtang	Hongzhi	1487-1505
Kangling	Zhu Houzhao	Zhengde	1505-1521
Yongling	Zhu Houcong	Jiajing	1521-1566
Zhaoling	Zhu Zaigou	Longqing	1566-1572
Dingling	Zhu Yijun	Wanli	1572-1620
Qingling	Zhu Changluo	Taichang	1620
Deling	Zhu Youxiao	Tianqi	1620-1627
Siling	Zhu Youjian	Chongzhen	1627-1644

While incarcerated as a POW, Zhu Qizhen's brother Qiyu was emperor between 1450 -1456.

The Underground Palace of Dingling. The emperor is entombed in the center, with his empresses on both sides.

Visit the beautiful Fragrant Hills in autumn when the leaves burn orange and red.

⑩ Fragrant Hills Park 香山公园 Xiāngshān gōngyuán ★★★

Imperial garden, famous for red leaves in autumn

Hours: 6am-6pm (winter), 6am-6.30pm (summer)
Entrance: RMB 10, half price for students. Azure
Cloud Temple (碧云寺) RMB 10
Suggested length of visit: 1-2 hours
Transport: Bus 360, 331, 318, 714, 733, 737 to
Fragrant Hills (香山)
No. 28, Qinghua Xilu, Haidian District. (86-10-
62591155)
海淀区清华西路28号
✗ *At the foot there are a lot of cheap restaurants.*

Shaped like an incense burner, Fragrant Hills, standing 557 m high, owes its name to the aromatic fruit and lilac groves that abound on its slopes. Once an imperial hunting ground, it's a wonderful place for people to hike and relax on weekends. Especially beautiful in autumn, the park ignites into a mass of red crunchy leaves, truly the best time to visit, but you won't be alone!

You can trek to the top on foot or take the cable car. At the foot, the Fragrant Hills Hotel is a good example of modernist architecture by IM Pei, and the **Azure Cloud Temple** (also containing the personal effects of Dr. Sun Yat-sen) is a tranquil sanctuary.

⑪ Beijing Miniature Park
老北京微缩景园
Lǎoběijīng wēisuō jǐngyuán ★

Mini-size old Beijing

Hours: 8am-6pm (summer), 8.30am-5pm (winter)
Entrance: RMB 45 (summer), 40 (winter)
Suggested length of visit: 1 hour
*Transport: Bus 919 at Deshengmen (德胜门) to
Chenzhuang (陈庄). **About 1.5 hours' journey.***
*Nankou Town, Changping District. (86-10-
69771805)*
昌平区南口镇

This 1:15 scale replica of old Beijing provides visitors with a giant's-eye view of 50 ha of landscape. Including a touring area, customs street, reception and administration area, the model recalls Beijing's Ming and Qing Dynasty heritage.

⑫ Silver Mountain and Pagoda Forest
银山塔林 Yínshān tǎlín ★

A grouping of pagodas

Hours: 24 hours
Entrance: RMB 20

*Suggested length of visit: 4-5 hours to the summit; 2
hours will be enough just for cultural and historical
sites.*
*Transport: Bus 345 at Deshengmen (德胜门) to
Changping Beizhan (昌平北站) and then change to
a mini-bus to the destination. **About 1.5 hours'
journey.***
*Xingshou Town, Changping District. (86-10-
89726426)*
昌平区兴寿镇
❌ *Yinshan Talin Restaurant (银山塔林餐厅, 86-
10-89726425), inside the gate. Meals RMB 20-50/
person.*

Nestled amongst the remote mountains, this site is almost un-visited and untouched by tourists.

It is a collection of five Jin pagodas, two Yuan Dynasty pagodas and 18 pagoda-style tombs, a cemetery for eminent monks and abbots whose life achievements and status are reflected by the grandeur of their stupas. Climbing to the summit is a challenge, and on your descent follow the route to the **Luoluodong** (落落洞), a two-story hall formed by a natural cave.

Pagoda Forest is right!

⑬ Badachu Park 八大处公园 Bādàchù gōngyuán ★★

Owing its name to the eight beautiful temples

Hours: daily 6am-6pm
Entrance: RMB 10
Suggested length of visit: 2 hours
Transport: Bus 347, 389, 972, 489 to Badachu (八大处)
Badachu, Shijingshan District. (86-10-88964661)
石景山区八大处

✗ *Zhaoxian Restaurant (招仙餐厅, 86-10-88964661 ext.2017), opposite the Temple of Divine Light (灵光寺). Offers Muslim food. About RMB 20-30/person.*

Located just south of Fragrant Hills, Badachu is home to eight temples dotted throughout its 332 ha. The most renowned is the **Temple of Divine Light** (灵光寺 Lingguangsi) which houses a tooth of the Buddha. Maintaining a temperate climate year round, in contrast to the extremes of the nearby city, the tree-clad hills make this one of locals' favorite hiking spots.

Badachu means "Eight Great Sites," among which is this Temple of Divine Light.

⑭ Fahai Temple 法海寺 Fǎhǎisì ★★

With murals rivaling Dunhuang

Hours: 9am-4.30pm (closed on Mondays)
Entrance: RMB 20 (closed for renovations until May 2008)
Suggested length of visit: 1 hour
Transport: Bus 运通112, 运通116, 311 to Moshikou (模式口)
North of Moshikou Village, Shijingshan District. (86-10-88715776/3976)
石景山区模式口村北

📷 *The temple lights are shut off to protect the murals, so borrow a flashlight from the employees to view the amazing artwork.*

Its entrance guarded by four stern-looking deva kings, the temple has 10 beautifully preserved **Buddhist murals** of the Ming Dynasty. The mural of Guanyin (Goddess of Mercy) is truly breathtaking. It's highly recommended for lovers of mural art.

⑮ Shijingshan Amusement Park 石景山游乐园 Shíjǐngshān yóulèyuán ★

Hours: daily 8 am-6.30pm (Apr 1-Oct 31), 9am-4.30pm (Nov 1-Mar 31)
Entrance: RMB 10 (all inclusive ticket: summer RMB 100, winter RMB 80)
Suggested length of visit: 1 day
Transport: Subway Line 1 to Baojiao Youleyuan (八角游乐园) or Bus 337, 389, 622, 354, 385, 327, 728, 941 to Jingyuan Lukoudong (京原路口东)
No. 25, Shijingshan Lu, Shijingshan District. (86-10-68874060) http://www.bs-amusement-park.com/ (in Chinese)
石景山区石景山路25号

The park houses a variety of amusements to entertain children and adults alike. The beautiful and unusual surroundings are a real treat, and a pleasant and enjoyable day can be spent wandering around.

⑯ Temple of Pool and Wild Mulberry 潭柘寺 Tánzhèsì ★★

A temple older than Beijing

Hours: 8am-5pm

Entrance: RMB 35

Suggested length of visit: 2 hours

Transport: Subway Line 1 to Pingguoyuan (苹果 园) and then change to Bus 931 to the temple. Or take the official tour bus at Tian'anmen Square (see p.315). **About 1.5 hours' journey.**

Before the Baozhu Peak, Tanzhe Mountain, Mentougou District. (86-10-60862500/2505)

http://www.tanzhesi.com.cn/ (in Chinese)

门头沟区潭柘山宝珠峰前

A s the saying goes, "there was Tanzhesi, then came the city of Beijing," this is Beijing's oldest temple, dating back to the Jin Dynasty and later the favorite worship site of Kublai Khan's daughter. In its heyday, monks from all over Asia came here to study.

As with many other ancient temples, its name has been changed over time; its current name honors the **Dragon Pool** (龙潭 Longtan) above the temple and the wild mulberry trees that blanket the surrounding hills.

The stupa grove nearby, the biggest and best of its kind in Beijing, is worth seeing. There are 75 stupas (monks' graves) in total, all of them different.

"Welcome friend, to the Temple of Pool and Wild Mulberry."

Sitting upon the Ordination Altar is Sakyamuni.

⑰ Temple of Ordination Altar 戒台寺 Jiètáisì ★★

Housing the most impressive white marble altar in China

Hours: 8am-5pm

Entrance: RMB 35, half price for students

Suggested length of visit: 1-1.5 hours

Transport: Subway Line 1 to Pingguoyuan (苹果 园) and then change to Bus 931 to the temple. Or take the official tour bus at Tian'anmen Square (see p.315). **About one hour's journey.**

Shimenying, Mentougou District. (86-10-69802232, 69806611)

门头沟区石门营

✖ *Jietaisi Restaurant (戒台寺餐厅, 86-10- 69802232/6611) inside the temple. Offers both vegetarian and meat dishes. RMB 20-30/person.*

A Ming Dynasty structure intricately carved with motifs of lotus petals, drifting clouds and 113 niches of Buddha. This is China's most impressive white marble altar; if you visit just one altar, let it be this one. Combine this trip with a visit to the **Temple of Pool and Wild Mulberry** (潭柘寺Tanzhesi), which is a 15-minute drive from here.

No skyscrapers, no subway: Cuandixia, an untouched quaint village.

⑱ Cuandixia Village
爨底下村 Cuāndǐxiàcūn ★★

The best-preserved Ming-and-Qing era town in suburban Beijing

Hours: 24 hours
Entrance: RMB 20, half price for students
Suggested length of visit: 3 hours
*Transport: Subway Line 1 to Pingguoyuan (苹果园), then take Bus 929 支 (7.30am-10.10am and 12.40pm-3.30pm) to Zhaitang (斋堂), then take a taxi (RMB 10-15) to the village gate. **About 2.5 hours' journey.***
Zhaitang Town, Mentougou District. (86-10-69819333/9090)
门头沟区斋堂镇
❌ 🍴 *The locals offer cheap accommodation and food at their home. Meals RMB 20/person; rooms RMB 10-25/bed.*

A stop on the ancient trade route between Shanxi Province and Beijing, this 400-year-old village is now under national architectural protection and attracts numerous tourists, photographers and filmmakers. 70 beautifully preserved courtyard houses, dating to the Ming and Qing dynasties, provide a bewitching view of two ancient Chinese architectural styles blended together. A winding street separates this village into upper and lower parts. Most residents in this village are surnamed Han (韩).

It is recommended to visit Lingshan Mountain (灵山) while in the area.

⑲ Lingshan Mountain
灵山 Língshān ★

Famed as "mini Tibet," it is the highest peak in Beijing

Hours: 24 hours
Entrance: RMB 35 and RMB 80 for the cable car, (free for children under 1.2 m)
Suggested length of visit: 4 hours; ride a horse or the cable car to shorten the time.

Lingshan offers a peek into distant Tibet.

Amazing hand-dug caves at Guyaju.

*Transport: Subway Line 1 to Pingguoyuan (苹果园), then take Bus 929 支 (7.30am-10.10am and 12.40pm-3.30pm) to Shuangtangjian (双塘涧), then take a taxi (about RMB 50) to the gate. **About 3 hours' journey.***

Northwest of Mentougou District (on the border of Mentougou District and Hebei Province). (86-10-61827994) http://www.lingshan.org/ (in Chinese)

门头沟区西北部 (门头沟区和河北省的交界处)

❌ ♿ *Baihualin Farmer's House (白桦林农乐园, 86-10-87012720), north of the Lingshan Scenic Area parking lot. Meals RMB 20/person; rooms RMB 10-40/bed. They also have a pick-up service (RMB 30 from Shuangtangjian to their place).*

Favored with gentle slopes and an alpine climate, at 2,302 m, the Lingshan Mountain is the highest point around Beijing. Similar to Tibet in geographical features, this place has been deliberately transformed into a "Tibetan plateau." A Tibetan-style village has emerged half way up where visitors can enjoy Tibetan performances and festivals as well as witnessing lamas chanting Buddhist scriptures. Yurt tents make for novel overnight accommodation.

The best time to visit is between July and September.

⑳ Guyaju 古崖居 Gǔyájū ★★
Mysterious cave complex

Hours: 24 hours
Entrance: RMB 40, half price for students
Suggested length of visit: 1 hour
*Transport: Bus 919快 at Deshengmen (德胜门) to Yanqing (延庆), then transfer to a mini-bus to Guyaju (古崖居). **About 2.5 hours' journey.***
Zhangshanying Town, Yanqing District. (86-10-69778491)
延庆县张山营镇

Nestled in a peaceful gorge to the northwest of Beijing, Guyaju is a 1,000-year-old cave complex. 117 stone rooms were hand-carved out of sheer cliffs in the gorge, an amazing feat. Theories as to the identities of the residents include outlaws, soldiers or refugees from fighting. Whoever created these labyrinthine dwellings however, certainly had a room with a view.

㉑ Museum of Peking Man Site at Zhoukoudian
周口店遗址博物馆
Zhōukǒudiàn yízhǐ bówùguǎn ★★
World-shaking find

Hours: 8.30am-5pm

The clever Peking man used tools and made fire.

Entrance: RMB 30, free for children under 1.2 m
Suggested length of visit: 2 hours
Transport: Bus 917 (Shidu Line 十渡线) at Tianqiao (天桥) to Zhoukoudian Lukou (周口店路口), then change to a mini-bus to the museum; or take the official tour bus at Tian'anmen Square to Zhoukoudian (see p.315). About 1.5 hours' journey.
No. 1, Zhoukoudian Dajie, Fangshan District. (86-10-69301272/1278) http://www.zkd.cn/ (in Chinese)
房山区周口店大街1 号

❌ *The restaurant inside the museum serves cheap dishes. RMB 10-20/person.*

📖 *With the Museum Pass you can get one free admission.*

A super-abundance of archeological remains dating back 200,000 to 500,000 years has revealed the home of "Peking Man," a distant human relative. The discovery, in 1921, of some paleo-fossils led to full-scale excavation that unearthed cave dwellings, hearths and "ape man" fossils in the following years.

Scientific research proves that Peking Man could walk upright and use tools and fire. The great number of paleo-fossils, stoneware and layers of ash displayed here, remain as testaments to the time passed.

㉒ Museum of the Yan Capital Site in Western Zhou
西周燕都城遗址
Xīzhōu yāndūchéng yízhǐ ★

Beijing of 3,000 years ago

Hours: 8.30am-4.30pm
Entrance: free
Suggested length of visit: 1 hour
Transport: Bus 917 支 at Tianqiao (天桥) to Shangzhou Yizhi (商周遗址)
Dongjialin Village, Liulihe, Fangshan District. (86-10-61393475). About 1.5 hours' journey.
房山区琉璃河镇董家林村

Discovered in the 1960s, this site was the capital of the State of Yan during the Western Zhou Dynasty (c.1100-771 BC). A wealth of cultural remains is on display, including bronze utensils and two pits of horses and chariots.

㉓ Zhangfang Old Plank Road
张坊古栈道
Zhāngfáng gǔzhàndào ★

The only ancient military defense route in Beijing

Hours: 8am-5pm (winter), 8am-6pm (summer)
Entrance: RMB 20, half price for students
Suggested length of visit: 1 hour
Transport: Bus 917 at Tianqiao (天桥) to Zhangfang (张坊). About 2 hours' journey.
Zhangfang Village, Zhangfang Town, Fangshan

Zhangfang Old Plank Road, underground safe haven.

District. (86-10-61339763)
房山区张坊镇张坊村

The Zhangfang Old Plank Road is northern China's oldest underground military defense line and definitely worth a visit for a cross-section of Chinese history. At 4 m deep, the original plank is estimated to be 1,500 m long, with only 400 m restored and open to tourists. On the approach, look out for the weapons, command rooms, living facilities and the chambers soldiers used to hide in. You can drop by this site on your way to Shidu.

㉔ Shidu National Geological Park 十渡国家地质公园
Shídù guójiā dìzhì gōngyuán ★★
Natural scenery of 10 bends; bungee jumping

Hours: 7.30am-6.30pm (summer), 8am-5.30pm (winter), closed from Nov 1 to Mar 31
Entrance: depending on specific sites in the park
Suggested length of visit: 1 day
*Transport: Bus 917 at Tianqiao (天桥) to Shidu (十渡). **About 2.5 hours' journey.***
Shidu Town, Fangshan District. (86-10-61340841)
房山区十渡镇

❌ 🍴 *Youshan's Home (有山家园, 86-10-61346396). Meals RMB 20-30/person; rooms RMB 50 (doubles). They sell tickets to Shidu Scenic Area at 20% off.*

"Shidu" or "10 Ferry Crossings" is a reference to the 10 bends along this part of the Juma River. Karst canyons and rock formations such as the Juma River Canyon, Dashi River Valley and Longmenxia Granite Canyon are true spectacles. It is in the running to become Beijing's first UNESCO designated world geological park. RMB 175 will buy an exciting 55-m tandem or solo bungee jump above the Juma River.

Come for an exciting bungee jump at Shidu.

Itinerary

Itinerary L: Three-day Excursion (Friday to Sunday)

Day 1: Badaling Great Wall—Ming Tombs (round trip: 226 km)

8am Wake up and eat, get ready and head to Tian'anmen Square. Take the **official tour bus** (see p.315) to **Badaling Great Wall** (see p.282). (⚡ *The tour bus has a guide, so follow the guide*)

11am Arrive at the Great Wall. Put your hiking boots on and explore this must-see wonder of the world for about 2 hours. For those with mobility issues, a cable car can be ridden up onto the wall. You will need to purchase a ticket for the ride up and/or the ride down.

1pm Eat lunch with your tour group, which is included in the price of the tour.

1.45pm Make your way back to where the bus dropped you off and head to the **Ming Tombs** (see p.286).

2.50pm Arrive at the Ming Tombs. Follow the guide and explore this resting place for 13 Ming emperors (70 minutes).

4pm Time to end the day and head back to town. After all that walking, you might just want a nice foot massage.

> **Expenses**
>
> **Official tour bus:** 160 (including bus fare, admissions to the Badaling Great Wall, Ming Tombs and lunch)

Day 2: Temple of Pool and Wild Mulberry—Cuandixia Village (round trip: 300 km)

8am Get up and get ready. Take Subway Line 1 to Pingguoyuan (苹果园) and then change to Bus 931 to the **Temple of Pool and Wild Mulberry** (see p.292).

10.30am Arrive at the temple. This temple is said to be older than Beijing. Learn the history and explore the amazing stupa grove nearby for about 1 hour.

11.30am Lunch at any surrounding restaurant and our next stop is **Cuandixia Village** (see p.293).

12.15pm With your hunger satisfied, head back to the same stop where you arrived and then take Bus 931 to the Hetan Lukoudong (河滩路口东) stop. Get off and head westward to the Chengzi Dajie (城子大街) intersection, turn right at the intersection and walk north for about 400 m and you'll see the Chengzi Dajie Nankou (城子大街南口) bus stop on the right side of the street. Take Bus 929支 (7.30am-10.10am and 12.40pm-3.30pm) to Zhaitang (斋堂), then take a taxi (RMB 10-15) to Cuandixia Village's front gate.

3pm Arrive at Cuandixia Village. Stroll around this mysterious Ming-and-Qing-era town for about 2 hours.

5pm End of the tour, time to head back to the city.

> **Temple of Pool and Wild Mulberry:** RMB 35
>
> **Lunch:** RMB 20
>
> **Cuandixia Village:** RMB 20
>
> **Transport:** RMB 64 (round trip)

Day 3: Museum of Peking Man Site at Zhoukoudian—Shidu National Geological Park (round trip: 220 km)

8am Prepare everything including your lunch. Arrive at the Tian'anmen Square. Take the **official tour bus** (see p.315) to **Zhoukoudian** (see p.294) and **Shidu** (see p.296). (⚡ *This official tour bus only operates between 6.30am-8.30am on weekends and official holidays from July to August; and for any less than 15 people the bus does not leave.*)

9.30am Arrive at Zhoukoudian. Spend about 1.5 hours here and learn about this significant archaeological find.

11am Time to be back to the tour bus, and be off to Shidu. Eat lunch on the bus.

11.45am Arrive at Shidu. Take a bamboo raft and enjoy the beautiful natural scenery for about 2 hours. The truly brave may want to try bungee jumping at their designated spot; the rest will no doubt enjoy watching.

2.45pm Time to head back to the tour bus for the trip back into town.

> **Official tour bus:** 80 (including bus fare, admissions to Zhoukoudian and Cuandixia Village)
>
> **Bungee jumping:** RMB 175

Total: RMB 554 (USD 76)

TRAVELERS' SURVIVAL GUIDE

Planning
Your Trip

Take a 4 lefts and I'm there.

The best laid plans are always the most successful—isn't that the phrase? Beijing's sheer vastness is most certainly conquered with a good plan tucked into your backpack. Be prepared and do some research before heading out, you stand to save yourself a lot of time, energy and money. Your best source of tourist information about Beijing is your local travel agencies or the website of the **Beijing Tourism Administration** (北京旅游局http://english.bjta.gov.cn/), which has the most up-to-date information on everything from Beijing maps in English to learning Chinese.

It's not easy to find up-to-date maps outside China. Although the **51 maps** in our book offer pretty much everything you need to navigate Beijing, you might still want a bigger size Beijing map. *Beijing Tourist Map* (北京旅游交通图) (in Chinese and English) is quite good for scale. It can be purchased at the airport bookstore, train stations, Foreign Languages Bookstore at Wangfujing and most tourist sites.

Visas and Customs

To apply for a visa you will need a passport valid for at least six months from the date of application and containing at least two blank pages. Visas are issued only from outside China through Chinese embassies, consulates, visa offices, and the consular department of the Chinese Ministry of Foreign Affairs, or at travel agencies authorized by the Ministry. You are suggested to apply for the visa two months before your departure date. If you need a special visa, or to change your visa, be sure to do so within 30 days of entering the country. This can be done at local public security bureaus.

All visitors must complete three forms: the **Traveler's Luggage Declaration Form**, the **Traveler's Health Declaration Card** and the **Entry Registration Card** upon arrival. The Traveler's Luggage Declaration Form is required to be produced again upon departure. All valuable personal items must be declared, including cameras, computers, etc.

Visa Types

The most relevant visa types are listed below. For a full list of up-to-date details and visa application forms, consult the Chinese embassy website for your country—easily found through most search engines. Remember that the embassy is likely to be closed on Chinese holidays, notably around May Day, Chinese New Year and (October) National Day. Visa applications cannot be processed by mail, Internet or express delivery. Submission and collection of the visa must be done in person (not necessarily by the applicant though!).

L Visa "tourist visa"
Issued to those who plan to visit China for the purposes of tourism, family or other personal affairs.

X Visa "student visa"
Issued to applicants who come to China for the purposes of study, advanced studies or intern practice for a period of more than six months.

G Visa "transit visa" Issued to those who need to stay in China for over 24 hours. Both single and double entry visas are available. This visa grants a period of 90 days to enter China, and is valid for 7-10 days per entry. Details for nationalities vary, so see website.

F Visa "business visa" Issued to those invited to China for research, lectures, business, or scientific, technological or cultural exchanges, or for short-term advanced studies or intern practice for a period of no longer than six months.

Visa Extension

Staying in China beyond the duration of one's visa can result in being fined or worse. L visas can generally be extended for 30 days; X and F visas will need sponsorship letters from an employer or school. Applications for a visa extension should be submitted at least five working days before the expiration date. Second extensions are like finding oneself alone on the Beijing subway—rare and unlikely! For more information about visa extension, check the website: http://www.bjgaj.gov.cn/epolice/qianzheng.htm.

Insurance

A hospital stay is never fun, and visiting a dentist is stressful at the best of times. Such things can be doubly daunting in a foreign country. Beijing has a number of quality health-care facilities to choose from but China does not provide free medical services to visitors, and international hospitals and clinics are particularly pricey. Comprehensive **medical and dental insurance** when traveling is strongly recommended. Some credit card companies and travel agencies provide a level of insurance. Check your coverage and know your options before you leave home. See p.329 for international hospital listings.

Getting There

By Air

Beijing Capital International Airport (北京首都国际机场), about 25 km from Tian'anmen Square, handles over 5,000 flights a week serving 88 Chinese and 69 foreign cities. Eleven domestic and

---

Where to apply for visa extension

Exit and Entry Management Section, Beijing Municipal Public Security Bureau (北京市公安局出入境管理处) *Hours: 8.30am-4.30pm*
Transport: Bus 44, 13, 116, 117, 106, 807, 特2 to Beixiaojie Huokou (北小街豁口) or Subway Line 2 to Yonghegong (雍和宫)
No. 2, Andingmen Dongdajie, Dongcheng District. (86-10-84020101 for 24-hour automated service in Chinese and English) 东城区安定门东大街2号

---

55 foreign airlines fly into the capital. It currently has two modern terminals. Most domestic and international flights arrive at Terminal 2. And for the 2008 Olympics, a new state-of-the-art terminal opened in February 2007.

Avoid the possibility of getting ripped off by avoiding all but the metered taxis outside arrival gates 5-9. Remember that the **expressway charge** is additional to what is shown on the meter. If you want something to eat in the airport, it's going to cost you an arm and a leg in most places. Your best bet is KFC at Terminal 1, where you can still get a burger, fries and drink for about RMB 20.

Beijing Capital International Airport 北京首都国际机场

Airport Expressway, Chaoyang District. (86-10/64564247/3220, lost luggage 64599523/4, arrival info 962580, customer complaint hotline 64571666) http://www.cia.com.cn/en/index.jsp 朝阳区机场路

Booking Air Tickets

Air tickets can be booked via your local travel agents, or online through individual airlines, travel companies, and agents. There are cheap flights out there; they may just not be behind the first travel agent's door. Shop around! Here are some tips to point you in the right direction:

- Avoid weekends and national holidays when, predictably, prices shoot up (see p.25 for holidays). Friday to Monday flights fill up first so, for the cheapest fares, look for flights in and out on Tuesdays, Wednesdays and Thursdays.

- Don't ignore cheap flights first to other cities such as Shanghai, from where you can take a train or bus to Beijing which is cheap and convenient. A bit of additional time may save you a lot of money, and you get to see more of China that way. Alternatively, a stopover in Bangkok or Delhi may allow you to grab a flight on a budget airline serving China.

- Check all airlines, not just your national carrier. SAS, Qatar, Qantas, China Southern Airlines and many more make stop-overs in Beijing.

Online Agencies

A convenient option; some offer free delivery if you are in China.

http://www.elong.net/flights/
http://english.ctrip.com/index.asp
http://www.yoee.com/

Beijing Capital International Airport welcomes 48.5 million passengers a year. Source: China Daily

Carriers

Air Canada 加拿大航空 *http://www.aircanada.com*
Air China 中国国际航空公司 *http://www.airchina.com.cn*
Air France 法国航空公司 *http://www.airfrance.com.cn/*
Air Ukraine 乌克兰航空公司 *http://www.airukraine.com/*
Alitalia 意大利航空公司 *http://www.alitalia.com*
Asiana Airlines 韩亚航空公司 *http://www.asiana.co.kr/*
Austrian Airlines 奥地利航空 *http://www.aua.com/*
British Airways 英国航空公司 *http://www.british-airways.com/*
Civil Aviation Administration of China 中国民用航空总局 *http://www.caac.gov.cn*
China Eastern 中国东方航空公司 *http://www.ce-air.com*
Hong Kong Dragonair 港龙航空公司 *http://www.dragonair.com/*
Japan Airlines 日本航空公司 *http://www.jal.co.jp/*
Korean Air 大韩航空 *http://www.koreanair.com*
Lufthansa German 德国汉莎航空公司 *http://www.lufthansa.com/*
Malaysia Airlines 马来西亚航空公司 *http://www.malaysiaair.com/*
Oasis Hong Kong Airlines 甘泉香港航空 *http://www.qatarairways.com*
Qantas 澳洲航空公司 *http://www.qantas.com.au*
Qatar Airways 卡塔尔航空公司 *http://www.qatarairways.com/*
SAS 北欧航空 *http://www.scandinavian.net*
Singapore Airlines 新加坡航空公司 *http://www.singaporeair.com/*
Swiss Air 瑞士航空公司 *http://www.swiss.com/*
Thai Airways 泰国航空公司 *http://www.thaiair.com/*
United Airlines 美国联合航空公司 *http://www.ual.com/*
Vietnam Airlines 越南航空公司 *http://www.vietnamairlines.com*

By Train

Beijing can be easily reached by train from most Chinese cities, as well as from several cities in neighboring countries, such as Russia and Vietnam. Beijing has four railway stations: **West Railway Station** (which handles most domestic routes), **North Station, South Station,** and **Beijing Railway Station** (near Tian'anmen Square).

All aboard! (at the Beijing West Railway Station)

International routes from Moscow, Pyongyang and Ulaan Baatar (Mongolian capital city) arrive at the Beijing Railway Station, while trains from Hong Kong and Lhasa arrive at the West Railway Station.

If you go to Beijing from other Chinese cities, booking your tickets four to five days in advance is highly recommended, especially during major Chinese holidays. When you are in China you can book train tickets at a local travel agency. Even if you are outside of China, you can still book train tickets through online travel agents like **www.chinatripadvisor.com** or **www.china-train-ticket.com**. You can't have the tickets sent abroad, but they can be waiting for you at a Chinese hotel, for a small service charge.

Guesthouse, Hostel or Hotel

Beijing has no shortage of places to stay, suiting every need and budget—from dorm beds at RMB 35 per night, to luxury hotels over RMB 1,000 and every point in between. Hostels with cheap dorm beds can be found in central Beijing, where most tourist sites are located. University areas such as **Wudaokou** (see p.168) are a magnet for budget hotels. Expensive high-end hotels can be found near most tourist sites or in east Beijing.

After selecting which location, budget and service options best meet your needs, it's advisable to call and inquire about specifics. For cheaper hotels, having asked "Do you have air conditioning?" and received the (truthful) answer "Yes," you might want follow that up with "Is it currently working?" This is not a joke; some establishments may indeed have A/C, but non-functioning, or yet to be turned on, (believing May/June not hot enough to justify it). Some hotels have an airport shuttle bus service and you can even arrange to have them meet you at the airport.

The main categories of accommodation are as follows, in ascending order of price. See area sections for listings.

Guesthouses 招待所

Watch for the sign of " 招待所 " (zhaodaisuo) which literally means "place to receive guests." These are cheap guesthouses for students and budget travelers, asking RMB 30-50/bed or RMB 90-120/ double room. Many are part of residential buildings, or even cheaper semi-basement (with poor ventilation as you can imagine). Don't expect many amenities; a TV, a bed and a shared WC are as much as you'll get. Showers will cost extra, either within the building or in a public bathhouse.

Hostels

There are many international youth hostels in Beijing, offering backpackers a great temporary dwelling. They typically cost RMB 35-60/bed, but remember to ask about their membership. Once you stay there, you'll get a discount on the next one. International youth hostels, known for being clean and modern, offer guests a bed, shared bathroom, and limited-hour hot water service. Some offer 24-hour hot water, Internet access, laundry service, bicycle rental and information desk. Famous ones are **Peking Down Town Backpackers Accommodation** (see p.87) and **Saga International Youth Hostel** (see p.86).

Hotels

Hotels with no rating, or one star rating, are inexpensive, their prices ranging RMB 100-150 per room, double occupancy. They have TV, telephone, private bathroom and limited-hour hot water, no Internet, no laundry or room service. Two-star hotels ranging RMB

Zhāodàisuǒ, memorize these characters and keep your eyes open if you are in the market for a dirt cheap room for the night.

150-250 per room, double occupancy usually offer TV, telephone, private bathroom and 24-hour hot water. They may have chargeable extras like Internet access, Internet café and/or laundry service. Hotels with three stars and upward cost about RMB 300 or more; they offer extra amenities such as room service, breakfast, laundry service, Internet, restaurant, bar, café, business center, and even a beauty salon and gym, so that you needn't disrupt your work-out routine.

Siheyuan/Garden-style Hotels

You can enjoy the authentic tradition and luxury of old Beijing by staying in a *siheyuan* (traditional courtyard house) hotel, tucked deep inside leafy *hutong* alleys. These can be as expensive as RMB 500 per night. Though embodying classical courtyard style, they have modern facilities you'd find at any high-end hotel, but with a most important extra—the environment. There are fewer than ten of this kind in Beijing and they don't come cheap, but the extra cost is definitely worth. Two such are listed in our guide, **Lüsongyuan Hotel** (see p.90) and **Bamboo Garden Hotel** (see p.90).

Accommodation prices

In our book, hostels, hotels and *siheyuan*/garden-style hotels are all listed **in order by price**. For hostels, prices of dorm beds, double and triple occupancy rooms are given. For hotels and *siheyuan*/garden-style hotels, prices are based on double-occupancy. Prices may vary at different times of the year. Generally prices are higher during festivals, holidays and special events, such as National Day and Spring Festival.

Online agents

Worth checking, often with some good prices. You could try:
http://english.ctrip.com/supermarket/hotel/hotelSearch.asp
http://beijing.asiaxpat.com/atoz.asp
http://www.beijingservice.com/hotels/cheaphotel.htm
http://www.trav.com/cities/hotels/beijing.html
http://www.sinohotel.com/hotel/city.html?cid=1
http://www.thebackpacker.net/travelhostels/4274_beijing_travelhostels.htm

---

Payment

Major international **credit cards** are accepted at most hotels, but you would be wise to check first and not assume. When booking a hotel via an online service, you'll be expected to join their membership program and pay first if you are a new user. Smaller hotels, guesthouses and hostels don't accept credit cards, so you'll need cash. Most Chinese merchants are completely unfamiliar with traveler's checks, so remember to cash those at major banks first.

Discounts

For the best deals, book hotels several weeks in advance. "Walk-in" discounts are rare and unless you **pre-book** you may pay through the nose for the same room. Bear in mind the places you want to visit and their **proximity** to the hotel; traipsing from place to place eats up time and money.

Always ask about discounts for stays longer than one night. They might not be offered but if you don't ask, you'll never know! Most hotels offer 20-50% off during **low travel seasons**.

How Much to Budget

Transport Expenses

From north to south Beijing is over 50 km in length; the same is true from east to west. Taking taxis every day could easily run you over RMB 100, over 10 times the cost of public transportation. Neither taxis nor buses are immune to Beijing's frequent traffic jams, but at least the bus has no meter ticking away racking up the cost.

Tickets

Tickets for Beijing sights are moderately priced. The major sights range RMB 50-80; common sights are RMB 10-30; museums and former residences of famous people are mostly RMB 5-20; and sights in the suburbs cost RMB 15-45. Use our budget tip suggestions (see p.341) to help cut down your costs. If you plan to visit Beijing in summer and want to use the **Museum Pass** (see p.341) to save on tickets, you really need to plan early, maybe ask a friend in Beijing to reserve one for you.

Accommodation Expenses

Beijing is a city of people on the move, which translates into a wide price range when it comes to accommodation (see p.305).

Food and Drink Expenses

Street-side restaurants offering "home-style" Chinese food cost RMB 15-30 per person for one meal. "Street" snacks sold by vendors who set up almost anywhere are RMB 1-2 and tummy-filling, but hygiene can be less than perfect, so exercise caution if you want to avoid the risk of diarrhea or worse. Dumplings, noodles and *gaifan* (rice topped with a cooked dish) can be found in most small and medium-sized restaurants, and only cost a few RMB. A small bottle of Tsingtao beer in a bar or club usually costs RMB 10-30, but is available from street shops for only RMB 2-3. **Hint: many expats down a few of these before hitting the bars**.

Other Expenses

Internet access averages about RMB 10 per hour in Internet cafés. Shopping is a big part of Beijing life and may account for a big part of your budget too. Hit the shops at the end of the day or the last day of your trip, perhaps at Qianmen (前门), Panjiayuan (潘家园) or other markets; buying souvenirs here is much cheaper than at tourist spots.

Average Daily Expenses (RMB)			
	Budget	**Middle-range**	**Expensive**
Breakfast	5	15	25
Lunch	10	20	55
Dinner	20	30	75
Transport	10 (bus)	50 (subway & taxi)	100 (taxi)
Accommodation	40 (dorm bed)	200	400
Sights	60	60	60
Total	145	375	715

What to Pack

Appropriate Clothing

···

In spring

Pack a warm sweater, a light jacket, long johns and sunglasses. A mask may be needed because of severe sandstorms.

···

In summer

Shorts, T-shirts, slacks or cotton dresses are ideal; waterproof shoes as well as an umbrella are good ideas (this is rainy season for Beijing).

···

In autumn

The finest season, long-sleeve shirts and slacks are the best for traveling.

In winter

Wrap up warm—this will involve at least one pair of long johns, two sweaters, a very warm feather-stuffed jacket, scarf, hat (covering the ears) and gloves. Your feet will thank you for warm socks and comfy boots.

Medicines and Toiletries

Most over-the-counter medicines are readily available in Beijing, but if you take regular prescription medication, be sure to bring enough for your trip and more. Also bring a copy of your doctor's prescription as back-up in case your medication gets damaged or lost. When flying, keep it in your "carry-on" baggage, in case your checked luggage is delayed in reaching you. Consult your doctor about bringing antibiotic meds with you. **Tampons** are NOT generally available in China.

Here's a checklist of essential and useful items you'll need.

Categories	Items	Notes
Identity Documents	passport	Plus a photocopy of relevant pages in case of loss. Also needed as ID for air travel within China and hotel registoation
	student's card	For discounts at certain sights
	driver's license	If you want to hire a car, but with this one exception, International and foreign driver's licenses are NOT legal for driving in China. If you plan to stay in China and drive, you will need to have your license translated into Chinese and pass a theory test first.
Gadgets	Camera, cell-phone, MP3, etc	Plus rechargers, universal adaptors and batteries

Getting
Around

Could you imagine if they were all driving cars?

I n a city as vast as this, taking "Bus No.11" (Beijing slang for walking) will not let you cover much ground. Beijing has a convenient yet complex network of public transport. Crowded buses and "stop-go" traffic often result in frustration. Beijing's subway system can still leave you miles from your intended destination, so foreign tourists most often travel by taxi. But you don't have to! This book gives the **low-down** on the public transport system.

Airport Shuttle Bus

U ntil the direct **Airport-Downtown subway line** is completed (scheduled for April 1, 2008), the best bet for a ride into Beijing is the **shuttle bus service**. At only **RMB 16** it takes 40-90 minutes depending on destination and traffic conditions. If you're in a hurry, or in a group sharing the cost, take a taxi, but it's going to cost at least RMB 60 to get downtown (excluding the expressway charge). To find the shuttle bus, keep your eyes open for a **white bus stop sign** outside **arrival gates 11-13**. Routes are marked in English

and Chinese. Go to a ticket seller sitting by the buses and then give your ticket to the driver as you board the bus. For buses to the airport, pay from the stop you get on. Buses leave every 15 to 30 minutes. There's a **24-hour information hotline** in Chinese only at 86-10-64594375/ 64594376.

When taking the shuttle ask around to find out which stop is nearest to your destination.

From the Airport to Town

● To Zhongguancun 中关村 (8am-10.30pm)

Capital International Airport 首都国际机场-Wangjing (Huajiadi) 望京(花家地)-Xiaoying 小营-Yayuncun (Anhui Qiao) 亚运村(安慧桥)-Xueyuan Qiao 学院桥-Zhongguancun Siqiao 中关村四桥

● To Beijing Railway Station 北京站 (7am-last flight)

Capital International Airport 首都国际机场 -Yuyang Hotel 渔阳饭店 -Dongdaqiao (bypassed after 10.30pm) 东大桥 -Chaoyangmen 朝阳门 -Yabao Lu 雅宝路 -Beijing Railway Station 北京站

● To Gongzhufen 公主坟 (7am-11pm)

Capital International Airport 首都国际机场 -China International Exhibition Center 国际展览中心 -Xibahe 西坝河 -Anzhen Qiao 安贞桥 -Madian Qiao 马甸桥 -Beitaipingzhuang 北太平庄 -Jimen Qiao 蓟门桥 -Friendship Hotel 友谊宾馆 -Beijing TV Station 北京电视台 -Zizhu Qiao 紫竹桥 -Hangtian Qiao 航天桥 -Gongzhufen (Xinxing Hotel) 公主坟 (新兴宾馆)

● To Xidan 西单 (7am-last flight)

Capital International Airport 首都国际机场-Sanyuan Qiao 三元桥-Dongzhimen 东直门 -Dongsishitiao Qiao 东四十条桥 -Xidan (Civil Aviation Building) 西单 (民航营业大厦)

● To Fangzhuang 方庄 (7.30am-10.30pm)

Capital International Airport 首都国际机场 -Liangma Qiao 亮马桥 -Hujialou 呼家楼 -Dabeiyao (World Trade Center) 大北窑 (国贸)-Panjiayuan 潘家园 -Shilihe (KingWing Hot Spring International Hotel) 十里河 (京瑞大厦)-Fangzhuang (Guiyou Shopping Mall) 方庄 (贵友大厦)

From Town to the Airport

● From Zhongguancun 中关村 (6am-7.30pm)

Zhongguancun Siqiao 中关村四桥-Beihang University North Gate 北航北门-Huixin Xijie (Anhui Building) 惠新西街 (安徽大厦)-Huixin Dongjie (SINOPEC) 惠新东街 (中国石化集团)-Capital International Airport 首都国际机场

● From Beijing Railway Station 北京站 (6am-9pm)

Beijing Railway Station 北京站 -International Hotel 国际饭店 -Dongzhimen (50 m east of the bridge) 东直门(桥东 50 米)-Jingxin Building West Gate 京信大厦西门 -Capital International Airport 首都国际机场

● From Gongzhufen 公主坟 (5.40am-9pm)

Gongzhufen (Xinxing Hotel) 公主坟 (新兴宾馆)-Friendship Hotel North Gate 友谊宾馆北门 -Beitaipingzhuang 北太平庄 -Anzhen Qiao 安贞桥 -Capital International Airport 首都国际机场

● From Xidan 西单 (5.40am-9pm)

Xidan (Civil Aviation Building) 西单 (民航营业大厦)-Dongzhimen (50 m east of the bridge) 东直门 (桥东 50 米)-Jingxin Building West Gate 京信大厦西门 -Capital International Airport 首都国际机场

● From Fangzhuang 方庄 (6am-7.30pm)

Fangzhuang (Guiyou Shopping Mall) 方庄 (贵友大厦)-Dabeiyao (China Southern Airlines Hotel) 大北窑 (南航大酒店)-Capital International Airport 首都国际机场

地铁
BEIJING SUBWAY

Many people cycle to the subway and then ride the subway to work.

Subway

Simple and quick, the subway (地铁 ditie) is a cheap and fast way to scoot around Beijing. Station entrances are identified with white-on-blue symbols and English writing, though the actual name of the station appears only in Chinese.

As of early 2008, Beijing has five subway lines: Lines 1, 2, 5, 13 and Batong Line (八通线). Massive expansion of the network in preparation for the 2008 Olympics will add Lines 4, 10, Olympic Line and a direct airport link (see the **Beijing Metro Guide** on p.312).

- **Line 1** (going east 5.10am-10.55pm; going west 5.05am-11.15pm) runs between Pingguoyuan (苹果园) in the west to Sihui East (四惠东) in the east.

- **Line 2** (clockwise 5.03am-10.45pm; counter-clockwise 5.09am-10.59pm) is the loop line.

- **Batong Line** (going east 6am-10.45pm; going west 5.20am-10.05pm) is an extension of Line 1 from Sihui (四惠) through to Tuqiao (土桥) in the far east suburbs.

- **Line 5** (going north 5.19am-11.10pm; going south 4.59am-10.47pm) is a new line running through the heart of the city from Tiantongyuan North (天通苑北) in the north to Songjiazhuang (宋家庄) in the south.

- **Line 13** (6am-11pm), the Light Rail (城铁 Chengtie), connects the stations of Dongzhimen (东直门) and Xizhimen (西直门) on the northeast and north-

west corners respectively of Line 2, in an extended loop via Huoying (霍营) in the far north suburbs.

Ticket

A one-way ticket now costs only 2 yuan, versus the previous 3 yuan. The 2 yuan is a flat rate for an entire journey, no matter how long the journey is or how many transfers a passenger makes. The new pricing system is also the cheapest among all the Chinese subway systems.

Check the maps on the station platform before making your way to the best exit for your destination. If you arrange to meet someone at a subway station, always specify which exit; there are usually at least two.

And it's not even rush hour yet!

Buses

Buses can get you pretty much anywhere in Beijing. It takes a little work to figure out the right route but it pays off in the end. Taxis can cost 10 or even 20 times more to reach the same spot. There are standard buses and air-conditioned ones. Check out our updated list of **Useful Bus Routes** at the end of each area chapter to help navigate your way around like a native. Usually one bus route has two lines heading opposite directions. To avoid taking a bus in a wrong direction, check the **arrow** on the bus stop board. Bus routes and stops may change as Beijing is undergoing a lot of road construction. You can call **96166** (in Chinese and English) for the latest bus information.

Downtown buses and trolleys (1-126) have a flat rate fare of RMB 1 and run between approximately 5am and 11pm; **night services** (201-212) have a flat rate fare of RMB 1 and run between 11pm and 5am. For most other routes **numbered under 900**, prices start from RMB 1; and the ones numbered over 900 start from RMB 1 or 2, depending on whether the bus is air-conditioned. The first bus is usually between 5 am and 6 am and the last comes around 8pm to 11pm. For information on **Superpass digital cards** (60% discount on most buses), see p.342. For information in English on how to use the complex but extensive public transport system to get from point A to B in Beijing, go to this website for help on buses and subway lines to take: **http://english.mapbar.com/enmodule/**. If you know Chinese, you can use the much handier, more detailed Chinese website: **http://ditu.mapbar.com/**.

Decoding Beijing buses

A major bus company, BPT, operates over 800 routes, including bus and trolley, minibus, tour bus and long-distance. A route number beginning with "1" is a **downtown bus** or a **trolley**, with "2" a night bus, with "3", "4", "6"or "7" an **uptown bus**, with "8" an air-con bus, and with "9" a long-distance **suburban bus**. Official day-trip tour buses are run by **Beijing Hub of Tour Dispatch** (北京旅游集散中心, 86-10-83531111, http://bjlyjszx.com, in Chinese only). Look for the sign "北京旅游集散中心" at the departure points (see p.315) and purchase tickets there. Some routes carry a Chinese character indicating something special about them.

特 -Tè, a double-decker.

快 -Kuài, meaning "express." It usually covers fewer stops.

支 -Zhī, "branch route."

专 -Zhuān, "commuter bus."

空调 -Kōngtiáo, A/C

内 -Nèi, meaning "inner ring" as the bus follows the ring roads clockwise.

外 -Wài, meaning "outer ring" as the bus follows the ring roads counter-clockwise.

区间 -Qūjiān, meaning "section." As the name indicates, it only covers one section of the original bus line.

运通 -Yùntōng, a bus company name. The bus is usually yellow with red letters.

Official Day-trip Tour Buses

Line	Departure Time	Departure Point	Destination	Fare (RMB) (round-trip bus fare and admission included)
World Cultural Heritage Tour A 世界文化遗产 A 线	6.30am-10.30am	Southwest and southeast of Tian'anmen Square 天安门广场西南角发车中心和天安门广场东南角分发车中心	Badaling Great Wall (八达岭长城) and Dingling (定陵)	160 (including lunch)
World Cultural Heritage Tour B 世界文化遗产 B 线	6.30am-10.30am	Southwest corner of Tian'anmen Square 天安门广场西南角分发车中心	Juyongguan Great Wall (居庸关长城) and Dingling (定陵)	125
World Cultural Heritage Tour C 世界文化遗产 C 线	7.30am-11.30am	Southwest corner of Tian'anmen Square 天安门广场西南角发车中心	Badaling Great Wall (八达岭长城)	90
Day Trips 一日游	6.30am-8am (Weekends and official holidays from April 7 to October 15)	Southwest of Tian'anmen Square 天安门广场西南角发车中心	Temple of Pool and Wild Mulberries (潭柘寺 Tanzhesi) and Stone Flower Cave (石花洞 Shihuadong)	145
	6.30am-8am (Weekends and official holidays from April 7 to October 15)		Zhoukoudian (周口店) and Shidu (十渡)	80
	6.30am-8am (Weekends and official holidays from April 7 to October 15)		Huanghuacheng Great Wall (黄花城长城)	75
	6.30am-9.30am		Simatai Great Wall (司马台长城)	95

Taxi

Standard Beijing taxis carry the sign TAXI on the roof and a red light in the windscreen if they are available for hire. RMB 10 (11) will take you 3 km and RMB 2 (2.4) for every further km; after 15 km, it's RMB 3 (3.4) per km. The bracketed numbers above indicate the higher rates that apply between 11pm and 5am.

You can ask your hotel to hire you a taxi for the day, for about RMB 300-700 depending on where you want to go and what you can bargain.

Having your destination address in Chinese characters to show the driver is a great help to everyone. Not many drivers can read Pinyin. Generally speaking, Beijing cab drivers are honest; but if you suspect, take down the number of the driver and the phone number for the complaint office. **Always** take the taxi receipt; that way if you leave anything in the cab, you can contact the taxi company. **Illegal taxis** (黑车 "black cars") are common, but potentially dangerous and you may be cheated.

Bicycle

Some say the best way to experience Beijing is by bicycle, cruising past the prisoners of the internal combustion engine as they stifle in traffic jams!

Take a detour into old *hutong* and get some exercise while sightseeing. It's easy to find **bike rentals** at tourist spots. This may cost RMB 10-20 a day or a few RMB per hour plus returnable deposit.

New convenient, public rental, 50,000 bikes available across the city: RMB 100/year or 20/day (RMB 400 deposit, refunded less rental fees), including repairs and old-for-new exchange. It's easy to spot these bright-colored rows of bikes in key spots all over the city. **Tandem** togetherness can be yours from rental outlets at **Houhai Lake** (后海), etc.

Coming for the 2008 Olympics? A bike may be your best bet to get around. If you are here for a while, you might even think about buying a new bike—they can be had for under RMB 200, but buy a good lock!

Who is copying whose fashion?

Useful Information

People are seen all over checking out the daily news on the street-side news boards as they pass by.

Banking

China's **banking services and facilities** are improving, but they are probably unlike what you are used to. Patience will go a long way to get what you need to accomplish. In some places you'll need to stand in line; in others you take a number and wait to be called. Expect only limited service in English.

As a WTO member, China fully opened its banking sector to foreign competition on December 11, 2006. This will mean better service and more diverse products.

Bank hotlines (in Chinese and English)

 中国银行 BANK OF CHINA 95566

 中国建设银行 China Construction Bank 95533

 招商银行 CHINA MERCHANTS BANK 95555

HSBC ⟨X⟩ 汇丰 8008208878

 citibank 花旗银行 8008301880

中国工商银行 INDUSTRIAL AND COMMERCIAL BANK OF CHINA 95588

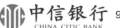 中信银行 CHINA CITIC BANK 95558

 Standard Chartered 渣打银行 65669888

Bank of China Headquarters on Chang'an Jie.

Exchanging Money

Sixteen currencies can be converted into RMB at the exchange rate quoted on the foreign exchange market for that day. They are Pound Sterling, US Dollar, Swiss Franc, Euro, Singapore Dollar, Swedish Krona, Danish Krone, Norwegian Krone, Japanese Yen, Korean Won, Canadian Dollar, Australian Dollar, Philippine Peso, Thai Baht, Hong Kong Dollar, and Macao Pataca.

Only the **Bank of China** (中国银行), several outlets of which can be found at the Capital International Airport, can convert all of them. The highest amount one can cash out per day is USD 5,000. But it's better to do so in **small amounts**, so as to avoid having to convert any RMB back to your original currency. When converting foreign currency into RMB at an authorized location, they will give you an **exchange slip**, which you should keep safe as you'll have to show it should you change your RMB back to foreign currency. Many large hotels are also approved for currency exchange, but the service is often reserved for guests. **Passport** identification is compulsory for all currency conversions, so be sure to bring it with you.

Traveler's checks

Traveler's checks are now accepted at most Chinese banks, and foreign exchange desks in hotels and some department stores. It is a much easier and safer way than carrying a lot of cash, though **0.75% commission** is payable on checks. But it is still a good idea to have some cash for emergencies.

The Bank of China handles more types of traveler's checks than other banks, for example those issued by **Thomas Cook** and **Barclays** of the UK, **American Express** and **City Bank** of the US, and **Sumitomo Bank**, **Bank of Tokyo-Mitsubishi, Ltd** and **Fuji Bank** of Japan. You need to bring your passport to cash traveler's checks of any amount under USD 5,000. You will need your passport and the contract you signed with the issuing company for your traveler's check to cash any amount over USD 5,000 (including USD 5,000).

Credit Cards

Credit cards are not as universally accepted in China as in the West. Major foreign credit cards likely to be accepted here are **MasterCard**, **Visa**, **American Express**, **JCB** and **Diners**. They can be used at most star hotels and some department stores. Paying by foreign credit card may entail a 4% **service fee**. Making cash withdrawal from a credit card is usually done in the form of a "cash advance," which can be particularly expensive, depending on your bank's policy and how long you take to repay the "advance." American Express card members can cash personal checks for USD 2,000-3,000 over a 21-day period at **CITIC Bank** *(Room 2313-14, Tower 1, China World Trade Center, No. 1 Jianguomenwai Dajie, 86-10-65052838, 建国门外大街1号国贸大厦1座2313-14室)*. Visa card members can withdraw money up to a daily limit of RMB 3,000 at **Bank of China** and **HSBC** branches.

ATMs

Beijing is quite an ATM-friendly city. Almost all banks have ATMs and many accept main foreign credit cards (see above) and bankcards connected to Cirrus, Plus, Amex, Visa and MasterCard. Check the logos posted at the ATM to see if it will accept your card. The top daily limit on withdrawals is RMB 20,000. **Transaction fees** will be deducted by your bank according to its exchange rate and policy prevailing at the time of transaction. If an ATM says that your transaction has been declined and asks you to contact your bank, this often just means that the international network is unavailable. You should try an ATM from another bank, or return the next day. Note that no matter which country/currency is associated with your ATM or credit card, the amount requested and withdrawn will be in RMB.

One-hundred, two-hundred, three...

Communications

B eijing's communications network is reliable and stable. Post, telephone and Internet services are readily available to all parts of the world.

Post

Look for the distinctive green livery and the words **China Post** (中国邮政). Here you can send postcards, letters, express mails and parcels to any place in the world. Some hotels and major sights such as the Forbidden City also have postal services. Post offices usually open from 9am to 6pm, 7 days a week.

When sending parcels, you must fill out a declaration form and items contained will be checked before shipping. You may even have to put the **purchase receipt** inside the parcel when goods are CDs, DVDs and clothes (or other items frequently pirated). When sending important, valuable or protected items such as antiques or cultural relics that are under customs control, forget mini-post offices in hotels; you must consult and get a customs check at **Beijing International Post & Telecommunications Office** (see below). In addition to regular postal services, it handles money orders, wire transfers, international phone calls, etc.

● **Beijing International Post & Telecommunications Office** 北京国际邮电局
Yabao Lu, Jianguomenwai Dajie, Chaoyang District (300 m north of Jianguomen Overpass). (86-10-65128114) 朝阳区建国门外大街雅宝路 (建国门桥往北300米)

● **Western Union**
The Agricultural Bank of China and China Post serve as Western Union agents. For a list of China Post branches offering this service, see http://html. bj183.com.cn/yyzn/yyzn_3.htm (in Chinese). For a list of Western Union agents of the Agricultural Bank of China, see http://www.95599bj.com.cn/information/XLRemit/MTAInBJ.htm (in English).

Telephone

Calls can be made from landline telephones in your hotel, some large post offices, public phones at newspaper kiosks and stores (often with a sign reading " 公用电话 " gongyong dianhua), or from telephone booths on the street.

Dialing in hotels saves a lot of fuss, though they charge a service fee. When dialling from a public phone you should pay cash after the call is finished. To use the telephone booths a prepaid card is needed. Calls within Beijing have a standard three-minute minimum charge, and additional time thereafter is charged by minute. Both IDD (International Direct Dial) and DDD (Domestic Direct Dial) are charged by minute. Note that sometimes phone numbers in Beijing have a computerized answering service first, if this happens, most likely you can press 0 to get someone you can speak to.

Most phone booths around require IC cards, but there are still some which will accept coins.

DDD Calls

DDD call rates are the same anywhere in China (excluding Hong Kong, Taiwan and Macao). Visitors should dial the domestic prefix 0, plus the area code and the number.

IDD Calls

There are two ways to place an international call: either dial "00" to connect with the IDD telephone system, then enter the country code, followed by the area code; or dial **108-888** to place a collect call or a credit card call (may not be available from every phone/public phone; check your hotel room phone first), then press zero or stay on the line and an **AT&T operator** will assist you.

Telephone Cards

Calling another city or country directly is expensive but telephone cards are godsend gifts to cut down your phone costs. There's quite a variety, but they can be categorized into three groups: 201 cards, IC cards and IP cards. They are all **prepaid calling cards** that can be bought at stalls in supermarkets, tobacconists and newsstands in denominations RMB 10 -200, often discounted. This means you can get RMB 100 worth of calls on a 201 card for around RMB 80, a RMB 100 IC card for RMB 50 and a RMB 100 IP card for RMB 35.

201 cards can be used to place local, DDD and IDD calls on any landline phone that has an outside line and at any IC telephone booth. They don't have local access charge.

IC cards must be inserted into the slot in a public phone booth.

IP cards are the cheapest of all cards for long-distance or international calls and they have very low local access

Colorful phone cards are now a collectable.

charge. You may see different IP cards like 17908, 17910, 17970, etc. Those numbers indicate the number you have to call to use the card. Check the expiry date on the card and remember that a card bought in Beijing does not work if you move to another city. For most cards listen past the initial Chinese instructions when you start to use the card and usually English instructions will follow.

IP Telephone Service Rates (RMB) (excluding local access charge of about RMB 0.1/min)			
Destination		**Rates**	**RMB 100 Card**
China's Mainland		0.30/min	333 minutes
Hong Kong, Macao, Taiwan		1.50/min	66 minutes
International	US, Canada	2.40/min	40 minutes
	UK, France, Italy, Germany, New Zealand, South Korea, Japan, Australia, Singapore, Malaysia, Thailand, Philippines, Indonesia	3.60/min	27 minutes
	Other countries	4.6/min	21 minutes

How to Use 201 and IP Cards

Scratch to reveal the card and password numbers. Dial the Access No. (2011 for 201 cards or 5-digit number for IP cards) + Language Code (for English, usually 2) + IP Card No+ PIN No + # + Country/Area Code + Telephone No + #. As mentioned above, English instructions often follow the Chinese, so be patient.

Night Discounts

If you place a long-distance or international call between midnight and 7am—not only is it easier to get through but calls are 60% of the daytime price. The same discount applies to 201 and IC cards for long-distance or international calls.

Internet

Beijing uses dial-up, broadband and wireless services. Increasingly more hotels (and some hostels) offer Internet access, some having in-room connections for use with your personal computer. **Internet cafés** are also popular; some even serve coffee! Hourly fees range RMB 3-10, and you'll need to show your passport to register. If you have your laptop, **free Wireless Internet (Wi-Fi)** service can be found at the following locations.

High speed = High popularity.

Wireless Internet (Wi-Fi)

Café
SPR Coffee East Gate Plaza SPR Coffee 北京东环广场店
SPR Coffee Jianwai SPR Coffee 北京建外店
Be There Or Be Sqaure Café 不见不散餐厅
GL Café Restaurant 金湖茶餐厅
GL Café Restaurant 金湖茶餐厅
Adria Restaurant 亚的里亚餐厅
Pink Loft Food & Drink 粉酷东南亚新菜
Sculpting in Time Café 雕刻时光咖啡馆
Sculpting in Time Café 雕刻时光咖啡馆
Fruity Mix 水果捞
Handsome 海上 Café
Raj Indian Restaurant 幕府拉兹印度餐厅
Pass By Bar 过客酒吧
Heaven and Earth Café 天与地茶餐吧
Ching 清阁西餐厅

Address	Tel
EA6C, East Gate Plaza, No.9 Dongzhongjie, Dongzhimenwai, Dongcheng District 东城区东直门外东中街 9 号东环广场 EA6C	86-10-64185718
1/F, Bailian Building, No.17 Jianhua Nanlu, Jianguomenwai Dajie, Chaoyang District 朝阳区建国门外大街建华南路 17 号佰联大厦一层	86-10-65688338
B1/F, Beijing Capital Times Square, No. 88, Xichang'an Jie 西长安街 88 号首都时代广场地下 1 层	86-10-83914077
Shop L132, 1/F, China World Shopping Mall, No. 1, Jianguomenwai Dajie, Chaoyang District 朝阳区建国门外大街 1 号国贸商城一层 L132 店	86-10-65056868
Shop 198, International Club, No.19, Jianguomenwai Dajie, Chaoyang District (Beside St. Regis Hotel) 朝阳区建外大街 19 号国际俱乐部 198 店（圣瑞吉斯饭店旁）	86-10-65328282
Central Park Club, No. 6, Chaoyangmenwai Dajie, Chaoyang District 朝阳区朝外大街 6 号新城国际会所	86-10-65970499
No. 6, Sanlitun Nanlu, Chaoyang District 朝阳区三里屯南路 6 号	86-10-65068811
No. 7, Weigongcun Lu (south gate of Beijing Institute of Technology) 魏公村路 7 号 (北京理工大学南门)	86-10-68946825
No. 1, Building 12, Huaqing Jiayuan, Wudaokou, Chengfu Lu (Wudaokou Light Rail Station) 成府路五道口华清嘉园 12 楼 1 号 (五道口城铁)	86-10-82867025
Shop 107, 1/F, Pacific Century Place, No. A2, Gongti Beilu, Chaoyang District 朝阳区工体北路甲 2 号太平洋盈科中心 1 层 107 店	86-10-65392279
Building 7, Sanlitun Beili, Chaoyang District 朝阳区三里屯北里 7 号楼	86-10-64178288
No. 31, Gulou Xidajie, Dongcheng District 东城区鼓楼西大街 31 号	86-10-64011675
Inside a *siheyuan*, No. 108, Nanluoguxiang, Jiaodaokou, Dongcheng District 东城区交道口南锣鼓巷 108 号四合院内	86-10-84038004
No. 2, Qianhai Beiyan, Xicheng District 西城区前海北沿 2 号	86-10-66571870
No. 76, Donghuamen Dajie, Dongcheng District 东城区东华门大街 76 号	86-10-65238775

Embassies

Foreign embassies are concentrated in the **Sanlitun** and **Jianguomenwai** areas in the east. Embassies usually work from 9am to 5pm, five days a week. They have holidays on both Chinese festivals and their own countries' festivals. Visa sections may have different working schedules than the rest of the embassy. It is always best to call before you go. If calling on a holiday, after hours, or for an emergency, listen to the recording for numbers to call in such cases. If you extend your stay in China and/or leave your tour, it is a good idea to "register" with your embassy according to its policies. For a complete list of embassies, log onto the following website: http://metrolife.chinadaily.com.cn/travel/embasy.html

Australia 澳大利亚使馆
No. 21, Dongzhimenwai Dajie. (86-10-65322331) www.austemb.org.cn
东直门外大街 21 号

Austria 奥地利使馆
No. 5, Xiushui Nanjie, Jianguomenwai. (86-10-65322061)
建国门外秀水南街 5 号

Belgium 比利时使馆
No. 6, Sanlitun Lu. (86-10-65321736) www.diplobet.org
三里屯路 6 号

Canada 加拿大使馆
No. 19, Dongzhimenwai Dajie. (86-10-65323536) www.beijing.gc.ca
东直门外大街 19 号

Denmark 丹麦使馆
No. 1, Dongwu Jie, Sanlitun. (86-10-65322431) www.dk-embassy-cn.org
三里屯东五街 1 号

Finland 芬兰使馆
26/F, South Tower, Beijing Kerry Center, No. 1, Guanghua Lu. (86-10-85298541) www.finland-in-china.com
光华路 1 号北京嘉里中心南塔楼 26 层

France 法国使馆
No. 3, Dongsan Jie, Sanlitun (86-10-85328080) www.ambafrance-cn.org
三里屯东三街 3 号

Germany 德国使馆
No. 17, Dongzhimenwai Dajie. (86-10-85329000) www.deutschebotschaft-china.org
东直门外大街 17 号

India 印度使馆
No. 1, Ritan Donglu. (86-10-65321908) www.indianembassybeijing.org.cn
日坛东路 1 号

Ireland 爱尔兰使馆
No. 3, Ritan Donglu. (86-10-65322691) www.ireland-china.com.cn
日坛东路 3 号

Israel 以色列使馆
No. 17, Tianze Lu. (86-10-65052970)
天泽路 17 号

Italy 意大利使馆
No. 2, Dong'er Jie, Sanlitun. (86-10-65322131) www.italianembassy.org.cn
三里屯东二街 2 号

Japan 日本使馆
No. 7, Ritan Lu, Jianguomenwai Dajie.
(86-10-65322361) www.japan.org.cn
建国门外大街日坛路7号

 Malaysia 马来西亚使馆
No. 2, Liangmaqiao Beijie. (86-10-65322531)
亮马桥北街2号

 Mexico 墨西哥使馆
No. 5, Dongwu Jie, Sanlitun. (86-10-65322574)
三里屯东五街5号

Netherlands 荷兰使馆
No. 4, Liangmahe Nanlu. (86-10-65321131) www.nlembassypek.org
亮马河南路4号

 New Zealand 新西兰使馆
No. 1, Dong'er Jie, Ritan Lu. (86-10-65322731) www.nzembassy.com/china
日坛路东二街1号

 Norway 挪威使馆
No. 1, Dongyi Jie, Sanlitun (86-10-65322261) www.norway.org.cn
三里屯东一街1号

Philippines 菲律宾使馆
No. 23, Xiushui Beijie. (86-10-65321872)
秀水北街23号

Poland 波兰使馆
No. 1, Ritan Lu, Jianguomenwai. (86-10-65321235)
建国门外日坛路1号

 Russia 俄罗斯使馆
No. 4, Beizhong Jie, Dongzhimennei.
(86-10-65322051) www.russia.org.cn
东直门内北中街4号

 Singapore 新加坡使馆
No. 1, Xiushui Beijie. (86-10-65321115) www.mfa.gov.sg/beijing
秀水北街1号

 Spain 西班牙使馆
No. 9, Sanlitun Lu. (86-10-65321986)
三里屯路9号

 Sweden 瑞典使馆
No. 3, Dongzhimenwai Dajie. (86-10-65325003)
东直门外大街3号

 Switzerland 瑞士使馆
No. 3, Dongwu Jie, Sanlitun (86-10-65322736) www.eda.admin.ch/beijing
三里屯东五街3号

Thailand 泰国使馆
No. 40, Guanghua Lu. (86-10-65321749)
光华路40号

 United Kingdom 英国使馆
No. 11, Guanghua Lu, Jianguomenwai (86-10-51924000) www.britishembassy.org.cn
建国门外光华路11号

 United States 美国使馆
No. 3, Xiushui Beijie, Jianguomenwai. (86-10-65323831) www.usembassy-china.org.cn
建国门外秀水北街3号

 Vietnam 越南使馆
No. 32, Guanghua Lu, Jianguomenwai. (86-10-65321155)
建国门外光华路32号

Good Manners and Bad Luck

Friendly, warm and pretty informal, Chinese people are usually easy to deal with. Sometimes though, cultural differences can give rise to difficulties. Keep in mind these taboos of which foreigners may be unaware:

If you need to use a toothpick after eating, cover your mouth with your other hand. Chinese people think it's gross and impolite to reveal this activity to others.

1

2

Most Chinese are very conservative and don't go in for hugging, so stick to shaking hands when greeting to avoid giving offence.

3

Don't tap your chopsticks on your bowl; not only is it an impolite sign of impatience, beggars do this in the street to attract attention.

Don't plant your chopsticks into your rice bowl pointing straight upward, unless you want your fellow diners to think you wish them dead. Why? Because pairs of incense sticks are placed like this next to graves.

4

Try not to let the spout of the tea-pot face anyone. It's considered impolite to do this, so remember to point it toward an empty spot, or toward yourself.

5

6

The Chinese word "钟" (clock) has the same pronunciation as the word for "death"; so don't ever give a Chinese a clock, even if it's a really nice one.

In China, "green hat" often refers to a man whose wife is cheating on him. In the unlikely event of you wanting to give your Chinese friend a hat, steer clear of green.

7

8

Don't offer to share your pear. "分梨" (share pear) sounds the same as "分离" (parting), a sad occurrence to be avoided as much as possible.

The Chinese word for "8" (ba) sounds similar to a word for prosperity, whilst the number "4" (si) shares the same sound as death. This is why people are willing to pay more for cell phone numbers and auto plates containing a lot of 8s and why most residential buildings don't have a fourth or 14th floor.

9

Health

Though Beijing's air quality and seasonal sandstorms bear potential threats of some respiratory illnesses, health levels are generally high, with life expectancy nearing **80**. Pharmacies, clinics and emergency centers can be found throughout the city, at many tourist attractions and at larger hotels. Pharmacies often stock many Western brand medicines. Look out for the sign " 药店 " (yaodian), meaning pharmacy. A recommended chain is Golden Elephant Pharmacy (金象大药房).

Medical Services

Beijing has a wide range of medical services encompassing traditional Chinese medicine and Western medicine, public Chinese hospitals and international hospitals. Many hospitals provide excellent care, with doctors of both TCM (Traditional Chinese Medicine)and Western medicine. Examples include the People's Hospital (人民医院) and Beijing Chinese Medicine Hospital (北京中医医院). In Chinese hospitals the important thing is to find someone to translate for you, and be prepared to stand in multiple lines and at various locations, as you make your way through the registration, testing, diagnosis, treatment and account settling procedures. This can be energy-draining and time-consuming. Alternatively, international hospitals with English-speaking staff, advanced treatment and equipment will ease your mind, but they can be very expensive for anyone without good medical insurance.

Traditional Chinese Medicine

Traditional Chinese medicine (TCM) has a history of more than 2,500 years and still plays an important role in China's healthcare. Most Chinese people, especially seniors, prefer Chinese medicine

Long line-ups can be seen in almost any hospital.

to Western medicine, as they believe herbs have fewer side effects.

A mystery to the outside world for a long time, TCM has gradually established its name in the international world by fighting some chronic diseases, such as cancer. Increasingly more foreign students and doctors come to China to study TCM, and the new millennium has seen more joint treatment using Chinese and Western medicines. Chinese medicine comes in sachets, liquid form, tablets or as the herb itself. It may look, taste and smell unpleasant, and may need to be taken in large dosages over potentially longer periods, but if your Western medicine is failing you, why not give it a try?

Where to call in emergency

First Aid / Ambulance: 120
International SOS Assistance: 64629100

International hospitals

Peking Union Medical College Hospital 北京协和医院
Hours: 24-hour emergency care
No. 1, Shuaifuyuan, Wangfujing, Dongcheng District. (Foreign patient reception is behind and to the left of the main building). (86-10-65295284) 东城区王府井帅府园 1 号 (接待外国人在主楼的左后方)

Sino-Japanese Friendship Hospital 北京中日友好医院
Hours: 24-hour
Yinghua Donglu, Hepingjie Beikou, Hepingli, Chaoyang District (Foreign patient reception is inside the east gate). (86-10-64222952/1122) 朝阳区和平里和平街北口樱花东路 (接待外国人在东门内)

Bayley & Jackson Medical Center 庇利积臣医疗中心
Hours: 8am-6pm (Mon-Fri), 8am-4pm (Sat), doctors on call (Sun)
No. 7, Ritan Donglu, Chaoyang District. (86-10-85629998 during working hours, 85629990 out of hours) 朝阳区日坛东路 7 号

Beijing International SOS Clinic 北京国际救援中心
Hours: daily 9am-5.30pm (Chinese and foreign doctors), after 5pm (Chinese doctors only)
Building C, BITIC Jingyi Plaza, No. 5, Sanlitun Xiwu Jie, Chaoyang District. (86-10-64629112; 24-hour service: 64629100) 朝阳区三里屯西五街 5 号北信京谊大厦 C 座

Beijing United Family Hospital 北京和睦家医院
Hours: daily 9am-5pm; 24-hour emergency care
No. 2, Jiangtai Lu, Chaoyang District (close to Holiday Inn Lido). (86-10-64333960; 24-hour service: 64332345) 朝阳区将台路 2 号 (丽都附近)

Hong Kong International Medical Clinic 香港国际医务诊所
Hours: daily 9am-9pm; 24-hour emergency care
9/F, office building of the Swisshotel, No. 2, Chaoyangmen Beidajie, Chaoyang District. (86-10-65014260) 朝阳区朝阳门北大街 2 号港澳中心办公楼 9 层

International Medical Center (IMC) 北京国际医疗中心
Hours: daily 24 hours
S106, 1/F, Lufthansa Center, No. 50, Liangmahe Lu, Chaoyang District. (86-10-64651561) 朝阳区亮马河路 50 号北京燕莎中心写字楼 1 层 S106

Beijing Massage Hospital 北京按摩医院
Hours: daily 7.30am-11.45am, 1.30pm-9.30pm
No. 7, Baochan Hutong, Xicheng District. (86-10-66168880) 西城区宝产胡同 7 号

Beijing Tongren Hospital 北京同仁眼科医院
Hours: 8am-12pm, 1pm-5pm (Sat and Sun afternoons off); 24-hour emergency care
No. 1, Dongjiaominxiang, Dongcheng District. (86-10-58269911) 东城区东交民巷1号

Elite Dental Clinic 精致口腔
Hours: daily 9am-5pm
Room 206, Building 2, New Start Garden, No. 5, Changchunqiao Lu, Haidian District. (86-10-82562566) 海淀区长春桥路 5 号新起点家园 2 号楼 206 室

Chinese Massage

Chinese massage (推拿 tuina) is one of the earliest medical treatments in the world. Dating back over 2,000 years, its earliest form was to rub, press, knead, pound or stamp in order to keep out cold, get rid of discomfort and treat various injuries. Today, it has developed into a practical

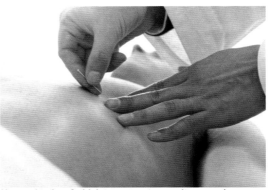

No need to be afraid, let acupuncture melt your pain away.

therapy that involves pressing at certain acupuncture points and/or manipulating joints so as to relieve stress and treat illness. Rhythmic thumping, clapping and pounding over parts of your body are also often part of the experience.

In recent years, blind massage and foot massage have become very popular. **Blind massage** is usually done by blind masseurs who are renowned for their keen sense of the joints and muscles. And what could be nicer than a **foot massage** after a hard day pounding the streets? There are establishments all over town which also offer other forms of massage, like Thai-style. One-hour full-body (feet excluded) massages cost about RMB 50.

But the quality varies, with some places even using fake blind masseurs. One of the reputable locations is **Aibosen Blindman Massage** (爱博森盲人按摩院 *No. 11 Liufang Beili, Chaoyang District, 86-10-64652044/64661247 朝阳区柳芳北里 11 号*) where the masseurs receive rigorous training.

Acupuncture

As part of TCM therapy, acupuncture has been used to diagnose, treat and prevent illness for over 2,000 years. It's especially effective for treating a variety of **pains** and some special needle treatment is claimed to even help you lose weight. Those needles may look scary, but they are actually very safe and you'll be surprised to find the treatment quite relaxing. You may feel a tingling or warmth while the needle is inserted.

Acupuncture treatment can be found in many Chinese medicine hospitals. If you visit a private clinic, make sure you check the therapist's license before receiving treatment.

The approval of the World Health Organization has re-

They can offer a relaxing massage even to the most ticklish feet.

sulted in wider acceptance and practice of acupuncture in other countries.

Smoking

China has the world's largest population of smokers, so expect to see people smoking in most restaurants and bars, on the streets, etc. Only a few restaurants have non-smoking sections.

Extra! Extra! Read all about it!

Places you aren't supposed to smoke in Beijing include theaters, museums, bookstores, libraries, hospitals, public transport and places with "no-smoking (禁止吸烟)" signs. Some people smoke anyway, but they are frowned upon and now frequently asked to stop.

Media

CTV (China Central Television) is the national TV station and has nearly 20 channels. When turning on your hotel TV, you'll most likely see **CCTV 9** (not necessarily found on channel 9), the English-language channel which is useful for news and weather. 7pm-7.30pm is the national prime time for news, followed by weather forecast. Foreign TV channels are limited, or non-existent, depending on your hotel service. **English-language magazines and newspapers** (see below) are available at bookstores, big hotels, restaurants and bars where expats hang out.

China Daily 中国日报 A daily newspaper covering Chinese current affairs. A free copy is available in big hotels. http://www.chinadaily.com.cn/

City Weekend 城市周报 Fortnightly listings magazine favored by expats. Free copies are available in most bars and restaurants. http://www.cityweekend.com.cn/beijing/

That's Beijing 城市漫步 Very popular monthly listings magazine—you won't need to look far to find a free copy. http://www.thatsbj.com

Public Toilets

Public toilets in China are almost all "squatter-style" and virtually none provide toilet paper. Some pay-toilets (RMB 0.5 per use) have toilet paper you can buy. So always carry tissues or be prepared to buy or borrow. Used toilet paper should not be flushed away, but placed in the basket beside the toilet. Pipework is small and blockages might ensue otherwise.

When asking people "Where is the nearest toilet?" most Chinese will understand if you use the phrase "**WC**" instead of "bathroom." There are blue **mobile toilets** (RMB 0.5 per use) on the street. Restrooms in large malls, hotels or major restaurants are a good resource and McDonald's and KFC are always a safe bet. Which door to choose? Many restrooms will have recognizable symbols, but it's useful to know the characters for **men** (男) and **women** (女). Thus, embarrassment can be avoided.

Religious Services

Buddhism, Christianity, Islam, Taoism... religion in Beijing is as diverse as its architecture; temples, churches, mosques and synagogues are all present. Call in advance to inquire if there is English-language service.

Islam

Beijing's over 40 mosques are testament to the substantial population of Muslims in China. Having arrived through trade links with Persia during the Tang and Song dynasties (618-1279), Islam became a fully accepted religion during the Yuan Dynasty (1271-1368). Today, the Xinjiang Uygur Autonomous Region is still home to the greatest number of Muslims in China.

Dongsi Mosque 东四清真寺

Service hours: daily 8am-5pm

Transport: Bus 101, 812, 116, 110 to Dongsi (东四)

No. 13, Dongsi Nandajie, Dongcheng District. (86-10-65251194)东城区东四南大街13号

Originally built in 1356 and rebuilt in 1447 by a general, it is home to the **Beijing Branch of the Chinese Islamic Association**. The mosque's library preserves the oldest manuscript of the *Koran*. Non-Muslims are not allowed to attend services.

Christianity

Records have Christianity first setting foot on Chinese soil in the 7th century, but it was later, with the arrival of the Jesuits in the 1670s and of the first protestant missionaries in 1807, that it really had an impact. Christianity was made legal by the Qing government following the Opium War (1840-42). Since the establishment of the People's Republic of China in 1949, it has become a fully accepted and widely practiced religion. Today there are approximately four million Catholics and 10 million Protestants in China.

Protestant

Beijing Protestant Church 基督教缸瓦市教堂

Service hours: 7pm-8pm (Tue); 8.30am-9.30am (Wed); 7pm-8.30pm (Thur); 8.30am-9.30am (Fri); 7.30am-8.30am, 9am-10am, 10.30am-11.30am, 7pm-8pm (Sun)

Transport: Bus 105, 102 to Gangwashi (缸瓦市) or 603, 808 to Xisi (西四)

The Dongsi Mosque.

No. 57, Xisi Nandajie. (86-10-66176181) 西
四南大街57号

Formally known as the **Bible Society**, this Western-style church was established in 1922 by the American Protestant Church. Service in Korean is available on Sundays 2pm-3.30pm. The rest is all in Chinese.

Chongwenmen Christian Church 崇文门堂

Service hours: 7pm-8pm (Tue), 7pm-8pm (Wed), 9am-11am (Thur), 9am-10am, 6.30-7.30pm (Fri), 8am-9.30am, 10.30am-12pm (Sun)

Transport: Bus 108, 44, 110 to Chongwenmen (崇文门)

No. D2, Hougou Hutong, Chongwen District (east of Tongren Hospital). (86-10-65133549/ 65229984) 崇文区后沟胡同丁2号 (同仁医院东侧)

Now the largest home of Protestant worship in Beijing, it was known as Asbury Church when it was established in 1870. As the first church set up by the American Methodist Church in north China, and still enjoying a high level of prestige, it combines style, architecture and rich culture. Services in Chinese but with interpretation into English.

Zhushikou Church 珠市口教堂

Service hours: 9am-10.30am (Tues); 7am-8am (Wed); 9am-10.30am (Thur); 9am-10.30am (Fri); 8pm-9.30pm, 10pm-11.30pm (Sun)

Transport: Bus 57, 105, 120 to Zhushikou Xi (珠市口西)

Intersection of Zhushikou Xidajie and Qianmen Dajie. (86-10-63016678) 珠市口西大街和前门大街交接处

A small church with simultaneous meetings on three floors, this church is not short of worshippers. An in-house video system makes sure that everyone can see what's going on. Services in Chinese only.

Roman Catholic

Church of St. Joseph (Dongtang Cathedral) 东堂

Service hours: daily 6.30am and 7am in Chinese; 6.15am in Latin (Sun)

Transport: Bus 103, 108, 111 to Dengshi Xikou (灯市西口)

No. 74, Wangfujing Dajie, Dongcheng District. (86-10-65240634) 东城区王府井大街74号

Formally called **St. Joseph's**, it may rank second in terms of importance among Beijing's Catholic churches, but it leads the way as a photo backdrop first for wedding pictures and tourist snaps. Built in 1655 and used as a residence for two foreign abbots in the mid-1600s, the church was renovated in 2000. Services in Chinese and Latin.

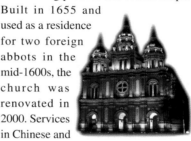

Our Lady of Mt. Carmel (Xitang Cathedral) 西堂

Service hours: 6.30am (Mon-Sat), 8am (Sun)
Transport: Bus 105 to Xinkai Hutong (新开胡同)

No. 130, Xizhimennei Dajie, Xicheng District. (86-10-66156619) 西城区西直门内大街130号

It's hard to think of a church established in 1723 as young, but this Catholic church is junior to its sisters to the north, south and east. Renovated in 1912 and featuring gothic arches and ornate pillars, the church is simultaneously somber and graceful. Service in Chinese only.

The grand Beitang Cathedral at mass.

St. Mary's (Nantang Cathedral)
南堂

Service hours: 6am in Latin, 6.30am and 7.15am in Chinese (Mon-Fri); 6am in Latin, 6.30am and 7.15am in Chinese, 6.30pm in Chinese (Sat); 6am in Latin, 7am and 8.30am in Chinese, 10am and 4pm in English (Sun)
Transport: Bus 102, 105, 109 to Xuanwumen (宣武门)
No. 141, Qianmen Xidajie, Xuanwu District. (86-10-66037139) 宣武区前门西大街141号

Also known as the **Cathedral of the Immaculate Conception**, the oldest Catholic Church in Beijing was established in the 16th century. It was then home to the Italian missionary Matteo Ricci. Services in Latin, Chinese and English.

Beitang Cathedral
北堂 (西什库教堂)

Service hours: 6am and 7am (Mon-Sat); 6am, 7am, 8am, 10am and 6pm (Sun)
Transport: Bus 103, 109, 101 to Fuyou Jie (府右街)
No. 33, Xishiku Dajie, Xicheng District. (86-10-66175198) 西城区西什库大街33号

With gothic style clearly evident on its blue and white façade that is reminiscent of Rheims Cathedral in France, this church was first completed in 1703 and was moved to Xishiku in 1886. Arguably this is one of the most beautiful houses of worship in Beijing. Services in Chinese.

St. Michael's Church
圣弥额尔天主教堂

Service hours: 6.30am and 7am (Mon-Sat); 7am, 8am and 6pm (Sun); 10.30am and 11.30am in Korean (Sun)
Transport: Bus 104, 103 to Chongwenmen (崇文门)
No. A13, Dongjiaominxiang, Dongcheng District. (86-10-65135170)东城区东郊民巷甲13号

Another gothic style Catholic church, St. Michael's was constructed in 1901 in a special zone then reserved for foreigners. Three main spires and ornate and delicate décor add to the ambiance and beauty of the architecture. Service in Chinese and Korean.

Scams to Avoid

● **Friendly students with an agenda.** When walking in Wangfujing, and other shopping areas popular with foreigners, you may be approached by a local "student" who starts chatting with you. They will often speak very good English and even help you shop or show you around "just to practice English." After a while comes the suggestion of a lovely teahouse nearby to rest a bit. You'll be served nice tea in a pleasant atmosphere and no one will mention the price until the bill comes. When it does arrive the amount will be ridiculous. Or they may bring you to an art gallery featuring works by their "art professor" or "fellow students" where you will be hit with a really hard-sell. **Never eat, drink or buy anything without knowing the price first.**

● **Taxi scam.** Jumping into a taxi from the airport, your driver may try to tell you that your hotel is pretty far and that the price will be high. This kindly gent will offer to turn off his meter for an agreed upon "flat rate," but you'll probably wind up agreeing to more than twice the metered fare. **Stay with the meter and** keep the receipt (automatically generated) in case you feel you have been taken advantage of.

● **Tour scam.** Practiced the world over, this common scam involves your tour stopping at places to buy souvenirs or gifts, almost always over-priced and of low quality. **Never feel obliged to buy anything and stay firm under pressure.**

● **Picture-taking scam.** Dressing up in traditional clothes for pictures at local tourist spots can be fun and memorable. It can also be expensive if you don't clearly negotiate the price and what the price includes. Often they will tell you after you and a friend have posed that the price negotiated was per person. Or they will tell you the price is for only the smallest size print.

● **Restaurant scam.** Pay attention, as you order, to the price of each dish you select. Keep a rough idea in your head about what your total bill should be. Sometimes a restaurant will add money

to your bill counting on the fact that you can't read it and haven't paid much attention. Should you contest anything or find a mistake, the server will smile and apologize. You may also find that the cheap beer on the menu is "out of stock" as they try to convince you that the more expensive one is best. When it comes to tea, don't feel compelled to buy expensive tea, no matter how emphatic they are about its virtues. Ask if they have **free tea** (免费茶 mianfei cha), and if they don't, order what **you** want to drink, not what **they** want.

● **Hutong rickshaw scam.** Strolling the *hutong* areas is fun but can also be tiring and you might want to take in the sights from the comfort of a rickshaw. Before climbing aboard, clearly negotiate the price for the tour and what it includes—duration, price per person, point-to-point, etc. Common scams are settling on a price for a tour (e.g. RMB 70) only to be told in mid-journey by your driver that this price is per person or per hour and your time is up and you'll have to pay more. **Always clearly detail how long your tour will be and where you will go.** Our "**Itinerary B Hutong Tour Route 2**" (see p.93) is an example

of what a *hutong* tour should look like.

● **Ticket scam.** When joining a tour, or being guided at a local sightseeing spot, you may be offered a higher priced ticket including a performance (acrobatics, Peking Opera show, etc) that you don't want to watch. **Always ask the price of the sight-only ticket.**

● **Counterfeit notes.** Always check change given by street vendors, especially larger notes. Things to look out for are the texture (fake notes often feel smoother than real ones), the watermark and drawn lines (they are more defined in counterfeits), the color (more pronounced in fakes) and the collar on Mao's jacket ("ribbed" and easy to feel on a real bill). Avoid accumulating old or tatty notes, but if you do, these can be exchanged at the banks (unfortunately, they won't exchange counterfeits!)

Security

Beijing is considered a very safe city compared with many other major cities in the world. Serious crimes against foreigners are rare, and common sense precautions can keep you safe and sound. Foreigners may experience whistles or calls, but curiosity, not aggression, is the sentiment behind this! **Petty crimes** such as pick pocketing and purse snatching occur more frequently, but you can take steps to avoid being an easy target. Be particularly alert in crowded places such as train stations, pubic transport, shopping areas, tourist destinations and parks.

For **emergencies** or **serious crime**, call **110**. For **lost and stolen articles**, contact **Beijing Municipal Public Se-curity Bureau** (84020101, English service) and your insurance company. Most insurance companies require you to file a record of your loss with the appropriate authorities within 24 hours of the loss being discovered. If you lose your passport you will need to contact both your **embassy** (see p.324) and the **Exit and Entry Management Section of the Public Security Bureau** (see p.302). Always get a receipt when taking a taxi, which will allow you or a Chinese-speaking friend to contact the taxi company directly if you leave something behind. Prompt action allows the company to call the driver, making the return of your things much more likely.

In crowded surroundings keep notice of your wallet at all times (taken at a train station during Chinese New Year).

How to use 110

In Beijing 110 is the emergency number equivalent to 911 in the US. You can dial this number free from any cell phone or pay phone in Beijing. Calmly ask for service in English and speak slowly and deliberately when transferred to an English-speaking officer. Be prepared to provide details on your location, why you're calling, your name and any other requested information. Remain where you are after you call, unless unsafe to do so. If you change your location, contact 110 again when possible with updated information. Leave things as they are at any crime scene to keep evidence intact.

Shopping Tips

What to Buy

Souvenirs like key chains, pins and T-shirts, etc., are universally available at any tourist sight. But for a bit more special Chinese items, you'll have to search at markets. Here we give you a list of recommended items to buy. Enjoy and bring an empty suitcase!

Brocade (织锦 **Zhijin**)
A type of silk. Colorful and more durable than other types of silk, its intricate patterns adorn many household items, such as pillows, curtains and tablecloths.

Batik
(蜡染 **Laran**)
Wax drawn on cloth and then dyed in indigo. After removing the wax a unique pattern emerges against the dark color.

Carpet (地毯 / 挂毯 **Ditan/Guatan**)
Wall carpets and floor carpets alike, of all sizes, adorned with beautiful Chinese designs.

Carved Lacquerware
(漆器 **Qiqi**)
Layered lacquer ornament (such as plate or vase) which is intricately carved by hand.

Silk
(丝绸 **Sichou**)
Fine, smooth and exquisite, China has been famous for silk products for hundreds of years.

Cloisonné (景泰蓝 **Jingtailan**)
First appearing in the 13th century, it is a local enamel handicraft made with rough-cast brass and copper wire inlay.

Ceramic (陶瓷 **Taoci**)

Chopsticks (筷子 **Kuaizi**)

Jade Carving
(玉雕 **Yudiao**)
Following a truly ancient trade, these hand-carved objects are both valuable and collectable.

Sandalwood Fan
(檀香扇 **Tanxiangshan**)

Chinese Writing Brush (毛笔 **Maobi**)

Ink Stone (砚 **Yan**)
Add water and grind the ink stick here to prepare your ink.

Ink Stick (墨 **Mo**)
Made from soot, and used in combination with an ink stone to make liquid ink for Chinese paintings and calligraphies.

Chop/Seal (印章 **Yinzhang**)
An unmistakable Chinese souvenir. Be sure to get the traditional red ink paste with it.

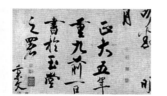

Chinese Calligraphy and Painting (书画 **Shuhua**)
Originals are very expensive, but you can find cheap, quality reproductions.

Kite (风筝 **Fengzheng**)

Pearl (珍珠 **Zhenzhu**)

Dough Figurine (面人 **Mianren**)
A typical Beijing handicraft made of wheat flour and glutinous rice flour.

Tea (茶 **Cha**)

Painted Snuff Bottle (鼻烟壶 **Biyanhu**)
Mostly made of glass, these little delicate bottles are painted from the inside.

Embroidery (刺绣 **Cixiu**)
Silky, colorful and delicate, the art of embroidery has several regional styles.

Qipao Dress (旗袍)

Quotations from Chairman Mao (毛主席语录)
Alias "The Little Red Book" with quotes from Mao on such diverse topics as War and Peace, the Mass Line, Women, Education, and Servitude. It can be bought at Pearl Market (see p.111).

Paper-cut (剪纸 **Jianzhi**)

Common Prices

While prices vary from store to store, there are places you can bargain and places you can't. In a famous retail outlet like Wal-Mart, common sense dictates you can't bargain there. On the street though, it's game on! Be prepared to haggle. And even in some large Chinese outlets, you can negotiate on expensive items of jewelry, or electronics. Small businesses and street stalls charge a large mark-up and you need to watch out or you could be cheated. Here are some common prices for general reference. There's no need for you to be a sucker!

In a store or a supermarket

AA battery: RMB 25/pair (for digital camera)
Beer: RMB 2/can, RMB 2-3/bottle
Coco-Cola: RMB 2/can, RMB 5/bottle
Film: RMB 20-30/roll (35mm)
Milk: RMB 1.7/pack
Purified/mineral water: RMB 1-2/bottle
Ice tea: RMB 3/bottle
Instant noodle: RMB 2-3/tub
Erguotou **alcohol**: RMB 2-4/small bottle

In a market

Backpack: RMB 40 +
Chopsticks set: RMB 25-60
Embroidered cloth: RMB 50 +
Embroidered silk handkerchief: RMB 50 +
Fan: RMB 10-50
Hat: RMB 20-50
His-and-hers watches: RMB 300/pair
Jacket: RMB 80-300 depending on materials
Jeans: RMB 80-120
Kite: RMB 10 +
Knick-knacks: RMB 10 +
Lacquer ware: RMB 50 +
Leather purse: RMB 60 +

Luggage: RMB 100 +
Mahjong set: RMB 100
Mao's Little Red Book: RMB 20 for one reprinted copy
Painting/calligraphy scroll: RMB 30 +
Pants: RMB 60-100
Paper-cut: RMB 5 +
Pearl necklace: RMB 20 +
Qipao dress: RMB 80 +
Seal: RMB 50 +
Shoes: RMB 80-200 depending on whether they are leather
Silk robe: RMB 100
Silver bracelets: RMB 100 +/pair
Silver earrings: RMB 40 +/pair
Skirt: RMB 50-100
Small cloisonné souvenir: RMB 20 +
Snuff bottle: RMB 30 +
Sunglasses: RMB 20-100
Sweater: RMB 80
Tie: RMB 10+
T-shirt: RMB 25-50

Other prices

Seal carving: RMB 25 +
Tailor-made suits: RMB 1000 +
Tailor-made *qipao* **dress**: RMB 600 +
6 megapixel digital camera: RMB 2,000+

Shoe Size Difference

Women's International Shoe Size										
China	35.5	36	37	37.5	38	39	39.5	40	41	—	42
USA/Canada	5	5.5	6	6.5	7	7.5	8	8.5	9	9.5	10
UK	2.5	3	3.5	4	4.5	5	5.5	6	6.5	7	7.5
Europe	35	35.5	36	37	37.5	38	38.5	39	40	41	42

Men's International Shoe Size										
China	38	39	39.5	40	41	—	42	43	43.5	44	44.5	45
USA/Canada	5	5.5	6	6.5	7	7.5	8	8.5	9	9.5	10	10.5
UK	4.5	5	5.5	6	6.5	7	7.5	8	8.5	9	9.5	10
Europe	37.5	38	38.5	39	40	40.5	41	42	42.5	43	44	44.5

Top 10 Budget Tips

There are plenty of ways while traveling to SAVE money and time, and still have a good time. Planning your trip before leaving home, learning how to get around, what to see and where to eat... we'll help you get the most out of your time and budget in Beijing. Here we give you a "Top 10" list of things to keep in mind. Many of the money-saving services are not widely known outside the Chinese community and may not provide English service. If so, try getting a Chinese friend to help—people are always keen to practice their English.

1

Free admission day

A fantastic budget saving trick is to take advantage of the "free admission day" at the city's 13 museums, which award the first 200 visitors free entry every Wednesday. The 13 museums are: **Capital Museum** (首都博物馆, see p.137), **Xu Beihong Museum** (徐悲鸿纪念馆, see p.71), **Ancient Bell Museum** (大钟寺古钟博物馆, see p.165), **Beijing Art Museum** (北京艺术博物馆, see p.139), **Cultural Exchange Museum** (文博交流馆, see p.63), **Beijing Ancient Coins Museum** (北京古代钱币展览馆, 86-10-62018073), **Beijing Art Museum of Stone Carvings** (北京石刻艺术博物馆, see p.138), **Lao She Memorial Hall** (老舍纪念馆, 86-10-65142612), **Zhengyangmen Gate** (正阳门, 86-10-65229384), **Da Jue Temple** (大觉寺), **White Dagoba Temple** (白塔寺, see p.60), **Confucius Temple** and **Guozijian Museum** (孔庙和国子监, see p.60) and **Beijing Ancient Architecture Museum** (北京古代建筑博物馆, 86-10-63045608).

On May 18, or the **International Museum Day**, museum-goers also enjoy free entrance. For a complete list of participating museums, please log on http://english.bjww.gov.cn/zwgk/jgsz_zsdw.asp.

2

Pass it on! Entrance tickets and Museum Pass

Many sights offer a choice of "access-all-areas" or "single-zone" tickets. Decide in advance which bits you do and don't want to see and buy the appropriate ticket at the entrance (Sometimes, it's much pricier to buy individual ones on the way round).

You can also get student discounts at many venues on presentation of a student card. Not all attractions offer this discount, but it's always worth asking!

Beijing Museum Pass (博物馆通票): This wondrous little pass is a godsend for Beijing visitors. For RMB 80, up to three adults can enjoy discounts (half price, three for one, etc. according to the attraction) to

nearly all the city's main museums as well as several temples and cultural sights. This can add up to very big savings. However, a limited number of these booklets are available between late December and late January each year. They are valid through the entire calendar year and can be bought at main branches of China Post offices or order them by calling **86-10-64177845** (in English), **86-10-622131256** (in Chinese); or from **www.piao.com.cn** (in English), **www.bowuguan.bj. cn** (in Chinese). But stocks run out quickly, so if you know you are coming to Beijing later in the year, perhaps it's worth arranging for a friend or colleague here to buy one for you.

Welcome to Beijing!
Upon arrival

Don't make the mistake of running straight for the first airport taxi you see; it is a fair distance and the meter won't be a pretty sight at the end. The **airport shuttle bus** (see p.310) or the subway to downtown (opening in 2008) will save you a hefty sum. Your hotel may arrange airport pick-ups, but if not, ask them which bus to take and where to get off. Some bus drivers speak little English, so be sure to have the name of your hotel written in Chinese and the driver tell you where to alight. It's a great introduction to the city, trust us!

Getting orientated

Park your bags and go check out the area around your hotel. Seek out bus lines in the near vicinity, and you may just be able to get to the sites without taking a taxi.

All change! Using
public transport

Public transport in Beijing seems a lot more stressful than it actually is, and is a great way to save money. Bus and subway routes are clear and logical and we offer bus and/or subway route information to all the sights listed (see relevant section). For a **bus map**, see http://www.mapbar. com (in Chinese and English).

A public transport "**Superpass**" (一卡通 yikatong) may help save money and time buying individual tickets. Three types of prepaid superpasses are now available:

- **Adults' card** For buses numbered from 1 to 499, there is a flat-rate fare of RMB 0.4; and for these numbered from 601 to 899, 40% of the normal ticket prices. For those numbered from 900, 80% of the normal ticket prices. Subways, NO discount. NO limit on duration.
- **Students' card** For buses numbered from 1 to 499, there is a flat-rate fare of RMB 0.2; and for those numbered from 601 to 899, 20% of the normal ticket prices. For those numbered from 900, 80% of the normal ticket prices. Subways, NO

discount. NO limit on duration.

● **Limited duration bus cards** are very handy for visitors: a 3-day card (maximum 18 rides) costs RMB 10; a 7-day card (maximum 42 rides) costs RMB 20; and a 15-day card (maximum 90 rides) costs RMB 40.

You can buy a superpass at China Post offices, subway stations or CITIC Bank branches.

◪ *There is a refundable RMB 20 deposit per card. To get back your deposit, visit one of the following places: Bus 328 terminal at Andingmen Xi (安定门西), Bus 15 terminal at Beijing Zoo (动物园枢纽站), and Bus 335 terminal at Fuchengmen (阜成门).*

When in "Rome"! Eating out

Eat where the locals eat. When you're in Beijing, Chinese food is always the cheapest. Look for **Chengdu Snack Food** (成都小吃) restaurants which can be seen everywhere in town. They serve cheap and cheerful dumplings, noodles and *gaifan* (盖饭 rice topped with dishes such as Kung-pow chicken 宫保鸡丁, approx. RMB 7/plate). **Street vendors** selling all kinds of snacks like *yangrou chuan* (羊肉串 lamb kebabs) and *jianbing* (煎饼 pancake) are extremely convenient when you're on the move.

Low-cost or free activities

One of the best ways to see a country is through the eyes of the local people. **Night-time dancing** in many public squares is a raucous and fun activity that foreigners can get involved in. Alternatively, a serene afternoon of **kite-flying** at Tian'anmen will thrust you into the middle of local life (and a kite only costs a few RMB!). If you're lucky enough to be around during the Spring Festival (Chinese New Year), you shouldn't miss the traditional **temple fair** (see p.26) where an eclectic range of foods is available.

Shop 'til you drop

A lot of "touristy items" are sold throughout the city. You do not have to buy a souvenir of a tourist site at the place itself. In Chinese markets it is often the late bird that catches the best worm. Vendors offer bigger discounts at the end of the day, so leave shopping until last (then you won't need to lug it around all day either!).

Don't go with the flow and shop at markets constantly mentioned in other travel guides, such as Pearl Market or Silk Street. Their prices tend to be **HIGHER** than others as they've become the most famous shopping spots among foreigners. Look for some new spots: for **cheap special souvenirs** go to **Tianyi Market** (see p.149); and stop at **Tianzhaotian Wholesale Market** (see p.149) for **women's accessories** at wholesale prices. Spend at least two hours at the wholesale market around **Beijing Zoo** (see p.149) for dirt-cheap wholesale clothes. For **a bit of everything, Golden Five-star Wholesale Market** (see p.181) should be your ideal stop. **Bargaining** (see below) is expected so make sure to haggle the price down or you'll be paying over the odds (see **Common Prices** on p.340).

9

Let your hair down: relaxing in Beijing

After a long day sightseeing, what better way to unwind than with a massage? Beijing's massages are first rate and extremely reasonable: for RMB 50 you can enjoy an hour-long **body** or **foot massage**. Alternatively, a *xitou* (洗头 head wash) is a vigorous shampoo and scalp, neck and shoulder massage. Almost all hair salons offer this for around RMB 10-15 (they may also throw in a hair cut too!).

10

Bicycle and walking tours

Beijing is huge—we can't repeat that often enough. That said, it is surprisingly easy to visit certain areas by pedal-power alone (see **Bike rental** on p.92). In "Historical Central" particularly, many of the main attractions including the Forbidden City, Tian'anmen Square, Beihai Park, Houhai and the Bell and Drum Towers are all within easy cycling distance from each other. And an easy stroll links the Lama Temple and Confucius Temple (see **Itinerary B** on p.92). Cycling or walking will save you money; but more than that, they are really enjoyable ways of truly experiencing the city.

Bargain tips

1. Bring along a sense of adventure and fun when shopping and be prepared to bargain.
2. Start by offering no more than 40% of the vendor's first price and smile through the process.
3. Once you've reached your limit, stand firm, but polite. Call the seller "*pengyou*" (friend).
4. If the vendor won't accept your price, walk away. They will often call you back. If not, their last price is really their last price, and if you want to buy the item (at least from them) that's the price you'll have to pay.
5. When buying multiple items, negotiate the single item price first, and then insist on a lower price for multiple purchases.
6. Don't feel sorry for the seller; there is no way they are losing money on a deal no matter how cutthroat a negotiator you are. At the end of the transaction, compliment them on their good selling and be prepared to be showered with praise for your excellent bargaining.

Useful Telephone Numbers

Emergency Calls

Fire: 119
Police: 110
First Aid / Ambulance: 120
Traffic Accident: 122
Beijing Public Security Bureau English Service: 84020101
International SOS Assistance: 64629100

Other Useful Numbers

BCNC Car Rental Toll-free: 800-810-9001
Beijing Customs: 65396114 (in Chinese)

Bus Hotline: 96166
Customer Complaint: 12315 or 96315 (in Chinese)
International Phone Directory: 115
Local Phone Directory: 114 (in Chinese)
Master Card: 65101090/95
Public Transport Superpass Hotline: 88087733 (in Chinese)
Ticket Booking Hotline: 64177845 or 800-810-3721
Tourist Information: 65130828
Weather Forecast: 121121 (in Chinese)

Weight and Measures

China uses metric system in weights and measures, but many people are still using traditional Chinese system which is more commonly applied in markets. The following conversion table between the old Chinese system, metric system and the other Western systems is made for your easy use.

	Metric System	Traditional Chinese System	British-American System
Units of Length	1 kilometer (1,000 meters)	2 *li*	0.621 mile
	1 meter	3 *chi*	3.281 feet; 1.094 yards
	0.1 meter	3 *cun*	0.328 foot; 0.109 yard
	1 centimeter	3 *fen*	0.394 inch
Units of Area	1 square kilometer	4 *square li;* 1,500 *mu*	0.386 square mile; 100 hectares; 247.1 acres
	1 square meter	9 square *chi*	10.764 square feet; 1.196 square yards
Units of Weight	1 kilogram	2 *jin*	2.205 pounds
	50 grams	1 *liang*	0.110 pound
	0.454 kilogram	0.907 *jin*	1 pound
Units of Capacity	1 liter	1 *sheng*	1.760 pints; 0.220 gallon
	4.546 liter	4.546 *sheng*	1 gallon

Language Guide

Pinyin

Pinyin is a system that uses the alphabet to represent the sound of Chinese characters. The sound of a Chinese character usually contains two parts: the front half (initial) and the second half (final), in addition to a tone. By combining these, the complete sound is made.

INITIALS

b, p, m, f, d, t, n, l, g, k, j, s, w, y, ch, sh are approximately the same as in English.

c = ts, as in "rats"
z = dz, as in "kids"
x = sh   q = ch   zh = j

FINALS

ai	=	eye
an	=	"and" without "d" sound
ang	=	ahng
ao	=	ow!
e	=	"u" sound as in "pull"
ei	=	"ay" sound as in "play"
en	=	"en" sound as in "then"
eng	=	"ung" sound as in "sung"
ia	=	"ya" sound as in "see ya!"
i	=	"ee" sound as in "meet"
ian	=	yen
iao	=	"yow" sound like when someone steps on your foot
iong	=	"yawng" sound as in "yawn" with an extra "g"
iang	=	"yanhg" sound
ie	=	yeah
iu	=	"eo" sound as in "leo"
o	=	"awe" sound as in "awesome" said with a British accent
ou	=	oh
u	=	normally "oo" sound as in "boot," but becomes "u" sound

after j, q, x, y as in French "est tu Brutus?"

ua	=	"what" without "t" sound
uan	=	"wan" sound as in "Juan," but becomes "yuan" after j, q, x, y
uang	=	"wahang" similar to "one"
un	=	"win" sound as in "window"
üe	=	similar to "yueah"
ui	=	"way" sound as in "sway"
uo	=	"wo" sound as in "wombat"

Tones

The most confusing part of speaking Chinese for foreigners (and for the Chinese people listening!) is the pitch of each syllable. Spoken Mandarin Chinese has four tones, variations of which can make great differences to the meaning of words, which when written in Pinyin seem identical. For example, "wén" (闻) means "to smell," while "wěn" (吻) means "to kiss." The following is a simple guide to get your head and tongue around the tones:

First tone ー A flat, level tone pronounced in a relatively high voice, the way we sing the note "la."

Second tone ╱ A tone that rises pronounced in the same way as a question, as in "far" when asking, "Is it far?"

Third tone ╲╱ A down and up tone pronounced with a dip in the middle, as when irritably saying, "So?"

Fourth tone ╲ A tone which goes from high to low, pronounced as if angry or giving an order.

Basic Chinese

These basic Chinese phrases and sentences will get you going in your first few days in China. All are presented in English, Chinese characters, Pinyin, and English pronunciation—everything you could need!

Numbers

Numbers	Chinese	Pinyin	English Pronunciation
0	零	líng	Ling
1	一	yī	E (Like the name of the letter)
2	二	èr	R (Like the name of the letter)
3	三	sān	San
4	四	sì	Suh
5	五	wǔ	Woo
6	六	liù	Leo
7	七	qī	Chee
8	八	bā	Bah
9	九	jiǔ	Geo
10	十	shí	Sher
11	十一	shí-yī	Sher-E
12	十二	shí-èr	Sher-R
20	二十	èr-shí	R-Sher
35	三十五	sān-shí-wǔ	San-Sher-Woo
100	一百	yī-bǎi	E-By
101	一百零一	yī-bǎi-líng-yī	E-By-Ling-E
225	两百二十五	liǎng-bǎi-èr-shí-wǔ	Liang-By-R-Sher-Woo
1,000	一千	yī-qiān	E-Chee-yen
10,000	一万	yī-wàn	E-Wan

● To say numbers 11-19, just add the extra digit after you say Ten, e.g. Ten-One (11), Ten-Two (12).
For numbers in the Twenties, Thirties and so on, add the digit before the Ten, i.e.: Two-Tens (20), Two-Tens-Four (24).

● When talking about quantity or price, 2 has another pronunciation, liǎng.

● To say numbers above 100, say the numbers in the order in which you see them, i.e.: One-Hundred-Zero-One (101).

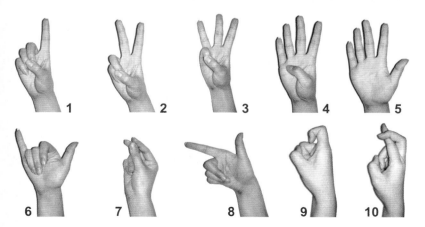

Learn these simple hand signs to give yourself a helping hand.

Phrases and Sentences

Courtesies

English	Chinese	Pinyin	English Pronunciation
Hello/ How are you!	你好！	Nǐ hǎo!	Knee how!
Nice to meet you.	很高兴认识你。	Hěn gāo xìng rèn shí nǐ.	Hen gow shing wren sher knee.
Goodbye！	再见！	Zài jiàn!	Dzai-jyen!
I'm sorry/ Excuse me.	对不起。	Duì bù qǐ.	Du-way boo chee.
It's ok/ It doesn't matter.	没关系。	Méi guān xi.	May gwahn she.
Thank you.	谢谢。	Xiè xiè.	Shyeah shyeah.
You're welcome.	不客气。	Bú kè qì.	Boo kuh chee.

Restaurants

English	Chinese	Pinyin	English Pronunciation
I'm looking for a restaurant.	我找饭馆儿。	Wǒ zhǎo fàn guǎn.	Wah jow fan gwar.
I want to eat this/that.	我想吃这个 / 那个。	Wǒ xiǎng chī zhè ge/nà ge.	Wah she-ahng chur juh guh/nay guh.
Beef	牛肉	Niú ròu	New row
Chicken	鸡肉	Jī ròu	Gee row
Fish	鱼	Yú	Ewe
Lamb	羊肉	Yáng ròu	Yang row
Pork	猪肉	Zhū ròu	Drew row
Vegetable	蔬菜	Shū cài	Shoe tsai
Bitter	苦	Kǔ	Koo
Salty	咸	Xián	Shyen
Sour	酸	Suān	Swan
Spicy	辣	Là	La
Sweet	甜	Tián	Tea-yen
I don't eat meat.	我不吃肉。	Wǒ bù chī ròu.	Wah boo chur row.
I'm a vegetarian.	我只吃素。	Wǒ zhǐ chī sù.	Wah jer chur sue.
It's delicious!	太好吃了！	Tài hǎo chī le!	Tie how chur la!
Miss/Sir, menu please/ bill please.	小姐 / 先生，菜单 / 买单。	Xiǎo jiě/Xiān shēng, Cài dān/Mǎi dān.	Shyow jay/Shyen shung, tsai dan/my dan.

Hotels

English	Chinese	Pinyin	English Pronunciation
I'd like to reserve a room.	我要订个房间。	Wǒ yào dìng gè fáng jiān.	Wah yow ding guh fahng jyen.
Single bed	单人间	Dān rén jiān	Dan wren jyen
Twin room	双人标间	Shuāng rén biāo jiān	Shoe-wahng wren b-yow jyen
Double bed	双人床	Shuāng rén chuáng	Shoe-wahng wren choo-wahng
A/C	空调	Kōng tiáo	Kong tea-yow
TV	电视	Diàn shì	D-yen sher
Telephone	电话	Diàn huà	D-yen hwa
Internet	上网	Shàng wǎng	Shahng wahng
Laundry room	洗衣房	Xǐ yī fáng	She e fahng
Check in/Check out	登记 / 退房	Dēng jì/Tuì fáng	Dung gee/Tway fahng.

Shopping

English	Chinese	Pinyin	English Pronunciation
Do you have a different color?	有别的颜色吗？	Yǒu bié de yán sè ma?	Yo byeah duh yen suh ma?
I need a bigger/ smaller size.	我要大 / 小一号。	Wǒ yào dà/xiǎo yī hào.	Wah yow da/ she-ow e how.
I want this/that.	我要这个 / 那个。	Wǒ yào zhè ge/ nà ge.	Wah yow juh guh/ nay guh.
How much is this?	多少钱？	Duō shǎo qián?	Doe shao chyen?
Make it cheaper.	便宜一点。	Pián yi yī diǎnr.	P-yen e e d-yen.
That's too expensive.	太贵了。	Tài guì le.	Tie gway la.

Questions

English	Chinese	Pinyin	English Pronunciation
A little faster, ok?	快一点儿，好吗？	Kuài yi diǎnr, hǎo mǎ?	Kwhy e d-yen, how ma?
Can I make international calls here?	可以打国际电话吗？	Kě yǐ dǎ guó jì diàn huà ma?	Kuh yee da gwo gee d-yen hwa ma?
Can you help me?	能帮我吗？	Néng bāng wǒ ma?	Nung bhang wah ma?
What time is it?	现在几点了？	Xiàn zài jǐ diǎn le?	Shyen dzai gee d-yen la?

English	Chinese	Pinyin	English Pronunciation
Where is the post of-fice/bank/washroom?	邮局 / 银行 / 厕所在哪里？	Yóu jú/Yín háng/ Cè suǒ zài nǎ lǐ?	Yo dju/Yin hung/ Tsuh swore dzai na lee?
How	怎么	Zěn me	Zen ma
What	什么	Shén me	Shen ma
When	什么时候	Shén me shí hòu	Shen ma sher hoe
Who	谁	Shuí	Shay
Why	为什么	Wèi shén me	Way shen ma

Questions you will hear from (a taxi driver, a vendor, a waiter...)

English	Chinese	Pinyin	English Pronunciation
Where are you going?	你去哪儿？	Nǐ qù nǎr?	Knee chew nar?
What country are you from?	你是哪国人？	Nǐ shì nǎ guó rén?	Knee sher nay gwore wren?
What's your name?	你叫什么名字？	Nǐ jiào shén me míng zi?	Knee gee-yow shen ma ming dzi?
How old are you?	你多大了？	Nǐ duō dà le?	Knee doe da la?
Are you married?	你结婚了吗？	Nǐ jié hūn le ma?	Knee jay Juan la ma?
How long have you been in Beijing?	你在北京多长时间了？	Nǐ zài běi jīng duō cháng shí jiān le?	Knee dzai beijing doe chahng sher jyen la?
How tall are you?	你有多高？	Nǐ yǒu duō gāo?	Knee yo doe gow?

Statements

English	Chinese	Pinyin	English Pronunciation
I can't understand.	我听不懂。	Wǒ tīng bù dǒng.	Wah ting boo dong.
I'm from the USA/UK/Canada...	我是美国人 / 英国人 / 加拿大人...	Wǒ shì měi guó rén/ yīng guó rén/ jiā ná dà rén...	Wah sher may gwore wren/ ying gwore wren/ jya nah da wren...
I'm lost.	我迷路了。	Wǒ mí lù le.	Wah mee loo la.
Just a moment.	等一下。	Děng yí xià.	Dung e shya.
My name is...	我叫...	Wǒ jiào...	Wah gee-yow...

Appendix

Beijing Olympics

That sound you heard on July 13, 2001 was the jubilant celebration by Chinese all over the world as Beijing was awarded "The Games of the XXIX Olympiad." The opening ceremony of the Beijing Olympics will take place at 8pm on the 8th day of the 8th month in 2008, a supremely auspicious combination of numbers, as the number "8" represents "prosperity" and "wealth" in China. The Games will wrap up on August 24th, but sports enthusiasts will not have to wait long for another "fix," since Beijing will also host the Paralympic Games September 6-17.

"One World, One Dream" is the theme for the 2008 Games, and Beijing residents have caught the fever as everyone focuses on improving their English. It's not just students, or the 100,000-plus volunteers practicing how to say "Welcome to Beijing" to 4.6 million overseas visitors expected in 2008. If taxi drivers want to continue driving during the Olympics, they too must learn some English and pass a test to prove their competence. There's some language learning involved with the five Olympic mascots too. Their individual names spell out in Chinese "Bei Jing Huan Ying Ni"—Beijing Welcomes You! The games have also prompted a commitment to "Going Green." Big time! An impressive RMB 280 billion (USD 38 billion) budget has been dedicated to improving Beijing's environment and infrastructure since the awarding of the Olympics in 2001. New subway lines, new and improved roads, and the wholesale relocation of factories are among the city's ambitious undertakings in the run-up to the games. Some wonder whether Beijing has perhaps bitten off more than it can chew, given the environmental challenges faced, but the smart money says that when 8pm of 08-08-08 rolls around, Beijing will unveil a new, fresh face to the world as it goes for Olympic Gold!

贝贝
Beibei

晶晶
Jingjing

Huanhuan

迎迎
Yingying

妮妮
Nini

Beijing Olympic Venues

This is what the Beijing Olympic venues, "Bird's Nest" and "Watercube" will look like when they are completed.

The 2008 Beijing Olympics will host 28 different types of sports, in 37 venues, most of those venues in Beijing. However, sailing events will be held Qingdao, equestrian in Hong Kong and football preliminaries in Tianjin, Shanghai, Shenyang and Qinhuangdao.

All venues are being newly built or renovated to Olympic standards—including the exciting "Bird's Nest" National Stadium and the "Watercube" National Aquatics Center, which will identify Beijing as a truly international, forward-looking city and leave Beijing citizens with a legacy of world-class facilities once the Games themselves are history.

All the Beijing competition and training centers are less than 30 minutes' drive from the Olympic Village. Most venues are concentrated in the north/northwest of Beijing, connected to the city center by purpose-built transport links. By 2008, the Olympic Subway Line will directly lead you to the Olympic Park.

Such is the enthusiasm for the Games here, construction of the new infrastructure and venues was proceeding so far ahead of schedule that the International Olympic Committee had to suggest slowing down a bit!

Olympic Green

Venue	Function
❶ National Stadium ("Bird's Nest") 国家体育场	Opening ceremony: 8.08pm, Aug 8 Closing ceremony: Aug 24 Football: Aug 23 Athletics: Aug 15-24
❷ National Indoor Stadium 国家体育馆	Handball: Aug 21-24 Trampoline: Aug 16, 18, 19 Artistic Gymnastics: Aug 9, 10, 12-15, 17-19

Venue	Function
❸ National Aquatics Center ("Watercube") 国家游泳中心	Swimming: Aug 9-17 Diving: Aug 10-13, 15-23 Synchronized Swimming: Aug 17-20, 22
❹ Fencing Hall, National Conference Center 国家会议中心击剑馆	Fencing: Aug 9-17 Modern Pentathlon: Aug 21, 22
❺ Hockey Field 奥林匹克公园曲棍球场	Hockey: Aug 10-23
❻ Archery Field 奥林匹克公园射箭场	Archery: Aug 9-15
❼ Tennis Center 奥林匹克公园网球场	Tennis: Aug 10-17
❽ Olympic Sports Center Stadium 奥体中心体育场	Football: Aug 9 Modern Pentathlon: Aug 21, 22
❾ Ying Tung Natatorium 英东游泳馆	Water Polo: Aug 10-20, 22-24 Modern Pentathlon: Aug 21, 22
❿ Olympic Sports Center Gymnasium 奥体中心体育馆	Handball: Aug 9-20

North

Venue	Function
⓫ Shunyi Olympic Rowing-Canoeing Park 顺义奥林匹克水上公园	Rowing: Aug 9-14, 16, 17 Canoe/Kayak (Flatwater): Aug 18-23 Canoe/Kayak (Slalom): Aug 11-14 Swimming: Aug 20, 21
⓬ Triathlon Venue 铁人三项赛场	Triathlon: Aug 18, 19

University Area

Venue	Function
⓭ University of Science and Technology Beijing Gymnasium 北京科技大学体育馆	Judo: Aug 9-15 Taekwondo: Aug 20-23
⓮ Peking University Gymnasium 北京大学体育馆	Table Tennis: Aug 13-23
⓯ China Agricultural University Gymnasium 中国农业大学体育馆	Wrestling: Aug 12-14, 16, 17, 19-21
⓰ Beijing Institute of Technology Gymnasium 北京理工大学体育馆	Volleyball: Aug 9-18

Venue	Function
⑰ Beijing University of Aeronautics & Astronautics Gymnasium 北京航空航天大学体育馆	Weightlifting: Aug 9-13, 15-19

West

Venue	Function
⑱ Capital Indoor Stadium 首都体育馆	Volleyball: Aug 9-24
⑲ Laoshan Velodrome 老山自行车馆	Cycling (track): Aug 15-19
⑳ Laoshan Mountain Bike Course 老山山地自行车场	Cycling (Mountain Bike): Aug 22, 23
㉑ Laoshan BMX Venue 老山小轮车赛场	Cycling (BMX): Aug 20, 21
㉒ Beijing Shooting Range Hall 北京射击馆	Shooting: Aug 9-17
㉓ Beijing Shooting Range Clay Target Field 北京射击场飞碟靶场	Shooting: Aug 9-12, 14-16
㉔ Wukesong Baseball Fields 五棵松棒球场	Baseball: Aug 13-16, 18-20, 22, 23
㉕ Wukesong Indoor Stadium 五棵松体育馆	Basketball: Aug 9-24
㉖ Fengtai Softball Field 丰台垒球场	Softball: Aug 12-18, 20, 21
㉗ Urban Road Cycling Course 城区自行车公路赛场	Cycling (road race): Aug 9, 10, 13

East

Venue	Function
㉘ Workers' Stadium 工人体育场	Football: Aug 15, 16, 18, 19, 21
㉙ Workers' Indoor Arena 工人体育馆	Boxing: Aug 9-20, 22-24
㉚ Chaoyang Park Beach Volleyball Ground 朝阳公园沙滩排球场	Beach Volleyball: Aug 9-22
㉛ Beijing University of Technology Gymnasium 北京工业大学体育馆	Badminton: Aug 9-17 Rhythmic Gymnastics: Aug 21-24

Olympic Venues Map

INDEX

* Map entries are colored.

Bold page No. = primary information

图书在版编目（CIP）数据

吝啬鬼游北京 英文/(加) 东方朔 (Glenn Alexander) 欧阳伟萍等编著. —北京：外文出版社，2007

ISBN 978-7-119-04621-1

I. 吝... II. ①东方...②欧阳... III. 旅游指南 —北京市 —英文 IV.K928.91

中国版本图书馆 CIP 数据核字 (2006) 第 114947 号

编　　著：G.C.A. (Glenn) Alexander　欧阳伟萍　Samantha Wilson　闫　红
选题策划：欧阳伟萍　何永妍　王京强
责任编辑：欧阳伟萍　何永妍
英文改稿：Chad Pearson　M. Tyson Darius　Chellis Ying
英文审定：Sue Duncan　韩清月　May Yee
设计创意：Edison Flores　何永妍　欧阳伟萍
插图绘制：李士伋
摄　　影：崔雁行　张　健　韩得群　Justin Hirschkorn　Tom Carter　王　虎
顾　　问：Andy Mckillop　Howard Aster　Tony McGlinchey　Stephen Horowitz
　　　　　Paul White　Gregor Kneussel
印刷监制：韩少乙

吝啬鬼游北京

©2007 外文出版社

外文出版社出版

(中国北京百万庄大街 24 号)

邮政编码 100037

http://www.flp.com.cn

北京外文印刷厂印制

中国国际图书贸易总公司发行

(中国北京车公庄西路 35 号)

北京邮政信箱第 399 号　邮政编码 100044

2007 年 (大 32 开) 第 1 版
2008 年第 1 版第 2 次印刷
(英)

ISBN 978-7-119-04621-1
08000 (平)
7-E-3764P